# The Metamorphosis of
# Leadership in a
# Democratic Mexico

# The Metamorphosis of Leadership in a Democratic Mexico

Roderic Ai Camp

OXFORD
UNIVERSITY PRESS
2010

# OXFORD
UNIVERSITY PRESS

Oxford University Press, Inc., publishes works that further
Oxford University's objective of excellence
in research, scholarship, and education.

Oxford   New York
Auckland   Cape Town   Dar es Salaam   Hong Kong   Karachi
Kuala Lumpur   Madrid   Melbourne   Mexico City   Nairobi
New Delhi   Shanghai   Taipei   Toronto

With offices in
Argentina   Austria   Brazil   Chile   Czech Republic   France   Greece
Guatemala   Hungary   Italy   Japan   Poland   Portugal   Singapore
South Korea   Switzerland   Thailand   Turkey   Ukraine   Vietnam

Copyright © 2010 by Oxford University Press, Inc.

Published by Oxford University Press, Inc.
198 Madison Avenue, New York, New York 10016

www.oup.com

Oxford is a registered trademark of Oxford University Press.

Library of Congress Cataloging-in-Publication Data
Camp, Roderic Ai.
The metamorphosis of leadership in a democratic Mexico / Roderic Ai Camp.
    p. cm.
Includes bibliographical references and index.
ISBN 978-0-19-974285-1
1. Political leadership—Mexico. 2. Democracy—Mexico.
3. Mexico—Politics and government—1946-1970.
4. Mexico—Politics and government—1970-1988.
5. Mexico—Politics and government—1988-2000. I. Title.
JL1281.C338 2010
320.972—dc22        2009053937

9 8 7 6 5 4 3 2 1
Printed in the United States of America
on acid-free paper

In memory of Charlie Hale,
Colleague, Scholar, and Friend.

# Contents

# The Metamorphosis of Leadership in a Democratic Mexico

# 1

# Introduction

Four decades ago, as a graduate student, I became interested in Mexican political leadership. In pursuit of a dissertation project, I developed a comparative study of the role of Mexican and U.S. economists in policy making, using a policy-making model developed by Charles O. Jones.[1] Through extensive correspondence, and later follow-up interviews in Mexico, I was introduced to an entire generation of Mexican public figures, many of whom lived through the Mexican Revolution of 1910 as children and who had made significant contributions to the postrevolutionary developments from the 1920s until the end of the twentieth century.[2] This generation of Mexican leaders, through their generosity and interest in my scholarly questions, steered me toward a lifelong project of exploring leaders and elites. I moved across professional boundaries, educating myself about Mexico's literary figures, artists, and others in the fascinating world of intellectual life; Catholic bishops and priests operating within the peculiar confines of Mexico's church and state history; capitalists and their tenuous relationship to the government; and the secretive officer corps, which succumbed to civilian supremacy while retaining protected spheres of autonomy long before its Latin American peers—all of whom were significantly linked, formally and informally, to political leaders.

Studying individual leaders is an indirect way of examining their institutions, regardless of whether they are businesses, churches, journals, interest groups, or armies. It is also a way of understanding how each of these many institutions relate to the Mexican state and the nature of the interactions that occur among them. After exploring these numerous leadership groups individually and then collectively, I decided to return a final time to politicians themselves, who initiated this focus, to fully understand how political leadership has evolved for most of the past century and where it

1. Roderic Ai Camp, *The Role of Economists in Policy-Making: A Comparative Case Study of Mexico and the United States* (Tucson: University of Arizona Press, 1977).

2. Most of these letters have been donated to the Nettie Lee Benson Latin American Collection, University of Texas, Austin, Texas.

appears to be headed in this century, after the remarkable election of 2000. For this, I am indebted to Peter Siavelis, who reawakened my interest, after I spent a decade analyzing citizen views of democracy and democratic politics, by inviting me to Wake Forest University for the first conference ever held on political recruitment in Latin America.[3]

Essentially, I wanted to address two broad, fundamental questions. First, how has Mexican political leadership evolved from the 1930s to 2010? Specifically, how has the changing model of Mexican politics from a semi-authoritarian, one-party dominant to a consolidating democratic, competitive, electoral system significantly altered Mexican leadership in ways which extend beyond their ideological preferences?[4] I want to make clear at the outset that I do not consider Mexico today to be a fully democratic political model. I view it as currently undergoing the process of consolidation.[5] Therefore, my definition of Mexico as a democracy refers only to it having achieved a competitive, accountable, electoral process governed by independent institutions that the majority of citizens support.[6] I also believe it has achieved a different if incomplete set of procedures that set it apart from the predemocratic era, implying a greater level of pluralism.[7]

3. The results of this groundbreaking conference can be found in Peter M. Siavelis and Scott Morgenstern, eds., *Pathways to Power: Political Recruitment and Candidate Selection in Latin America* (University Park: Pennsylvania State University Press, 2008).

4. My first foray into this topic, "Political Recruitment, Governance, and Leadership in Mexico: How Democracy Has Made a Difference," appears in Siavelis and Morgenstern, *Pathways to Power*, 292–315.

5. Dorothy J. Solinger provides a valuable comparative analysis of Mexico's arrival at the point of consolidation based on six structural factors: decades of elections, the existence of at least one opposition party during those decades, eventual electoral reforms, a high level of corruption and fraud in the ruling party, one or more fissures from the dominant party, and a charismatic opposition leader. "Ending One-Party Dominance: Korea, Taiwan, Mexico," *Journal of Democracy* 12, no. 1 (January 2001): 31.

6. For a comprehensive discussion of scholarly views of democracy, including its very definition, see Steve Ellner's insightful "Latin American Democracy in 'Post-Consolidation' Literature: Optimism and Pessimism," *Latin American Politics and Society* 43, no. 1 (Spring 2001): 127–42. For my views in more detail, see Roderic Ai Camp, *Politics in Mexico: The Democratic Consolidation* (New York: Oxford University Press, 2007), 291ff. I have been most influenced in my own definition of democracy by Terry Lynn Karl's conceptualization and analysis of democracy in Latin America, "Dilemmas of Democratization in Latin America," in Roderic Ai Camp, ed., *Democracy in Latin America: Patterns and Cycles* (Wilmington: Scholarly Resources, 1996), 21–46.

7. For a careful analysis of the components of Mexican democracy and the difficulties in its transition, see Guy Poitras's excellent "Mexico's Problematic Transition to Democracy," in Philip Kelly, ed., *Assessing Democracy in Latin America* (Boulder, Colo.: Westview Press, 1998), 63–75. For an in-depth analysis of emerging pluralism, Claudio Holzner uses Philip Oxhorn's terminology but labels it neopluralism, describing it as "characterized by a weakening of organized interests, a fragmented civil society, the persistence of clientelist forms of organization, technocratic elements in the government's dealings with individuals and groups, and the channeling of political participation into a narrow set of activities that don't effectively convey interests or affect policy." Claudio Holzner, *Poverty of Democracy: The Institutional Roots of Political Participation in Mexico* (Pittsburgh: University of Pittsburgh Press, 2009) and Philip

My second question is whether leadership changes between these two eras have been extensive, and if so, which features of Mexican leadership have been most altered by new institutional patterns, when did these changes actually take place, and why did they occur?

Given the resources available to me, I hoped to empirically test many questions that these broader issues raised. I devised two comprehensive data sets, which have taken forty years to complete. The most comprehensive is a data set that begins chronologically at June 1935, when Lázaro Cárdenas was president and freed himself from behind-the-scenes intervention and influence of his original mentor, Plutarco E. Calles, and continues through June 2009, during the third year of Felipe Calderón's presidency. This data set, a subset of my Mexican Political Biographies Project, contains extensive, detailed biographical information on nearly 3,000 influential national leaders, including cabinet secretaries, assistant secretaries, and *oficiales mayores* who represent the executive branch; supreme court justices, who represent the judicial branch; and repeating deputies and senators, who represent the legislative branch.[8] All state governors are included as representatives of the most prominent regional leaders and because they have carved out a major role in national political leadership, a role that is definitely on the increase since the 1990s.[9] Finally, I included influential political figures who do not qualify according to their more formal public positions, including guerrilla leaders, presidential candidates and party leaders of smaller political parties, and others who exerted a significant influence on elections and public policy.

To complement the information coded in the biographical data bank, I have attempted to bring the analysis of the data alive by incorporating extensive research based on published interviews in regional newspapers as well as appropriate, insightful excerpts from nearly a thousand interviews and personal correspondence from political figures representing every generation from the 1880s through the 1960s. These personal sources range from interviews and letters from seven presidents, dozens of cabinet members, assistant secretaries, supreme court justices, senators, governors, party presidents, and leading figures from all of the parties from the

Oxhorn and Graciela Ducantenzeiler, eds., *What Kind of Market? What Kind of Democracy? Latin America in the Age of Neoliberalism* (University Park: Pennsylvania State University Press, 1998).

8. These biographical entries are based on thousands of published sources including biographies, autobiographies, political histories, pamphlets, regional and national newspapers, regional and national magazines, scholarly articles, and books.

9. For example, see Rogelio Hernández Rodríguez, "The Renovation of Old Institutions: State Governors and the Political Transition in Mexico," *Latin American Politics and Society* 45, no. 4 (Winter 2003): 97–127, his *El centro dividido, la nueva autonomía de los gobernadores* (Mexico: El Colegio de México, 2008), and Rafael Morales Ramírez, "El Regreso de los gobernadores," *Este País* (February–March 2004): 39–43.

far left to the far right. Such sources provide a wealth of personal insight and observation in response to many of the questions raised in this study. To test the numerous assumptions and hypotheses I have examined, I divided this data set into three chronological eras. The *predemocratic era* is defined by the years 1935 through 1988, incorporating the nine presidencies of Lázaro Cárdenas (1934–40), Manuel Avila Camacho (1940–46), Miguel Alemán (1946–52), Adolfo Ruiz Cortines (1952–58), Adolfo López Mateos (1958–64), Gustavo Díaz Ordaz (1964–70), Luis Echeverría Alvarez (1970–76), José López Portillo (1976–82), and Miguel de la Madrid (1982–88). The second era, which I believed would produce significant differences from the preceding half a century, can be viewed as an era of *democratic transition*, consisting of the presidencies of Carlos Salinas de Gortari (1988–94) and Ernesto Zedillo (1994–2000). Finally, the third era, the *democratic period*, marked by the election of the first opposition party candidate for president since 1929, surveys the political leadership serving during the administrations of Vicente Fox (2000–2006) and Felipe Calderón (2006–2009).

Using the same criteria for inclusion of individual politicians in the 2009 project, I also made use of a data set I created in 1994, also part of the larger Mexican Political Biographies Project, which examined leading public figures from 1884 through 1934, beginning with Porfirio Díaz and culminating with the first year of the Cárdenas administration. Thus, the two data sets combined, containing biographical entries for nearly 4,000 individual political figures, allows comparisons covering more than 125 years. As far as I know, this combined data set is the largest, most detailed compilation of political elites from the nineteenth century to the contemporary period that exists for any country.[10]

In addition to being able to analyze the data on the basis of the presidential administrations that populate the three distinct analytical eras, I created variables that allow us to analyze the data on the basis of the generation (the decade in which they were born) to which they belong, on whether they held positions in any individual presidential administration, and on the presidency during which they held their first-time high-level office qualifying them institutionally for inclusion in the data set. The justification for creating and using a broad generational category for analysis is that generations, not presidential administrations, often provide insights into significant shifts in leadership characteristics well before they exert

10. Most of the biographical data for the 1994 data set can be found in my *Mexican Political Biographies, 1884–1935* (Austin: University of Texas Press, 1991). The biographical data for the 2009 data set will be available in *Mexican Political Biographies, 1935–2009*, 4th ed. (Austin: University of Texas Press, 2011), which will include a CD.

an impact in a given presidential period.[11] Also, generally two generations largely dominate individual presidential administrations.[12] The argument favoring the creation of a broad category of first-time office holders by administration is that it allows us to see the influence of each president on the changing composition of Mexican political leadership and introducing trends that may have an impact on that leadership for decades to come.[13]

Using these data, I began to address several more questions. First, how does the changing role of political institutions influence the characteristics and experiences of influential political leadership? For example, one would expect in a political model that underwent a change from a centralized political system to a democratic, decentralized system that the political setting and the new institutional political culture would promote an increase in the importance of local political experiences, elective or appointive.[14] Political scientists have argued that local political experience in the United States played an influential role in the careers of important future politicians.[15] Moreover, studies of Mexico conclude that the local political context is "a central feature affecting how one views the national political system" and that "local context, perceptions of the system, and political behavior are intimately connected."[16] There is no reason to believe that their findings would not apply to local politicians who eventually succeeded at the national level. Thus, an increase in the diversity and depth of local experiences also affects leadership behavior. I discovered, however, that some of our intuitive judgments anticipating these changes, as logical as they might seem, turn out to be incorrect.

To illustrate this very point, the evidence from the data shows that between 1935 and 2000 the percentage of prominent national political leaders who

11. Some of the sources on generational influences that most have affected my own vision include Karl Mannheim, "The Problem of Generations," in *Essays on the Sociology of Knowledge* (London: Routledge and Kegan Paul, 1959), 276–322; Philip H. Burch, *Elites in American History*, 3 vols. (New York: Homes and Meier, 1981); Alan B. Spitzer, "The Historical Problem of Generations," *American Historical Review* 78 (December 1973): 1353–85; and Marvin Rintala, "A Generation in Politics: A Definition," *Review of Politics* 25 (1963): 509–22.

12. I discovered this pattern in the early 1970s and discuss it in *Mexico's Leaders: Their Education and Recruitment* (Tucson: University of Arizona Press, 1980), 49–50.

13. I explore these arguments in more detail in "Age as a Variable in Political Recruitment," in *Political Recruitment across Two Centuries, Mexico, 1884-1991* (Austin: University of Texas Press, 1995), 37–57.

14. For the changing levels of regional participation, contributing to a more favorable environment toward electoral competition, see my "Province versus the Center: Democratizing Mexico's Political Culture," in Philip Kelly, ed., *Assessing Democracy in Latin America* (Boulder, Colo.: Westview Press, 1998), 76–92.

15. Joseph A. Schlesinger, *Ambition and Politics: Political Careers in the United States* (Chicago: Rand-McNally, 1966), 33–34.

16. John T. Hiskey, "Local Context and Democratization in Mexico," *American Journal of Political Science* 49, no. 1 (January 2005): 57.

formerly were mayors reached its highest level under President Díaz Ordaz (1964–70), who many analysts would describe as the most (or at the very least among the most) authoritarian of the predemocratic presidents.[17] But as the data revealed, there is a logical explanation for this earlier upsurge. On the other hand, the far more important pattern that emerges to illustrate the broader trend over time and support the intuitive notion grounded on early studies of the American democratic model, is that the highest number of former mayors reaching national posts occurred under Fox and Calderón, the two democratic presidents.[18] Moreover, from 1988 to 2000, as the democratic transition ensued, the pattern of increased local electoral experience among politicians became well established, increasing dramatically in contrast to all prominent politicians serving from 1970 to 1988.[19]

A second, equally broad question focuses on the extent to which informal (in contrast to formal) characteristics have an impact on leadership composition. For example, are informal qualities, such as kinship ties, as affected by democratic electoral competition as institutional consequences are? Throughout my previous leadership studies, I have noted the importance of family ties in Mexican politics as a means of linking political generations together and as a critical variable in determining access to and upward mobility through the leadership ladder.[20] One means of defining a changing leadership, especially one that might be altered by institutional change in the political model, is the degree to which the pool of politicians is altered by a more open and competitive process.

Political experience, measured by the type of offices a generation of political figures held previously, suggests certain changes, but not more than the extent to which politicians in one era were the products of important

17. For example, see George Philip's argument that Díaz Ordaz "was an outsider...who had made it to the top. Insecurity of status allied to personal ambition may have accentuated his interest in order and power, and his lack of sympathy with democracy or the 'values of 1968.'" *The Presidency in Mexican Politics* (New York: St. Martin's Press, 1992), 63.

18. For example, see the evidence presented in Joy Langston and Francisco Javier Aparicio, "Political Career Structures in Democratic Mexico, 1997–2006," paper presented at the American Political Science Association, Boston, August 28–31, 2008.

19. Interestingly, an international organization founded in 1989, Partners for Change Democratically, began training individuals to implement democracy through increased participation and negotiation. Mexico is one of their country partners, and their affiliate is Socios México/Centro de Colaboración Cívica, A.C. See www.partnersglobal.org/network/mexico, May 7, 2010.

20. Roderic Ai Camp, "Family Relationships in Mexican Politics: A Preliminary View," *Journal of Politics* 44, no. 3 (August 1982): 848–62, and "Camarillas in Mexican Politics, the Case of the Salinas Cabinet," *Journal of Mexican Studies* 6, no. 1 (Winter 1990): 85–108. For a comparative view, see Keith R. Legg, "Interpersonal Relationships and Comparative Politics: Political Clientelism in Industrial Societies," *Politics* 7, no. 1 (May 1972): 1–11. For another Latin American country, see Peter McDonough, *Power and Ideology in Brazil* (Princeton, N.J.: Princeton University Press, 1981).

political families in another. In other words, how different is the pool of democratic politicians from their predemocratic and transitional peers? Because the data set is so chronologically broad, I have been able to trace such familial linkages through more than ten generations.[21] Perhaps even more interesting, I also have tracked to some degree the extent to which contemporary politicians are related to historically important figures from the Porfirian elite or to their opponents among the revolutionary leadership, civilian and military alike.[22]

No variable is more difficult to ascertain than a politician's family background and socioeconomic origin. I have been able to provide precise, reliable information on these informal qualities for approximately half of the politicians analyzed. The rapid expansion of the Internet in Mexico allowed me to delve into local newspapers and other valuable local and national sources, adding significantly to our knowledge about individual politicians and their extended families. If anything, I would argue that my figures substantially undervalue the extent of such linkages, whether one is referring to historically important family ties extending back to the nineteenth or early decades of the twentieth century or to extended family members who have been deeply involved in local, state, and national politics.[23]

A single example analyzed in the chapter on local politics illustrates that during the years of the combined data sets from the 1880s to the present, four families in one community were known to have held the post of mayor nearly two-thirds of those years, from the first to the present decade.[24]

21. The depth of family linkages vary from one culture to another, with North America characterized by weak linkages. Although he emphasizes these differences as a basis for formulating social policies, David Sven Rehner offers interesting insights into the importance of such patterns in "Family Ties in Western Europe: Persistent Contrasts," *Population and Development Review* 24, no. 2 (June 1998): 203–34.

22. For a comparative, historical perspective from Brazil, see Linda Lewin, "Some Historical Implications of Kinship Organization for Family-Based Politics in the Brazilian Northeast," *Comparative Studies in Society and History* 21, no. 2 (April 1979): 262–92. For linkages within the Porfirian elite, see Armando Razo, *Social Foundations of Limited Dictatorship: Networks and Private Protection during Mexico's Early Industrialization* (Stanford, Calif.: Stanford University Press, 2008).

23. For extensive examples at the state and regional levels, see Mark Wasserman, *Persistent Oligarchs: The Political Economy of Chihuahua, Mexico, 1880-1940* (Durham, N.C.: Duke University Press, 1993); Stuart Voss, "Northwest Mexico," in Diana Balmori, Stuart Voss, and Miles Wortman, eds., *Notable Family Networks in Latin America* (Chicago: University of Chicago Press, 1984); and Hector Aguilar Camín, *La frontera nomada: Sonora y la revolución mexicana* (Mexico: Siglo XXI, 1977). One of the most comprehensive studies of family political ties straddling the revolutionary period through the 1990s is Javier Hurtado's outstanding *Familias, política y parentesco, Jalisco 1919-1991* (Mexico: Fondo de Cultura Económica, 1993).

24. These four families were represented forty-one out of sixty-seven times in Espinal, Oaxaca. The names can be found in the Espinal Web site through www.e-local.gob.mx/wb2/elocal. For comparable data on family influence among mayors in Brazil, and their ability

Thus, informal variables can sustain influences across historical periods and different political models, having their own impact on who reaches political office and thus on decision making.

A third question that has particular relevance to the arrival of democratic politics in Mexico concerns the extent of partisanship among Mexican politicians and how the importance of active party involvement and office-holding has changed as the institutional influence of political parties grew dramatically in the past two decades. I previously compared small groups of National Action Party (PAN) and Institutional Revolutionary Party (PRI) politicians, which revealed some important differences between the two groups.[25] But the role of partisanship among leading politicians has not been well examined largely because we have not accumulated adequate data to accomplish such an exploration over multiple decades.[26] Most analysts believe that during the years PRI maintained a virtual monopoly over the executive and judicial branches (which allowed few opposition victories in the legislative branch and none among state governors) that PRI partisanship would be extensive given its centralized control and party discipline.[27]

As I discovered, however, the reality of strong partisanship during the predemocratic era did not follow this expected pattern. Indeed, I found that only a small minority of PRI members (one in three) ever held a party position. In contrast, nearly eight out of ten PAN members held state or national party posts. When I surveyed political leaders' level of militancy, I discovered that only a third of PRI politicians during the predemocratic era could be considered militant rather than nominal party members! On the other

to transcend the change from dictatorship to democracy, see Claudio Ferraz and Federico Finan's conclusion that 31 percent of influential political families within a municipality were able to survive the change. "Political Power Persistence and Economic Development: Evidence from Brazil's Regime Transition," paper presented at the Conference on the Role of Elites in Economic Development, United Nations University-Wider, Helsinki, Finland, June 12-13, 2009, 6.

25. Roderic Ai Camp and Donald Mabry, "Mexican Political Elites 1935-1973: A Comparative Study," *Americas* 31, no. 4 (April 1975): 452–69.

26. The classic studies in American politics are Lewis Bowman and G. R. Boynton, "Recruitment Patterns among Local Party Officials: A Model and Some Preliminary Findings in Selected Locales," *American Political Science Review* 60, no. 3 (September 1966): 667–76, and Lester G. Seligman, "Political Recruitment and Party Structure: A Case Study," *American Political Science Review* 55, no. 1 (March 1961): 77–86, but they provide only limited insight into politicians pursuing national political careers. The best work remains Joseph A. Schlesinger, *Ambition and Politics: Political Careers in the United States* (New York: Rand McNally, 1966).

27. For comments on the degree of centralized control within the party, see Dale Story, *The Mexican Ruling Party: Stability and Authority* (Westport, Conn.: Praeger, 1986), 77ff. For the changes in disciplinary control by the party, see Joseph Klesner, "The End of Mexico's One Party Regime," *PS: Political Science & Politics* 34 (2001): 107–14.

hand, an examination of PAN members in the democratic era, in contrast to PRI, revealed the importance of party militancy among its leading politicians, including those achieving top posts in the executive branch. As I demonstrate in chapter 3, institutional variables, including the structure and role the party has played in the evolution of PAN's leadership, explains the huge differences in militant levels between PRI versus PAN and Party of the Democratic Revolution (PRD) politicians. Nevertheless, I also discovered that the larger political setting characterized by competitive electoral politics since 2000 produced similar recent trends among PRI politicians.

A fourth question I hoped to address in this study is to what extent has the advent of a democratic electoral process altered basic demographic characteristics among Mexican leadership, including their social and geographic origins? A number of demographic changes occurred among prominent political leadership over the past century. Not surprisingly, Mexican public life is overwhelming dominated by individuals who came from middle-class backgrounds. Middle-class politicians reached their apex under President Fox, but more interesting is the fact that the truly significant shift in the distribution of working and middle-class politicians actually occurred under Luis Echeverría, long before the democratic transition or the democratic era itself began.[28] One can offer several explanations for this change, including the fact that the beginning of Echeverría's presidency followed two decades of sustained economic growth.[29] It is also worth noting that the generations that dominated his presidency were the immediate products of postrevolutionary Mexico in the 1920s and 1930s. I also discovered the significance of social class in determining career preferences among leading politicians by branch of government, and how working class politicians have nearly disappeared from the judicial and executive branch leadership since the initiation of electoral democracy at the presidential level in 2000.[30]

28. Middle-class origins of national politicians is common in most other societies. For example, see Anthony Mughan and Samuel C. Patterson, eds., *Political Leadership in Democratic Societies* (Chicago: Nelson Hall, 1992), 119ff.

29. It is worth keeping in mind that Ronald Inglehart, using a wealth of data from the World Values Survey, has reached the conclusion that that "a massive body of evidence suggests that modernization theory's central premise was correct: economic development does tend to bring about important, roughly predictable changes in society, culture, and politics. But earlier versions of modernization theory need to be corrected in several respects." See Ronald Inglehart and Christian Welzel, "How Development Leads to Democracy: What We Know about Modernization," *Foreign Affairs* (March–April 2009): 37.

30. Social class, defined by levels of income, also produce significant differences among ordinary Mexican citizens in their basic conceptions of democracy, especially the principles of freedom of expression, liberty, equality, and the right to choose one's leaders. See Pablo Parás and Ken Coleman, *The Political Culture of Democracy in Mexico: 2006*, Latin American Public Opinion Project, December 2006.

Throughout these many years, I have been interested in gender issues related to leadership. As a result of that interest, and my earlier studies before the democratic transition began, I predicted (along with other analysts) that women would benefit from the advent of a democratic electoral process because they were heavily involved in grassroots organizations with participatory, democratic structures. These organizations honed women's skills in negotiating and leadership based on the principle of compromise.[31] To examine gender patterns and their impact carefully over long periods of time, I looked at women who were elected only once as members of congress and the senate, similar to the criteria I applied to early members of PAN and the Left before they achieved broad access to top political offices, to create a sufficient sample from which to draw credible conclusions.

Thus, I wanted to test whether the advent of electoral competition did indeed enhance the representation of women among leading political figures. As I will demonstrate, there is no question that women have increased their presence among top leadership since 2000, more than doubling their numbers. What is even more interesting, however, is that significant increases in female politicians already were occurring toward the end of the predemocratic era in the 1970s and 1980s, even before the democratic transition—but the transition reinforced and expanded their presence. One of the major discoveries in my analysis of gender patterns is that by altering the institutional patterns of how deputies would be selected and elected, the PRI enhanced political opportunities for women, who were best represented in the legislative branch.

By increasing the presence of women, the appearance of a democratic model also altered the overall composition of leading Mexican politicians. This is because the women elected differed from the elected men in many ways, including their educational levels and emphasis, political career experiences, and concentration on elective careers in the legislative branch. I discovered (and this finding is reinforced elsewhere in the study) that democratic change produced far greater consequences in the legislative branch than in any other institutional arena in government. The data also demonstrated that the expanded presence of women provided an equally important increase in party militancy, which in turn was linked to a career focus within the legislative branch, both national and state. In the long run, these and other changes wrought by women (because legislative careers rose in importance for leading politicians under Calderón), affect

31. I made this argument in "Women and Men, Men and Women: Gender Patterns in Mexican Politics," in Victoria Rodríguez, ed., Women's Participation in Mexican Political Life (Boulder, Colo.: Westview Press, 1998), 176.

the composition of leadership in the other branches of government, notably in the executive.[32]

My dissertation research led me indirectly to the theme of the importance of economists in Mexican public life. Economist-politicians took on greater visibility under President Salinas in the late 1980s, as they did elsewhere in Latin America. As I discovered in the late 1960s, their influence was already well under way, and they began making their mark in the administrations of José López Portillo and Miguel de la Madrid.[33] If we think of technocratic leadership, whatever its credentials, as having altered the makeup of Mexican politicians, we can go as far back as the *científicos* during the Porfiriato.[34] Having identified the growing influence of certain educational credentials among leading politicians in earlier studies, I began to see the importance of formal educational credentials defining a new generation of leaders well before the highly publicized technocratic generation at the end of the twentieth century.[35]

Has Mexico been characterized by more than one technocratic generation, and how has that generation molded top leadership generally? I make the argument that Mexico has witnessed two technocratic waves in the twentieth century and the beginning of a third wave under President Calderón. The initial technocratic wave is represented by the rise of civilian lawyers under Miguel Alemán, the first full-term civilian president since 1920. His generation represents the influence of college-educated leadership in Mexican politics, the importance of college professors and students in the recruitment of political leadership, and the dominance of

32. It also has been empirically demonstrated that those members of congress who have prior experience as a deputy or a senator are far more likely to obtain positions as committee chairs in the Chamber of Deputies, regardless of party. See D. Xavier Medina Vidal, Antonio Ugues Jr., and Shaun Bowler, "Experience Counts: The Revolving Door of the Mexican Chamber of Deputies," paper presented at the Western Political Science Association, Vancouver, British Columbia, 2009.

33. For the various versions of these public figures in individual Latin American countries, see Jorge I. Domínguez, *Freeing Politics and Markets in Latin America in the 1990s* (University Park: Pennsylvania State University Press, 1997). For the best description of the evolution of this movement, see Veronica Montecinos and John Markoff's excellent studies "The Ubiquitous Rise of Economists," *Journal of Public Policy* 13, no. 1 (1993): 37–68 and "From the Power of Economic Ideas to the Power of Economists," in Miguel A. Centeno, ed., *The Other Mirror: Essays on Latin America* (Princeton, N.J.: Princeton University Press, 2001). Raymond Vernon, a leading economist, was the first scholar to take note of this growing influence in his prescient *The Dilemma of Mexico's Development: The Roles of the Private and Public Sectors* (Cambridge, Mass.: Harvard University Press, 1965).

34. For a detailed characterization of this group, see Charles A. Hale's wonderful *Transformation of Liberalism in Late Nineteenth-Century Mexico* (Princeton, N.J.: Princeton University Press, 1989), 121ff.

35. "The Middle-Level Technocrat in Mexico," *Journal of Developing Areas* 6 (July 1972): 571–82 and "Education and Political Recruitment in Mexico: The Alemán Generation," *Journal of Inter-American Studies and World Affairs* 18 (August 1976): 295–321.

the two national educational institutions on the recruitment and socialization of Mexican leadership, both centered in the Federal District. The
Alemán generation reinforced the importance of the federal executive
branch and highlighted national bureaucratic office as the most desirable
post for future ambitious politicians to seek.

The Alemán generation's influence extends well beyond providing a
technocratic precedent early in the twentieth century. The characteristics
of this generation establish institutional patterns that affect the composition of leadership for the remainder of the century, as well as after 2000;
therefore, they are examined extensively. For example, two patterns this
group accentuated—geographic concentration from the Federal District and
the influence of two institutional sources of leadership in the same locale—
affect the presence of dozens of other background variables, many of which
are influential among politicians from other eras or cultures. Young people
who develop political ambitions and are successful in filling those ambitions
understand these patterns and take measures to become part of them. Thus,
they move to the Federal District because they realize beforehand that they
will be able to associate with others who can open the doors to their political ambitions. In making that choice, they devalue other sources of institutional recruitment, such as local political office and local party activities.
Furthermore, Alemán and his collaborators failed to expand political liberties and participation, a goal many of them professed as student activists.
The Alemán generation's disciples perpetuated many of these patterns and
perceptions, and they continued to do so for years to come.

The emergence of the more well-known economic technocrats of the
Salinas era actually contributed to the deep divisions within PRI leadership, which fomented democratic change in the 1980s. Precisely the
conflict between this wing and the nontechnocratic PRI wing led by
Cuauhtémoc Cárdenas and Porfirio Muñoz Ledo resulted in the splintering
of the party and the founding of the PRD shortly after Cárdenas's land-
mark but unsuccessful opposition presidential campaign in 1988.[36] This
second technocratic wave boasted its own set of credentials, establishing
Mexican leadership as having postgraduate education, specialized training
in economics, and most important, advanced studies from U.S. Ivy League
schools.[37]

36. For the critical consequences of this election, see my "Mexico's 1988 Elections: A
Turning Point for Its Political Development and Foreign Relations," in Edgar W. Butler and
Jorge A. Bustamante, eds., *Sucesion Presidencial: The 1988 Mexican Presidential Election*
(Boulder, Colo.: Westview Press, 1991), 245–62. This book provides the most comprehensive
views on this benchmark election.
37. "The Technocrat in Mexico and the Survival of the Political System," *Latin American
Research Review* 20, no. 1 (1985): 97–118.

The initiation of democratic politics moderated the impact of the second technocratic wave while introducing a third wave, notable for its different educational specializations extending well beyond economics into numerous contemporary fields, including communications, computer technology, and advanced engineering in multiple, esoteric disciplines. This wave took on additional features that were defined by the presence of PAN members in the most influential policy-making positions and reversed some of the more pronounced trends found in the second wave, including the emphasis on U.S. graduate education. Democratic politics increased the diversification of educational training in this third wave while simultaneously continuing to place an emphasis on specialization.

The basic characteristics found among all prominent politicians are not homogeneous. In fact, when essential demographic and career experiences of leading public figures in Mexico are examined, significant patterns that strongly impact diversity within that leadership quickly surface. I speculated that since the democratic era began, electoral democracy would increase the regional diversity of Mexico's leadership. The logic underlying this assumption was that the increasing competition—opening the doors to candidates from other parties—occurred unevenly at the local and state levels.[38] Is this the case? For example, an examination of leading politicians' career paths suggests that those figures who represent executive branch careers are much more likely than all other prominent politicians to have come from the Federal District. In fact, four out of ten assistant secretaries of cabinet-level agencies come from this single entity. Given the appointive powers of cabinet secretaries and the fact that numerous assistant secretaries go on to hold cabinet posts, the importance of this geographic bias increases. A comparison of the regional origins of predemocratic with democratic executive branch officials and supreme court justices (representing the judicial branch) reveals a huge increase in politicians coming from the capital. This is also the case in the legislative branch, but the overall percentages are no match for the portions found in the other two branches. One would expect some increase in leading figures coming from the Federal District since its population from 1920 to 1950 nearly doubled from 6 to 12 percent. But the percentage of leading politicians far exceeds

---

38. Interestingly, at least among Western democracies, once democratic institutions were in place, little variation in geographic origins occurred over time. Joel D. Aberbach, Robert D. Putnam, and Bert A. Rockman, *Bureaucrats and Politicians in Western Democracies* (Cambridge, Mass.: Harvard University Press, 1983), 78. In the transition from communism to the first phase of democracy in Russia, a survey of the literature suggests that considerable continuity in leadership at the local level existed, but so did substantial change. Stephen White and Olga Kryshtanouskaya report these conclusions in "Russia: Elite Continuity and Change," in Mattei Dogan and John Higley, eds., *Elites, Crises, and the Origins of Regimes* (Lanham, Md.: Rowman and Littlefield, 1998), 126.

those percentages, regardless of the generation examined. Democracy definitely has produced a change in the distribution of birthplaces among leading political figures, but it has reduced rather than increased geographic diversity.[39] 

Throughout much of the book I use generational data to test a number of questions, believing that age provides a critical measurement of identifying and analyzing new leadership trends. This is because generations are distributed among presidencies, whether they are confined to first-time high-level officeholders or include repeat performers. I believe that generational differences influence ideological differences, which affect policy positions and the ability of politicians to accomplish legislative compromise.[40] I expected that the two former opposition parties, especially the PAN, would consist of younger politicians compared to their counterparts in the PRI. Again, if one thinks of democratic competition and a democratic opening as diversifying the pool of leading political figures, the distribution of birthdates among leading figures confirms that hypothesis. Generally, PRD partisans were even younger than their PAN peers; more important, both were significantly younger than the PRIistas, thus increasing the presence of a younger generation in the mix of ages in this leadership.

Career differences are equally valuable in understanding the distribution of informal characteristics. Intuitively, one might expect democratic competition to decrease the percentage of top political figures who were related to other individuals active in politics. Does this turn out to be confirmed by the data? Overall, nearly half of all cabinet secretaries were related to other political figures. When this figure is compared to the post-2000 era leaders, the percentage of cabinet secretaries with such kinship ties does decrease significantly, suggesting that the appearance of PAN and to a lesser degree PRD politicians in larger numbers has broadened the pool

39. In my earlier work on a highly selective group of influential figures from all sectors of society, I found that 70 percent of these "power elites" spent most of their adult lives in just three cities: Mexico City, Guadalajara, and Monterrey. Birthplace and residence have significant consequences for political, economic, and social networking. Roderic Ai Camp, *Mexico's Mandarins: Crafting a Power Elite for the Twenty-first Century* (Berkeley: University of California Press, 2002), 67ff.

40. Christopher Díaz, in his study of bill initiation in the Chamber of Deputies from 1994 to 2003, found that PRI members were, "with their colleagues in other parties, very much involved in strengthening the Chamber as a political institution by, among other activities, initiating legislation.... Were it not for the democratic transition, it seems unlikely that any of the changes in PRI deputy behavior discussed in this study would have taken place. For PRI deputies in particular, the advent of divided government has challenged them to become more active in promoting their party's interests, and by extension their own interests, than previous generations of PRI deputies." "Do 'Nuevo PRI' Deputies in Mexico Legislate Differently Than Their 'Dinosauro' Predecessors? A Preliminary Analysis of Bill Initiation in the Mexican Chamber of Deputies," paper presented at the Latin American Studies Association, Las Vegas, Nevada, October 7–9, 2004. 13.

of potential political leaders. However, this is not universally true because little decline occurred among top figures in the judicial branch.

Career patterns also affected the source of politicians' education. Again, as was the case of kinship ties, democratic electoral change produced numerous trends contributing to the diversity of political leadership. Perhaps the most notable was the decline in graduates from public universities in Mexico City, particularly the National University, and the concomitant rise of state universities as the alma mater among numerous younger politicians.[41]

Of all the variables examined in this study, perhaps the most controversial is the degree to which non-violent and violent alterations in a political model produce similarly dramatic changes. I believed that democratic change would produce consequences for political leadership that would affect as many variables as violent change. What I discovered, however, is that non-violent change can be as dramatic, or more so, than violent change, and that some of those changes may actually occur in the opposite direction.

I want to be explicit, as I am in chapter 8, that I am referring to the major conflicts that occurred during the decade of 1910–20. I do not attempt to define that violence in any other way for the purposes of my analysis, especially not implying the degree to which Mexico actually underwent a social revolution, a highly contentious issue among historians, as a result of these civil conflicts.[42] What we do know is that approximately two million Mexicans (out of fifteen million) were lost to Mexico, because they either died directly or indirectly from the conflicts that took place during this decade, or were never born, and those experiences affected the vast majority of Mexicans for decades after.[43] As Jack Womack Jr. has suggested, violence can be defined in many ways, including doing violence to the Mexican poor. He also stated that other, singular violent events took place after these conflicts, including the assassination of Luis Donaldo

41. For my early speculations about these educational patterns on political life, see my "Review: Education and Politics, Politics and Education, Mexico in the 20th Century," *History of Education Quarterly* 25 (Summer 1985): 215–20.

42. For a detailed analysis of how revolution and democracy have been used in the Latin American context, see Alan Knight's enlightening, in-depth overview in "Democratic and Revolutionary Traditions in Latin America," *Bulletin of Latin American Research* 20, no. 2 (2001): 147–86.

43. Robert McCaa, "Missing Millions: The Demographic Costs of the Mexican Revolution," *Mexican Studies/Estudios Mexicanos* 19, no. 2 (Summer 2003): 367–400. These figures include "excess deaths," lost births, and a small percentage of emigrants. For the long-term impact on ordinary families, see Linda S. Stevenson and Mitchell A. Seligson, "Fading Memories of the Revolution: Is Stability Eroding in Mexico?," in Roderic Ai Camp, ed., *Polling for Democracy: Public Opinion and Political Liberalization in Mexico* (Wilmington: Scholarly Resources, 1996), 59–80.

Colosio during the presidential campaign of 1994, which clearly produced its own political consequences.[44] Whatever other forms of violence have occurred in Mexico, none approached the impact of the extensive armed violence of that decade and its potential consequences for altering political leadership.

In an era when four-fifths of Mexicans lived in villages and towns of fewer than 2,500 residents, one would expect the violent upheavals that took place in the decade of 1910-20 to have dramatically increased the percentage of politicians from rural backgrounds in the 1920s' administrations. The percentage of politicians with rural birthplaces from the 1920-28 administration's dominant generation did increase, but by only 12 percent. As a consequence of nonviolent electoral change in 2000, the rural backgrounds of the 1950s generation unexpectedly increased by 20 percent, exceeding the extent of the change occurring eighty years previously.

Equally important changes occurred in the place of birth among Mexican politicians. I expected the numbers of leading figures born in the Federal District to decline significantly, complementary to the increase in rural birthplaces, because most of the combatants in the revolution were products of the provinces. This was indeed the case, as the politicians from the capital declined dramatically by 64 percent, the highest regional change among all seven regions. Nevertheless, the democratic era witnessed a dramatic 72 percent increase in politicians *from* the Federal District—again greater than what took place after a decade of violence. In six out of the seven regions, nonviolent periods resulted in significantly more dramatic change than did violent periods.

If some of the most influential informal characteristics of prominent Mexican political figures are examined, similar patterns are encountered. For example, I would predict that in both cases of violent and nonviolent change, the numbers of politicians with family members who held important political and military posts would decline, given the altered pool from which a new generation of politicians emerged in the 1920s and 2000s. Given the deep ideological and social class differences between the prerevolutionary and postrevolutionary cohorts, I would expect those changes to be far more dramatic among the generations produced by violent conflict. Politicians with such family connections do decrease in both decades, but by the same percentages, with the democratic generation having slightly fewer such family ties.

Perhaps the most interesting of the variables that might be affected by a change in the political model is politicians' prior career experiences. Several such experiences that I examined included local offices, business management or ownership, and military careers. Among

44. Personal communication with the author, March 7, 2009.

postrevolutionary leadership I might expect the percentage holding local political offices and having reached the rank of colonel in the military to increase significantly, given the origins of those generations. On the other hand, I would also expect important business backgrounds, common in the Porfiriato, to decline substantially. Local office holding increased by nearly half, whereas business backgrounds declined by nearly three-quarters. Politicians with military backgrounds increased 15 percent. Eighty years later, after the election of 2000, an examination of the same variables revealed that politicians with local political experience increased a whopping 170 percent, and those with business backgrounds, which I also would have expected to increase, did so by an equally dramatic 140 percent.[45] Politicians with military careers declined by nearly two-thirds, an equally significant figure. In short, a comparison of all three variables, regardless of the direction of the change, clearly demonstrates nonviolent consequences to be more formidable than their violent counterparts.

To speculate about the future of national leadership, I also explore the impact of governorships on prominent national politicians and on the composition of that leadership. Given the fact the five of the six leading candidates for the presidency in 2000 and 2006 were former governors, it is not unreasonable to expect that former governors may play an increasingly influential role in determining the composition of the future political elite as cabinet secretaries and presidents.[46] The fundamental question raised by this pattern is the following: are governors and former governors who hold national political office different from other leading politicians in their formal and informal background variables, and if so, what are these differences and their potential consequences for national leadership in the coming decades?

45. It is worthwhile to note that a recent examination of Chinese leadership concluded that the Central Committee of the Communist Party made a decision in the 1980s to promote lower level bureaucrats to the top on the basis of performance targets, for example, their ability to attract foreign investment. Thus, skills valued in the private sector, which have become increasingly found among Mexican politicians since 2000, have been identified along with political skills as essential to success in China. See Xiaowei Zang, "The Elite Incentives and Capacity in Governing Growth in China," paper presented at the Conference on the Role of Elites in Economic Development, United Nations University-Wider, Helsinki, Finland, June 12-13, 2009, 17-19.

46. In a comparative study of Argentina, Mexico, and Colombia, Tulia Falleti argued that as a consequence of decisions made by a technocratic leadership, beginning during the administration of José López Portillo, by 1999, on the cusp of the democratic shift, the power of subnational executives (specifically governors) increased. "Governing Governors: Decentralization Trajectories and Balance of Power in Argentina, Mexico, and Columbia, 1978-1999," paper presented at the American Political Science Association, Boston, August 29-September 1, 2002, 36. Falleti published a broader argument of her decentralization theses in "A Sequential Theory of Decentralization: Latin American Cases in Comparative Perspective," *American Political Science Review* 99, no. 3 (2005): 327-46.

Some of the broader findings mentioned here can be attributed to the presence of prominent leaders with backgrounds as state governors.[47] Governors, for example, are increasingly from rural origins and have prior experiences in elective local office as mayors and state legislators, have business administration degrees and degrees from regional public institutions, are not college educated or have graduate training from schools other than those in the United States, have significant business experiences, have prior legislative careers, and have family with political or revolutionary experiences.

Finally, although I have excluded the impact of the consequences of the many patterns discovered in my analysis on generations of politicians' policy decisions (because it goes well beyond the scope of this study and involves variables too numerous to incorporate), I have added a final chapter on the Alemán generation, which consists of his college generation (1926–30), his preceding college generation (1921–25), and the immediately following college generation (1931–35). This analysis is based on data and extensive interviews and correspondence with numerous members of his generation, including Alemán himself. I have explored in detail the impact of this generation on the structure of Mexican political leadership, describing the actual and potential consequences on recruitment and socialization, or what Alan Knight aptly labels the modus operandi or way of doing politics, especially as it applies to the mass public. "One has to be careful not to mask how leaders get, retain and use power, by focusing on leadership characteristics."[48] I also have devoted equal attention to this generation's views and that of North American and Mexican scholars' interpretations of the impact of this group on public policy, exploring the linkage between what they claimed to have valued as a generation and the degree to which they actually concretely implemented those goals.[49] I believe this analysis demonstrates that this generation did have a long-term effect on the sources of

47. For fascinating insights into how recruitment patterns altered the selection of governors and increased the time frame from which local political leaders could conceivably be elected governors, see the views of a public policy official in the Mexican presidency: Alain de Remes, "Democratization and Dispersion of Power: New Scenarios in Mexican Federalism," *Mexican Studies* 22, no. 1 (Winter 2006): 175–204. De Remes further analyzes the important impact these changes have had on federalism.

48. Personal communication with the author, February 24, 2009. As Knight correctly notes, for example, one cannot just examine the continuity of political families through different eras, but the way in which those particular political figures function in the political world and how they interact with other political actors, including various constituencies.

49. One of the few efforts I have come across that links elite views empirically to public policies, in this case poverty alleviation, in Latin America, is Elisa P. Reis's recent examination of Brazil, "Poverty and Inequality in the Eyes of the Elites," paper presented at the Conference on the Role of Elites in Economic Development, United Nations University-Wider, Helsinki, Finland, June 12–13, 2009.

political leadership and therefore on the structure of the political system, given the PRI's monopoly. The changes that took place under this generation in the composition of leadership was as dramatic (or more so) as those that occurred under Fox and Calderón, suggesting just how influential this group came to be through its impact on the predemocratic era. In contrast, although they did have a significant impact on public policy, especially the issue of political order and unity, state intervention in the economy, and pragmatic decision making, they failed to implement another crucial leading tenet of their early beliefs—political liberty—which helped perpetuate the political model through the second half of the twentieth century.

# 2

# All Politics Is Local

## Mexico's Local Path to Democracy?

One of the founding principles in the recruitment literature on American politics is that local political activity initiated the careers of most leading national politicians. Early studies suggested that American politicians in the mid-twentieth century earned their political spurs through participation in local political and party posts.[1] Numerous politicians pointed to their experiences as mayors, state legislators, and governors, often leading to elected positions as members of Congress and the Senate. Mexico has an important historical political tradition of regionalism, suggesting that local political experience also became a critical variable in the emerging careers of ambitious politicians.[2] Mexico, however, never fully solved the tension between regionalism and centralism, a major theme in the nineteenth century, even though local autonomy became a major issue in the Mexican Revolution of 1910, especially among northern revolutionaries.[3]

After the revolution, the victorious politician generals confronted a series of rebellions in the 1920s and constructed an institutional vehicle in 1929, the National Revolutionary Party (PNR), designed in part to strengthen national political leadership and centralize political control.[4] Thus, during the evolution and consolidation of this apparatus for reinforcing the power of national political leadership, the party served as an organization through which the presidency of Mexico and leading executive and party figures attempted to control the nomination and election

---

1. C. Wright Mills, *The Power Elite* (New York: Oxford University Press, 1959), 229; Joseph A. Schlesinger, *Ambition and Politics: Political Careers in the United States* (Chicago: Rand-McNally, 1966), 33–34.

2. For a thorough discussion of Mexican regionalism, see Eric Van Young, ed., *Mexico's Regions: Comparative History and Development* (La Jolla: Center for U.S.-Mexican Studies, University of California, San Diego, 1992).

3. This particular theme is well developed in Michael Meyer, *Pascual Orozco and the Mexican Revolution, 1910-1915* (Lincoln: University of Nebraska Press, 1967).

4. See Luis Javier Garrido, *El Partido de la Revolución Institucionalizada* (Mexico: Siglo XXI, 1982), for a detailed explanation of its founding.

of deputies, senators, and governors. It is important to note, however, that contrary to popular myth, presidents and their representatives did not choose all politicians for these high-level positions.[5]

Mexico introduced new political structures and institutions in the 1930s that combated decentralizing forces, moving Mexico away from an incipient postrevolutionary democratic direction. This was reflected in the independence of many representatives in the federal congress (who until 1934 could be reelected consecutively), as well as among state governors, who represented diverse local interests and political groups. This produced numerous factions. For example, Guanajuato and Tabasco have lengthy, well-known histories of such internal rivalries in the 1930s, 1940s, and 1950s.[6]

The fundamental question addressed in this book is the degree to which nondemocratic and democratic structures impacted leadership and the extent to which changing leadership influenced those same structures. One of the arguments I offer from my earlier work is that in Mexico and elsewhere political observers need to pay greater attention to informal features of the political system, which are of equal importance to established institutional structures. I have identified the extraordinary significance of social networking in Mexico, which is not only fundamental to understanding the interactions among politicians but, indeed, among all leadership groups.[7]

The argument can be made that the influence of social networks, specifically familial ties, has withstood the impact of political structures and institutions over time, regardless of their democratic or nondemocratic features. Many scholars, myself included, warned during the years of Mexico's democratic transition (1988-2000) that democracy would not necessarily lead to the specific changes one might expect from electoral competition at the local level. In some locales, politics might become less rather than more competitive.[8] Recently, the Mexican government introduced an Internet

5. See my article on governors for evidence of this statement: "Losers in Mexican Politics: A Comparative Study of Official Party Precandidates for Gubernatorial Elections, 1970-75," in James W. Wilkie and Kenneth R. Ruddle, eds., *Quantitative Latin American Studies: Methods and Findings. Statistical Abstract of Latin America Supplement Series*, vol. 6 (Los Angeles: UCLA Latin American Center, 1977), pp. 23-33.

6. For example, see Ernest Gruening, *Mexico and Its Heritage* (New York: D. Appleton-Century, 1928), a book based on Gobernación's agents' own observations of these rival factions in numerous states.

7. *Mexico's Mandarins: Crafting a Power Elite for the Twenty-first Century* (Berkeley: University of California Press, 2002).

8. For an excellent analysis of changing behavior locally toward federal projects within a larger democratic context, see John Stolle-McAllister's case study, in which he concludes that "local activists took advantage of that space [democracy] and, building on their own perspectives and experiences, voiced opposition to the projects, reinterpreted nationalist ideologies

resource of considerable value to scholars that can shed some light on the impact of family linkages in local politics. Known as e-local, this encyclopedic Web site for every municipality in the country follows a consistent format and contains comparable demographic and economic information.[9] One feature of interest to the present argument is the government's request that each community list its *presidentes muncipales* (mayors). Many sites have done so since 1917, and others from more recent periods to the present. Espinal, Oaxaca, took the opportunity to provide a list from 1882 to the present covering the presidencies of Porfirio Díaz to Felipe Calderón.[10] What is extraordinary about this list is that from 1882 to 1892, the four names Toledo, Castillejos, Dehesa, and Benitez appear, accounting for five of the eight individuals who held the mayor's post. In the first decade, Toledo reappears on the list nine different times, most recently 2001-3; Castillejos appears twelve times, most recently 1999-2001; Dehesa appears seven times, most recently 1945-46; and Benitez nine times, most recently 1947-48. Furthermore, these original four families frequently intermarried in later years. Thus, the four families have been represented in this office forty-one out of sixty-seven times!

The case of Espinal suggests that in some cities, despite major political events and upheavals, extended families have dominated local leadership over multiple generations. This particular pattern is indicative of the importance of local influence, including networking ties, on political leadership. Surprisingly, Espinal produced two native sons who form part of the nearly 3,000 prominent national figures included in the broader study. The first is Demetrio Vallejo, a self-educated son of Zapotec Indians outside the circle of local elites, who exerted tremendous influence on the democratizing unions in Mexico as early as the 1950s and became a prominent figure in the Mexican Workers Party (PMT).[11] The second is an earlier figure, Wilfrido Cruz Castellijos, who was related to one of the dominant local political families. He became a lawyer, judge, two-time member of congress from Oaxaca, and senator under President Cárdenas.[12] Neither of these men, however, were

---

about land and revolution, and built cross-sectoral alliances that promoted a different kind of political project." "What *Does* Democracy Look Like? Local Movements Challenge the Mexican Transition," *Latin American Perspectives* 32, no. 4 (July 2005): 33.

9. See www.e-local.gob.mx/wb2/elocal. One can go to the Web site directly, then to each individual state, and a listing of municipalities. However, a general search of the Internet will bring up any topic listed in an individual e-local municipal site.

10. It omits a ten-year period from 1921 to 1931.

11. See www.loscuentos.net; www.Proceso.com.mx, 2008; *Hispano Americano*, March 21, 1983, 7; *Excélsior*, December 26, 1985, 1.

12. Ronald Hilton, *Who's Who in Latin America: Mexico* (Stanford, Calif.: Stanford University Press, 1945), 32; Salvador Novo, *La vida en México en el periodo presidencial de Miguel Alemán* (Mexico: Empresas Editoriales, 1967), 286.

involved in local politics; therefore, such experiences were not significant in their choice to pursue political careers, nor did such experiences become influential stepping stones in their national career ladders.

Are these men the exception or the rule, and to what extent has local political experience played a significant role in the careers of national politicians since the 1930s?[13] What table 2.1 clearly illustrates is that 7-10 percent of prominent political figures in Mexico born before 1940 could list having been a mayor among their career credentials. Little variation occurred among those born before 1889 through 1939.

Interestingly, since 1940, Mexican politicians increasingly have served as mayors of their home community, more often than not from the town in which they were born. Only one out of ten politicians could claim this experience, but the last three generations essentially doubled the incidence of holding this office in their early political careers (table 2.1).

State capitals, not surprisingly, have been significantly more influential than other cities in producing national politicians. A notable case is that of Toluca, México, only an hour's drive from Mexico City, the national capital. Since 1940, twenty-three individuals have administered the fortunes of this dynamic provincial city. Nearly half of these politicians eventually reached important national posts, and several were extremely influential in Mexican national politics. Of the eleven mayors who reached influential posts, three became governors of México state,[14] ten served as members of congress or as senators, and two held posts on the national executive committee of the Institutional Revolutionary Party (PRI). Seven were prominent enough to qualify for inclusion in the national data set.[15]

Two individuals, Carlos Hank González and Emilio Chuayffet Chemor, reached influential cabinet posts as head of the Federal District Department (1976-82) and Secretariat of Government (1995-98), respectively. Hank González became one of the most influential political figures in Mexico in the last third of the twentieth century, serving in two other cabinet posts under President Carlos Salinas and creating one of the most extensive political networks, exceeding that of many presidents, in the second half of the twentieth century.[16] His son became mayor of

13. For the importance of local politics and the role it has played in the democratization of Mexico, see Andrew D. Selee's, *Democracy Close to Home? Decentralization, Democratization, and Informal Power in Mexico* (University Park: Pennsylvania State University Press, 2010).

14. Juan Fernández Albarrán, Carlos Hank González, and Emilio Chuayffet Chemor.

15. For a detailed analysis of the political linkages of PRI politicians in the state of México, see Claudia Abigail Morales Gómez, "Las elites gobernantes Priístas del estado de México: Su conformación y redes, 1942-2005," *Convergencia* 13, no. 40 (January–April 2006): 189-229.

16. Roderic Ai Camp, Mexican Political Biographies Project, 1993. Hank González counted dozens of successful politicians as members of his political group or *camarilla*. See

**Table 2.1.** Generations of National Politicians
Who Were Mayors

| Generation | Mayors (%) |
|---|---|
| Pre-1889 | 7 |
| 1890–99 | 10 |
| 1900–9 | 7 |
| 1910–19 | 8 |
| 1920–29 | 10 |
| 1930–39 | 7 |
| 1940–49 | 12 |
| 1950–59 | 14 |
| 1960– | 22 |

*Source*: Mexican Political Biographies Project, 2009.

Tijuana and ran for governor of Baja California. Two mayors came from politically active families. Yolanda Sentíes de Ballesteros, who served as mayor in the late 1970s, is the daughter of a prominent cabinet figure and former member of congress.[17] Enrique González Isunza, twice a member of congress, is the son of a member of congress who served from 1949 to 1952.[18]

The most important conclusion that can be reached from analyzing this specific example of an important provincial capital is that for decades being a mayor provided a significant stepping stone to Mexico's national legislative branch, specifically as a member of the lower house. When a candidate from the National Action Party (PAN) won the Toluca post for the first time in 2000, he resigned to run successfully for congress at the end of his term (this happened again with another PAN candidate in 2003).[19] This pattern is replicated widely across Mexico; consequently, local elective office becomes an important means through which individuals can achieve national office. In some cases, such individuals attract the attention of national political leaders and are able to propel themselves on to important executive branch posts.

---

my description in "Camarillas in Mexican Politics, the Case of the Salinas Cabinet," *Mexican Studies/Estudios Mexicanos* 6, no. 1 (Winter, 1990): 85–107.

17. She was also the first female mayor of Toluca and senator from the state of México. *Excélsior*, March 1, 1982, 26; *Diccionario biográfico de México* (Mexico: Presidencia de la República, 1992), 351–52.

18. *Quién es quién en el Congreso, diputados y senadores de la LVII Legislatura* (1997–2000) (Mexico: ITED, 1998), 170.

19. Juan Carlos Núñez Armas, 2000–2003, and Armando Enríquez Flores, 2003–6. See http://www.e-local.gob.mx/work/templates/enciclo/mexico/mpios/15106a.htm, 2007.

Perhaps the most pronounced example of a city that has become a training ground for Mexican politicians is that of Atlacomulco, known to any
politician who is a product of the state of México. When one glances down
the list of Atlacomulco mayors from 1940 to the present, a single family
name stands out: Monroy. Out of the twenty-eight individuals who have
served as mayor, nine have been Monroys. What makes Atlacomulco a special example is that it has produced the largest, most influential group of
national politicians of any small town in Mexico, and these family linkages
extend back at least 100 years.

The governor of México state, Enrique Peña Nieto (2005–11), considered a strong early contender for his party's presidential nomination in 2012, was born in Atlacomulco in 1966. Peña Nieto is related
to four previous governors of his home state.[20] Through his mother,
he is related to Arturo Montiel Rojas, who preceded him in office and
was originally considered the favored candidate of a PRI faction for its
presidential nomination in 2006 until a scandal forced him to withdraw.
Montiel Rojas's father was mayor of Atlacomulco in 1971–72, and his
grandmother comes from the Monroy family. Peña Nieto's grandfather
Enrique Nieto Montiel, who in 1953–54 also held the post of mayor of
Atlacomulco, married the sister of Governor Salvador Sánchez Colín,
who therefore is his great uncle and another favorite son of Atlacomulco.
A daughter from this marriage is the wife of Governor Alfredo del Mazo
González's (1981–85) cousin. Del Mazo, in turn, is the son of Alfredo
del Mazo Vélez, also governor of México (1945–51), who is the cousin of
Mario Colín Sánchez, a native of Atlacomulco and a three-time member
of congress. Peña Nieto's brother also served as mayor of Atlacomulco
from 1994 to 1996.

The Atlacomulco clan began with the distinguished international
career of Isidro Fabela Alfaro (1882–64), who left the city to study law at
the National University in Mexico City. Fabela soon returned to his home
state, serving as a member of congress in 1912–14 and again in 1922. He
also became secretary of foreign relations under Carranza, and governor of México in 1942. While serving in the senate, he resigned in 1946
to accept an appointment as judge of the International Court of Justice.
Fabela extended his political influence well beyond the state of México and
beyond his own generation as a mentor to Adolfo López Mateos, whom
he chose while governor to direct the Scientific and Literary Institute of
Mexico in 1944. He then selected López Mateos as his alternate senator in
1946. This opened the way for López Mateos to hold the position of senator
until 1952, bringing him to the attention of the PRI's president as well as

20. See www.eluniversal.com.mx, February 11, 2005.

to Adolfo Ruiz Cortines, whose presidential campaign López Mateos managed in 1952.[21]

Three native sons of Atlacomulco, who were contemporaries of López Mateos, distinguished themselves in national politics. Roberto Barrios Castro, also Fabela's disciple, became secretary general of the National Peasant Federation (CNC) in 1947 and then a member of López Mateos's cabinet as head of the Department of Agrarian Affairs and Colonization. Alfredo del Mazo Vélez, also Fabela's disciple, in addition to serving as a senator and governor, joined López Mateos's cabinet as secretary of Hydraulic Resources. Del Mazo's father and grandfather both were mayors of Atlacomulco. Finally, Salvador Sánchez Colín, who served as governor of Mexico from 1951 to 1957, became López Mateos's alternate when he took over the senate post from Fabela.

Two of these politicians, del Mazo Vélez and Sánchez Colín, along with Adolfo López Mateos and Fabela, helped the stellar career of Carlos Hank González. Hank González came to know Fabela when the former was a schoolteacher in Atlacomulco from 1947 to 1951 and as head of the Ideal Republic Club in that city.[22] The remaining native son of Atlacomulco, who also appears among our leading politicians, is Arturo Martínez Legorreta (born 1938), who served as a two-time member of congress and president of PRI in the state of México.[23]

There is no question that serving as a mayor of small or influential communities in Mexico can serve as a jumping-off point for an important political career.[24] As opposition parties grew significantly in strength in the

---

21. *Hispanic American Historical Review* (February 1972): 124–25; *Enciclopedia de México* (1977), 3, 628; www.atlacomulco.com.mx, 2008. See Mario Colín's biography of Fabela as governor, in *Isidro Fabela, un gobernante intelectual (1942-1945)* (Toluca: Instituto Científico y Literario del Estado de México, 1946), and for his early career, see María Teresa Jarquín's excellent *Isidro Fabela: Pensador, político, y humanista, 1882-1964* (Zinacautepec: El Colegio Mexiquense, 1996).

22. Personal correspondence from Carlos Hank González; *Excélsior*, April 22, 1977, 6; *Proceso*, January 1, 1990, 6–9; *Hispano Americano*, January 31, 1972, 31, 34; *Hispano Americano*, December 21, 1964, 9; *Excélsior*, February 28, 1974; *Hispano Americano*, June 24, 1974, 38; *Hispano Americano*, December 20, 1976, 22; *Diaro de Yucatán*, August 20, 2001; and Joaquín Herrera, *Las elites del poder, el caso Hank* (Mexico: Ediciones Herrera, 1997).

23. A fascinating comparison among religious elites can be found. The tiny community of Cotija in Michoacán has produced a disproportionate number of prominent bishops and archbishops in the second half of the past century. Michoacán itself accounted for 30 percent of Mexico's bishops in 1969. This distortion has to do with historical events and environment, including Michoacán's role in the Cristero rebellion against the government in the late 1920s. Roderic Ai Camp, *Crossing Swords: Politics and Religion in Mexico* (New York: Oxford University Press, 1997), 183. Another community in an earlier era, Alamos, Sonora, produced an important but disproportionate generation of revolutionary leaders. Mexican Political Biographies Project, 1993.

24. For comments from other former local leaders, see the collection edited by Dalia Barrera Bassols and Alejandra Massolo, *Mujeres que gobiernan municipios: Experiencias,*

Table 2.2. Growth of Party Competition in Mexico by Year

|  | 1988 | 1990 | 1992 | 1995 | 1996 | 1997 | 2001 |
|---|---|---|---|---|---|---|---|
| Percentage of Mexicans governed at the state or local level by parties other than PRI | 3 | 10 | 14 | 24 | 38 | 50 | 61 |

Source: Roderic Ai Camp, *Politics in Mexico, the Democratic Consolidation* (New York: Oxford University Press, 2007), 110, table 5-1.

early 1990s, scholars began to notice the importance of opposition growth in cities and towns, rather than nationally. This deserves to be highlighted because the growth is dramatic and corresponds strongly to the three democratic periods I have chosen. As the data in table 2.2 make clear, the opposition's phenomenal growth occurred in a twelve-year period from 1988, when just 3 percent of the population was governed by opposition parties, to 61 percent, twenty times that figure, in 2001.

In national elections, an analysis of the electoral data demonstrated the repeated strength of the PAN in particular districts and states since 1946.[25] If the increase in the presence of prior experience as mayors in the backgrounds of prominent national politicians during the past century is examined, it becomes clear that this position can be associated with opposition parties' increased strength as well as with the implementation of democratic electoral competition. Among the nearly 300 individuals in our study who were PAN members, 16 percent counted service as a mayor in their public careers. Among those individuals who were born in the 1940s, 1950s, and since the 1960s, a dramatic rise is apparent in those who were mayors, reaching the level of one out of four PANistas born since 1950. In contrast, among PANistas born between 1900 and 1939, only 3 percent held this local post.[26]

---

*aportes, y retos* (Mexico: El Colegio de México, 1998).

25. I provide a list of states and in some cases towns from the 1946 through 1988 presidential elections. Roderic Ai Camp, "Political Modernization in Mexico: Through a Looking Glass," in Jaime Rodríguez, ed., *The Evolution of the Mexican Political System* (Wilmington: Scholarly Resources, 1992), 211–28. Specifically, the opposition won 30 percent or more of the vote in 1946, 1952, 1982, and 1988 in Baja California, the Federal District, Guanajuato, Jalisco, México, Michoacán, and Morelos.

26. It took PAN almost ten years after its founding before it was able to be recognized as winning control of a city government, when Manuel Torres Serranía became its first ever mayor in Quiroga, Michoacán, in 1947. This is the same year it won its first state legislative position, also in Michoacán, when Dr. Alfonso Hernández Sánchez represented the important town of Zamora in the state capital. Miguel Ramírez Munguía became the first member of congress from PAN in 1946, representing the district of Tacámbaro, Michoacán. See

Serving as mayor has taken on a dramatic importance among national PAN politicians, providing them with executive experience and the means of developing local roots and reputations, which became critical among future gubernatorial and congressional candidates. No other party in Mexico has benefited more from this type and level of political experience, nor has any other party used this position to the same extent to help engineer a democratic opening. By 2004, PAN controlled 276 municipalities, accounting for eighteen million people.

By breaking down politicians' experience as mayors on a partisan basis, it becomes clear why this distinction is crucial in our analysis. The Party of the Democratic Revolution (PRD), Mexico's third leading party and the youngest of the three major parties (1989), counts being a mayor among only half as many of their leading politicians' careers as do their PAN counterparts. However, this figure does seem to be following a similar upward trend, with more than a quarter of PRD's prominent members born since 1960 also having served in such a capacity. One structural explanation for this significantly lower figure among PRD members generally is that many top politicians are former members of PRI. Indeed, among those hybrid PRDistas, not one had served as mayor.

More important, the vast majority of leading PRD figures prior to 1989 were members of Mexico's fractured left, including the Unified Socialist Party of Mexico (PSUM), the Revolutionary Workers Party (PRT), the Socialist Workers Party (PST), the Mexican Communist Party (PCM), the Popular Socialist Party (PPS), the Workers Party (PT), and the Popular Party (PP). Among the prominent figures of the Left in Mexico in recent years, only 6 out of 102 were mayors. Again—and it is important to emphasize this point—among those born since 1950, the numbers have increased to a figure comparable to that of their PAN peers.

During the extended reign of PRI locally and nationally, one out of ten PRIistas could claim experience as a mayor. Yet beginning with the 1940 generation, an upsurge of interest in this post can be seen, culminating in 37 percent of PRI politicians born after 1960 having been elected to this position. These figures suggest that even among the PRI members, those who began their careers during the democratic transition already sought this position in greater numbers as a means of fulfilling their political ambitions, just as their counterparts in PAN had been doing for several generations. Whereas PAN politicians chose this post because in many cases it was the only competitive office available to them in the predemocratic

---

www.pancoahuila.org.mx, 2008. The achievement of these first three posts in one state, Michoacán, again suggests the importance of certain states to the long history of political opposition in Mexico.

era, PRI members began doing so as it became clear that electoral competition and fair elections mandated stronger constituency relations, and as the decisive influence in selecting party nominees rapidly devolved from national to local leadership. Joy Langston reached this same conclusion in her revealing analysis of PRI senatorial candidates.[27]

The growing influence of elective executive experience in Mexican politics follows a clear pattern from one presidential administration to another. In some respects, the predemocratic period from the 1930s to the 1980s, short of when Carlos Salinas was inaugurated in 1988, suggests the most interesting changes. An examination of the longitudinal data presented in table 2.3 suggests that in the 1930s, 1940s, 1950s, and 1960s, of the more than 1,000 prominent national politicians holding office, 1 in 10 counted being mayor among their prior public experience. These administrations were populated with national figures, including presidents, who often had pursued careers at the local level. Indeed, Gustavo Díaz Ordaz (1964–70) was the last president for two generations who spent many years in the 1930s and 1940s serving in local and state public offices after graduating from the University of Puebla in 1937.[28] Many of his collaborators were colleagues from his time as a member of congress from 1943 to 1946, and his local career experience partly explains why the incidence of having served as a mayor rose to its highest level among presidential administrations between his years in office and the administration of Vicente Fox in 2000.[29] Politicians who have pursued careers in the legislative branch are more likely to have served in elective offices, including that of mayor, at the local and state level.

The most dramatic change in the levels of experience as mayor among leading politicians occurs between the presidencies of Díaz Ordaz and Luis Echeverría Alvarez (1970–76). Echeverría himself marked a new career

27. Joy Langston, "The Changing Party of the Institutional Revolution: Electoral Competition and Decentralized Candidate Selection," *Party Politics* 12, no. 3 (2006): 395–413.

28. Díaz Ordaz served as an office boy in the Palacio de Gobierno in Puebla in 1931. His grandfather had been the political boss of numerous communities, including San Andrés Chalchicomula, Puebla, in 1911. What is most striking about Díaz Ordaz's local experience in Puebla is that he apparently replicated a technique he used there as secretary general of Government to suppress a strike by university students in his tragic management of the student massacre in Mexico City in 1968. Sergio Aguayo reports this prior experience in *La charola, una historia de los servicios de inteligencia en México* (Mexico: Grijalbo, 2001), 135ff.

29. For example, among the politicians he met in the thirty-ninth legislative session as a member of congress who served in his administration were Carlos A. Madrazo, his president of the national executive committee of PRI; Ruffo Figueroa Figueroa, governor of Quintana Roo; Jesús Yurén Aguilar, senator from the Federal District; Cosme Aguilera Alvarez, member of congress; Antonio J. Hernández, member of congress; Heliodoro Hernández Loza, member of congress; Eduardo Luque Loyola, senator; and Rafael Murillo Vidal, governor of Veracruz.

**Table 2.3.** Percentage of Politicians Who Were Mayors

| Presidency | Former Mayors (%) |
|---|---|
| Cárdenas | 10 |
| Avila Camacho | 7 |
| Alemán | 9 |
| Ruiz Cortines | 5 |
| López Mateos | 9 |
| Díaz Ordaz | 15 |
| Echeverría | 7 |
| López Portillo | 7 |
| De la Madrid | 6 |
| Salinas | 10 |
| Zedillo | 14 |
| Fox | 19 |
| Calderón | 21 |

*Source:* Mexican Political Biographies Project, 2009

path among leading national politicians. His entire career, beginning with his education at the National Preparatory school in 1938, took place in Mexico City. All of his political experience was confined to national political offices in the PRI and in the federal executive branch.[30]

Each of the preceding presidents were born in the provinces, developing significant political networks there. Many of Lázaro Cárdenas's cabinet and subcabinet colleagues established close personal and political ties with him in the 1920s in Morelia, when he served as military commander and governor of his home state. Cárdenas provides an excellent example of a president and political figure who relied heavily on regional experiences in developing his political network. One of his staunchest local supporters (and that of his son, Cuauhtémoc Cárdenas) was Natalio Vázquez Pallares, a member of congress and the senate from Michoacán in the 1940s and 1950s. Vázquez Pallares's maternal great-grandfather, a Liberal soldier, held numerous posts in Coalcomán, Michoacán, in the nineteenth century. His grandmother was the daughter of a local judge, and his father, Natalio Vázquez Sánchez, became the second alcalde of Coalcomán in 1910 and later a local judge. During the Cristero rebellion in 1929, Cárdenas set up his military headquarters in Vázquez Sánchez's

---

30. The only non-national position Echeverría ever held was as president of the PRI in the state of Guanajuato, a post he held only briefly and was appointed to by the National Executive Committee of the PRI, most likely by his patron, Rodolfo Sánchez Taboada, the party's president.

widowed mother's home on the town square. He often visited her to converse over coffee, where he came to know the then-sixteen-year-old Natalio. Natalio and his brother held numerous judicial posts in the state, and Natalio competed unsuccessfully for his party's nomination as a candidate for governor of Michoacán in 1962. Two of Cárdenas collaborators in his state administration later held important cabinet posts in his administration.[31]

Manuel Avila Camacho, Cárdenas's successor in the presidency, pursued a professional career in the army, serving as Cárdenas's chief of staff when he commanded troops in Michoacán. Both of his brothers were governors of his home state, Puebla, and Avila Camacho's family dominated the state's politics for decades.[32] Miguel Alemán (1946–52), who is responsible for introducing and emphasizing the importance of national bureaucratic careers, was governor of his home state in the late 1930s before joining the national cabinet in 1940. Although he represents an older generation, Adolfo Ruiz Cortines, Alemán's successor in the presidency, served as secretary general of the government of Veracruz (akin to lieutenant governor) before becoming governor, after which he, too, joined the cabinet in 1948.[33] Adolfo López Mateos, who preceded Díaz Ordaz in office, developed extensive ties with future collaborators in his native state of México, where he not only directed the state's leading university in Toluca but, before graduating from the local law school, became the private secretary to the governor of México in 1930.[34]

31. They were Gabino Vázquez Oseguerra, his secretary of government in Michoacán, who headed the Department of Agrarian Affairs, 1934–40, after having first worked for Cárdenas as a stenographer; and Raúl Castellano Jiménez Jr., who functioned as secretary of the State Superior Court of Michoacán in 1929, and then as a justice, and became attorney general of the Federal District, 1934–37, chief of staff to President Cárdenas, 1938–39, and head of the Department of the Federal District, 1939–40.

32. See Sergio Valencia Castrejón, *Poder regional y política nacional en México: El gobierno de Maximino Avila Camacho en Puebla (1937-1941)* (Mexico: Instituto Nacional de Estudios Históricos de la Revolución, 1966), and Alejandro Quintana, *Maximino Avila Camacho and the One-Party State: The Taming of Caudillismo and Caciquismo in Post-Revolutionary Mexico* (Lanham, Md.: Lexington Books, 2010). Wil Pansters provides an outstanding analysis of Puebla politics in *Politics and Power in Puebla: The Political History of a Mexican State, 1937-1987* (Amsterdam: CEDLA, 1990).

33. Ruiz Cortines met Alemán when the latter was governor of Veracruz. Alemán recommended Ruiz Cortines to fill the position of federal congressman from Tuxpan in 1937. When Alemán left the governorship to run Avila Camacho's presidential campaign, he appointed Ruiz Cortines as the campaign's treasurer. Apparently, during the revolution, Ruiz Cortines had served as an accountant and administrator to Alemán's father, General Miguel Alemán González. *Mexican Political Biographies, 1935-1993* (Austin: University of Texas Press, 1994), 628-29.

34. Clemente Díaz de la Vega, *Adolfo López Mateos, vida y obra* (Toluca: Terra Nova, 1986).

As suggested, 1970 marks a demarcation from the presence of local and state experiences among presidents and their collaborators. The years from 1970 to 1988 can also be viewed as crucial transition from provincial to Mexico City-born politicians, from politicians with elective to executive careers, and from generalists to economic technocrats. The semi-authoritarian reign of PRI continued during these three administrations but under a distinctively different type of PRI leadership. More than 700 politicians reached prominent national positions for the first time during these two administrations, but fewer than 7 percent served as mayors, well below the average figure for all leading political figures since the 1930s.

The democratic transition period from 1988 to 2000—when the opposition parties strengthened their presence among numerous cities and some states, as well as in the national legislative branch—reveals a significant and consistent return to the importance of having been elected a mayor before reaching national political offices, elective or administrative. Beginning with Salinas's administration, one out of ten influential politicians were mayors, a figure that increased to 14 percent under Zedillo. The figure from Salinas's administration nearly doubled among officeholders in the Fox and Calderón administrations. Thus, beginning with the democratic era in Mexican politics (2000), the importance of local elective office becomes clear and is found among the backgrounds of one in five prominent national political figures.

One other local position stands out as an indicator of the broader, changing patterns in Mexican politics marking the importance of the three presidential periods: that of local deputy (state legislator). Given the dominance of PRI governors on state politics until the 1990s, this career position has receive little (if any) attention, with the notable exception of Caroline Beer's revealing analysis, which demonstrates its importance during the democratic period.[35] Surprisingly, having served as a state legislator has been more common in the political credentials of Mexican politicians than any other local post, including that of mayor.

To understand the role serving as a state legislator has played in the backgrounds of Mexican political figures, we separate national political figures according to party affiliation and generation. Of all the political parties, PAN members again have used local office as a stepping stone to national prominence. What is extraordinary about local deputyships in the career backgrounds of prominent national PAN members is that its presence becomes significant as early as the generation born in the 1930s, the

35. Caroline Beer, *Electoral Competition and Institutional Change in Mexico* (Notre Dame, Ind.: University of Notre Dame Press, 2003).

same generation led by Miguel de la Madrid (1982–88) in the PRI. These politicians most typically would have held such local positions beginning in the 1950s and 1960s, when PAN achieved a foothold at the local and state levels for the first time. One in four prominent politicians among this early generation of PANistas achieved success in competing for state legislative seats. In contrast, only one national figure out of thirty-five peers from the fractured leftist parties that existed during some of these earlier decades served in a similar capacity.

It seems natural for PANista politicians to have relied on this local career path because it was more difficult for them to compete for the office of mayor and obtain funds from PRI-controlled governors to achieve success as local executives. As I suggested, until 2000, PAN's only access to national positions, with a few exceptions in the executive and judicial branches, was confined to congress. This practical restriction at both the national and local levels, therefore, contributed to the viability of the opposition pursuing this particular elective post. What is so significant among PAN members is a persistent increase in the representation of state legislators in each succeeding generation's careers, doubling to more than two-fifths among all PAN politicians born since 1950 and more than half by 1960.[36] On average, PRD politicians can claim this career experience in equal numbers to their counterparts in PAN. Since the 1930s, one in four served as state legislators; more than a third of the youngest generation now claims such experience.

Patricio José Patrón Laviada, the former PAN governor of Yucatán, provides a superb illustration of a local political figure who reaches national prominence. His family also illustrates the significance of social networks and local roots, as well as the increasing linkages between PAN and PRI political families in the twenty-first century. Patrón Laviada grew up in Mérida, the state capital and largest city, where he was born in 1957. As was the case with most PAN leaders, he pursued a career in the private sector as a manager of numerous firms, having completed his preparatory education in his birthplace. As early as the 1970s, Mérida provided an opening for PAN members with political ambitions.[37] In 1986 Patrón Laviada

36. Among the pre-PRD leftists, nearly a quarter of the 1940s generation and half of the 1950s generation served in state legislatures, including that of the Federal District Assembly.

37. This opening largely can be attributed to the career of Víctor Manuel Correa Racho, who directed the state PAN party just a decade after it was founded in Yucatán in 1950 and successfully defeated the PRI candidate for mayor of Mérida in 1967. In 1969, he ran for governor against Carlos Loret de Mola in a highly disputed race marked by fraud. Many observers believe he won that election. Interviews with the author, Mérida, Yucatan, 1972, and Carlos Loret de Mola, *Confesiones de un gobernador* (Mexico: Editorial Grijalbo, 1978), 47.

joined PAN, where he served as secretary of organization of the Mérida branch. After completing four years in this capacity, he was elected to the state legislature in 1994. The following year, he ran for mayor of Mérida, completing his term in 1998, followed by the local presidency of his party from 1998 to 2001. During this period, he coordinated the grassroots organization Amigos de Fox in Yucatán, a group crucial to Fox's electoral victory nationwide, and he became the party's candidate for one of the state's senate seats, which he won. He resigned his seat in 2001 to run successfully for governor. Early in his political career, he developed a relationship with Roger Cicero, a prominent local PANista, through his maternal uncles, and married Cicero's daughter, Silvia Cicero Cáceres, in 1998. His brother married Pilar Cevera, the daughter of one of Yucatán's most powerful regional PRI politicians, former congressman, senator, governor, and cabinet member Víctor Cervera Pacheco. Patrón Laviada is also the cousin of Hugo Laviada, a PAN senator from Yucatán in the Calderón administration, and of Emilio Gamboa Patrón, chief of staff to President Miguel de la Madrid and cabinet member in the Salinas administration.[38]

When comparing PAN and PRD politicians' careers with PRI politicians' trajectories, the difference is pronounced. Overall, extending back to the earliest generations who began holding national office in the mid-1930s, only one in six politicians (nearly all PRIistas) were elected from their local district to serve in the state capital. Thus, long before the democratic transition began, the PRI did not place a high value on that particular prior elective position. On the other hand, beginning with the 1950s generation, PRI members also emphasized experience in the state legislature, slightly exceeding the percentages from the PRD. Since 1950, over a quarter of nationally prominent PRI public figures served in the state legislature.

The similarities found among the most successful politicians from the three parties after 1950 suggest the important effects of electoral competition, which, similar to contests for mayor, emphasize the known qualities of politicians boasting local networks and experiences. This political maxim applies as much to PRI as it does to PAN and PRD. It is more pronounced for PAN because this party used the elective legislative route to achieve public office for a much longer historical period than the other two parties; therefore, PAN made this transition sooner. We know from past research that important mentor-disciple relations are often established through career contacts, resulting in the reality of disciples sharing the same careers as their mentors, not just because mentors are biased in selecting like types

---

38. See www.eluniversal.com.mx, October 25, 2005; *Quién es quién en el Congreso, diputados y senadores del LVII Legislatura, 1997-2000* (Mexico: Editorial ITED, 1998), 313; www.medigraphic.com.mx, 2008; www.diputadosfederales.panyucatan.org.mx, 2007.

Table 2.4.  Percentage of Politicians Who Were State Legislators

| Presidency | Former State Legislators (%) |
| --- | --- |
| Cárdenas | 12 |
| Avila Camacho | 15 |
| Alemán | 9 |
| Ruiz Cortines | 16 |
| López Mateos | 16 |
| Díaz Ordaz | 11 |
| Echeverría | 11 |
| López Portillo | 12 |
| De la Madrid | 12 |
| Salinas | 16 |
| Zedillo | 18 |
| Fox | 30 |
| Calderón | 35 |

Source: Mexican Political Biographies Project, 2009

but also because their connection occurred from precisely that specific career circumstance.[39]

As was the case among politicians who were mayor, equally revealing patterns appear when the careers of national politicians who served as state legislators are examined by the presidential administrations in which they first achieved prominence (table 2.4). During the administrations prior to 1988, one out of ten counted serving as a state legislator as part of his or her career experience. An increase of nearly 20 percent occurred among politicians with local legislative experience prior to 1970 and the last two predemocratic presidencies (1976–88). This increase is not as dramatic as among those politicians who were mayors. However, as soon as the 1988–2000 administrations are examined, a more significant upward trend in the number of national politicians who claim state legislative experiences becomes apparent. By the Fox and Calderón administrations, more than three out of ten figures had served previously in a state legislature.

Given the fact that executive posts were impermeable to opposition parties for much longer than legislative posts were, it is not surprising that PAN members in particular followed this local electoral path, and that such experience would be useful to the national legislative careers pursued by numerous influential PANistas.

President Calderón's sister, for example, served as a state legislator from their home state of Michoacán just three years after she graduated

39. Camp, Mexico's Mandarins, 38.

from college. Two years after leaving that post in 1988, she ran successfully for congress, serving in the first congressional session of Salinas's administration. In 2000, she represented PAN in the senate during Fox's presidency.[40]

Politicians who began their careers as mayors or local legislators could pursue alternative paths to national leadership, moving from municipalities and legislative and congressional districts to state-level posts, including that of state party chairperson, senator, and governor. Serving as mayor was not a stepping stone to the most important national legislative post—that of senator. Only one in ten prominent senators were likely to have served as mayors, compared to one in four of their counterparts in the lower chamber. Interestingly, that level of experience was more pronounced among predemocratic politicians who served in the Cárdenas administration. Nevertheless, senators holding office since 2000 have more than doubled their experience as mayors, suggesting the same patterns that have evolved among many members of congress.

The most logical elective office that a mayor and member of congress might ultimately pursue in Mexico is that of governor. Reaching a governorship has been important in the past as a stepping stone to the presidency, just as is the case in the United States.[41] Cárdenas, Alemán, and Ruiz Cortines all reached a governor's post before they served in the cabinet and then became the PRI presidential nominee. López Mateos and especially Díaz Ordaz held state offices, but neither reached the state's highest position.[42]

If cabinet members during these years are examined, especially from 1970 to 2000, it was just as common to serve first in the cabinet and become a governor as to have served as a governor prior to joining the executive branch. A dramatic shift occurred once again at the presidential level starting in 2000, when all three candidates from the leading parties were governors. This pattern repeated itself among the PRI and PRD candidates in

40. *Directorio del Congreso mexicano, LVIII Legislatura, 2000-2003* (Mexico: Senado de la República, 2001), 318-19; *Quién es quién en el Congreso, LVIII Legislatura, 2000-2003* (Mexico: ITED, 2002), 295; and Presidencia de la República, *Diccionario biográfico del gobierno mexicano* (Mexico, 1989), 410.

41. For an interesting comparison of gubernatorial careers leading to posts in the U.S. Senate, see Frank Codispoti, "The Governorship-Senate Connection: A Step in the Structure of Opportunities Grows Weaker," *Publius*, 17, no. 2 (Spring 1987): 41-52.

42. López Mateos was personal secretary to the governor of México, 1930; secretary of the state PNR committee in Toluca, 1931-34; and as mentioned, president of the state university in Toluca, 1944-46. Díaz Ordaz, as mentioned, served as an office boy at city hall in Puebla and secretary general of government, 1941-45. However, he also graduated from his state university in 1937; served as a professor and vice president of his alma mater; was a local prosecutor in Tehuacán, Puebla; was president of the state arbitration board, federal agent in Tlatlauqui, Puebla; and was a judge of the state supreme court.

2006, and in a sense even held true for Calderón, who ran for governor of Michoacán but lost the election. Since 2000, the single most important position that gains a politician national recognition sufficient to win a party's presidential nomination has been that of governor.

It is essential to understand career paths leading to the governorship in Mexico to understand future national leadership. This argument is fully developed in chapter 9. The data in table 2.5 demonstrate the significance of being a mayor en route to becoming a governor in Mexico. Even more clearly, they demonstrate the extent to which the three political periods differed in emphasizing the linkage between administering a town and becoming a state executive. During the predemocratic period (1934-88), fewer than one in five governors had been mayors. Under Miguel de la Madrid, this figure increases significantly, to nearly a third. In the twelve years of the democratic transition (1988-2000), mayors again achieve an increased presence in the backgrounds of Mexican governors, averaging two-fifths of all governors. In the democratic period, the average increases again to more than half of all governors. In addition, in the first two years of the Calderón administration, an extraordinary 70 percent of all governors held this local position.

**Table 2.5.** Percentage of Governors Who Were Mayors

| Presidency | Former Mayors (%) |
| --- | --- |
| Cárdenas | 15 |
| Avila Camacho | 17 |
| Alemán | 18 |
| Ruiz Cortines | 6 |
| López Mateos | 18 |
| Díaz Ordaz | 29 |
| Echeverría | 9 |
| López Portillo | 22 |
| De la Madrid | 31 |
| *Subtotal* | 17 |
| | |
| Salinas | 38 |
| Zedillo | 41 |
| *Subtotal* | 39 |
| | |
| Fox | 46 |
| Calderón | 71 |
| *Subtotal* | 51 |

*Source*: Mexican Political Biographies Project, 2009

Among those approximately 300 individuals who were mayors in the national leadership sample, few have been sought as assistant secretaries or secretaries of cabinet agencies. Only a tiny percentage of these leading executive branch officeholders have ever held this local elective post. Furthermore, the presence of mayor in the backgrounds of the most influential policy makers in the federal bureaucracy has not changed from the predemocratic, transitional, or democratic periods. In fact, under Fox and Calderón, appointees with this experience in their résumé are actually below the average for all the previous administrations.

The one remaining path that might be affording to an elective, local officeholder is through the respective party bureaucracies. An examination of those national politicians who have held important party posts at the state or national levels indicates that across all three leading parties, approximately one in ten have also been mayors. In the case of PAN, it is surprising to discover that not one of sixteen politicians who have risen to the position of president of the party's national executive committee had previously been a mayor. Given the importance of local elective positions to national PAN politicians in most other respects, this is unexpected. Although there is a slightly increased presence of having been a mayor among state party chairs, it is not significant. This same distribution among presidents and regional party chairs applies to the PRD as well.

Within the PRI there exists a much stronger linkage between local officeholders and party leadership. Although the overall percentage of party officeholders who were elected mayor is comparable to the levels found within the other parties, one party position, that of state chairperson, is the exception. More than a third of PRI state party chairpersons who attained nationally prominent careers served as mayors. After 2000, many analysts in Mexico began writing off the PRI as a party on its way out of office. But following the presidential election, the PRI continued to perform well at the local and state level, achieving percentages generally higher than it received in recent presidential races. This continued success can be explained by a number of factors, but among them is the caliber of the party's grassroots organization. One important characteristic inherent in this strength is the tie between state party leadership and strong roots in local communities.

## CONCLUSIONS

These data suggest that an important linkage exists between elective positions at the local level and elective positions at the national level, a pattern confirmed by Joy Langston among ordinary (rather than elite) members of congress.[43] I also argue that an important explanation for the existence of different patterns among the three leading parties can be attributed to the way the PRI structured access to national positions, the degree to which these elective positions were influential on policy making, and the breakthrough that electoral competition exerted on increased access to these positions as well as their importance during the transitional administrations, especially that of Ernesto Zedillo.

Among all leading politicians in Mexico, only one in six has served as a state legislator. However, of these individuals, more than 80 percent became federal legislators, and a fourth of all leading members of congress, nearly half of all politicians represented in the data, have been state legislators.[44] Similarly, more than three-quarters of the mayors in our sample became members of congress. Furthermore, a link exists between the two local elective positions, at least in the careers of national politicians, considering that two-fifths of prominent politicians who were mayors also had been elected to the state legislature. An examination of members of congress who were state legislators by presidential administration again reinforces the consistency of patterns described above and also reinforces conclusions about the three distinct periods of democratic or nondemocratic governance.

During the administrations from Cárdenas through López Portillo, little variation occurred in the state legislative experience of prominent politicians who served in congress. Beginning with López Portillo's administration, a persistent rise in the percentage of members of congress who previously served as state legislators becomes apparent. In just twelve years, under President Salinas, the percentage who were state legislators rapidly grew by half, from 21 to 31 percent. Twelve years later, at the beginning of Calderón's presidency, this figure jumped sharply once again, accounting for nearly half of all members of congress. These dramatic increases correspond with the years of democratic transition and with the highly competitive postdemocratic presidencies of Fox and Calderón.

---

43. Langston examined all federal deputies who held office from 1997 to 2003. We examine members of congress who served two or more times in either the upper or lower house or who held other nationally prestigious posts in the judicial or executive branch. She found that 90 percent of them came directly from positions in the public sector, 70 percent came directly from a local or state office, 20 percent from a national position, and 65 percent returned to a local or state position after leaving the chamber. See Joy Langston and Francisco Javier Aparicio, "Political Career Structures in Democratic Mexico, 1997–2006," paper presented at the American Political Science Association, Boston, August 28–31, 2008, 3.

44. In Kathleen Bruhn and Kenneth Greene's survey of candidates for congress from the PRD and PAN in 2006, 57 and 58 percent, respectively, had held elective positions. Thirty percent of the PRD candidates and 41 percent of PAN candidates had been state legislators.

For reasons already identified, one would expect the opposition parties to produce higher percentages of politicians who used national legislative careers to achieve prominence and therefore form part of the data set. This is unquestionably the case. For example, even by the 1910 generation, nearly three-quarters of prominent PANistas passed through the halls of congress. In the 1920s, 1930s, and 1940s generations, during the formative years of the party, this figure averaged an extraordinary 90 percent and higher.

There is another explanation for this pattern, which has never been identified in the literature. Among those PANistas whose fathers' or uncles' careers are known, nearly all those who became politically active in the 1940s or 1950s were PAN candidates for congress who failed to win their seats. In a few cases, they also won congressional seats. Many fathers of successful PAN politicians also were state legislators. These conclusions are based on a comprehensive online search of family names through all the published records of every session of congress since 1917 and similar records for some important state legislatures.[45] Unlike other trends in leadership careers, the percentage of PANistas who were former state legislators has declined somewhat among the younger generations. Naturally, this can be explained by the fact that younger partisans can now reach national political prominence as governors, jurists, and members of the executive branch, opportunities available to PRIistas since the 1930s.[46]

PRD leaders follow the same pattern as PAN members among early generations, but unlike PAN, its percentage never declines because the PRD has had little opportunity to place its leaders in national executive positions, never having won the presidency.[47] Therefore, congress has become an almost necessary and exclusive path for PRD figures to follow, just as was the case for PAN from 1940 to 2000.

The PRI represents a different pattern from the other two parties. Nearly half of all PRI politicians have served in the lower chamber over time, and traditionally this was a more important career path among the oldest PRI generations. It becomes less important among those politicians

45. See www.cronicadiputados.gob.mx, which often lists the congressional electoral results by district and year for each party's candidate in the August or September records of congressional sessions. Many sons have run successfully in the same districts twenty years after their fathers.

46. Given the distribution of local legislative seats to each party, the presence of local deputies in the backgrounds of national congressional politicians from each party will continue to be significant. In 2007 PAN held 30.2 percent, PRD 20.4 percent, PRI 20.4 percent, and other parties 12.2 percent of state legislative seats. See Consulta Mitoksky, "Los Congresos estatales en México," April 5, 2007, www.consulta.mx.

47. In the interest of bipartisanship, Fox offered two important cabinet posts to leading members of the PRD, but the party leadership refused to allow them to accept the offer.

who populate the Echeverría and López Portillo administrations, but it begins again to rise under De la Madrid and Salinas. By the time the 1940s generation is on the scene, more than half of prominent PRI figures have served in congress, a level that increased to 61 percent among PRIistas born after 1950.

The PRI pattern is explained by the fact that they have had to adjust their career patterns to rely largely on legislative seats and governorships to achieve national prominence, somewhat akin to the PRD pattern. But a less well-developed argument than the structural one brought about by the way in which electoral democracy was achieved in Mexico is the fact that as early as the late 1970s and 1980s, PRI members of the legislative branch began to express dismay at their own lack of autonomy as legislators. In the biographical surveys the PRI leadership collected within a legislative session, a reading of each individual response reveals that a small number of PRI members openly expressed criticism of the autocratic congressional leadership.[48] In some respects, some members of congress, although they exerted little influence on the outcome of government legislation until the Salinas administration, exercised greater independence than their peers in the executive branch or the party bureaucracy. A classic example of such a legislator during this period was Víctor Manzanilla Schaffer; during his third term in congress (twice as a deputy and once as a senator), he voted against President López Portillo's amendment to Article 27, a rare occurrence among PRI members of the legislative branch in that era.[49]

Today, members of congress or members of the executive branch who have served in congress account for a significantly larger percentage of prominent national politicians than in the past, when they averaged in the mid-fortieth percentile for most of the century. Under Zedillo and Fox, their numbers increased to the mid-fiftieth percentile and then to more than two-thirds of all prominent politicians under Calderón. Regardless of which party wins the 2012 presidential race, the level of prior experience in congress will continue to remain higher than in administrations prior to

48. Copies of these helpful documents were made available to me by the oficiales mayores of the Chamber of Deputies for all the sessions in the 1970s and 1980s, long before official directories, which included the legislative branch, were published by the Mexican presidency from 1984 to 1993.

49. Manzanilla Schaffer's father was a prominent revolutionary leader in Yucatán who founded the Anti-Reelectionist Party there and served in congress. Manzanilla Schaffer allegedly turned down the PRI nomination for governor of his home state in 1969 because he wanted to control appointments to several decentralized federal agencies in his state. He later became governor of Yucatán in 1988, but resigned three years into his tenure. Roderic Ai Camp, *Mexican Political Biographies, 1935–1993*, 3rd ed. (Austin: University of Texas Press, 1995), 432–33; and *Por Qué*, October 23, 1969, 22.

2000 and is likely to increase further in the short run if PAN is victorious for a third consecutive presidency.

The increasing importance of local elective office as a path to national elective office obviously has a long history in Mexico, which in part corresponds to the importance and impact of regionalism in that country. But trends in the importance of local political positions are affected by an individual's party affiliation because Mexico was controlled by a single party for seventy-one years, using its monopoly over most national offices to restrict opposition party career paths to specific positions. Moreover, at the federal level the constitution was amended to prohibit consecutive reelection in the legislative branch after 1934, thus eliminating the ability of a politician using the legislative branch as a means for establishing permanent ties with a constituency, thereby creating the means for a political base independent from that of the federal executive branch and national party leadership.

The revival of the importance of local elective office, executive and legislative, is indisputable from the data. The one intervening variable which exerts the potential for modifying the importance of the changing patterns brought about by democracy is the persistence of social and familial networking among Mexican politicians. It is difficult to judge the impact of this variable because of all the variables examined in the data set, it is the most difficult about which to provide complete information. Since the 1930s, at least more than a third of prominent political leaders were related to other Mexicans who reached influential national or state political offices. From the 1930s to 1970, at least two-fifths of national politicians claimed such kinship ties. During the administrations from 1970 to 1988, approximately a third retained such ties. Under Salinas and Zedillo, a decline began, dropping to about only one in four by the Calderón administration. This decline can be explained in part by the fact that the older the politician, the more likely such relationships can be identified, and the increasing statistical probability that their grandchildren's generation also had opportunities to pursue public careers unavailable to the younger generations with fewer adult descendants. PANistas, of course, are disproportionately younger compared with the PRI sample; this contributes to the pronounced differences between the post 2000 and pre-2000 generations. More important is the fact that at least a third of politicians who were local deputies, mayors, and members of congress shared these familial ties.

As we shall see, the democratic opening has introduced many differing characteristics among Mexico's postdemocratic leadership, to be expected as the result of a competitive electoral arena. But the importance of local, familial networking has not appeared to have changed significantly. Therefore, partisan groups are altering their career choices and patterns, and a high percentage of those same leaders are products of well-established families in Mexican politics, families who for whatever reason continue to influence politics locally and nationally.

Much of the data point to the importance of institutional changes that encouraged greater electoral competition and distinguishes the pre-democratic period from the transitional and democratic periods. Yet even after opposition parties won the presidency, the need for those political skills learned in the legislative branch, whether at the state or national level, became increasingly apparent. This explains Calderón's stronger legislative credentials in contrast to his predecessor. A major analysis of Latin American legislators found a similar pattern.[50] Local political experience and local political networks also increased in importance, as parties turned to candidates for congress and governorships who had already achieved favorable grassroots recognition, instead of imposing them from above (the PRI's typical pattern in the past). As those choices became increasingly competitive, it increased the relevance of local and local elective political experience for all parties.

50. María del Mar Martínez Rosón, "Legislative Careers: Does Quality Matter?," in Manuel Alcántara Sáez, ed., *Politicians and Politics in Latin America* (Boulder, Colo.: Lynne Rienner, 2008), concluded from three surveys of Latin American legislators from 1993 to 2005 that their elective experience increased significantly from only 25 to 41 percent during that period. Interestingly, unlike prominent Mexican politicians who were legislators, however, their prior experience in the federal legislative branch declined significantly, from 41 to 33 percent. She makes the point—correctly—that their representative experience is much more varied than was the case in the earliest survey. Table 11.1, 239–40.

# 3

# The Fall and Rise of Party Militants

The role of political parties in Mexico differs widely from the role they have played in U.S. politics or in other settings where they were established and operated within a democratic electoral context.[1] The parties themselves boast different features and functions during the three periods I have delineated as the basic chronological divisions in the present analysis of Mexican democratic politics. Furthermore, it is necessary to keep in mind that the long reign of the Institutional Revolutionary Party (PRI) and its relationship to the electoral process molded the functions and structures of other political parties in Mexico, determining to a great extent how Mexican citizens actually view political parties to this day.[2]

One of the original misconceptions about Mexican politics in the predemocratic era was the role played by the PRI in maintaining the long reign of its representatives in national government and the level of militancy required among national leadership. Prominent scholars such as Robert Scott mistakenly argued that the party governed Mexico.[3] In reality, the PRI always functioned as an actor subordinate to the president and his appointees in the executive branch.[4] The party was responsive to the bureaucratic elite, rather than producing and controlling that elite, as was the case of socialist authoritarian models in the Soviet Union and China. This serious analytical confusion was perpetuated in the minds of ordinary Mexicans by referring to the government and the party interchangeably as the PRI, which is analogous to calling the U.S. government the Democrats

1. For example, see Lester G. Seligman's enlightening discussion "Political Parties and Party Structure: A Case Study," *American Political Science Review*, 50 (March 1961): 77–86.

2. "Democracy through Latin American Lenses," Grant, Hewlett Foundation, principal investigator, Roderic Ai Camp, June 1998, and "Democracy through U.S. and Mexican Lenses," Grant, Hewlett Foundation, principal investigator, Roderic Ai Camp, September 2000.

3. Robert Scott, *Mexican Politics in Transition*, 2nd ed. (Urbana: University of Illinois Press, 1964).

4. Frank Brandenburg, in his classic *The Making of Modern Mexico* (Englewood Cliffs, N.J.: Prentice Hall, 1964), first captured this reality most clearly. See his chapter "The Liberal Machiavellian," 141–65.

Table 3.1. National Officeholders and Party Officials

| Party | National Officeholders Who Held Party Positions (%) |
|---|---|
| PAN | 79 |
| PRD | 63 |
| PSUM/PRT/PPS/PCM/PST/PT/PP | 58 |
| PRI | 30 |

Source: Mexican Political Biographies Project, 2009.

PAN positions: president, secretary general or secretary of the National Executive Committee, national adviser to the National Executive Committee, and president of a state party. PRI positions: president of state party, member of National Council of PRI, general delegate of the National Executive Committee of PRI to states. PRD positions: president, secretary general or secretary of the National Executive Committee, state party president. PSUM etc. positions: president, secretary general or secretary of the National Executive Committee.

or Republicans. Adding to this serious misconception was the belief that the "PRI-government" was the same as the state.

The National Action Party (PAN), of the three leading Mexican political parties, might be considered most likely during all three periods to have relied heavily on its party organization to identify leaders and candidates for national office. The data in the study overwhelmingly confirm this assertion. Four-fifths of all prominent members of PAN in our study have been important state or national party officials (table 3.1). This surprisingly distinctive party role can be attributed to the fact that PAN essentially had to rely exclusively on politicians who pursued careers in local elective offices as mayors and state legislators, or in national elective offices as members of congress for most of the period from its founding in 1939 to its first victorious gubernatorial race in 1989 in Baja California.

One of the most important features of PAN in its early years is that its national founders and executive committee members were often state party chairs.[5] An excellent example of such a politician is Efraín González Luna, who is a household name among PAN militants, having co-founded the party with Manuel Gómez Morín in 1939.[6] He led his home state organization from 1939 to 1952, becoming the party's presidential

5. For historical background on its evolution and founding, see Donald Mabry, Mexico's Acción Nacional: A Catholic Alternative to Revolution (Syracuse, N.Y.: Syracuse University Press, 1973), and Soledad Loaeza, El Partido Acción Nacional, la larga marcha, 1939-1994 (Mexico: Fondo de Cultura Económica, 1999).

6. Roderic Ai Camp, Mexican Political Biographies, 1935-1993 (Austin: University of Texas Press, 1995), 307; www.autlan.gob.mx, 2007; www.jalisco.gob.mx, 2008; and Mexican Political Biographies Project, 2009.

candidate in 1952. In fact, as PAN began to expand its reach to other states, it often relied on members with party experience in their home states to serve as chairs in other states to help develop the party's grassroots appeal elsewhere in Mexico.

Only a handful of PAN party officials reached national prominence during the nine presidencies from 1934 to 1988, regardless of whether their party posts were at the national or state level. This is explained by the fact that few members of PAN were able to break into congress, the only national position open to them during those years. From 1949 to 1964, before plurinominal/party seats were introduced, PAN averaged only five seats in each session of congress.[7] This pattern did not change until the Zedillo administration. PAN party officials during the second half of the democratic transition period made inroads in other positions, accounting for 11 percent of all prominent national political figures from 1994 to 2000.

Democratic politics engineered a sea change among politicians in the linkage between holding a party position and a nationally prominent office during the six years of Fox's tenure in the presidency. One out of five party officials achieved a prominent national post during that administration. In the first two years of Calderón's tenure, this figure continues at a similarly high level. These figures suggest that the PAN's presidential victory in 2000 opened up all three branches of government to PAN partisans, and among PAN members, having been an important party official served as valuable training for both elected and appointed posts at both the state and national levels.

If the position of state party chair is examined more closely and from an historical perspective, the importance of having served in this position can be seen as strongly linked to success in the state legislature, as mayor, and as a member of congress or the senate.[8] Complete lists of party chairs from Jalisco, a state that has been historically important to PAN's regional strength and Mexican politics generally, illustrate some commonalities with PAN officeholders who were mayors of important provincial cities.

From 1939, when the Jalisco party organization was founded simultaneously with the national party, state party chairs have gone on to national

---

7. Roderic Ai Camp, *Politics in Mexico: The Democratic Consolidation* (New York: Oxford University Press, 2007), 206, table 8-1.

8. For comparisons with the United States, see Lewis Bowman and G. R. Boynton, "Recruitment Patterns among Local Party Officials," *American Political Science Review* 60 (September 1966): 667-76, and elsewhere, Joseph A. Schlesinger, "Political Careers and Party Leadership," in Lewis D. Edinger, ed., *Political Leadership in Industrialized Societies* (New York: Wiley, 1967), 266-93.

Table 3.2. Presidents of the PAN in Jalisco

| Party President | Tenure | National Office |
| --- | --- | --- |
| Efraín González Luna | 1939-52 | Congress and presidential candidate |
| Salvador Urzua | 1952-55 | |
| Ramón Garcilita Partida | 1955-57 | Congress |
| Jesús Obregón Reynoso | 1957-60 | |
| David Alarcón Zaragoza | 1960-63 | Congress and gubernatorial candidate |
| Guillermo Ruíz Vázquez | 1963-66 | Congress |
| Ignacio González Morfín | 1966-69 | |
| Guillermo Baeza Somellera | 1969-72 | Congress |
| Carlos Petersen Biester | 1972 | |
| José Herrera Herrera Marcos | 1972-75 | |
| Ramón Garcilita Partida | 1975-79 | Congress |
| Adolfo Martín del Campo | 1979-81 | |
| Ernesto Espinoza Guaro | 1981-82 | |
| Héctor Pérez Plazola | 1982-87 | Congress and senate |
| Gabriel Jiménez Remus | 1981-90 | Congress, senate, National Committee |
| José G. Tarsicio Rodríguez | 1990-96 | |
| Herbert Taylor Arthur | 1996-99 | Alternate member of congress |
| Emilio González Márquez | 1999-2002 | Congress and governor |
| José Antonio Gloria Morales | 2002-5 | Congress |
| Eduardo Rosales Castellanos | 2005-8 | |

*Source*: Mexican Political Biographies Project, 2009; www.panjal.org.mx, 2008.

office more than half the time. A third of these state party officials are included in our highly selective sample of leading national political figures (see table 3.2). Few career experiences characterize prominent PAN national figures as commonly as having been a state party chair. A more detailed examination of Jalisco suggests some significant career patterns about these party officials. Reaching the presidency of the state organization is clearly a likely stepping stone to a single national office: member of congress. Without exception, all of the individuals who achieved national prominence did so through this elective post.[9] In our national sample of prominent politicians, four-fifths of PAN party officials as well as PAN members served in the congress.

What table 3.2 fails to convey in detail, however, is that among the early PAN state leaders, many were repeatedly candidates for elective

9. In several cases, these politicians became members of congress while serving in the state party position or prior to holding that party office.

office as mayors, state legislators, and congress members. Illustrative of these repeated efforts by early PANistas to achieve office is the career of Guillermo Ruíz Vázquez, who joined the party in 1944. Within ten years he had become an active member of the state PAN committee, serving as the press and studies secretary from 1955 to 1960. In 1955, he ran for the state legislature without success. Significantly, in the case of Jalisco, PAN candidates had more success obtaining a seat in congress than one in the state legislature. Not until 1973, thirty-four years after its founding, did Adolfo Martín del Campo, state party chair from 1979 to 1981, and Francisco Ramírez Acuña, secretary general of the state party in 1977, win the first two seats in this state-level electoral body.[10] Ruíz Vázquez ran unsuccessfully three times for a congressional seat in 1946, 1955, and 1958. Finally, in 1964, twenty years after joining the party, he competed successfully for a seat in congress, and he repeated his success six years later.[11]

This brief case study of Jalisco confirms even more strongly a finding from the national data set having long-term national consequences on the recruitment of Mexico's national politicians. Changes in electoral laws at the national level beginning in 1964 allocated additional seats (plurinominal or party) in congress to opposition parties based on their percentage of the vote received nationally for all congressional candidates. Thus in the 1964 legislative session, PAN seats in the lower chamber jump from five in 1961 to twenty, an extraordinary increase. This important change in the electoral law produced three major, long-term consequences on national recruitment.

First, as seen previously from more detailed career data locally or nationally, it became easier for opposition party politicians to achieve a national elective office than a local or state-level position. Thus, an institutional reform, allowing for increased representation among opposition parties, channeled a huge influx of successful candidates into the national legislative branch. This structural reform reinforced an established perception of Mexican politics in the predemocratic era that, typically, civil rights abuses, including rights related to electoral transparency, could more commonly be found at the local level, especially in smaller, rural communities,

10. Ramírez Acuña ran unsuccessfully for a seat in congress in 1973 and 1979, but won a state legislative seat a second time in 1983. He was the youngest state legislator in Mexico when he took office in 1974. He went on to become mayor of Guadalajara in 1998, governor of Jalisco in 2000, and secretary of government in Calderón's administration in 2006. He also was president of PAN in the First District of Guadalajara, as well as the secretary of organization of youth action. *Quéhacerpolítico,* December 10, 2006; *Los Angeles Times,* November 28, 2006; *Diario de Yucatán,* November 28, 2006; www.heraldextra.com, June 16, 2008; and Mexican Political Biographies Project, 2009.

11. Camp, *Mexican Political Biographies,* 633. His son, Pedro Ruiz Higuera, won a seat in the state legislature in 2006.

than at the national level, particularly in highly competitive, urban districts in major cities.[12]

A breakdown of reported election results, in which opposition parties achieved high percentages of the votes, confirms this argument.[13] The higher the socioeconomic demographics and the more urbanized the geographic setting, the higher the percentage of votes for the opposition, especially for the PAN.[14] David Shirk reinforces the importance of the consequences of urbanization for PAN from a cultural perspective, arguing that the party benefited significantly from the changing "patterns of behavior, political beliefs, and attitudes demonstrated in the 1980s and 1990s."[15]

The second truly notable impact of this law is that it altered the grassroots nature of PAN's battle for elective offices, shifting the emphasis from competitive legislative majority district seats to those seats assigned solely on the basis of the party's national congressional vote by region. The impact can be seen clearly in the election results reported in table 3.3. It actually took PAN more than twenty years to win more seats on the basis of district competition than was true in 1961, the last time they competed for congressional district seats without plurinominal seats. In 1964, 1967, and 1970, the party won a minuscule two, one, and zero seats, respectively. During those nine crucial years, only three members of PAN won (or were awarded) seats where they had a close constituency connection. In the following two sessions of congress, they held only four of these seats, having decided not to run a presidential candidate in 1976. Collectively, from 1949 to 1988, nearly forty years, PAN was only able to win 47 competitive district seats, reinforcing ties between their candidates and their local district constituencies,[16] compared to 282 party seats, accounting for 86 percent of all PAN congressional seats.[17]

12. Conversations with friends who hosted local balloting stations in their homes confirmed the integrity of the voting in many middle-class congressional districts in the Federal District since the 1970s.

13. See, for example, the work of José Luis Velasco, *Insurgency, Authoritarianism, and Drug Trafficking in Mexico's "Democratization"* (New York: Routledge, 2005).

14. To illustrate, since 1979, the opposition parties collectively received 45 percent or more of the votes in high-income states. By contrast, it took them until 2000 to capture that same percentage in low-income states. See table 8.3, in Camp, *Politics in Mexico*, 215.

15. David A. Shirk, *Mexico's New Politics: The PAN and Democratic Change* (Boulder, Colo.: Lynne Rienner, 2005), 39.

16. Of course, it very likely they lost many seats through fraud.

17. For a detailed analysis of the evolution of these reforms and their impact on elections and the composition of the legislative branch, see Camp, "Mexico's Legislature: Missing the Democratic Lockstep?" in David Close, ed., *Legislatures and the New Democracies in Latin America* (Boulder, Colo.: Lynne Rienner, 1995), 17–36. For a historical analysis of how PRI used the no-reelection rule in the legislative branch, which was not incorporated into any provisions in the 1917 constitution but introduced in 1934, see Luisa Bejar Algazi,

**Table 3.3.** PAN Seats in the Chamber of Deputies, 1949 to 1988

| Session | District Seats | Party Seats |
|---|---|---|
| 1949 | 4 | – |
| 1952 | 5 | – |
| 1955 | 6 | – |
| 1958 | 6 | – |
| 1961 | 5 | – |
| 1964 | 2 | 18 |
| 1967 | 1 | 19 |
| 1970 | 0 | 20 |
| 1973 | 4 | 21 |
| 1976 | – | 20 |
| 1979 | 4 | 39[a] |
| 1982 | 1 | 50 |
| 1985 | 9 | 32 |
| 1988 | 38 | 63[b] |

*Source:* Roderic Ai Camp, *Politics in Mexico: The Democratic Consolidation* (New York: Oxford University Press, 2007), 206, table 8-1.

a. Party deputies were increased to the fixed number of 100. There were 300 district seats.
b. Party deputies were increased to the fixed number of 200. The district seats remained at 300.

In making these reforms, PRI produced a third grave consequence for PAN, in effect giving its national party leadership the ability to ultimately determine the lists by which party seats were awarded, rather than assigning those decisions solely to local party officials and active members to make their nominations and to voters to determine electoral outcomes, at least when those local elections were honest.[18] Steve Wuhs, a leading expert on PAN, confirms that before 1999, the years during which the effect of this pattern was most pronounced, the party's National

---

"La reelección parlamentaria inmediata: Un reto en la agenda política de México," *Revista Mexicana de Ciencia Política* 46, no. 187 (January–April 2003): 203–27.

18. As I have pointed out elsewhere, the plurinominal system has the same impact on the PRI and the PRD, allowing each party to choose long-standing, older party activists at the national level to populate their respective lists. This condition explains why the two sets of deputies, based on their status as plurinominal or majority district regardless of party, differ substantially in their composition and attitudes. Joy Langston and Francisco Javier Aparicio discovered the same pattern in their examination of all deputies elected in 1997 and 2000. See "Political Career Structures in Democratic Mexico, 1997–2006," paper presented at the American Political Science Association, Boston, August 28–31, 2008.

Executive Committee exercised significant discretionary control over the nominations.[19]

The electoral laws helped weaken PAN as a grassroots party, while strengthening the voice of the national party leadership. These structural reforms reinforced PAN's self-imposed pattern to limit its membership since its founding in 1939.[20] The party's limitations were designed to maintain cohesive leadership and a homogeneous ideology and to protect the party from embracing mass-oriented democracy.[21]

A strong argument can be made that the electoral reforms favoring party versus district seats and PAN's own leadership preferences significantly delayed its expansion from a regional party to a national party with strong grassroots support throughout the republic. In 1988, when it won more than 10 percent of the majority district seats in congress, four-fifths of those seats were from just five cities.[22] Even as late as 1997, after most electoral fraud was eliminated in 1994, PAN did not win a single district in fourteen out of thirty-two states, and the Party of the Democratic Revolution (PRD) did not win a single district in twenty-two out of thirty-two states.

19. Steve Wuhs, in a letter to the author, describes the decisions in practice before and after 1999: "Mostly the system hasn't changed all that much—it's pretty centralized and based on the proposals that PAN state party committees make to the CEN [National Executive Committee] for the formation of the plurinominal lists within their plurinominal district. The most significant change that did occur was in 1999, when they established a process that the CEN of the PAN had to follow in pooling the state party nominees and ordering them into a plurinominal list. Before the reform, the CEN had significant discretion—could bump to the top folks that they were sympathetic to, that sort of thing. After 1999, they established a rotating process that removed that discretion, so that nominees from states 1, 2, 3, 4, 5 in plurinominal district 1 were added to the list in alternation. The exceptions, of course, were reserve spots on the lists. Normally the top two spots on all plurinominal chamber lists are reserved for the party leadership." September 19, 2008. David Shirk also confirms Wuhs's account. Personal letter to the author, September 20, 2008. See Wuhs, *Savage Democracy: Institutional Change and Party Development in Mexico* (University Park: Pennsylvania State University Press, 2008), for an excellent comparison of PAN and PRD candidate selection rules and their consequences.

20. Yemille Mizrahi, *From Martyrdom to Power: The Partido Acción Nacional in Mexico* (Notre Dame, Ind.: University of Notre Dame Press, 2003).

21. Shirk, *Mexico's New Politics*, 118. For a detailed discussion of the consequences of the three leading parties' internal nomination process for the legislative branch since 2000, see Joy Langston's excellent analysis in "Legislative Recruitment in Mexico," in Peter M. Siavelis and Scott Morgenstern, eds., *Pathways to Power: Political Recruitment and Candidate Selection in Latin America* (University Park: Pennsylvania State University Press, 2008), 143–63; Steven T. Wuhs, "Democratization and the Dynamics of Candidate Selection Rule Change in Mexico, 1991-2003," *Mexican Studies/Estudios Mexicanos* 22 (2006): 33–55; and Joy Langston, "The Changing Party of the Institutional Revolution: Electoral Competition and Decentralized Candidate Selection," *Party Politics* 12 (2006): 395–413.

22. See my historical analysis of the regional growth of political opposition in "Mexico's 1988 Elections: A Turning Point for Its Political Development and Foreign Relations?," in Edgar Butler, ed., *Sucesión Presidencial: The 1988 Mexican Presidential Election* (Boulder, Colo.: Westview Press, 1991), 95–114.

At the state level, PAN party chairs, in spite of difficulties in obtaining a seat in the state legislature, have held this post second only to serving in congress. The national data on PAN party officials bear out the experiences of Jalisco state officials, because three out of ten party leaders have been elected to their respective state legislatures. The office of mayor in the resumes of party officials who have achieved prominence is not nearly as common as it is among all PAN members, including other party and nonparty officials.[23]

The most successful Jalisco PAN party official in recent years is the state governor (2007–13) Emilio González Márquez, who became the state party chair in 1999. González Márquez boasts a long history of party offices, state and national, extending back to the most conservative wing of the PAN, as a member of the Mexican Democratic Party (PDM), an organization with ties to the Sinarquista movement in western México. He joined the PDM in 1982 at the age of twenty-two, while studying for an accounting degree at the University of Guadalajara. Six years later he became a member of its national committee and briefly served as president. In 1991, he left the PDM to become a member of PAN, joining the state organization two years later. González Márquez held a series of state party positions as secretary of electoral action, organization, and political promotion in the mid-1990s. He was elected mayor of his home town, Lagos de Moreno, a community located in the heart of the 1920s pro-Catholic antistate Cristero rebellion, and became the first PANista member of the Guadalajara city council before achieving a party seat in 1997, like most of his PAN peers, in congress. He served as mayor of Guadalajara immediately before running for governor.[24]

PAN, unlike PRI, performed the typical functions of a political party; it identified, nominated, and elected its members to office. The PRI, on the other hand, functioned far more often as a vehicle that promoted the government's candidates for elective office, rather than playing a decisive role in identifying or nominating its candidates. For most of the decades, its members dominated Mexico's political scene, but it essentially sought to stay in power rather than to win power away from its political opponents.

---

23. Data provided by the PAN state organization in Coahuila, a northern state where PAN has strong historic roots, suggest the difficult path of winning such local elections. From 1978, when it won its first mayoral election in Monclova, through 1988, it won only five elections, four of them in Monclova. In the next decade, from 1991 through 1999, it achieved sixteen victories in ten different municipalities. From 2003 to 2006, it already claimed ten victorious elections. www.pancoahuila.org.mx, 2008.

24. *Quién es quién en el Congreso, 1997–2000* (Mexico: IETD, 1998), 37; www.cddhcu.gob.mx; www.pan.org.mx; www.jalisco.gob.mx; www.gilbertoperez.blogspot; Mexican Political Biographies Project, 2009.

Despite this significant difference in roles, the original National Revolutionary Party (PNR) was an umbrella organization that brought together numerous state and local parties.[25] Therefore, in the early years, despite the efforts to centralize control over the party in Mexico City, local parties exerted considerable influence when confronting numerous divisions among personal political factions. Of all the parties in Mexico, including the minor leftist parties, the presence of party offices in the backgrounds of PRI politicians have been less important, particularly so during the early predemocratic period from 1934 to 1958, when only 15 percent shared that experience. An excellent example of a politician whose adult life spanned the founding and twentieth-century evolution of the PRI and its antecedents is Leopoldo Hernández Partida, who was born in the early 1900s. He left his hometown of Guadalajara to attend the National Preparatory School and the National School of Law from 1928 to 1932. As a first-year law student, he supported General Alvaro Obregón's reelection campaign with other students, including Luis I. Rodríguez. Four years later, he joined the PNR after directing the party's magazine *La Revolución* during the chairmanship of Emilio Portes Gil, one of his favorite professors. He joined the National Peasant Federation (CNC), the largest union affiliate of the party's agrarian sector, becoming private secretary to its famous agrarian leader, Graciano Sánchez. He became secretary of the new Mexican Revolutionary Party popular sector under his fellow student's leadership, Luis I. Rodríguez, from 1938 to 1940. Three years later, he was elected to congress from the twelfth district in Mexico City, and he served twice more in the chamber of deputies in 1967-70 and 1982-85. He became private secretary to Javier Rojo Gómez, a major figure in Mexican politics and also leader of the CNC, supporting him as a candidate for president in 1945-46, and then completed another stint on the National Executive Committee of PRI as secretary of agrarian action in 1964-65. He served as interim chair of the PRI in the Federal District in 1965. His career successfully intertwined his posts in the agrarian union sector, the party bureaucracy, and the congress.[26]

During the entire predemocratic period (1934-88), one in four PRI politicians who reached national influential offices served as an important state party official (see table 3.4). The presence of party offices in their backgrounds increases significantly during the transitional years, during which time more than a third of prominent PRI politicians were veterans of party posts.

25. For a discussion of this phenomenon, see Luis Javier Garrido, *El partido de la revolución institucionalizada, la formación del nuevo estado en* México (Mexico: Siglo XXI, 1982), 20-62.

26. Personal communication, July 22, 1974.

Table 3.4. Prominent PRI Officeholders Who Were PRI State Party Officials

| Prominent PRI Officeholders | State Party Officials (%) |
| --- | --- |
| Predemocratic presidencies 1934-88 | 24 |
| Democratic transition presidencies 1988-2000 | 37 |
| Democratic presidencies 2000-2009 | 60 |

Source: Mexican Political Biographies Project, 2008.

PRI party officials include state party presidents and other state party posts.

By the democratic period, a whopping 60 percent had served in state and regional party positions. This dramatic change is reflected in the fact that in the democratic period, the only PRI members who had achieved nationally prominent positions in the Fox and Calderón administrations, with a few exceptions, were governors, senators, and members of congress—that is, individuals who established their reputations through elective office, both executive and legislative. Regardless of the period examined, leading members of congress in Mexico were much more likely to have been party activists than elsewhere in Latin America. In the case of Argentina, from 1991 to 1999, only a fourth of repeating members of congress shared such party experiences.[27]

Drawing on complete data from the state of Jalisco, thus providing a direct comparison between the state party leaders of PAN and PRI since their founding in this influential state, table 3.5 reveals some truly significant patterns in the relationship between PRI state party presidencies and national political careers. The most extraordinary finding is that of the forty-three different politicians who chaired the state party organization, more than 90 percent served in the national congress. As was the case with PAN state party officials, those politicians who reached national political office were state party officials, and they typically did so through congress. PRI state party chairs in all states appear to correspond closely with the figures from a complete sample of Jalisco officials. Nearly nine out of ten prominent politicians who were elected to congress since 1934 served as chair of their respective state party organizations.

Out of the national sample of 1,482 members of congress, nearly 60 percent held some party posts. Among all prominent national PRI politicians in the sample, 2,249 individuals, or 8 percent, served as state party chairs. Even more surprising, more than half of the Jalisco state party presidents achieved national political prominence beyond that of serving

27. Mark P. Jones, "The Recruitment and Selection of Legislative Candidates in Argentina," in Siavelis and Morgenstern, Pathways to Power, 60.

**Table 3.5.** Presidents of the PRI in Jalisco

| Politician | Year(s) President | Position Held |
|---|---|---|
| Rodrigo Camacho Cafuentes | 1929 | Congress |
| David Orozco | 1930 | Congress |
| Antonio Valadéz Ramírez | 1930 | Congress, senate, governor |
| Luis F. Ibarra | 1930 | Congress |
| Martiniano Sendis | 1930 | Congress |
| Esteban García de Alba Larios | 1930–31 | Congress, cabinet, National Executive Committee |
| Antonio Valadéz Ramírez | 1931 | Congress, senate, governor |
| Sebastián Allende | 1931 | Congress, governor |
| José de Jesús González Gallo | 1932–34 | Congress, governor, cabinet |
| Manuel Ochoa Arambula | 1934 | mayor of Guadalajara |
| Clemente Sepúlveda | 1934–36 | Governor |
| Florencio Topete Valencia | 1936 | Congress, mayor |
| Salvador Galvéz Gutiérrez | 1937 | |
| Florencio Topete Valencia | 1937–40 | Congress, mayor |
| Margarito Ramírez Miranda | 1940 | Congress, governor, cabinet |
| Lucio González Padilla | 1941–44 | Congress |
| Florencio Topete Valencia | 1944 | Congress, mayor |
| Miguel Moreno Padilla | 1945 | Congress, senate |
| Angel F. Martínez | 1946–47 | Congress, mayor of Guadalajara |
| Ramón Castellanos Camacho | 1947–53 | Congress |
| Guillermo Ramírez Valadéz | 1950–53 | Congress, senate |
| Juan Gil Preciado | 1953–56 | Congress, governor, cabinet |
| José de Parres Arias | 1956 | Legislature, rector |
| Salvador Corona Bandin | 1956–1961 | Congress, senate |
| Sergio Corona Blake | 1961 | Alternate congress, legislature. |
| Raul Padilla Gutiérrez | 1961 | Congress, oficial mayor |
| Felipe Hernández Colunga | 1964–65 | Congress |
| Filiberto Rubalcaba Sánchez | 1965–68 | Congress |
| Jesus Bueno Amezcua | 1968 | Congress |
| José Martín Barba | 1969–72 | Congress |
| Arnulfo Villaseñor Saavedra | 1972–76 | Congress, senate, mayor |
| Reyes Rodolfo Flores Zaragoza | 1976–79 | Congress |
| Carlos Rivera Aceves | 1979–82 | Congress, governor |
| Eugenio Ruiz Orozco | 1982–83 | Senate, candidate for governor |

Continued

**Table 3.5.** Continued

| Politician | Year(s) President | Position Held |
|---|---|---|
| Ricardo Chávez Pérez | 1983–85 | Congress, National Executive Committee |
| Francisco Javier Santillán Oceguera | 1985–88 | Congress |
| Oscar de la Torre Padilla | 1988–89 | Congress, assistant secretary |
| Enrique Chavero Ocampo | 1989–91 | Congress |
| Eduardo Rodríguez Rodríguez | 1992 | |
| Raúl Juárez Valencia | 1992–94 | Congress |
| Rafael González Pimienta | 1994–95 | Congress, assistant secretary |
| José Manuel Correa Ceseña | 1995–97 | Congress, legislature |
| Francisco Javier Morales Aceves | 1997–2000 | Congress |
| Ramiro Hernández García | 2000–04 | Congress, senate |
| Javier Alejandro Galván Guerrero | 2004–08 | Legislature |

Source: Mexican Political Biographies Project, 2008; Roderic Ai Camp, *Mexican Political Biographies, 1884-1934* (Austin: University of Texas Press, 1991); www.prijalisco.org.mx/presicde, 2008.

in congress for a single session (for inclusion in the national sample, one would have to have held two or more congressional or senate positions or have served as an oficial mayor or higher in the executive branch, as a justice of the supreme court, or as a state governor). For example, more than six out of ten PRI senators held party positions, and nearly half served as state party chairs. Many of these officials served multiple times as members of congress, as senators, and in several cases as assistant secretaries and secretaries of cabinet-level agencies.

A number of the initial presidents of the Jalisco state PRI organization, before Cárdenas became president in 1934, were prominent politicians, having served as governors or as members of congress for multiple terms. This pattern seems to be typical, given the fact that the party was organized at the national level by former president Plutarco Elías Calles and his closest allies.[28] Calles himself became the first president of the party in his home state of Nuevo León in 1929, the same year the PNR was founded.[29] This pattern is reminiscent of the PAN state organization, in which one of the leading co-founders of the party served as its first chair for many years.

The other position that stands out in the backgrounds of PRI state party officials is that of state legislator. More than a fourth of all state presidents

28. Garrido, *El partido de la revolución*, 63ff.
29. See www.prinl.org/expresidentes, 2008.

in Jalisco served in this position, several of them two or three times. What is surprising is that only a small number of party presidents were elected mayors in Jalisco, most of them in Guadalajara, the state capital. However, this is not the norm among all PRI state party officials in our sample of national politicians. Approximately one in ten prominent politicians have been mayors, but among all PRI state party chairs who have achieved national prominence, one in three were mayors.

Of all the Jalisco party presidents since 1934, the most successful figure nationally was Juan Gil Preciado. His father, the humble mayor of Juchitlán, Gil Preciado's home town, had to abandon the city for Guadalajara during the Cristero rebellion because of the persecution of peasants. Eventually, this move permitted Gil Preciado to study at the University of Guadalajara, where he obtained a teaching certificate, becoming a high school principal in rural Jalisco in 1927. Gil Preciado became an auxiliary major and teacher for the Army's 32nd regiment, allowing him to travel widely around Mexico. He soon attached himself to General Ruperto García de Alba, who after briefly serving as interim governor of Jalisco was appointed governor of the federal territory of Baja California del Sur in 1931, where Gil Preciado served as his personal secretary and then secretary general of government. In the late 1930s, he worked for the PNR national committee, and through his contacts with party officials, became a member of congress from Jalisco's thirteenth district. Using his connections in the capital, he began working in the agricultural ministry, rising to the influential position of personal secretary to Oscar Flores Sánchez, assistant secretary of agriculture, before returning to Guadalajara in 1952 at the end of the Alemán administration. In 1953, he became president of the PNR in Jalisco and was elected to the state legislature. During his tenure as state party president, he represented the National Executive Committee as its delegate to Tamaulipas. Two years later he received his party's nomination as a candidate for mayor of Guadalajara, and he served in that capacity until 1958, after which he won the Jalisco gubernatorial race in 1959. In 1964, Gustavo Díaz Ordaz named him secretary of agriculture.[30]

The short political history of the PRD beginning in 1989, and the fact that its National Executive Committee only identified six states as having state organizations in 2009, precludes examining its state party leadership in detail. As noted previously, the electoral structure of Mexico's political

---

30. His first mentor, General Ruperto García de Alba, was the brother of Esteban, who was president of the party in Jalisco, and secretary general of the PNR from 1936 to 1938, when Gil Preciado worked for the National Executive Committee. At the same time, Esteban was oficial mayor of government, which would have allowed him to recommend Gil Preciado as a possible congressional candidate to the secretary of government, a key player in determining those nominations. Mexican Political Biographies Project, 2009; Camp, *Mexican Political Biographies, 1935-1993,* 262, 282.

system prior to 2000 distorted its national leadership largely into elective posts, the most numerous and common being a member of congress. If those party members who had served in any important party post or multiple local party posts are surveyed, we discover that 92, 79, and 47 percent of such PRD, PAN, and PRI party militants, respectively, were members of congress. Because the PRD has essentially achieved no access to national executive office, this is not a surprising figure. Thus, the criteria for achieving national political prominence are largely confined to elective national posts, especially in the lower chamber.

An examination of the executive branch and comparison of the party leadership experiences of cabinet-level secretaries and assistant secretaries, reveals significant differences between PAN and PRI members. What is most striking about the data in table 3.6 is the lack of partisan political experience among PRI executive and judicial branch leaders. I have argued in earlier studies that few assistant secretaries have held PRI party positions. Most of them have risen through the ranks of the bureaucracy, typically as department and division heads. This is borne out by the fact that only one out of ten PRI assistant secretaries ever served in a national party position on the executive committee, whereas slightly more have held any party post, local, state, or national.

Not surprisingly, if one thinks that holding any party post implies party militancy (rather than just nominal party membership) and therefore greater partisanship, PRI militants are more likely to have obtained the most influential positions as cabinet secretaries compared to assistant secretaries, who are more frequently chosen for other reasons, including their expertise and specialized experience. Nevertheless, unlike senators and members of congress, only a small minority of executive branch leaders in the past eighty years, regardless of their position, were products of the party bureaucracy.

Table 3.6. Party Experiences of Leading Politicians in the Executive and Legislative Branches

| Party Position | Government Post (%) | | |
|---|---|---|---|
| | Cabinet Secretary | Assistant Secretary | Supreme Court Justice |
| PAN CEN | 53 | 31 | 100 |
| PAN Other | 72 | 75 | 100 |
| PRI CEN | 14 | 10 | 3 |
| PRI Other | 19 | 14 | 2 |

Source: Mexican Political Biographies Project, 2009.

There is perhaps no better example of a successful PRI party activist's career on both the state and national level than that of Ernesto Uruchurtu Peralta, who made good in the executive branch, succeeding in serving four consecutive presidents. Uruchurtu Peralta came from a large, prominent family in the northern border state of Sonora, and he grew up in the state capital, Hermosillo, in the first decade of the twentieth century. Ernesto's older brother, Gustavo Adolfo, served on the medical staff of General Alvaro Obregón and was elected to congress and the senate. Both Ernesto and his brother were second-generation politicians; their paternal uncle, Manuel Uruchurtu Ramírez, served in the lower chamber in 1912. While a member of congress, Manuel established a national reputation for his nephews when he perished in the sinking of the *Titanic*, after giving up his seat in a lifeboat to a woman with a baby.[31] Their maternal uncle, Francisco Martínez Peralta, also a member of congress and a senator, was a career army officer who achieved the top rank of division general.

His uncles and older brothers served as natural political mentors to Ernesto, but he was by far the more successful politician. After studying at the Normal School in Hermosillo, Ernesto traveled to Mexico City to attend the National Preparatory School and the National School of Law, a significant decision that decidedly affected his political career. This choice allowed him to become part of one of the most influential political groups in Mexico after the revolution: the Alemán generation, a cluster of future politicians who attended both schools with Miguel Alemán, president of Mexico from 1946 to 1952. Initially, however, after graduating, Uruchurtu returned to Sonora to open a law practice in Ciudad Obregón. He served as a judge and became a state supreme court justice in 1937. That same year he obtained his first party post as chair of the state committee. In 1939, he returned to the capital, where he became a legal adviser in the ministry of agriculture and then at the National Bank of Ejido Credit, an agency he directed on an interim basis. Most important, however, Alemán, who had become secretary of government under Manuel Avila Camacho in 1940, the most influential cabinet post in that administration, appointed his former classmate as director of government in the same agency. When Alemán resigned to run as the PRI's presidential candidate, Uruchurtu became his assistant secretary during the campaign. Uruchurtu played an important role on the PNR national council, which, in response to Alemán's strong wishes, transformed the party from the PNR into the PRI. Uruchurtu was designated the first secretary general of the new PRI in December 1946.[32]

31. See www.elimparcial.com, April 13, 2008.
32. He was surely influential in this capacity in having his uncle, Francisco Martínez Peralta, appointed to the new National Executive Committee as secretary of agrarian affairs.

In the Alemán administration, he continued in the government ministry as the assistant secretary, becoming the acting secretary when his boss died in 1948 and remaining assistant secretary when Adolfo Ruiz Cortines became the new secretary. In 1951, when Ruiz Cortines, following in Alemán's footsteps, became PRI's presidential candidate, Uruchurtu again became secretary, remaining until the end of 1952. Ruiz Cortines appointed his collaborator as head of the Department of the Federal District in 1952, where he was subsequently reappointed by presidents López Mateos and Díaz Ordaz. Uruchurtu was the only Mexican to serve consecutively in the same cabinet post for three administrations, and one of a handful of politicians in eight decades to have served in the cabinet in four consecutive administrations.[33] In 1958, he was a serious precandidate for the PRI presidential nomination.[34]

In contrast to the PRI and its antecedents, most observers would expect PAN to be less partisan in its choices for the executive branch. In certain respects this is true, reflected by the fact that Fox appointed many independents with no known party affiliation and, consequently, no party experience. A few other appointees were members of the PRI. But of the PAN members who had served in the cabinet in the last three administrations, three-quarters held party offices at the state or national level, and more than half served on the National Executive Committee.[35]

These significant differences in the role of political party experiences in the backgrounds of Mexico's most prominent national leaders can again be explained by the different roles the two parties played. As I suggested at the beginning of this chapter, the PAN leadership remained cohesive and in charge of the party's fortunes, in contrast to the PRI's trajectory typically being decided by prominent figures in the executive branch, most notably individual presidents. Uruchurtu's career illustrates this difference. His party activity did not bring him to the attention of influential mentors. Rather, those mentors, notably Alemán, relied on his friendship and his evaluation of Uruchurtu's performance as a division head in a

---

Later, his uncle also served under him as the director of traffic in the Federal District, a position traditionally assigned to a career military officer.

33. Camp, *Mexican Political Biographies, 1935-1993*, 710; Mexican Political Biographies Project, 2009; www.ssh.org.mx, 2008; www.es.wikipedia.org.mx, 2008.

34. See my "Mexican Presidential Pre-Candidates, Changes and Portents for the Future," *Polity* (Summer 1984): 588-605, for an in-depth discussion of this decision.

35. Zedillo was the only PRI president to have appointed a PAN member to his cabinet, Fernando Antonio Lozano Gracia, as attorney general, thus setting the stage for a bipartisan cabinet. Lozano Gracia was not just a nominal PAN member but a member of the Regional Committee for the Federal District, the National Executive Committee, and became secretary general of the party. He also practiced law with Diego Fernández de Ceballos, who was the PAN presidential candidate against Zedillo, to whom Zedillo allegedly first offered the position. *Proceso*, December 5, 1994, 29-30, and Mexican Political Biographies Project, 2009.

cabinet agency to assess his qualities as a politician. In PAN's case, however, it is not surprising that many individuals moved from party positions to elective office and then, when the opportunity became available in 2000, to executive branch positions.

The contrast between PAN and PRI is furthered demonstrated in the figures for supreme court justices. It is clear from the minuscule percentages of justices who experienced careers in the PRI party bureaucracy that anyone with ambitions for a successful public legal career during PRI's reign would not have pursued a path in the party bureaucracy at the state or national levels. Among PAN justices, who account for only a small percentage of the total number of justices, all have held party posts. Again, this suggests the role the party has played in PAN and its importance in originating and promoting potential public figures in all branches of government.

One can grasp the significance of the changing face of partisanship in Mexican politics over time by comparing the party affiliations of all prominent national officeholders in each presidential administration. This allows us to gain a stronger sense of the characteristics of officials who reached a certain level of influence in each successive administration, including their partisan backgrounds. An examination of the trends in table 3.7 suggest the extraordinarily restricted access to important national offices available to PAN members and early leftist party members from the Cárdenas administration through the end of the Miguel de la Madrid administration in 1988.

Table 3.7. Partisan Affiliation of Prominent National Officeholders, 1935–2009

| | Party Affiliation (%) | | | | | |
|---|---|---|---|---|---|---|
| Presidency | None | PAN | PRD | PRI | Left | All Others |
| *Predemocratic* | | | | | | |
| Cárdenas through De la Madrid | 0.9 | 0 | 0 | 96.8 | 0 | 2.3 |
| *Democratic transition* | | | | | | |
| Salinas | 6.1 | 0 | 0 | 84.3 | 0 | 9.6 |
| Zedillo | 9.5 | 11.3 | 3.4 | 71.7 | 2.1 | 2.0 |
| *Democratic period* | | | | | | |
| Fox | 15.6 | 24.0 | 7.1 | 48.7 | 2.3 | 2.3 |
| Calderón | 9.8 | 35.3 | 9.8 | 35.3 | 2.7 | 7.1 |

*Source*: Mexican Political Biographies Project, 2009.

Left = PSUM, PPS, PRT, PST, PCM, PT, and PP; All Others includes PAN, PRD, PDM, Sinarquista, and Left before Zedillo, but only PDM, PRI/PRD, PRI/PAN, PVEM, and Convergencia after Zedillo.

Basically, of the 2,949 individuals who held prominent national offices in these nine administrations from 1935 to 1988, 97 percent were PRI members. Of the ninety-three individuals who were not affiliated with PRI, twenty-five had no party affiliation, and sixty-eight belonged to other parties, essentially PAN and the Left because the PRD was not formed until 1989.

I have broken down the democratic transition and postdemocratic periods into individual presidencies because important changes occur between each of those four administrations, unlike the predemocratic presidencies. The first decline in the percentage of PRI politicians in top positions during a Mexican presidency occurs under Salinas (1988–94). It is important to note that the first significant representation of unaffiliated individuals occurs in this administration. All other parties combined increased their representation more than threefold from approximately 2 percent in the previous nine administrations, to one out of ten under Salinas. In some respects, these trends are surprising because most analysts view Salinas as reasserting a stronger, more authoritarian presidency in comparison to his predecessor, Miguel de la Madrid.

Zedillo, however, truly presided over the fundamental transformation of the political system represented by the significant decline in the PRI's partisan affiliation in top political offices, as he did in so many other respects. Opposition parties doubled their presence in his administration over that of his predecessor. Compared to all previous administrations through Miguel de la Madrid, just six years earlier, opposition party members under Zedillo accounted for nearly a fourth of all influential politicians.

The Fox and Calderón administrations not only represent a significant and expected change from Zedillo, the last PRI-controlled presidency, but equally important, they reveal politically significant distinctions from each other. Under Fox, the former opposition parties account for more than a third of the officeholders in his administration, not quite double that of Zedillo. What is more surprising is that PRI party members remained nearly half of all influential officeholders under Fox, double that of the 24 percent of party members from the president's own party, PAN.

Fox's presidency, measured by party affiliations of politicians who served in all three branches of government during his administration, represents three significant changes from the past. First, unlike the PRI-controlled administrations prior to 2000, the president's own party accounts for a minority of party-affiliated politicians. Second, if one thinks of the PAN as the incumbent party and all other parties as the electoral opposition, those parties collectively, in combination with independents, total an astonishing 75 percent of officeholders. Finally, as analysts have noted previously, Fox opened the door widely to nonpolitical appointees, including numerous individuals whose careers were in the private rather than the public sector. Unaffiliated officials reached a high point in his administration, third in total numbers only to PRI and PAN members, respectively.

Calderón's administration represents some equally important additional alterations in trends of partisan affiliations among top office-holders. Reversing the trend instituted by Fox, Calderón appointed many more active party militants to his important cabinet positions. The over-all percentage of PANistas in his administration, when all officeholders are combined, including representatives of the legislative and judicial branches, suggests a significant increase from 24 to 35 percent. Calderón instituted this partisan change because he believed many of the legislative failures of Fox's administration could be attributed to a lack of party and political experience among Fox's appointees. The most dramatic change, however, is the decline among PRI-affiliated politicians, who drop from nearly half in Fox's presidency to the same level as PAN politicians, 35 percent. Furthermore, when one considers the outcome of the 2006 presidential race, where the vote was largely split by PAN and PRD, with the PRI earning a distant third place among voters, officeholders' party affiliations (with the exception of PAN), do not correlate in the slightest with their actual level of electoral support.

The most notable pattern in party affiliation among officeholders in the Calderón administration is the extreme underrepresentation of the PRD. The PRD's own behavior in large part is responsible for this low figure. As suggested previously, Fox specifically offered major cabinet posts to two well-known PRD politicians after his election. The PRD refused to allow its members to accept these offices, thereby preventing them from developing bipartisan reputations as executive branch administrators as well as exercising their ability to appoint numerous assistant secretaries who also would have an opportunity to earn such credentials. Second, PRI members continue to exercise a significant role in many public settings, suggesting that in addition to their prominent legislative posts, many of their members were valued by Calderón for their expertise and management skills as well as their abilities to persuade an opposition-controlled congress to join with PAN in support of influential and often controversial legislation.

Most observers of Mexican politics since the establishment of the PRI in 1929 have suggested that PRI militants dominated each administration. Instead of surveying the presence of just party officials or party affiliation in the backgrounds of leading politicians by administration, an analysis of militant party members provides an entirely different picture of officeholders. Our data set incorporates 4,524 officeholders during the period from 1935 to 2009, consisting of 2,973 different individuals. In reality, the vast majority of officeholders were nominal party members, not active party officeholders or campaigners. Beginning with Cárdenas, who presided over the first full presidential administration since the party was founded, one is struck by the fact that only one out of five individuals can be described as a PRI militant. The remaining four-fifths of his administration, except for three individuals, were not militants of any party.

What is striking about the patterns in the data in table 3.8 is that for the first three administrations, including that of Alemán, who founded the PRI in 1946, militants accounted for only one-quarter or fewer of officeholders. As I have argued for many years, based on conversations with politicians who held office in these early administrations, many leading politicians (the vast majority) were only nominal party members, equivalent to registered Democrats or Republicans in the United States.

Through the mid-1960s, barely more than a third were active PRIistas. During the five PRI-controlled administrations over the next thirty years, PRI militants account for more than two-fifths of all officeholders. Under Zedillo, a reversal in the upward trend among PRI militants to a level comparable to the late 1950s emerges. Naturally, under Fox and Calderón, one would expect to witness a decline among PRI militants countered by a concomitant rise in PAN and PRD militants. This is the case, accompanied by a slight decline in nonmilitant officeholders. However, what remains most interesting is that nominal party members and independents are equal in numbers to the PAN and PRI militants combined.

**Table 3.8.** Party Militants in Presidential Administrations

| Presidency | Militancy (%) | | | |
|---|---|---|---|---|
| | None | PAN/PDM | PRD/Left | PRI |
| Cárdenas | 78.2 | 0.4 | 0.8 | 20.6 |
| Avila Camacho | 75.7 | 0.4 | 0.8 | 23.1 |
| Alemán | 72.2 | 1.1 | 1.5 | 25.1 |
| Ruiz Cortines | 65.6 | 1.1 | 1.8 | 31.6 |
| López Mateos | 61.3 | 0.4 | 1.1 | 37.3 |
| Díaz Ordaz | 56.3 | 0.3 | 1.1 | 42.2 |
| Echeverría | 56.2 | 0 | 1.3 | 42.5 |
| López Portillo | 52.1 | 0.5 | 1.8 | 45.6 |
| De la Madrid | 52.7 | 1.4 | 2.5 | 43.5 |
| Salinas | 47.9 | 4.8 | 4.5 | 42.8 |
| Zedillo | 48.3 | 8.8 | 6.5 | 36.5 |
| Fox | 44.8 | 17.9 | 8.2 | 29.1 |
| Calderón | 45.7 | 23.7 | 10.1 | 20.5 |

*Source*: Mexican Political Biographies Project, 2009.

Conclusions from the comparative literature on the impact of fresh leadership after a democratic shift are mixed. For example, a number of studies have emerged about the democratic transition in Russia, especially because it was one of the few countries where political leadership has been examined carefully in the predemocratic period. Sharon Werning Rivera discusses the contradictory findings and ultimately concludes from two comprehensive studies that Russia's new national leadership was populated with numerous politicians whose origins could be found in regional governmental positions and party structures, similar to the present findings about local offices and state party positions, and that the old elite was not replicated in the postdemocratic era.[36]

Politicians who enter national politics through their activities as party militants provide an important channel for past and future national leaders. Given the fact that nearly a third of all officeholders had been militants early in their careers, it is valuable to understand how these politicians are recruited into their respective party activities. Many politicians' interest in politics occurs at a young age, often in their high school or undergraduate years, and party registration dates confirm this fact among hundreds of Mexican politicians.

An excellent example of such an early interest is the career of PANista Francisco José Paoli Bolio, who was born and raised in Mérida, Yucatán, the son of a hacienda owner. During his preparatory school years he became involved in a social Christian study group that discussed the Catholic encyclicals and worked with extremely poor Mexicans. They tried to establish a social democratic movement incorporating various groups, including a group from PAN. This group attempted, without success, to convert PAN into a social Christian party; instead, under Paoli Bolio's leadership, the group existed independent of the party.

In the 1960s, Carlos Madrazo, then president of the PRI, attempted to democratize the PRI through municipal primaries, taking away control over nominations for mayors and other local offices from political bosses and governors.[37] When President Díaz Ordaz intervened and prevented Madrazo from implementing this strategy further, Madrazo resigned. Paoli Bolio, impressed with Madrazo's attempts to democratize the PRI from within, contacted this influential politician through mutual friends, and

36. "Elites in Post-Communist Russia: A Changing of the Guard?," *Europe-Asia Studies* 52, no. 3 (2000): 416. See David Lane and Cameron Ross, "The Changing Composition and Structure of the Political Elites," in David Lane, ed., *Russia in Transition: Politics, Privatization and Inequality* (New York: Longman, 1995), 75.

37. Rogelio Hernández Rodríguez, *La Formación del político mexicano: El caso de Carlos A. Madrazo* (Mexico: El Colegio de México, 1998), and Enrique Krauze, *Biography of Power* (New York: HarperCollins, 1998), 684.

together they attempted to organize a new party, for which they never were able to achieve registration.

After graduating from law school, Paoli Bolio represented a social Christian union. During this period, a group of former political prisoners from the 1968 student massacre, including Heberto Castillo Martínez, a political activist, and Demetrio Vallejo, a prominent labor leader, founded the Mexican Workers Party (PMT) in 1974, where Paoli Bolio served on the executive committee with Vallejo. After leaving the party in 1981, he abandoned his political militancy altogether from 1981 to 1991, devoting himself to his academic career, eventually becoming president of the Autonomous Metropolitan University, Xochimilco campus. In 1991, thirty years after Paoli Bolio had tried to convert it to a social Christian party, PAN underwent this change, and its leaders asked him to be a candidate for a plurinominal seat in the Chamber of Deputies. He won that seat without any formal affiliation to PAN, joining the party two years later during his last year in congress. He rapidly became secretary of studies of the National Executive Committee at the invitation of the party president at the time, Felipe Calderón Hinojosa, and competed for but lost the PAN nomination as a candidate for governor of the Federal District. Instead, he served in the Assembly of the Federal District (its state legislature) for three years, and then again, at the invitation of Calderón, he was placed first on the list of party deputies for the Federal District in 1997, becoming president of the lower chamber in 1999–2000, during the first congressional session in which the PRI had lost majority control. He again served on the National Executive Committee from 1999 to 2002 and resigned from his party post to become assistant secretary of government in the Fox cabinet.[38]

Paoli Bolio represents another pattern among militant party members that has received little attention. A small but important group of party officials and militants, similar to Paoli Bolio, shifted their allegiance or roots from one party to another. In recent years, the most common transformation occurred among PANistas who formerly were members of the PRI or of one or more small leftist parties in the 1960s and 1970s who joined or helped found the PRD in 1989. One of the most interesting examples of a highly successful PRI politician with unusual ideological roots is the career of Santiago Oñate Laborde, whose father, a lawyer and professor at the National University, was a PAN leader mentored by Adolfo Christlieb Ibarrola, PAN's president from 1962 to 1968. When Oñate Laborde's father

38.  See www.larevista.com.mx, September 26, 2005; www.gobernacion,gob.mx/portal, 1997; *Diccionario biográfico de México* (Mexico: Presidencia de la República, 1994), CD; and Mexican Political Biographies Project, 2009.

died at age fifty, Christlieb tutored Santiago and his brothers. Santiago's mother was the daughter of Hernán Laborde, longtime leader of the Mexican Communist Party and their presidential candidate against General Lázaro Cárdenas in 1934.

Instead of becoming a PANista or Communist Party militant, Oñate Laborde joined the PRI in 1974, shortly after completing his law degree and spending a year studying sociology in Italy. He joined the party during the presidency of Jesús Reyes Heroles, who attended elementary school with Santiago's father. Ten years later, Oñate Laborde served a term in congress, where he became friends with Luis Donaldo Colosio, who served on the Rules Committee presided over by Oñate Laborde. While they were in congress together, Colosio became oficial mayor of the PRI National Executive Committee in 1987, and Oñate Laborde became legal director of the PRI. After Colosio became the party's president in 1988, under the influence of his mentor, Carlos Salinas Gortari, he appointed Oñate Laborde as secretary of ideological divulgation in 1990, while Oñate Laborde, similar to Paoli Bolio, was serving in the Assembly of the Federal District. After holding several top appointed posts, including another under Colosio, who had joined Salinas's cabinet, he became the party's secretary of international affairs when Colosio became the PRI presidential nominee in 1993. After Colosio's assassination during the campaign, Oñate Laborde continued to direct the PRI during Zedillo's presidential campaign, eventually joining Zedillo's cabinet as secretary of labor. In 1995, following his mentor's footsteps, he, too, became the party's president.[39]

Many of those party militants who are not hybrids of multiple party backgrounds are products of long family traditions in the party. For example, Felipe Calderón points to his father's activities as a leading PANista in initiating his own interest in politics and in the party.[40] Among PRI militants, given the party's lengthy life span, some are third-generation activists today.[41] Most party officials who achieved national prominence

---

39. *El Financiero*, December 1, 1994, 51; Notimex, April 5, 1994; *Christian Science Monitor*, August 12, 1995, 6A; www.opcw.org.mx, 2008; *El Financiero*, January 30, 1995, 2; personal interview with the author; www.fortunecity.com, 2008; *Diccionario biográfico de gobierno mexicano* (Mexico: Presidencia de la República, 1992), 267; and Mexican Political Biographies Project, 2009.

40. As a young child, Felipe accompanied his father, Luis Calderón Vega, an important intellectual and author, during his participation in political campaigns. Two of President Calderón's siblings have held national office and multiple party positions at the state and national level.

41. Some interesting examples include Rafael Moreno Valle Rosas, senator from Puebla, 2006–12, whose grandfather was secretary of political action of the national PRI, governor of Puebla, and secretary of health. Although Rafael was an active member of PRI, and served

as I have suggested did so through the legislative branch. Miguel Osorio Ramírez, a native of Guerrero and a three-time member of congress, was exposed as a young child to the National Executive Committee of the PRI because when he was a child, his father, who became the party's secretary general, regularly took him to party headquarters. A student political activist, he joined the party at age fourteen. Just two years later, he participated in Adolfo Ruiz Cortines's presidential campaign, and when he was only twenty-two, Miguel became director of the PRI National Youth Action for six years, an important party post that typically leads to higher party and elective offices. In the 1960s, he presided over the party as state chair in Nayarit, represented the National Executive Committee in several states, and became private secretary to the party president in 1966. He also served in the executive branch as an assistant secretary of agrarian reform and authored an important book on the PRI.[42]

## CONCLUSIONS

Party posts at both the state and national level have played a crucial role in the careers of numerous influential national politicians. The structure of Mexican politics and the function of political institutions, including parties, have exercised the most decisive influence on the impact of party positions in the backgrounds of political leadership over the past eight decades.

The most surprising general revelation in the long-term chronological data on party militancy is the extraordinary percentage of politicians who were only nominal party members or who were not known to have any party affiliation. Given the fact that the PRI controlled access to the political process for seven decades, it is unexpected that more Mexican politicians were nonmilitants than were militants. These figures can be explained by the lesser role of the party in contrast to the decisive role of the federal bureaucracy in determining most of the candidates for appointed and elective offices, including those making up the PRI National Executive Committee (CEN). This fact alone explains why twice as many members of PAN and PRD held party offices as their PRI counterparts (see table 3.1).

on the party's National Council, he resigned from the party following a scandal with the state governor before running for senator.

42. Personal communication to the author; *Proceso*, June 12, 1978, 25; *Excélsior*, December 26, 1981, 16; *Diccionario biográfico del gobierno mexicano*, 541; www.suracapulco. com.mx, August 18, 2000; and Mexican Political Biographies Project, 2009.

The functional realities of the political parties during the decades prior to 2000 also influenced the presence of party offices in the backgrounds of prominent PAN and PRD politicians. The most striking example of this presence, as I discovered, was the reinforcement of the PAN's national party leadership as a consequence of congressional electoral decisions in the 1960s that assigned opposition parties national offices in the legislative branch based on party affiliation rather than on winning competitive district seats. These assigned seats—essentially the only rewards opposition parties could assign their most faithful and able politicians—reinforced the national party leadership's power in making these decisions. Thus PAN awarded ninety-eight congressional seats versus winning only seven seats in the first fifteen years these laws were in effect (table 3.3). Given the location of this decision-making authority, ambitious politicians desiring national political careers naturally sought national party offices. Furthermore, in the democratic era, studies show that plurinominal deputies, because they boast more legislative experience, were much more likely to obtain positions as committee chairs in the legislative branch, regardless of party affiliation.[43]

Equally important to the decisive impact of the electoral laws themselves was the impact of the larger democratic electoral trends in Mexico. Many analysts would suggest that as the democratic transformation ensued in the 1990s and the democratic consolidation began in 2000, opposition parties, especially PAN, spearheaded the increase in younger and recent nationally prominent politicians with party experience. Yet the longitudinal data also clearly show that the PRI's own members have dramatically increased their party activities to the point where since Vicente Fox's election nearly two-thirds boast having held important state and national party posts compared to approximately only a fourth from the predemocratic era (table 3.4). PRI members were reacting to not only the same electoral trends as PAN and PRD but also the dissatisfaction expressed among many party activists toward technocratic politicians, without any party or elective experience, dominating its leadership. This antitechnocratic attitude led to a dramatic reform in party statutes in the 1996, introducing a specific requirement that nominees for national office be PRI militants who had previously held elective office.[44]

43. D. Xavier Medina Vidal, Antonio Ugues Jr., and Shaun Bowler, "Experience Counts: The Revolving Door of the Mexican Chamber of Deputies," paper presented at the Western Political Science Association, Vancouver, British Columbia, 2009, 17.

44. For evidence of the important consequence of these internal rules, see Joy Langston, "Why Rules Matter: Changes in Candidate Selection in Mexico's PRI, 1988–2000," *Journal of Latin American Studies* 33 (2001): 485–511, and Frederic Cady's excellent "Filling the

A third significant and broad finding is that politicians who successfully pursued national careers and stressed party organizational experience in their backgrounds typically did so following national elective office, especially in the lower chamber of congress. Whether all members of congress in the data set are examined or individual state party organizations are explored, the linkage is overwhelmingly strong. Our national sample of nearly 1,500 members of congress reveals that nearly 60 percent held some party posts.

Nevertheless, despite the linkage between national elective office and party experience, PAN members alone (when compared with the PRI) demonstrate nearly equally high figures for the executive branch. The presence of party backgrounds in PAN cabinet secretaries and assistant secretaries can also be explained in part by the fact that PAN's most prominent political figures, including President Calderón, were equally products of the legislative branch and the party apparatus, especially the CEN, prior to 2000. Whereas very few PRI members in the executive branch served on their party's CEN or in some other party post, an extraordinary three-quarters of PAN cabinet and assistant secretaries held party posts, and half the cabinet were former members of the CEN. The fact that so many PAN assistant secretaries share such a militant background suggests that party organizational activities will characterize future PAN executive branch leaders for years to come.

Mexico illustrates that a country undergoing democratic transformation after decades of experiencing a one party-dominant state, cannot dramatically shift its leadership to entirely new figures or to leaders who come from parties other than the previously dominant organization.[45] Fox, as noted, actually presided over twice as many members of the PRI as his own party during his administration. Calderón, after six years of PAN being in power, could select from a newly established pool of experienced executive branch party members, and he increased his PAN appointees and top elected officials to a level equal to those from the PRI. This shift has been accompanied by a decline in nominal party members and independents and a rise in all partisan politicians, from nearly 80 percent nonmilitants under Cárdenas to fewer than half today

Power Void: Candidate Selection Changes in the Partido Revolucionario Institucional (PRI) in Mexico," paper presented to the Midwest Political Science Association, Chicago, Illinois, April, 2005, for a discussion of the post-2000 changes.

45. For valuable comparisons with other Latin American legislatures in the early 1990s, see David Close, "Introduction: Consolidating Democracy in Latin America—What Role for Legislatures?," as well as the individual case studies in his edited volume *Legislatures and the New Democracies in Latin America* (Boulder, Colo.: Lynne Rienner, 1995). For an historical analysis of Latin American legislatures, excluding Mexico, see Weston Agor, ed., *Latin American Legislatures: Their Role and Influence* (New York: Praeger, 1971).

(table 3.8). It remains to be seen whether the increased party experiences combined with increased legislative backgrounds will enhance Mexico's decision-making process and the ability of opposing parties to compromise on national legislation, or instead will increase obstacles to negotiating successful legislative outcomes.[46]

46. It is worth speculating that the recent increase in trust in political parties in Mexico, second only to Canada in the Americas, may be attributed to the increased presence of party affiliations in leadership, as well as to the role parties were perceived to have played in the democratic shift. These data are presented in the Americas Barometer polls, which suggest an average trust level of 4.2 on a 7-point scale. We don't have comparable data using a similar scale, but generally prior to 2006 only 25–30 percent of Mexicans express confidence in parties. See Margarita Corral, "(Mis)Trust in Political Parties in Latin America," *Americas Barometer Insights*, no. 2 (2008): 1–6.

# 4

# Democratic Demographics

## Does Democracy Alter Politicians' Origins?

The transition to a democratic political model produces numerous changes in the institutional careers of politicians, and Mexican politicians are no exception to this pattern. The data suggest some truly significant shifts (or lack thereof) in career backgrounds from a semi-authoritarian to a democratic political model, including active party membership, party officeholding, and elective state and local political offices. An even more basic set of characteristics are described by a candidate's origins, including the type of community an individual was raised in and the community's location, the socioeconomic setting of his or her family upbringing, ethnicity, and the consequences of such personal background variables on the credentials and institutional choices each politician must make in early adulthood. Without question, demographic variables determine many characteristics in a politician's background and critical career choices.

What has intrigued analysts most about the backgrounds of elite politicians globally is their family origins, most significantly their socioeconomic status. This interest is partly due to the importance of citizen perceptions of their leaders. For example, does the political culture emphasize positive views of elite origins, the case in Britain for much of the twentieth century, or of popular origins, the case of the United States, represented notably in the nineteenth century by Abraham Lincoln's "log cabin" origins.

In Mexico, two intertwining, important political variables drive expectations about a national leader's background. First, during the pre-democratic phase, an imposed political ideology and rhetoric helped reinforce certain personal qualities. For example, one would expect China's socialist, authoritarian regime after the communist victory in 1949 to promote a new generation of leadership from working-class backgrounds, given the regime's extensive persecution of wealthy families in the 1950s and the penalties they levied against their descendants in the 1960s and 1970s. In fact, since 1949 China largely has been led by middle-class (not working-class) elites, similar to elite leadership in most other political models and cultures.[1]

In Mexico, which also underwent a major violent revolution, the doors to the elite political class opened briefly to a larger group of individuals from modest social backgrounds. Mexico developed its own mythology about the 1910 revolution—a mythology that reinforced positive public perceptions of a leader's humble background.[2] Such views of modest origins became particularly pronounced among the postrevolutionary military leadership.[3]

The second political variable is the political model's institutional features. Mexico created a semi-authoritarian model after the revolution to sustain the victorious revolutionary leadership and that leadership's ideology. The model was semi-authoritarian, but it viewed itself as a one-party democracy, boasting such a broad ideological umbrella that it welcomed all social classes, including the children and grandchildren of the very opponents it defeated in the revolution and subsequent violent rebellions in the 1920s.

From the 1930s through the 2000s, the distribution of social backgrounds among Mexican politicians appears unremarkable. The data in table 4.1, incorporating all prominent leaders serving under each presidential administration, is notable for its gradual but generally increasing dominance of political figures from middle- and upper-class backgrounds. These social class distributions among politicians are extremely slow to change. For example, although two of every five politicians in the Cárdenas administration emerged from blue-collar backgrounds, their highest level for the past eighty years, the figures from Manuel Avila Camacho (1940–46) through Gustavo Díaz Ordaz (1964–70) largely remain unchanged, with

1. Robert North and Sola Pool, "Kuomintang and Chinese Communist Elites," in Harold D. Lasswell and Daniel Lerner, eds., *World Revolutionary Elites* (Cambridge, Mass.: MIT Press, 1966), 381.

2. Even as late as 1978, in a meeting sponsored by former president Miguel Alemán, a heated discussion arose about this issue during my presentation of a paper on postrevolutionary intellectuals. The Twentieth National Sociology Congress, Mexico City, June 1978.

3. Secretaries of national defense, as late as the 1980s, would sometimes mention their modest social origins in public presentations, even if such origins were fabricated, to reinforce the notion that the army was a popular institution stemming from the people. For example, General Félix Galván, secretary of national defense (1976–82), told journalists, "The army comes from the people. I myself am a product of campesinos. We, truthfully—this isn't a word, a phrase or posture—truthfully, we are the people of the people. The enlisted men are campesino boys who we recruit; the officers also come from the popular classes." Roderic Ai Camp, *Mexico's Military on the Democratic Stage* (Westport, Conn.: Praeger and CSIS, 2005), 66–67. A top general pointed out to me that several of the defense ministers making these claims were actually the sons of modest middle-class families, not rural peasants.

Table 4.1. Socioeconomic Origins of Mexican Political Leadership

|  | Social Origins (%) | |
| Presidential Administration | Working | Middle/Upper |
| --- | --- | --- |
| Cárdenas | 40.8 | 59.2 |
| Avila Camacho | 34.1 | 65.9 |
| Alemán | 31.3 | 68.7 |
| Ruiz Cortines | 33.3 | 66.7 |
| López Mateos | 38.6 | 61.4 |
| Díaz Ordaz | 38.5 | 61.5 |
| Echeverría | 24.1 | 75.9 |
| López Portillo | 23.2 | 76.8 |
| De la Madrid | 18.6 | 81.4 |
| Salinas | 19.3 | 80.7 |
| Zedillo | 18.3 | 81.7 |
| Fox | 15.8 | 84.2 |
| Calderón | 16.7 | 83.3 |

Source: Mexican Political Biographies Project, 2009.

approximately one-third from modest family origins and the remainder from middle- and upper-class backgrounds.[4]

The only exception to this pattern during those years occurred under Alemán, who was again well ahead of his time in terms of highlighting numerous characteristics among future Mexican politicians. Between 1935 and 1970, individuals from middle-class backgrounds reached their highest levels during his administration. These numbers decline in subsequent administrations and do not surpass the numbers of the Alemán administration until the Echeverría presidency began in 1970.[5]

The second significant revelation within these data is the sudden decrease in 1970, by nearly 40 percent, of politicians from working-class backgrounds. This dramatic change was not due to any alteration in the political model because the predemocratic transition did not begin until the 1980s. Why is 1970 a benchmark date for this social change? An

4. Only 5 percent or fewer politicians in the middle and upper social category are from wealthy families, which explains why they are not separated into two distinct groups.

5. It is worthwhile noting that most members of these generations who graduated from college view their fellow students as lower middle class, or as one member of the Alemán generation described it, "poor middle class." Few were wealthy, and few were extremely poor. The students from this latter group "went to school barefoot, with clothing made from the cheapest cloth, with the patches on their clothing occupying areas a little bit larger than those patches on the clothing of the middle class students." Personal communication from Clemente Bolio, July 18, 1974.

important generational demarcation occurred between the presidencies of Echeverría and Díaz Ordaz. Like most Mexican presidents, the largest generation represented in their administration is their own or the previous or next youngest cohorts. The most well-represented generation under Díaz Ordaz, who was born in 1911, is the 1900 group, followed by the 1910 group. In his administration, 58 percent of the politicians born in these two generations came from middle-class backgrounds. However, Echeverría, born in 1922, is most strongly represented by the 1920s and 1930s generations, 83 percent of whom were products of middle-class families, suggesting a significant generational change in the composition of Mexican politicians before and after 1970.

The third significant figure that appears in table 4.1 is that politicians from working-class origins reach their lowest point under Fox. This pattern may be associated with a change in the political model. Is democracy closing the doors to broader socioeconomic patterns in Mexican leadership? The answer to that question is yes and no. In the first place, perhaps the most important conclusion one can reach from table 4.1 is that politicians from lower socioeconomic origins always have been significantly underrepresented in the backgrounds of Mexican politicians, in both the nineteenth and the twentieth centuries.[6] This is starkly illustrated by the figures for the general population, which show that working-class Mexicans accounted for 91 percent of the population in 1895, 85 percent in 1940, 80 percent in 1950, and 75 percent in 1960. The middle class during those years ranged from 8 to 21 percent.[7]

Politicians in Mexico have never come close to representing the social origins in each of their respective generations among the general population, the vast majority of whom have been members of the working or "popular" classes. Even though the middle class has expanded as a percentage of all socioeconomic groups in Mexico, and therefore one would expect middle-class representation to also increase among political leadership, politicians' middle-class origins have increased far more rapidly than among the population generally.

The democratic era did not significantly alter socioeconomic backgrounds among Mexican political leaders generally. Definitively, it did not

---

6. Considering that working-class Mexicans accounted for an overwhelming percentage of the total population, their underrepresentation was even more exaggerated prior to 1935. From 1884 to 1935, only twice, under Díaz's brief 1910 administration and Venustiano Carranza (1914–20), did they account for a third of Mexico's leadership. See Roderic Ai Camp, *Political Recruitment across Two Centuries: Mexico, 1884–1991* (Austin: University of Texas Press, 1995), 174.

7. See Roderic Ai Camp, *Politics in Mexico: The Democratic Consolidation* (New York: Oxford University Press, 2007), 275, table 102.

Table 4.2. Socioeconomic Patterns across Generations of Mexican Politicians

| | Social Origins (%) | |
| --- | --- | --- |
| Generations | Working Class | Middle/Upper Class |
| Pre-1889–1919 | 35 | 65 |
| 1920–29 | 29 | 71 |
| 1930–59 | 16 | 84 |
| 1960+ | 8 | 92 |
| All generations | 24 | 76 |

Source: Mexican Political Biography Project, 2009.

produce an opening in socioeconomic terms by ushering in an expanded group of politicians from modest social origins. Clearly, authoritarian and nonauthoritarian political processes have not influenced these social characteristics in different directions in Mexico since the mid-1930s. Instead, having eight out of ten leaders from middle-class backgrounds has been a consistent pattern since Miguel de la Madrid.[8] The other explanation for the trend toward middle- to upper-class backgrounds among politicians under Fox, similar to the more dramatic change introduced under Echeverría, results from the introduction of a new, younger generation of politicians born after 1960, 92 percent of whom come from higher socioeconomic families (table 4.2).

Finally, if the sample of prominent national politicians is limited to only those individuals in a given administration *who reached such a level for the first time*, allowing us to examine more closely those politicians each president first promoted to the top echelon, a similar pattern is apparent in the presence of middle-class backgrounds, slightly more exaggerated in favoring middle-class politicians but with two more noteworthy distinctions. Calderón's first-time elite middle-class political appointees exceeded the percentages under Fox; more important, two decades after Cárdenas left office, Adolfo López Mateos reversed the upward middle-class trend in politicians' backgrounds, boasting the same percentage of working-class politicians in his administration (41 percent) as found thirty years earlier in Cárdenas's era.

This is an interesting finding because a controversial theory in analyzing Mexican presidencies argues that during the predemocratic era, each

8. For an early analysis of the social class backgrounds which PAN contributes to this growing pattern, see Roderic Ai Camp, "The PAN's Social Bases, Implications for Leadership," in Victoria E. Rodríguez and Peter M. Ward, eds., *Opposition Government in Mexico* (Albuquerque: University of New Mexico Press, 1995), 65–80.

presidency could be viewed as contributing to an ideological shift within the revolutionary ideological umbrella that allowed the left and right wings of the Institutional Revolutionary Party (PRI) to be represented over time. Labeled the pendulum theory, it has been shown to be inconsistent in certain measures, but each president has been thought to represent a position along that broad ideological continuum.[9] López Mateos, for example, has been classified by analysts as representing the far Left within the PRI, most closely approximating Cárdenas among those presidents from 1934 to 1970. For example, he distributed more land under the government agrarian reform program than any president since Cárdenas. It is interesting, therefore, that his choices (or those of his immediate collaborators) opened up leadership to a larger percentage of politicians from blue-collar backgrounds.

Another pattern occurs in the distribution of social backgrounds across administrations that cannot be attributed to democratic change. If the scope of the politicians surveyed is limited to only those individuals who were first-time top-level officeholders who held cabinet-level positions, a different relationship is revealed between those specific politicians and their class backgrounds. These individuals have been the most influential figures on policy making in Mexican politics, and each one was chosen personally by the president, thus representing more than any other influential position a group of decision makers that can be classified as the president's own.

These data suggest that politicians from middle-class backgrounds have dominated cabinet-level posts at a figure far higher, generally, than among all politicians because more than eight out of ten came from such families. Even more surprisingly, several early presidents chose middle-class cabinet ministers in percentages far greater than all other members of their administration, including Ruiz Cortines (90 percent); López Mateos (81 percent); Echeverría (95 percent); López Portillo, De la Madrid, Salinas, and Zedillo (89–90 percent); and Fox (96 percent). Nevertheless, it is equally interesting to note that when measured by the number of top offices each political figure achieved, those individuals who served in four or more positions were more likely to have come from modest social circumstances (one-third compared to one-fifth) than top politicians generally.

One of the explanations for the rapid rise of more complex middle-class socioeconomic backgrounds is the relationship between the level

9. The theory was originally offered by Martin C. Needler, *Politics and Society in Mexico* (Albuquerque: University of New Mexico Press, 1971). For discussion of some of the features of the theory, see Robin Grier and Kevin Grier, "Political Cycles in Non-Traditional Settings: Theory and Evidence from the Case of Mexico," *Journal of Law and Economics* 43 (April 2001): 45–64.

of political interest expressed among Mexican families and the influence such interest bears on a young person's choice to become politically active. Many of the personal anecdotes that pepper the pages of this book reinforce the importance of such an environment to deciding to pursue a career in public life at a young age. This is a link I discovered many years ago that is also found among politicians globally.[10] Such an environmental setting varies widely from community to community and region to region. For example, in the World Values Survey in 1990, Mexican respondents were asked: How often is politics discussed? There was a clear relationship between the size of the community and the response, with 45 percent of those living in villages under 2,000 responding that they never discussed politics, compared to only 11 percent in cities of 50,000 to 100,000.[11]

It is not sufficient to examine family background solely from a social perspective. Political systems and their preferred institutional processes can alter the pool of politicians in numerous ways. Family social status is also related to other contextual variables, as already suggested. One of the most important of these demographic relationships is the linkage between social status and place of birth. If we separate politicians' social backgrounds by their region of birth, we discover two significant influences (table 4.3).

Most significant, the region that has supplied the largest number of national politicians, the Federal District, has produced a disproportionate percentage of Mexico's middle-class politicians. These data add to the previous conclusion about the sudden rise of middle-class politicians in Echeverría's administration. Echeverría was the first president born in the Federal District, establishing a pattern among his successors that remained unbroken for thirty years until Vicente Fox. A 61 percent increase in top politicians born in the Federal District occurred between the presidencies of Gustavo Díaz Ordaz and Luis Echeverría. The West (Aguascalientes, Baja California del Sur, Colima, Durango, Jalisco, Nayarit, and Sinaloa), which is significantly underrepresented among middle-class politicians' backgrounds, declined by 17 percent among the backgrounds of Echeverría's collaborators. Fox and Calderón broke the pattern,

10. Roderic Ai Camp, *The Making of a Government: Political Leaders in Modern Mexico* (Tucson: University of Arizona Press, 1984), especially the chapter "Choosing a Political Career," 7–27.

11. See my detailed analysis of these and other data, which reveal that politics is discussed nearly twice as frequently in the Federal District and the North as in the South. "Province versus the Center: Democratizing Mexico's Political Culture," in Philip Kelly, ed., *Assessing Democracy in Latin America: A Tribute to Russell H. Fitzgibbon* (Boulder, Colo.: Westview Press, 1998), 76–92.

Table 4.3.  Socioeconomic Patterns among Politicians' Place of Birth

| Social Class | Region of Birth (%) | | | | | | | | |
|---|---|---|---|---|---|---|---|---|---|
| | Federal District | East Central | West | North | South | Gulf | West Central | Foreign | Totals |
| Middle/upper class | 93 | 68 | 62 | 73 | 73 | 76 | 72 | 96 | 76 |
| Working class | 7 | 32 | 38 | 27 | 27 | 24 | 28 | 4 | 24 |

*Source*: Mexican Political Biographies Project, 2009.

having been born in the provinces, specifically in two West Central states (Guanajuato and Michoacán), both National Action Party (PAN) strongholds historically. More important, however, in spite of their own place of birth being different, they did not reduce the Federal District's presence in the birthplaces of all other politicians; indeed, it reached an all-time high under Calderón.

An even broader linkage between family social origins and place of birth can be found in the size of a politician's birthplace. The earliest generations of officeholders, beginning with the Cárdenas administration, came from small rural villages and towns, communities that dominated the Mexican landscape.[12] In part, these rural origins explain the higher percentage of politicians from humble family origins. Politicians from rural communities have come in almost equal percentages from working- and middle-class families, much more in line with the actual distribution of social origins in the general population. Politicians from urban birthplaces, more than eight out of ten individuals, are overwhelmingly from middle-class families.

12.  President Cárdenas not only appointed larger numbers of public figures from rural, humble backgrounds to influential positions during his administration, he also encouraged a generation of younger individuals, born during the first decade of the twentieth century, who were children growing up during the violent years from 1910 to 1920. Pedro Daniel Martínez García, who devoted most of his life to pediatric diseases, and eventually became assistant secretary of health in 1964, came under Cárdenas's influence. Born in the small community of Purépero, Michoacán, his family suffered significantly during this period. His father had no formal education but taught himself to read and write. Martínez García graduated from the National School of Medicine in 1923 and returned to his home state when Cárdenas was governor, where he began visiting dozens of small villages to study and prevent communicable diseases, sometimes traveling with Cárdenas. From 1929 to 1936, he practiced medicine in a small clinic in Apatzingán, Michoacán. When Cárdenas became president, he appointed Martínez García as director of Coordinated Services for Health and Welfare in the state of Michoacán in 1938. Personal communication, February 1974.

## EL MAESTRO IN MEXICAN POLITICS

The perfect illustration of the intersecting relationship between a rural birthplace and family socioeconomic status is best illustrated by the number of rural schoolteachers among those who became Mexican politicians. Among the most common previous professions among politicians, that of elementary and secondary teachers ranked sixth after college-educated lawyers, economists, engineers, physicians, and accountants and business administrators. In Mexico, the "maestro" and the local parish priest are the two positions most admired by average citizens. Mexicans who achieved upward social mobility through teacher training were the civilian equivalents of those who achieved upward social mobility through the armed forces.[13]

For most of the period under examination, obtaining a teaching certificate from a normal school would be the equivalent of completing a middle school or secondary education. Because schoolteachers were not required to attend college, and because numerous normal schools were located in rural areas, individuals from modest circumstances could attend these schools while they continued other employment.[14] Four percent of all politicians in the study were elementary or secondary teachers before Mexico required a college degree in education to teach.

The linkage between rural birthplaces and parents' social status is clearly illustrated in table 4.4. In the first place, nearly a fourth of all prominent politicians come from the Federal District, which, as suggested, is nine out of ten times someone from a middle-class family. But the Federal District accounts for only 6 percent of politicians who were elementary and secondary teachers, 73 percent less than for all politicians. Furthermore, the West, which produced the largest percentage of Mexican politicians from modest social backgrounds (table 4.3), is responsible for a fourth of

---

13. For an interesting historical comparison of the role of rural teachers as development leaders and popular political figures, see John Lauglo, "Rural Primary School Teachers as Potential Community Leaders? Contrasting Historical Cases in Western Countries," *Comparative Education* 18, no. 3 (1982): 233–55.

14. Manlio Favio Tapia Camacho, a former mayor of Veracruz, state legislator, and senator, describes an interesting situation between the university and the Normal School in Jalapa from 1946 to 1950, when he attended law school at the University of Veracruz. Many times their intense athletic competition led to social clashes in a period when many students became involved in politics as a means of improving their social situation. Given the importance of networking, the Law School was in a much better position to establish mentoring relationships leading to a public career. His class consisted of twenty-three students, but enrollments in the Normal School were much larger than the Law School. Despite its small size, Tapia Camacho's professors included Angel Carvajal, governor, secretary of government under Ruiz Cortines, presidential precandidate in 1958, and supreme court justice; Mario G. Rebolledo Fernández, chief justice of the supreme court; and Fernando Román Lugo, attorney general of the Federal District under López Mateos. Personal communication, June 27, 1974.

Table 4.4. Politician Schoolteachers by Birthplace

| | Region of Birth (%) | | | | | | | | |
|---|---|---|---|---|---|---|---|---|---|
| | Federal District | East Central | West | North | South | Gulf | West Central | Foreign | Totals |
| Teachers only | 6.3 | 15.9 | 26.2 | 14.3 | 15.1 | 12.7 | 9.5 | 0 | 100.0 |
| All politicians | 23.3 | 13.2 | 15.0 | 14.9 | 8.4 | 11.9 | 12.3 | 1.1 | 100.0 |

Source: Mexican Political Biographies Project, 2009.

all teacher-politicians, 75 percent more than would be expected given the percentage of politicians who come from that region. Similarly, the South (Chiapas, Guerrero, and Oaxaca), Mexico's poorest region economically, containing three of seven states with the largest percentage of indigenous people, is responsible for an even higher proportion of teacher politicians than the West, compared to all politicians from that region.[15] Together, these two regions alone account for two out of five teacher politicians.

The disproportionate rural origins of teacher politicians enhance the likelihood that they come from modest family backgrounds. The explanation for this is that half of all prominent politicians from rural communities grew up in working-class family settings, compared to only 16 percent of politicians from urban origins. Only slightly more than a fourth of all prominent politicians came from such rural beginnings, but more than half of all teacher politicians shared such origins. Therefore, it is not surprising that basically half of all teacher politicians are from blue-collar families.

Teacher politicians in Mexico reached their peak in the 1900 and 1910 generations, accounting for more than 7 percent of all politicians in those years. These two generations alone were responsible for nearly half of all teacher politicians in the last seventy-five years. Their influence declined precipitously among the 1940s generation and was eliminated altogether among the post-1960s generations, attributable to the fact that a normal teaching certificate was no longer an adequate credential to teach.

There is no better example of a successful teacher politician from this earlier era than that of Edgar Robledo Santiago, who was raised in the small village of Motozintla, Chiapas, the son of *campesinos*. Robledo

15. In his excellent study of mid-level national bureaucrats, Miguel Centeno also found that the South produced fewer well-educated public servants. See *Democracy within Reason: Technocratic Revolution in Mexico* (University Park: Pennsylvania University Press, 1994), 118, n. 30.

Santiago, given his family circumstances, alternated between attending elementary school and working as an agricultural laborer. He completed his elementary education at the Motozintla Rural School and the Ilhúicamina Elementary School in his village, eventually finishing the sixth grade at the Cuauhtémoc School in Huixtla, Chiapas. He began teaching in 1934 in a rural elementary school; the following year he was awarded a scholarship to attend the Rural Normal School of Cerrahueco, Chiapas. After graduating, he continued teaching, eventually furthering his teaching credentials by attending and graduating from the Normal Urban School in Chiapas's capital city of Tuxtla Gutiérrez in 1949. In 1952, he became a federal inspector of rural normal schools for the Secretariat of Public Education. During those years he was active in the National Teachers Union and eventually became secretary general of the national union in 1964. After completing his union term, he served in congress, leaving that position in 1968 to become director general of the Federation of Government Employees' Unions, Mexico's largest federation of government employees.[16] He won a senate seat in 1970, but he left that post when President Echeverría appointed him director general of the cabinet-level Institute of Insurance and Social Services of Federal Workers.[17]

Although the data suggest the disappearance of the traditional rural school teacher from the top political leadership, a few individuals since the 1940s have reached influential positions, and some, such as Elba Esther Gordillo Morales, even played influential roles in the democratic transition. Gordillo, like Robledo Santiago, is a native of Chiapas, having been born in Comitán. Her father died when she was two, and her mother, who was also a teacher, was not able to support her family without her daughter's help, forcing Gordillo to begin working at the age of twelve. She left home at fourteen, finding employment in a hotel as a receptionist and waitress and then a year later as a rural elementary teacher. Gordillo obtained a teaching credential three years later, in 1963, from the Federal Teaching Institute after marrying a fellow teacher who died shortly thereafter.

Gordillo joined the National Teachers Union and the PRI during her first year of teaching. She moved to Mexico City in 1964, where she

16. *Justicia*, April 1973; *Hispano Americano*, September 2, 1975, 10; *Hispano Americano*, April 5, 1971, 14; and Mexican Political Biographies Project, 2009.

17. See www.diariodechiapas.com, May 17, 2008. Probably the most successful teacher politician from this earlier, predemocratic era was Carlos Hank González. During his career, as mentioned in a previous chapter, he held four cabinet-level posts, including head of the Federal District Department and secretary of agriculture and secretary of tourism, and was governor of México. Hank González also was among the most successful Mexican politicians in the private sector, whose family wealth was valued by *Forbes* at $1.3 billion at the time of his death in 2001. His wife, Guadalupe Rhon García, also was a teacher. www.diariodeyucatán, August 20, 2001.

taught elementary school in the fastest growing working-class community in the country, Ciudad Netzahualcóyotl. A year later, she began teaching high school history in Tlalpan, another neighborhood in the capital. After a decade of teaching, Gordillo held several positions in Local 21 of the National Teachers Union; by 1975, she was coordinating regional campaigns for the PRI presidential candidate. In 1977, she became secretary general of Local 36, covering the Valle de México region, a heavily populated and politically influential area of México, and successfully ran for congress from the Ciudad Netzahualcóyotl congressional district. In the 1980s, she became a member of the Executive Committee of the National Teachers Union, and again served in congress from 1985 to 1988, during which time she was appointed to a key party position as secretary of organization on the National Executive Committee of PRI. When her term in congress came to an end, she became secretary general of the National Teachers Union, serving two consecutive terms, from 1985 to 1995.

Her union was incorporated into the most influential umbrella organization representing middle-class groups, the National Confederation of Popular Organizations. This made her eligible to become secretary general of this organization from 1996 to 2001, while simultaneously serving as senator from her home state. A controversial union leader and politician, Gordillo became secretary general of the PRI in 2002, using her influence in an attempt to establish a working relationship between the party and the Fox administration. After winning another seat in congress for the third time in 2003, she headed the PRI delegation. Unable to convince PRI leadership under then-party president Roberto Madrazo Pintado to collaborate with Fox, she became secretary general once again of the National Teachers Union and resigned from the PRI in 2005, creating her own political organization, the New Alliance Party, which helped Calderón defeat Madrazo and the PRI in 2006.[18]

Increasing credentials for certain professions is likely to have an important impact on who can pursue public careers, civilian and military alike. For example, the Mexican army recently upgraded its educational requirements to become an officer. Previously, an applicant to the Heroic Military College, which trains nearly all future career officers, only needed a secondary education because the college provided its equivalent of a civilian preparatory education. Officers achieving general rank almost without exception completed a college degree equivalent at the

18. See www.territolibre.blogspot.com, 2008; www.expreso.com.mx, 2008; Ricardo Romero Aceves, *La mujer en la historia de México* (Mexico: Costa Amic, 1982); and Mexican Political Biographies Project, 2009.

Higher War College, and the most successful officers continued their education and obtained master's degrees in national security from the National Defense College. What is important about these changes in the armed forces is that few Mexicans from modest backgrounds ever complete a preparatory education making them eligible for this historic upwardly mobile career.

The demise of the teacher politician is analogous to this situation in the army. By increasing the educational requirements for a teaching career, fewer future politicians from modest backgrounds are likely to pursue that profession. Such increases in credentials are the product of an increasingly complex economy and economic development generally, having little to do directly with Mexico's political opening.

The decreasing presence of working-class backgrounds among prominent politicians can be tied directly to the democratic transition because socioeconomic origins vary significantly among politicians according to their party affiliations. Consequently, electoral competition and the subsequent PAN victory in 2000 naturally increased the presence of PAN and Party of the Democratic Revolution (PRD) members.

Among the 290 PAN members in this study, only 2 were teachers, and among PRD members, only 1 out of 65 was a teacher. The increased percentages of politicians from these two parties in top positions since 2000 are important because it also helps explain the continued decline in working-class backgrounds. Basically, a fourth of all PRI members are from working-class origins, compared to only a tenth of PANistas and a fifth of PRD members.[19] It is relatively easy to explain why PAN members have not been teachers. Mexican public education has long generated ideological debate, including the movement toward socialist educational principles in the late 1920s and early 1930s, which actually encouraged the party's founding in 1939.[20] For years PANistas have been critical of the public school curriculum, especially on social issues, such as sex education. Furthermore, in Mexico the federal government controlled public education until the end of the twentieth century, and most public schoolteachers were affiliated with the National Teachers Union (Sindicato Nacional de Trabajadores de la Educación). This union, like most other major Mexican unions, was affiliated with the PRI. Because the PAN viewed unions as active collaborators of the PRI and as corrupt institutions, it would be

19. This is ironic because the PRD's ideology presents itself as the representative of Mexico's downtrodden.

20. See Michael J. Ard, *An Eternal Struggle: How the National Action Party Transformed Mexican Politics* (Westport, Conn.: Praeger, 2003), 64. Manuel Gómez Morín, the central figure in founding the PAN, fought against Marxist influences as rector of the National University.

unlikely that an individual in such a profession would become a PAN member.[21]

The other group of party members other than the PRIistas, the Left, is most strongly associated with careers in teaching. Leading politicians from the small leftist parties are more than twice as likely as all their peers to be teachers. They also come from modest social backgrounds in numbers slightly higher than the average politician.

The low incidence of teachers among prominent politicians also influences career choices. Generally speaking, as a politician's educational level increases, he or she is less likely to pursue a career in congress or the state legislature. For example, although fewer than one in seven politicians served in their local state legislature, among teacher politicians, more than a fourth held this post. If we examine PRI politicians, who accounted for the majority of teachers in national politics, an extraordinary three-quarters of them became members of congress, more than any other educational category. Among leftists politicians, nine out of ten served in the national lower house.

Thus, a rural birthplace determines certain choices, and those choices in turn determine certain types of political careers. Such choices, if they are eliminated or reduced, also decrease the diversity of individuals who make up the pool of likely national political figures. The individuals most affected by the decline in rural birthplaces among politicians are Mexicans from lower socioeconomic backgrounds and the indigenous, who are ethnically and economically in the minority.

How do politicians from modest backgrounds who grow up in isolated rural communities make it to the top? Two personal histories are revealing. The first of these is the fascinating example of an indigenous female Mexican, among the most underrepresented demographic in Mexican politics based on her ethnicity, gender, economic status, and rural origins. Cirila Sánchez Mendoza was born in Santa Cruz Tepenixtlahuaca, a member of the Chatina indigenous group. To obtain an elementary education, her parents sent her at age nine to live with her grandfather in San Miguel Panixtlahuaca, four hours away on foot, where she began her primary studies. When she returned after a short stay, her parents realized they needed to send her farther away, this time to Santa Catarina Juquila, where she lived with a family and worked as a maid while attending school.

Realizing the difficulty of her situation and her anguish from being so far from her family, her parents asked her to return home, but Cirila decided

---

21. An excellent overview of the evolution of the role of the National Teachers Union can be found in Maria Lorena Cook, *Organizing Dissent: Unions, the State, and the Democratic Teachers' Movement in Mexico* (University Park: Pennsylvania State University Press, 2004).

to remain, choosing to live with a neighboring woman who owned a small bakery, where she worked selling bread and milk from 5 A.M. to 9 A.M. each day before attending school. She continued this exhausting schedule until she completed elementary school and then went to live with her aunt in the capital city, Oaxaca, where she studied secondary at the Institute for Research and Social Integration, a special school for bilingual children. She completed the equivalency of high school in bilingual culture at age eighteen and returned to her native community. Her alma mater offered her a scholarship to return and study as a technician in social promotion, and after three years of training, she returned again to her native village as an employee of the Spanish-language educational program. She became director of the Juquila Regional Indigenous Educational Division, but eventually was fired because of her repeated complaints that teachers were not fulfilling their responsibilities in her community.

She pursued other activist positions in the interest of her indigenous community, after which the local PRI asked her to run as a candidate for the state legislature in 1983. She won the seat, becoming the first female indigenous member of a Mexican state legislature. After completing her term, as was true of many former members of congress, the party nominated her as their successful candidate for the Oaxaca eighth district in 1988, the first indigenous women to hold a congressional seat. She returned to her home state, serving as the state attorney for the defense of indigenous people. In 1994, she won a senate seat, again becoming the first indigenous woman to do so, and was selected as president of the Indigenous Affairs Committee in the upper chamber. In 2000, PRI leadership appointed her as the secretary of indigenous action on the National Executive Committee.[22]

The second example of an individual from a modest, provincial background accomplishing a distinguished career in public life is that of Dr. José Enrique Villa Rivera, twice president of the National Polytechnic Institute from 2003 to 2009, one of Mexico's leading public institutions in engineering and science. Villa Rivera grew up in rural Sinaloa in the 1950s, the son of two rural schoolteachers and the grandson of a woman who founded an elementary school. He attributes his scholarly success to the academic discipline he learned from his parents, having obtained his elementary education under them, which naturally required that he be the best student. He was ultimately chosen as the outstanding student in Sinaloa in the sixth grade as part of the Knowledge Olympics contest and in 1965

22. See www.criterios.com, 2008; *Diccionario biográfico de gobierno mexicano* (Mexico, D.F.: Presidencia de la República, 1992), 832; www.indesol.gob.mx, 2008; *Quién es quién en el Congreso, 1997–2000* (Mexico: IETD, 1999), 333–334; and Mexican Political Biographies Project, 2009.

was sent to Mexico to meet Agustín Yáñez, secretary of public education, and President Díaz Ordaz. After completing his preparatory studies at the University of Sinaloa, he decided, on the advice of his father, to enroll at the National Polytechnic Institute (IPN). Along with six other friends from Sinaloa, armed with a letter of introduction from a friend's cousin, they met with the founder and former president of the IPN, Juan de Dios Bátiz, who assisted all seven in enrolling in the university. Ninety-five percent of all students who enroll in IPN are from the provinces. Villa Rivera went on to complete a master's degree and a doctorate in petroleum engineering science at the French Institute of Petroleum, after which he returned to his alma mater to teach. He later became director of graduate studies in chemical engineering and then director of science and technological research before Fox appointed him as university president.[23]

## RELIGION AND POLITICIANS' RELIGIOUS BELIEFS

Demographic variables extend well beyond ethnicity and social class as a means of measuring the diversity within the pool of Mexicans from which most top politicians are selected. Most of us tend to believe that given democracies' institutional processes, electoral competition increases the potential for greater diversity and broader inclusiveness in values, attitudes, and experiences. However, this may not be the case, depending on the composition of the existing pool of future politicians at the time when the democratic transformation begins or when it eventually achieves a fuller consolidation. Such a pattern is clearly reflected in the decline among Mexican politicians with working-class backgrounds, attributable to a higher percentage of politicians from those circumstances affiliated with the PRI, whose representation among all prominent politicians decreased significantly after 2000.

Another way to measure increased diversity introduced by a political model that increases different levels of party participation and corresponding leadership is through fundamental attributes, such as race and religion. One of the most fascinating changes Mexico's democratic opening has produced among politicians is a fresh, strong diversity in religious beliefs. Religious affiliation always has been a significant demographic variable in participatory democracies, often producing casual relationships between one's religion and one's party preferences and affiliations.

23. See www.reneavilesfabila.com.mx, 2008; www.ipn.mx, 2008; www.presidencia.gob.mx, 2008; www.jornada.unam.mx, November 9, 2006; and Mexican Political Biographies Project, 2009.

In the past, in the analysis of U.S. politics, a breakdown among Catholics, Jews, and Protestants was a significant explanatory variable in explaining voting patterns as well as leadership's social characteristics.[24] The world has witnessed the tragic tendencies of intensely held religious and ethnic divisions and their violent personal and political consequences in the past two decades.

Religious beliefs in Mexico were paramount in the country's political development in the nineteenth and twentieth centuries, producing serious political conflict and civil war in the 1850s and 1860s and reinforcing antirevolutionary sentiments in the 1910 revolution. Mexico emerged from that revolution with the 1917 constitution, a document that definitively imposed severe restrictions on religious influences in politics, and on the legitimacy of religious institutions.[25] These restrictions, including the lack of any legal status for religious institutions, sent a bold message that the postrevolutionary leadership viewed itself as anticlerical and devalued the impact of religious and spiritual beliefs on Mexican politics and behavior, and led to another religious conflict in the late 1920s, the Cristero Rebellion. Those views were ingrained in the instruction and textbooks in the federally controlled public education system and were deeply embedded in the postrevolutionary rhetoric.[26]

The democratic transition and opening, by increasing the percentage of PAN and PRD politicians among top officeholders, altered the makeup of politicians' religious beliefs, but in ways different from what is typically found in U.S. and European democracies. These broad political transformations did not significantly alter the level of religious affiliation among politicians, who remain more than 85 percent Catholic, similar to their Mexican constituencies and despite evangelical Protestant inroads in some states.

However, two religious variables other than church affiliation appear to be highly significant in recent Mexican politics: the level of active citizen involvement in religious organizations and the number of individuals who claim no religious beliefs. For example, in the 2006 Mexican presidential election, voters who maintained active membership in religious organizations were 22 percent more likely to have voted for Felipe Calderón than for Andrés Manuel López Obrador (table 4.5). Among Mexicans who had no

---

24. See the American politics classic: Angus Campbell, Philip. E. Converse, Warren E. Miller, and Donald E. Stokes, *The American Voter* (New York: Wiley, 1960), 296ff.

25. Richard Roman, "Church-State Relations and the Mexican Constitutional Congress, 1916–1917," *Journal of Church and State* 20 (Winter 1978): 79.

26. Peter Reich, "Mexico's Hidden Revolution: The Catholic Church in Politics since 1919," unpublished Ph.D. dissertation, UCLA, 1991, and Stanley E. Hilton, "The Church-State Dispute over Education in Mexico from Carranza to Cárdenas," *Americas* 21, no. 2 (October 1964): 163–83.

Table 4.5. Presidential Preferences of Mexican Voters in 2006 by Participation in Religious Activity

| | Religious Organizations (%) | |
| --- | --- | --- |
| Presidential Choice | Active Member | Not a Member |
| Calderón | 38.0 | 31.1 |
| Madrazo | 25.7 | 15.3 |
| López Obrador | 31.1 | 41.4 |

Source: 2006 Mexico Panel Survey, Second and Third Waves, April–May and July 2006, in Roderic Ai Camp, "Exercising Political Influence, Religion, Democracy, and the Mexican 2006 Presidential Race," *Journal of Church and State* (Winter 2008): 101–22.

affiliation with a religious organization, a nearly equal percentage favored López Obrador, who attracted 19 percent more voters than Calderón did from this category.[27] Thus, activity or inactivity in religious organizations may exert more importance than different religious affiliations.[28]

Differences in the religious activities of citizens, despite Mexicans' overwhelming belief in God and Catholicism, also are quite apparent among the politicians representing the three leading parties. For example, in the Chamber of Deputies more than half of PAN members reported attending church weekly compared to only one out of ten and one out of twenty deputies from PRI and PRD, respectively.[29] However, more recently, religious intensity, as measured by attendance, is not quite as exaggerated. Among congressional candidates in the 2006 elections, 50 percent of PAN versus 23 percent of PRD contestants reported weekly church attendance. Among PRD candidates, nearly 60 percent rarely or never attended church services.[30] Perhaps an even more interesting indicator of religious influence among PAN and PRD politicians is the fact that 51 percent of these

27. Roderic Ai Camp, "Exercising Political Influence, Religion, Democracy, and the Mexican 2006 Presidential Race," *Journal of Church and State* 50, no. 1 (Winter 2008): 101–22.

28. For interesting differences among American Latino Christians, see Gastón Espinosa, "Latino Clergy and Churches in Faith-Based Political and Social Action in the United States," in Gastón Espinosa, Virgilio Elizondo, and Jesse Miranda, eds., *Latin Religions and Civic Activism in the United States* (New York: Oxford University Press, 2006), 301. Espinosa concludes that "there does appear to be a correlation between religious participation and political and social action."

29. Based on interviews with members of the 1994–97 legislature. See Antonia Martínez, "Diputados, clivajes (cleavages) y polarizacíon en México," *Perfiles latinoamericanos*, 11 (December, 1997), 57.

30. Kenneth Greene and Kathleen Bruhn, "Survey of Candidates for Federal Deputy from PRD and PAN, June 6 and June 30, 2006," 2006 Mexico Panel Survey Project.

PAN candidates were members of religious organizations compared to only 20 percent of their PRD peers.[31]

The differences in religious intensity and activity found among the three parties' members of or candidates for congress, and just as likely to be found among the same party members in other branches of government, is a reflection in part of the socioeconomic distribution and place of birth of party members. Their religious values, in combination with these basic demographic variables, also affect their educational choices. For example, among working-class politicians, not surprisingly nine out of ten have attended public elementary schools. The differences in values emphasized by private and public schools in Mexico is substantial, and private schools, given the lack of scholarships, are overwhelmingly accessible to only middle- and upper-class citizens.[32] Not quite half of all middle-class politicians have attended private elementary schools compared to less than 10 percent of their working class peers.

Even sharper differences in social values are likely to be stressed in religious versus nonreligious schooling. If the academic preparatory education of Mexican politicians is examined, the data reveal that those individuals who have attended private secular or religious institutions in the Federal District, where the highest percentage of middle-class political families in Mexico reside, come from that middle class. The same pattern is true among provincial secular and religious preparatory schools, although not quite as exaggerated as the differences found in Mexico City.

The significance of religious schooling has been noted by President Vicente Fox in interviews and in his memoirs. As he suggested:

> All education is a process from the very early years of schooling. My own education was with the Jesuits in Jesuit schools and at a Jesuit university, the Ibero-American University. In that learning environment, you get something that you cannot get anywhere else and that knowledge is not just technological know-how—it is inspiration, it is leadership, it is commitment, and it is motivation. This is the philosophy of the founder of the Jesuit order, St. Ignatius of Loyola; you will only find your self-satisfaction, your self-joy, your self-accomplishment of your dreams through being for others, working for others, serving others. That became one of my key components of my thinking, which I nourished myself with all my life in school.[33]

31. Camp, "Exercising Religious Influence," 55.

32. Although he focuses on higher education, Daniel Levy discusses some of these issues in *Higher Education and the State in Latin America: Private Challenges to Public Dominance* (Chicago: University of Chicago Press, 1983), 34ff.

33. Elaine Loveland, "Mexico Rising: An Interview with Vicente Fox, Former President of Mexico," *International Educator* (May–June 2008): 31. For more details about specific professors and their impact on his co-students, see his memoir, *Revolution of Hope: The Life, Faith, and Dreams of a Mexican President* (New York: Viking, 2007), 45ff.

If we examine these same attendance figures but compare politicians from PAN and PRI, the significant differences in their educational influences becomes apparent, part of which can be attributed to the socioeconomic background differences characterizing the two groups of politicians.[34] In the first place, the most influential preparatory education in Mexican political history has been the National Preparatory School in Mexico City, responsible for the education of at least 500 of the nearly 3,000 leading politicians. Slightly more than one out of ten of those preparatory graduates were from working-class families. Among PRI politicians, however, more than half of its ranks came from such socioeconomic backgrounds. A third of PRI politicians graduated from this institution compared to only one-fifth of PAN members.

The differences between the PAN and the PRI are even sharper when we compare the percentage of politicians who were religious and private secular school graduates. More than a fifth of PAN politicians graduated from religious schools in the provinces or Mexico City and 10 percent from private secular schools. Nearly half of all PAN politicians were known to have graduated from these two types of schools at the elementary or preparatory level. In sharp contrast, only 10 percent of all PRI politicians were educated in private institutions, and only 5 percent, one-fourth as many as PANistas, attended religious schools.

These differences suggest the importance that families of future PAN and PRI politicians place on religious education and on the importance of spiritual values within their families. Whatever those values consist of, they largely have been excluded from the views of Mexican politicians before the 1990s and from the policy agenda of presidential candidates and presidents.[35]

Mexican voters, similar to U.S. voters, often identify more strongly with a presidential candidate's persona, not his political views and positions. During the 2006 presidential race, it became clear early on that voter support for candidates often contradicted their evaluations of candidate qualifications and policy positions.[36] In relation to this, it is quite possible that a

34. For the first comparative study of PAN and PRI, where some of these distinctions became apparent, see the Roderic Ai Camp and Donald Mabry, "Mexican Political Elites 1935-1973: A Comparative Study," *Americas* 31, no. 4 (April 1975): 452-69.

35. The leftist party leadership is also distinctive in two ways. A third has never completed preparatory education, but among all the parties, it boasts the highest percentage of graduates from the National Preparatory School. Contrary to what might be expected however, most of those graduates were from middle-class and not working-class families.

36. Roderic Ai Camp "Democracy Redux? Mexico's Voters and the 2006 Presidential Race," in Jorge Domínguez, Chappell Lawson, and Alejandro Moreno, eds., *Mexico's Choice: The 2006 Presidential Campaign in Comparative Perspective* (Baltimore, Md.: Johns Hopkins University Press, 2009), 29-49.

politician's profession, or even an imaginary view of his professional attri-butes, might benefit his candidacy in an electoral contest. In a poll taken in 2006, when asked to describe the three candidates as something other than a politician, in response to the question: Who would be the best [given five occupations]? López Obrador (PRD) was identified most strongly as a ship captain and teacher, Calderón (PAN) as a teacher and priest, and Madrazo (PRI) as a gambler and boxer.[37] Given the fact that teachers and priests elicit the strongest sense of trust and confidence of any occupations in Mexico, being identified with that profession would be a helpful boost to a politician's successful public career.[38]

The differences found in early educational patterns among differ-ent party members, which hearken back to place of birth and family circumstances, continues through the college years. Such differences increase the institutional diversity in the training of future politicians and definitely affect their social, economic, and political values. When the educational data among Mexican politicians are analyzed, it becomes apparent that the presence of PAN politicians has produced a significant change in the educational backgrounds and socialization of all post-democratic politicians. Of the four most important institutions attended by PAN leaders, nearly the same percentage attended the National University as the other three private institutions (two secular and one Jesuit) combined. The Left, who, similar to PRI, are most often graduates of the National University, come in equal numbers from working- and middle-class backgrounds (see table 4.6).

Socioeconomic backgrounds and their distribution among politicians according to party affiliation dramatically affect not only the location of their primary, secondary, preparatory, and college education but also politi-cians' interest in and ability to teach in preparatory schools and universities. Six out of ten politicians from middle-class backgrounds have taught at these two levels compared to only a third of their working-class peers. The decline in working-class backgrounds among politicians since the democratic open-ing, largely the result of the smaller numbers of PAN politicians coming from such socioeconomic backgrounds, is likely to increase the importance of educational contacts and influences among leading political figures.

As I have suggested elsewhere, the sources of institutional experiences' impact on two significant political relationships in Mexico: mentor–disciple relationships and the building of important political networks or cama-rillas. Among Mexico's political power elite, educational experiences as

37. Survey by *Reforma* of 1,515 voters, November 11–14, with a 2.5 percent margin of error, available at www.terra.com.mx/presidenciables, 2006.

38. For comparative data on citizen trust in various professions and institutions, see Camp, *Politics in Mexico*, 57.

Table 4.6.  Politicians' Socioeconomic Backgrounds and College Choices

| Party and Socioeconomic Origin | Significant Institutions Attended (%) | | | |
|---|---|---|---|---|
| | UNAM | ITESM | ELD | Ibero |
| PAN | | | | |
| Middle class | 27 | 8 | 10 | 8 |
| Working class | 6 | – | – | – |
| PRI | | | | |
| Middle class | 53 | 2 | 0.1 | 0.2 |
| Working class | 24 | 1 | – | – |
| Non-PRD Left | | | | |
| Middle class | 58 | – | – | – |
| Working class | 18 | – | – | – |

*Source*: Mexican Political Biography Project, 2009.

UNAM = National University of Mexico; ITESM = Monterrey Technological Institute of Higher Studies; ELD = Free Law School; Ibero = Ibero-American University.

teachers and/or students provide the source of nearly half of all mentor-disciple relationships. Among this same elite group of politicians, educational institutions account for six out of ten networking relationships with fellow politicians, twice that of institutional contacts occurring in other career positions.[39]

## CAREERS AND CLASS: THE CHOICES OF WORKING-CLASS POLITICIANS

I noted earlier the increasing importance of local officeholding for pursing national political careers. Another variable that has affected the likelihood of local officeholding in a politician's background, especially in the past, is working-class family origins. Working-class origins increased the likelihood of a national politician having been elected mayor by nearly 60 percent compared to politicians from middle-class backgrounds. Interestingly, the increased numbers among politicians from working-class backgrounds

39. See Roderic Ai Camp, *Mexico's Mandarins: Crafting a Power Elite for the Twenty-first Century* (Berkeley: University of California Press, 2002), 29, 43. The sources of mentor disciple relationships were 45 percent, 42 percent, and 13 percent for education, career and family respectively. The sources of networking among top politicians were educational institutions (61 percent), career (28 percent), family (7 percent), and social engagements and civic organizations (4 percent).

is even more pronounced among PRI politicians. Among PAN members, class background has produced few differences in mayoralty experiences.

The most commonly held local office among all leading politicians was that of state legislator. Nearly one in seven politicians was elected to the state legislature. Among politicians from working-class families, however, nearly a fourth could count state legislative experiences in their careers, almost double that of politicians who grew up in middle-class circumstances (table 4.7).

What is most fascinating about the impact of a politician's social origins on career choice is that the relationship between modest social origins and elective, local political experience increases in importance as the office becomes more influential. Again, of all the politicians in our data from modest socioeconomic backgrounds, more than a fourth became governors compared to only a sixth from middle-class origins. One could make the argument than in the absence of democratic electoral politics in the semi-authoritarian era, social class diversity, measured by a larger percentage of politicians from modest social origins, produced its own distinctive patterns. Some of these patterns, notably the emphasis on local officeholding, are now enhanced by a competitive, electoral political model instead of the class origins alone.

Of the 351 governors in our data set (a nearly complete sample of all governors since June 1935), 90 percent were PRI members. Among PRI governors, nearly two in five came from modest family circumstances. Thus, becoming a governor during the PRI's reign was a career path attainable by such politicians. By contrast, of all the PAN governors who have been elected since 1989 during the democratic transition and consolidation eras, only 13 percent came from working-class origins.

At the national level, the same distortion in socioeconomic origins continues among elective legislative offices. Those politicians who were

Table 4.7. Working-Class and Middle-Class Politicians' Elective Career Choices

| Office Held | Percentage from Socioeconomic Class Who Held Specific Posts | |
| --- | --- | --- |
| | Working Class | Middle Class |
| Mayor | 13.4 | 8.5 |
| State legislator | 22.7 | 12.7 |
| Governor | 27.7 | 16.3 |
| Deputy | 59.3 | 45.1 |
| Senator | 37.3 | 24.9 |

Source: Mexican Political Biographies Project, 2009.

members of congress and the senate were again disproportionately more likely to come from modest than from middle-class families. The differences in class origins are not as great as those that characterize state and local elective offices; nevertheless, the social bias is still significant. The impact of the three political eras on the socioeconomic backgrounds of senators, the most important national elective office other than president, is apparent, even if a decrease in the percentage of Mexicans in the working class during these time periods is taken into account (table 4.8).

Elective office is just one important route taken by Mexican politicians to achieve national office. A more common route is through state and national bureaucracies. Several positions in these institutions stand out in the backgrounds of prominent national figures. One out of ten Mexican politicians have served as a private secretary at the state level, typically to a governor, or at the federal level to a cabinet secretary. Because this position requires a high level of trust between the private secretary and his boss, it typically reflects a mentor relationship between the superior and the secretary, often leading to the secretary's successful political career. Politicians from working-class families, however, are only half as likely to have ever served in such a position as they climb the political ladder.

A less common appointed position than that of private secretary found in the backgrounds of successful national politicians is that of secretary general of government, a state position somewhat analogous to lieutenant governor. Politicians from working-class families are 30 percent more likely to have used this post as a stepping stone than their middle-class peers, the only position analyzed for which this was true.

As we continue the analysis of exclusively federal appointed posts, including three top positions, a clear pattern emerges. In each case, whether we are evaluating the position of oficial mayor, the third ranked administrative post in cabinet-level agencies, or that of assistant secretaries or cabinet secretaries, politicians with working-class origins are significantly less likely than their middle-class peers to hold these positions (see table 4.9). With the exception of being appointed as a state secretary general (lieutenant governor), politicians from working-class backgrounds have not been as

Table 4.8. Working-Class Origins of Senators across Political Periods

| Political Periods | Senators from Working-Class Origins (%) |
|---|---|
| Predemocratic era (1935–88) | 36 |
| Democratic transition (1988–2000) | 25 |
| Democratic consolidation (2000–2009) | 12 |

Source: Mexican Political Biographies Project, 2009

Table 4.9. Working-Class and Middle-Class Politicians' Appointed
Career Choices

| | Percentage from Socioeconomic Class Who Held Specific Posts | |
|---|---|---|
| Office Held | Working Class | Middle Class |
| Private secretary | 5.5 | 11.0 |
| Secretary general | 8.2 | 6.1 |
| Oficial mayor | 5.2 | 11.5 |
| Assistant secretary | 14.1 | 28.3 |
| Cabinet secretary | 12.7 | 18.1 |
| Supreme court justice | 3.6 | 6.1 |

*Source*: Mexican Political Biographies Project, 2009.

likely to count the most significant executive branch policy-making posts
in their career trajectories in Mexican politics.

One explanation for politicians who come from rural, humble family
backgrounds being less likely to achieve influential posts in the federal
bureaucracy may be linked to the way many of those successful Mexicans
are recruited to such executive branch careers: through the classroom. As
we have witnessed during various periods in Mexican political history,
especially since the Alemán administration, professors have exercised a
critical role in recruiting able students to bureaucratic careers. Therefore,
one's ability to take advantage of such mentoring relies on a student's
socialization skills. Dr. Martínez García argued that "the social interaction between students and professors of his generation were determined,
in large part, by the students' socio-economic level (those who enjoyed a
better situation formed a subgroup and they had greater interactions with
professors)."[40] This argument has not been well developed and is not the
result of social prejudice felt toward certain groups of students by the professors, but rather stems from the inability of many of the students from
such limited circumstances to easily fit into this environment.[41]

---

40. Personal communication, February 13, 1974. As Pedro Martínez García pointed out,
what influenced him most were not his professors but two years he spent in Michoacán in the
antileprosy service, during which time he examined 2,000 cases of leprosy in individual homes.

41. When I raised this issue with Daniel Cosío Villegas, one of Mexico's leading intellectuals, he was incensed with this response. Although it is true that nearly all of my respondents reported such interactions with their professors, Cosío Villegas and others perhaps
lacked sensitivity to how individuals from extremely modest families in reality reacted to
their circumstances in Mexico City. One of the few works to explore this issue of fitting in
academically, focused on minority and poor students who become educators, universally
reported sentiments analogous to Dr. Martínez García's comments. See C. L. Dews, ed.,

The peculiar corporative structure of Mexican politics traditionally provided two separate paths through which an individual with political ambitions from a humble background could achieve political success. As was the case with schoolteachers who became successful leaders in the National Teachers Union, other influential unions existed and provided career paths for politicians. One out of ten prominent politicians held major union leadership posts at the state or national level. As one might expect, individuals from working-class backgrounds were much more likely to be found in such union executive positions.

In Mexico, nearly a third of all politicians from blue-collar families held union positions and were five times more likely to do so than their middle-class peers. This is a huge difference. Union leadership no longer typically leads directly to top political offices, except among PRI nominees for elective positions. Thus, major union leaders can and do attempt to influence government policy in their own right rather than seeking positions inside the government.

Pursuit of a military career, for a tiny percentage of officers of general rank, leads to important positions in the naval and defense ministries. Given the different social origins between career military officers and Mexican politicians, in which nearly two-fifths of officer politicians were raised in working-class families, it is not surprising that twice as many career officers as politicians have come from such backgrounds. This channel, however, has been restricted for some time to a narrower group of individuals because career officers no longer compete against civilians for gubernatorial nominations, nor do they run for congressional or senate seats.[42]

One additional career experience deserves mention. The family socioeconomic origins of politicians not only affect their career choices in public life but also produce strong patterns outside of government. One of the dramatic changes introduced by a larger percentage of PAN candidates for elective office, and by successful politicians generally, is the increasing presence of public figures that founded and headed their own businesses or were top-level managers of large companies. This is true for a fourth of PAN members in national politics, but is only true of 6 percent of PRI members, suggesting that PAN is introducing another form of diversity, experience and values learned in the private sector. A huge disparity in class origins characterizes those politicians with high levels of private sector experience because only one in every forty-three politicians from

---

*This Fine Place so Far from Home: Voices of Academics from the Working Class* (Philadelphia: Temple University Press, 1995).

42. Retired officers now account for only 1 or 2 individuals out of 500 members of congress.

a working-class setting ever achieves such a business career, compared to every tenth middle-class politician.

Finally, can the presence of one of the most influential informal characteristics of Mexican politics—family kinship ties in public life—be attributed to a person's social class origin? If we think of democracy as broadening the scope of individuals who are included in the pool of potentially important politicians, what role does one's social class origins exert on this variable? Slightly more than half of middle-class politicians were known to be related to someone holding an influential state or national political post, compared to only slightly more than a fourth of politicians from modest social origins. Thus, the decline in working-class backgrounds among Mexican politicians in the postdemocratic era is also likely to increase the percentage of politicians who are related to family members in public life, further narrowing the recruitment pool of potential leaders.

## CONCLUSIONS

Demographic characteristics have shifted significantly among leading Mexican politicians over the decades. One of the most interesting of those characteristics, an individual's social class origins, has changed dramatically from the 1930s to the 2000s. However, the major shift in social origins actually took place at the apex of the predemocratic era during the Echeverría administration (1970–76), rather than as a result of Mexico's democratic transformation. As revealed in the data, middle-class politicians always have been overwhelmingly overrepresented compared to the size of the middle class in the general population. The sizable drop in politicians from working-class families in the 1970s can be traced in large part to Mexico's rapid urban growth in the 1940s and 1950s and the increasing reliance on future politicians from Mexico's most urbanized metropolis, the Federal District. Nevertheless, the democratic opening, by bringing in an increased percentage of PAN militants to top posts, explains in part why that social class reached its highest level of representation among any political leadership group under Vicente Fox.

Another broad conclusion about demographic variables is that one's social origins exercise a tremendous impact on the type of political career a politician may pursue. For example, I discovered that prominent public figures from humble origins are much more likely to find success in elective office, including as members of congress or the senate. On the other hand, politicians who are products of middle-class families are much more dominant in the executive branch at the highest levels as cabinet secretaries and assistant secretaries. Thus, despite an ambitious individual's abilities and skills, a person's social origins in Mexico, over which they have no control, impacts significantly the degree to which certain career channels are more or less open. Complementary to politicians' social origins is their place of birth, specifically if they are products of small villages and communities or larger urban centers. A strong relationship exists between rural origins and modest social circumstances.[43] Despite the fact that Mexico has increased its level of urbanization, successful politicians from such origins have far exceeded the distribution of ordinary Mexicans from larger communities. I have used the important rural school teacher's role in political leadership as an example of the influence of combined rural birthplaces with modest social origins. The PRI encouraged this type of individual in its ranks, a career channel that has essentially disappeared in recent years. PAN's victory, and its presence in the executive branch since 2000, has contributed to the accelerated decline in Mexico's rural poor achieving national political prominence. In short, democracy has increased social and geographic homogeneity, specifically middle-class and urban origins, among many types of politicians.

Mexico's democratic transformation has not led solely to increased homogeneity in the past decade or so. A democratic opening, as Mexico clearly illustrates, can also simultaneously enhance differences among public figures. In opening up the political system to representatives from the PAN and the PRD, electoral democracy has contributed to an increasing diversity in religious and social values. These differences, as we learned from the analysis, are related to the intensity of politicians' religious activities to the extent they are personally involved in religious organizations. Their values also are differentiated by their educational experiences.

PAN middle-class politicians in many cases have been educated in environments different from PRI and PRD politicians. These differing environments are the results of diverse types of schooling, including private secular, private religious, and public institutions at all levels of education. Middle-class politicians from all three parties often have experienced socializing educational experiences in different geographic locations and similarly often are the products of different disciplinary training. The diversity of political party representation among prominent politicians introduced by the democratic transformation has generated diversity among leaders in belief systems and personal experiences.

43. One of the most revealing accounts of the transformation of a single rural community during the critical years covered by our study is Luis González's wonderful *San José de Gracias: Mexican Village in Transition* (Austin: University of Texas Press, 1991), which details the changes occurring in this municipality in Michoacán.

Finally, it can be concluded that all leading politicians are not created equal. Given their particular family origins and place of birth, which affect their location and level of educational achievement, politicians are recruited differently, come in contact with different groups of citizens, and follow different career tracks more easily than others. Democratic transformation has played a role in the distribution of basic demographic characteristics that enhance or detract from such choices, while simultaneously altering as well as reinforcing the existing composition of leading politicians.

# 5

# Has Democracy Favored Women Politicians?

The introduction of a democratic model provides numerous vehicles through which one can observe an altered political leadership. I argued in 1998 that during the transition period, women were likely to benefit from an electoral opening because female national politicians typically and in greater numbers than men have early political experiences as party leaders and as activists in nongovernmental organizations (NGOs) and unions at the local level. Democratic electoral competition, I suggested, would enhance such credentials.[1] A recent comparative study demonstrates that women who were party loyalists and strongly involved in parties were more likely to be elected to national legislative office.[2] An opposing viewpoint, focused only on civic organizations, has been offered by María Luisa Tarrés, who suggests that if democracy became firmly entrenched in Mexico, the prestige of NGOs and their political importance would likely decline. Basically, she believes this because these organizations developed as alternative channels for expressing demands outside institutions provided by the predemocratic model. Once democracy was achieved, functions previously performed by civic organizations would be replaced by traditional institutional channels incorporated within the democratic model.[3]

1. Roderic Ai Camp, "Women and Men, Men and Women: Gender Patterns in Mexican Politics," in Victoria Rodríguez, ed., *Women's Participation in Mexican Political Life* (Boulder, Colo.: Westview Press, 1998), 167–78.
2. See María Escobar-Lemmon and Michelle M. Taylor-Robinson, "How Do Candidate Recruitment and Selection Processes Affect the Representation of Women?," in Peter M. Siavelis and Scott Morgenstern, eds., *Pathways to Power: Political Recruitment and Candidate Selection in Latin America* (University Park: Pennsylvania State University Press, 2008), 347, 367.
3. María Luisa Tarrés, "The Role of Women's Nongovernmental Organizations in Mexican Public Life," in Victoria Rodríguez, ed., *Women Participation in Mexican Political Life* (Boulder, Colo.: Westview Press, 1998), 193–203.

In the predemocratic period, the role of women in national politics was slow to emerge.[4] It should be remembered that women were not allowed to vote in national elections until the presidential administration of Adolfo Ruiz Cortines (1952–58).[5] Top Institutional Revolutionary Party (PRI) officials from that era have explained to me in interviews that effective female suffrage was purposefully delayed because of their belief that women were politically less sophisticated than men, were sympathetic to Catholic teachings, and would be likely to support the National Action Party (PAN) given its important Catholic roots.[6]

Social values regarding gender roles also have undoubtedly contributed heavily to the likelihood that women would pursue political careers. In one of the earliest studies cited by Rogelio Díaz Guerrero in his classic work on Mexican psychology, 91 percent of men residing in Mexico City in 1952 gave a definitive positive response to the question: Do you believe that a woman's place is in the home? Only 1 percent fewer women responded with the same answer.[7] When given their first opportunity to vote in a presidential election in 1958, only 48 percent of women (compared to 82 percent of men) indicated they had done so.[8] It is important to keep these beliefs in mind when exploring explanations for the chronological expansion of women politicians.

The data presented in table 5.1 suggest several insightful trends about Mexican female politicians. In the first place, they did not really achieve a presence in political life until the 1920s generation, well represented for the first time in the Echeverría presidency (1970–76). The upsurge of

---

4. For these early developments, see Carmen Ramos Escandón, "Women and Power in Mexico: The Forgotten Heritage, 1880–1954," in Victoria Rodríguez, ed., *Women's Participation in Mexican Political Life* (Boulder, Colo.: Westview Press, 1998), 87–102, and Jocelyn Olcott, *Revolutionary Women in Postrevolutionary Mexico* (Durham, N.C.: Duke University Press, 2005).

5. María Emilia Farías, "La participación de la mujer en la política," *México 75 años de revolución, Desarrollo social* (Mexico: Fondo de Cultura Económica, 1960), 693–816, and Ward Morton, *Women Suffrage in Mexico* (Gainesville: University of Florida Press, 1962). Under Miguel Alemán, legislation was passed that allowed women to vote and participate fully as candidates in municipal elections.

6. Personal interview with Agustín Salvat Rodríguez, June 23, 1975. Salvat Rodríguez organized youth groups in Manuel Avila Camacho's presidential campaign (1940), was the personal representative of Adolfo Ruiz Cortines to the Federal District during his presidential race, 1952, and served as treasurer on the National Executive Committee of the PRI from 1952 to 1964.

7. Rogelio Díaz Guerrero, *Psychology of the Mexican* (Austin: University of Texas Press, 1975), 67. In 1965, also in Mexico City, he conducted a survey in three high schools, all male, coed, and all female. Eighty-four percent responded similarly in the all-male school, 87 and 90 percent of males and females responded positively in the coed high school, and 74 percent agreed with that statement in the all-female school (163).

8. William J. Blough, "Political Attitudes of Mexican Women," *Latin American Society and Politics* 14, no. 2 (May 1972): 206.

Table 5.1. The Rise of Women Politicians across Generations

| Generation | Politicians Who Were Women (%) | Generational Source of All Female Politicians (%) |
|---|---|---|
| Pre-1889 | 0 | 0 |
| 1890–99 | 0 | 0 |
| 1900–1909 | 1.9 | 3.5 |
| 1910–19 | 3.0 | 5.5 |
| 1920–29 | 8.3 | 13.4 |
| 1930–39 | 10.5 | 20.4 |
| 1940–49 | 10.2 | 24.4 |
| 1950–59 | 12.8 | 26.4 |

*Source*: Mexican Political Biographies Project, 2009.

I have left out the figures for the 1960s generation because its members still have not fulfilled their probable share of prominent national posts, which will not occur until 2024.

female politicians in this generation may also be explained in part by the changes in suffrage instituted by Presidents Alemán and Ruiz Cortines, which occurred when these women reached their twenties and thirties. Second, beginning with the 1930s generation, women achieved a firm plateau in which one out of every ten leading political figures was female. This level of representation was maintained for twenty years among women born between 1930 and 1949.

The 1950s generation, which dominated politics in the Calderón administration, achieves the highest level of female representation ever, but it remains to be seen whether the youngest generation, born after 1960, will be as well represented as its predecessor. Finally, perhaps the most notable figure emerging from the data reported in table 5.1 is that over 70 percent of prominent female leaders came from three successive generations: the 1930s, 1940s, and 1950s.

Presidents can exercise a large impact on female representation in top posts because many of these positions are appointed. Prior to 1994, to some extent even legislative and judicial posts among PRI members were strongly influenced by presidential preferences. No women served in important national political offices until Miguel Alemán reached office in 1946. Two women served in his administration. The tiny numbers of women who reached top posts remained under 3 percent during the Alemán, Ruiz Cortines, and López Mateos administrations. Beginning with Díaz Ordaz's presidency, women accounted for 5 percent of all leading officeholders.

As suggested previously, a major breakthrough for women occurred under Echeverría's presidency. The total percentage of women serving during his administration does not significantly increase over that of his predecessor, Díaz Ordaz, but the percentage of first-time female office-holders expands notably to 10 percent. The level of female officeholders reached 12 percent under López Portillo, the highest percentage ever achieved until Calderón was inaugurated, when women established a new plateau of 15 percent. Viewed differently, of the 206 women who form part of this elite group of politicians, 17 percent of first-time female officehold-ers served during the López Portillo administration.

Guillermina Sánchez Meza de Solís, a member of the 1930s genera-tion, is representative of the influx of female politicians who first achieved prominent political posts in the López Portillo administration. Born in the Federal District, she attended the public Benito Juárez elementary school and Secondary School No. 11, the same institutions as the presi-dent. She continued her education at the National Preparatory School and the National University, becoming one of the first future women pol-iticians to graduate in economics. In addition to her economics degree, she obtained a second degree in consular law and diplomacy from the Women's University of Mexico, where she also taught. She joined the PRI in 1949, shortly after graduating. She held a number of posts in the pri-vate sector and the federal bureaucracy and became active in an impor-tant PRI-affiliated corporatist interest group, the League of Revolutionary Economists, eventually achieving the presidency of this organization. In 1970, she was elected a member of congress from the twenty-second dis-trict in the Federal District as a representative of the PRI umbrella organi-zation the National Federation of Popular Organizations (CNOP). In 1976, she became oficial mayor of foreign relations, one of the first women to achieve that administrative level in a cabinet-level agency, and in 1978, she was appointed assistant secretary of that agency. At the beginning of Miguel de la Madrid's presidency, she became oficial mayor of the National Executive Committee of the PRI, the first woman in Mexico to achieve this post.[9] Sánchez Meza de Solís's highly successful career in the 1970s and 1980s helps set the stage for the next generation during the democratic transition after 2000.

Does the democratic opening actually enhance women's opportunities in these recent administrations? The percentage of women in the three periods did undergo a significant change from one period to the next (table 5.2). But these figures hide a more significant pattern, administra-tion by administration. A careful breakdown within those periods suggest

　　9. *Excélsior*, June 22, 1979, 19; Rosalia d'Chumacero, *Perfil y pensamiento de la mujer mexicana* (Mexico: Editores Mexicanos Unidos, 1974), 303–5; *Directorio general de presun-tos Diputados al xlvii Congreso de la Unión* (unpublished), 1971, 184–85; Mexican Political Biographies Project, 2009.

Table 5.2.  Democratic Transformation and the Presence of Female Politicians by Era

|  | Predemocratic 1935–88 | Democratic Transition 1988–2000 | Postdemocratic 2000– |
|---|---|---|---|
| Women politicians (%) | 5.2 | 8.6 | 12.5 |

Source: Mexican Political Biographies Project, 2009.

that a major transformation in the percentage of women politicians already was occurring under José López Portillo (1976–82) and Miguel de la Madrid (1982–88), and that instead of women increasing their presence during the transition period from 1988 to 2000, their numbers declined slightly under Salinas and significantly under Zedillo. During the democratic era, the presence of women recovers slightly under Fox but does not achieve the same level as under Salinas. Only under Calderón do we witness the significant increase identified.

These increases under López Portillo and de la Madrid are attributable to both their personal attitudes toward women in public office and to the importance of the 1920s and 1930s generations to their presidencies. Nevertheless, they are also attributable to electoral reforms, which increase the presence of opposition party representation in the legislative branch, therefore opening the door to more prominent women politicians who are much more likely than men to have held congressional seats. In 1979, in the mid-term congressional elections, the number of seats overall increases from 238 to 400, and the seats obtained by the opposition increases from 41 to 104, a pattern that continued under de la Madrid.[10]

Thus, a structural decision, as part of an earlier attempt by the PRI to legitimate itself by allowing for greater opposition representation in the legislative branch, unintentionally enhanced leadership diversity on the basis of gender, given the fact that already women were better represented in the legislative branch than in the executive branch. This is an important finding because although the increased electoral competition was pronounced in the 1988 elections, with the PRI barely winning half the vote in a fraudulent contest, it had little impact on increasing the presence of women among the political leadership. Instead, presidentially mandated changes in the electoral laws automatically increased opposition representation in the lower chamber, thereby simultaneously increasing opportunities for ambitious female politicians prior to 1988.

10. Roderic Ai Camp, *Politics in Mexico: The Democratic Consolidation* (New York: Oxford University Press, 2007), 206, table 8-1.

The increased representation of women is also linked to the increased presence of PAN members in presidential administrations. The first female member of PAN to reach a top position occurred in López Portillo's presidency, and she is the only female from PAN to do so. No new women from PAN achieved this stature under De la Madrid, and only one more new female PAN member was added under Salinas. The upsurge in representation of PAN women among first-time officeholders produced even larger numbers under Zedillo, doubled under Fox, and increased nearly 40 percent again under Calderón.

Expressed differently, 13, 26, and 36 percent of all female PAN political leaders can be found in the Zedillo, Fox, and Calderón presidencies, respectively. Zedillo provides this boost because nearly a fourth of all members of congress in the 1994–97 session were PAN members.[11] The same pattern develops under Calderón, where two-fifths of all members of congress are from PAN and more than a fourth from the Party of the Democratic Revolution (PRD). PAN alone provided 45 percent of the 116 female members of congress serving in the sixtieth legislative session (2006–9).[12]

Mexico's democratic transition, by increasing the presence of opposition parties in the legislative branch and therefore the percentage of women who achieved top political posts, altered the career experiences of all politicians given the fact that women's career experiences often differ from those of men. Indeed—and this is a fundamental point—democratic opening produces the most explosive consequences by altering the composition of political leadership in the legislative branch of government. By comparison, the composition of political leadership changes more slowly within the executive and judicial branches. Significant differences in the pace of altering leadership from one branch to another suggests that democratic electoral-produced changes in leadership composition in the legislative branch are far more responsive to new individuals than the other branches of government, whose leadership is indirectly the product of other politicians elected to higher office.

There exist four major potential explanations for these differences. First, male and female politicians, regardless of party affiliation, have pursued different careers. Thus, an increase in female politicians increases or alters the distribution of those career experiences. Second, differing levels of female and male politicians characterize each party. Therefore, any change in the distribution of leadership from one party to another alters the composition of politicians, including gender balance. Third, women

11. Camp, *Politics in Mexico*, 206, table 8–1.
12. See www.sitl.diputados.gob.mx, March 15, 2007. Twenty-three percent of all deputies were women. The Ecologist Green Party of Mexico, with seventeen members, had the highest percentage of females (41).

(compared with men) are more inclined and prepared to compete for posts in the electoral arena, especially stressing careers in the legislative branch. Fourth and finally, beginning with the democratic transition period, the PRD in 1990 established a fixed quota for women congressional candidates, and the PRI followed suit in 1996. Shortly after the democratic consolidation began, the Mexican Congress passed legislation imposing a 70 percent limit on one gender being nominated for congressional candidates from all parties, which also applied to the senate.[13] This latter legislation, which went into effect in 2003, contributed to the significant increase in women leaders under Calderón.

In the chapter on the importance of holding local offices, I found that in recent years obtaining a seat in the state legislature has been an important stepping stone to national political office, especially in the legislative branch, even for members of the PRI.[14] Prior to the democratic transition, about 15 percent of leading politicians, mostly men, served in the state legislature. In recent administrations, a fourth of all politicians could claim this experience. However, female politicians were much more likely to have served in state legislative posts then their male counterparts.[15]

Women politicians in Mexico at the national level have been most successful in the legislative branch since more than three-quarters of them have served in the lower chamber, continuing the trend women already share with their state-level legislative experiences. No other position in the national political careers of successful men or women has been held as frequently as being a member of congress.

A dramatic shift in career experiences between women and men is revealed when we examine elective executive offices. We see a reverse pattern, but a pattern that is even more extreme at the state compared to the local level (table 5.3). Women are much less likely than men to have been

13. The PRD began with a 20 percent quota and changed it to 30 percent a year later (imposing the same distribution on its National Executive Committee). The PRI accepted this same limit in 1996, to take effect in the 1997–2000 session. In 2001, the PRI increased those figures to 40 percent. The law passed by congress went into effect for the 2003–6 session, and the percentage of women members rose from 16 to 23 percent. Some state legislatures have imposed similar quotas. It is important to remember, however, that candidates are not automatically translated into seats obtained by women. For the best discussions of this system and its impact, see Lisa Baldez, "Elected Bodies: The Gender Quota Law for Legislative Candidates in Mexico," *Legislative Studies Quarterly* 29, no. 2 (May 2004): 251, and Kathleen Bruhn, "Whores and Lesbians: Political Activism, Party Strategies, and Gender Quotas in Mexico," *Electoral Studies* 22, no. 1 (March 2003): 101–19.

14. A fourth of all leading members of congress were state legislators.

15. For valuable comparisons and insights, see Susan Thomas, "Women in State Legislatures: One Step at a Time," in Elizabeth Ardell Cook, Susan Thomas, and Clyde Wilcox, eds., *The Year of the Woman: Myths and Realities* (Boulder, Colo.: Westview Press, 1994), 141–60.

Table 5.3.  Elective Careers of Female Politicians

| Positions | Women (%) | % Difference | Men (%) |
|---|---|---|---|
| *Legislative* | | | |
| State legislature | 21.4 | +42.6 | 15.0 |
| Congress | 77.7 | +62.5 | 47.8 |
| *Executive* | | | |
| Mayor | 6.3 | –40.0 | 10.5 |
| Governor | 2.4 | –87.4 | 19.1 |

*Source*: Mexican Political Biographies Project, 2009.

elected mayor, indeed, equal to the same percentages of men who were less likely to share experiences in the state legislature. The most notable comparison, however, is as governors of their home states.

A fifth of all prominent politicians have been governor, but of the 529 governors in our study (more than 90 percent of all governors), only 5 (fewer than 3 percent of leading female politicians) held this post. This is a crucial figure in light of the importance of governors as future candidates for the most important elective executive position in Mexico, the president. As suggested earlier, five of the six candidates for president from the three leading parties in 2000 and 2006 were governors. If that career experience continues to be essential in presidential races, and it is definitely likely to be the case among the opposition parties, the PRI and the PRD, in 2012, then women are at a distinct disadvantage because they are eight times less likely than men to have held this office.

When women politicians' appointive careers are carefully examined, a completely different picture from that of men emerges. Women are woefully underrepresented in all appointed executive positions regardless of the level of government (table 5.4). The most influential appointed executive position at the state level is that of secretary general. Of the more than 200 women who are in our study, only 1 ever served in this capacity. This is the central administrative post in state government, combining the functions of lieutenant governor, chief administrator, and the political portfolio in a state cabinet rolled into one. Given the secretary general's role, an accomplished and ambitious politician can use it as a significant vehicle for achieving his or her party's nomination as a gubernatorial candidate.[16]

---

16. Roderic Ai Camp, "Losers in Mexican Politics: A Comparative Study of Official Party Precandidates for Gubernatorial Elections, 1970–75," in James W. Wilkie and Kenneth R. Ruddle, eds., *Quantitative Latin American Studies: Methods and Findings*, Statistical Abstract of Latin America Supplement Series, vol. 6 (Los Angeles: UCLA Latin American Center, 1977), 23–33.

Table 5.4. Appointed Executive Branch Careers of Politicians
by Gender

| Positions | Women (%) | % Difference | Men (%) |
|---|---|---|---|
| *State* | | | |
| Secretary general | 0.5 | -93.3 | 7.5 |
| *State and federal* | | | |
| Private secretary | 2.4 | -73.9 | 9.2 |
| *Federal* | | | |
| Oficial mayor | 5.3 | -50.5 | 10.7 |
| Assistant secretary | 14.1 | -40.5 | 23.7 |
| Secretary | 7.8 | -49.0 | 15.3 |

*Source*: Mexican Political Biographies Project, 2009.

Data from our study confirm the strategic importance of this career experience in reaching a governorship. Three times as many governors in Mexico compared to all other prominent politicians—15 percent—were secretary generals.

Another influential administrative position, chief of staff (private secretary) at both the state level (to the governor) and the federal level (typically to cabinet secretaries and assistant secretaries) is also strongly underrepresented in female politicians' backgrounds. This individual, whether at the state or national level, is the gatekeeper for his or her boss, interacting on a firsthand basis with other influential politicians who seek access to and appointments with his or her superior. Because the position of private secretary requires one's superior to have complete confidence in that individual, it is a position that always places a public servant in the center of a boss's political group. Again, few women are given an opportunity to use this position to their advantage in seeking higher political office.

Figures for these state offices raise a significant question about certain career positions. Why should women be so deeply underrepresented in these posts, even when they compare favorably in influential national positions that qualify a person for inclusion among Mexico's most prominent leaders? One potential answer is that state and local constituencies and their leaders are more socially conservative than national leadership and therefore were slower to open the doors to women. Second, women who were appointed to national political offices in the federal bureaucracy more often than not earned their spurs by making contacts with fellow politicians at institutions of higher education. These political contacts themselves rose to positions that allowed them to make those appointments.

The earliest example of a woman using such educational contacts is that of María Emilia Téllez Benoit, who first achieved the position of oficial mayor in the federal bureaucracy. Téllez Benoit was the daughter of Manuel C. Téllez, a public figure who held multiple influential cabinet-level positions from 1925 to 1932 as ambassador to the United States, secretary of government, and secretary of foreign relations. Téllez Benoit had the good fortune of graduating with her fellow student, Luis Echeverría Alvarez, in the 1944 law school class at the National University. She joined the Foreign Service as a vice consul in 1946 and rose up the ranks of Mexico's Foreign Relations ministry, having served as a department head in multiple regions and as a director general of international organizations from 1964 to 1970, when President Echeverría appointed her as oficial mayor of foreign relations.[17]

Six years later, President López Portillo chose her as assistant secretary of foreign relations. Her friendship with López Portillo also went back to her school years. The president preceded her in law school by one year and, more important, joined her in a student protest march against the American embassy in Mexico City, during which López Portillo was struck in the head with a brick and Téllez Benoit came to his rescue. She jokingly remarked in an interview that when she was oficial mayor and he was secretary of the treasury, she would remind him of holding his head in her lap when she needed assistance from his agency.[18]

The national position most frequently held by women is that of assistant secretary. Of all the top positions in government it is the least likely to be achieved by party militants. Only a fourth of assistant secretaries were linked strongly to political parties compared to nearly half of all other influential officeholders. Thus, a higher percentage of appointees are likely to be appointed for meritorious reasons focusing on their expertise and experience than for their partisan, ideological credentials. Success in reaching this office suggests that as merit becomes more influential in determining an appointment, gender becomes less important.

In addition to appointed posts in local, state, and national bureaucracies, many politicians have pursued careers in the smallest of the three branches of government, the judiciary. The judiciary is an especially important institution for women in Latin America with political ambitions because it has often provided more opportunities for them than the other government branches. Even as early as the 1950s, women were having an impact on the Mexican judiciary.[19] Elsewhere, Elsa Chaney found that women made up a large percentage of judges in the Chilean judiciary, attributing their

17. *Hispano Americano,* December 14, 1970, 20; personal communication to the author; Mexican Political Biographies Project, 2009.
18. Personal interview, July 28, 1974.
19. *Time Magazine,* October 12, 1959, reported that twelve of sixty government prosecutors and thirteen federal judges were women.

Table 5.5. Judicial Careers of Politicians by Gender

| Positions | Women (%) | % Difference | Men (%) |
|---|---|---|---|
| *Local* | | | |
| Local judges | 2.4 | –52.0 | 5.0 |
| *State* | | | |
| State superior judge | 1.5 | –57.1 | 3.5 |
| Federal district judge | 2.4 | | 2.4 |
| *National* | | | |
| Supreme court justice | 4.4 | –15.3 | 5.2 |

*Source*: Mexican Political Biographies Project, 2009.

presence in that branch to it being financially less attractive to men than a career in a private law firm.[20] She argued that women also were better represented in this branch in Mexico; she suggested that the reason was not financial but that women sought these posts because they were less competitive and required fewer political skills.

I offer a different potential explanation. Women initially often made headway in the judicial and legislative branches because male politicians, who controlled access to these positions, were aware that prior to the 1990s neither branch exercised much influence on politics or policy making. This alternative argument has been confirmed in a broader examination of female political ambition.[21]

The judicial experiences of the most successful female politicians in Mexico reveals the same distinctive patterns found among women's elective and appointed executive experiences (table 5.5). The most striking finding in these data is that once again women are seriously underrepresented at the local level and only half as likely as men to have served as local and state superior court (supreme court) judges. These data reinforce the seemingly strong differences in perceptions of women's abilities at the state and local compared to the national level, where they are strongly underrepresented as mayors, secretaries generals, and governors. The exception to

20. Elsa Chaney, "Women in Latin American Politics: The Case of Peru and Chile," in *Female and Male in Latin America* (Pittsburgh: University of Pittsburgh Press, 1973), 119, and *Supermadre: Women in Politics in Latin America* (Austin: University of Texas Press, 1979). In an interesting reappraisal of her book, Chaney provides many examples of women in Peru and Chile who clearly had little or no political ambition and did not wish to continue a political career. See her brief comments in "*Supermadre* Revisited," in Victoria Rodríguez, ed., *Women's Participation in Mexican Political Life* (Boulder, Color.: Westview Press, 1998), 78–83.

21. Susan J. Carroll, "Political Elites and Sex Differences in Political Ambition: A Reconsideration," *Journal of Politics* 47, no. 4 (1985): 1241.

this local versus national bias is their success in state legislative and federal congressional seats and of course in party offices.

Other than differences in gender biases between national and local/state officials, one peculiar explanation would apply to all judicial offices, not just state and local positions. Women, especially from the older generations, as will be demonstrated, have been much less likely (18 percent) to have graduated from college, automatically eliminating them from consideration for any judicial position. Perhaps even more significant, among those men and women who graduated from college, 44 percent of men compared to only 29 percent of women obtained law degrees, further reducing the number of women eligible to become judges. To a much smaller degree, social class may play a role because law school graduates predominantly come from middle-class family circumstances, and women politicians from such backgrounds are slightly underrepresented compared to men.[22]

What is interesting about these career data is that women and men who have achieved national political prominence have equally been appointed to the Federal District superior court, which, because of its location in Mexico City, was viewed as the most prestigious judicial position after that of a supreme court justice. In some respects the position could have been considered a national appointment until the Federal District elected its own governor and legislature in the 1990s. Prominent women politicians proportionate to their overall numbers have been well represented on the supreme court (9 out of 156), and because our data at this level provide a nearly complete sample of all justices serving since 1935, these patterns are conclusive. Although the presence of local judgeships in the backgrounds of women politicians generally are much lower compared to men, among only supreme court justices a third of men and women have served in that capacity, and little difference exists on the basis of gender.

What distinguishes women from men who reach the supreme court, however, is that a fifth of all male justices served as judges in the highest court at the state level, either in their home state or elsewhere. Women justices, on the other hand, never held this judicial office. Instead, most female justices have held federal judgeships selected by a federal judicial council under the auspices of the supreme court. In fact, many women and men have spent most of their careers as federal circuit court judges assigned to different judicial districts. Those justices, having served long years in this capacity, rightly can be viewed as having pursued judicial nonpolitical careers.

22. Interestingly, the case of Mexican female politicians is different from the findings of U.S. politicians. See Edmond Costantini and Kenneth Craik, "Women as Politicians: The Social Background, Personality, and Political Careers of Female Party Leaders," *Journal of Social Issues* 28 (1972): 217–38.

This career difference between women and men suggests that state superior court experiences are on the decline and that women, who were denied this career opportunity by state governors in earlier decades, are reinforcing a new selection pattern following a more professionalized federal judicial career.

In my initial exploration of women politicians' careers, I discovered that a greater percentage of women in the predemocratic era boasted experience in women's organizations or unions, many of which were affiliated with the PRI.[23] This finding was reinforced in the careful field research of David Schers, a doctoral student who interviewed many rank-and-file PRIistas in the 1970s.[24] It is striking that in the two organizational positions I examined—head of a state or national union and secretary general of the state CNOP, the middle-class professional sector of the PRI—prominent women were as well or better represented in these posts than were men (see table 5.6).[25] Their activism in feminine organizations proved to be a useful channel through which to obtain party positions.[26] It also proved to be a significant channel for women to gain their party's nomination for congress.[27]

Women's active involvement in their parties plays an important role in determining their career paths while at the same time increasing partisanship. Broadly speaking, women are better represented by substantial

23. "Women and Political Leadership in Mexico: A Comparative Study of Female and Male Political Elites," *Journal of Politics* 41 (May 1979): 417–41.

24. See his "The Popular Sector of the Mexican *PRI*," unpublished Ph.D. dissertation, University of New Mexico, August 1972, 184–85.

25. For a discussion of how women have fared generally as union leaders, see Regina Cortina, "Gender and Power in the Teacher's Union of Mexico," *Mexican Studies/Estudios Mexicanos* 6 (Summer 1990): 241–68.

26. For an outstanding analysis of a classic case of a local female boss who used the union structure, see María Teresa Fernández Aceves, "Exgendering *Cacquismo*: Guadalupe Martínez, Heliodoro Hernández Loza and the Politics of Organized Labour in Jalisco," in Alan Knight and Wil Pansters, eds., *Caciquismo in Twentieth-Century Mexico* (London: Institute for the Study of the Americas, 2005), 201–24.

27. For example, of the sixteen women who were members of congress in the 1973–76 session, thirteen were from the PRI. Of those, five were from CNOP and two were from the National Peasant Federation (CNC), the largest umbrella organization representing the party's agrarian sector. Alejandra Massolo also has concluded that "A significant change that is occurring in Mexico, particularly since the dramatic presidential election of 1988...is the transfer of women activists in urban popular movements and community organizations to the electoral arena, especially for *regidor* [city council] positions in local government." See her excellent evaluation of these early trends in "Women in the Local Arena and Municipal Power," in Victoria Rodríguez, ed., *Women's Participation in Mexican Political Life* (Boulder, Colo.: Westview Press, 1998), 202. Paul Haber, in his revealing *Power from Experience: Urban Popular Movements in Late Twentieth-Century Mexico* (University Park: Pennsylvania State University, 2007), 143ff., also confirms Massolo's views of the significance of these experiences for women.

**Table 5.6.** Organizational Positions of Politicians by Gender

| Positions | Women (%) | Men (%) |
|---|---|---|
| Secretary general CNOP | 2.9 | 1.8 |
| Union leader | 10.7 | 11.0 |

*Source*: Mexican Political Biographies Project, 2009.

**Table 5.7.** Party Militancy of Politicians by Gender

| Parties | Women (%) | Men (%) |
|---|---|---|
| PAN and PDM | 12.1 | 8.3 |
| PRD, PRT, PSUM, PST, PCM, PRD | 6.8 | 5.4 |
| PRI | 39.3 | 26.8 |

*Source*: Mexican Political Biographies Project, 2009.

margins in the PAN and PRD than in the PRI. Interestingly, this is not the case of the more than 100 members of the small leftist parties, perhaps because of the increased personal risk of belonging to some of these parties in the 1950s, 1960s, and 1970s. If we take the next step and only examine party militants, not nominal members, we discover an important universal pattern among women politicians.

Women across the three leading parties are significantly more likely to be party activists (see table 5.7).[28] This level of activism can be explained by their career trajectories within party bureaucracies and organizations affiliated with their parties. It can also be explained by the closer link between parties and elective, legislative positions, the same positions held and sought by women.

As demonstrated previously, in many respects the democratic open-ing has advanced the cause of women politicians. The greater presence of women, however, increases partisanship. Perhaps even more important, their presence also increases the percentage of PRI politicians who have held party positions during their careers. PRI men have been woefully underrepresented compared to women in influential party positions. This is not the case with the other three groups, the PAN, the PRD, and the small

28. For interesting comparative insights, see Kent M. Jennings and Norman Thomas, "Men and Women in Party Elites: Social Roles and Political Resources," *Midwest Journal of Political Science* 12, no. 4 (November 1968): 469–92.

Table 5.8. Party Members Who Held Party Leadership Positions by Gender

| Party | Women (%) | Men (%) |
|---|---|---|
| PAN | 77.4 | 81.6 |
| PRD | 77.7 | 92.8 |
| PRI | 67.9 | 29.4 |
| PSUM/PRT/PPS/PCM/PST/PT/PP | 50.0 | 65.6 |

Source: Mexican Political Biographies Project, 2009.

PAN positions: president, secretary general, or secretary of the National Executive Committee; national adviser to the National Executive Committee; and president of a state party. PRI positions: president of a state party, member of National Council of PRI, general delegate of the National Executive Committee of PRI to states. PRD positions: president, secretary general or secretary of the National Executive Committee, or state party president; PSUM etc. positions: president, secretary general, or secretary of the National Executive Committee.

leftist parties. Women are more than twice as likely as men within the PRI to have held important regional positions (table 5.8).

An important illustration of such a PRI member from the 1950s generation is Roberta Lajous Vargas, who comes from a distinguished intellectual and political family. Lajous is the daughter of Adrián Lajous Martínez, director general of the National Foreign Trade Bank in the early 1980s.[29] She attended the Colegio de Mexico's prestigious international relations program, and taught both at the Colegio and National Autonomous University of Mexico.

Lajous attributes her career success on the National Executive Committee of the PRI—first in 1989 as founder and director of the party's magazine Examen, and in 1992-94 and 2005-6 as secretary/coordinator of international relations—to contacts made inside the party bureaucracy and more important to colleagues from her days at the Colegio de Mexico. She joined the party at the invitation of Abraham Talavera, a companion from the Colegio, who was serving as secretary of political training in 1989. During her directorship of Examen, she came to know Roberto Madrazo, who functioned as secretary of organization on the National Executive Committee under party president Luis Donaldo Colosio, the PRI presidential candidate assassinated

29. See www.fundacion.christlieb, 2008. Roberta Lajous's siblings include Luz, twice a member of congress and oficial mayor of CNOP, who was married to Ignacio Madrazo Reynoso, assistant secretary of the treasury; Alejandra Lajous, official chronicler of the presidency; Adrián Jr., director general of Pemex under President Zedillo and husband of Soledad Loaeza Tovar, distinguished intellectual and social scientist, brother-in-law of Enrique Loaeza, director general of Aeroméxico, and son-in-law of PAN founder Enrique M. Loaeza. President López Portillo's son, José Ramón, is married to a relative of Loaeza.

in 1994. She also came to know Mariano Palacios Alcocer, who directed the 21st Century Foundation for Change. Both of these men later became president of the PRI. She traveled to Washington, D.C., with Palacios and Colosio and made an impression on them with her knowledge of the U.S. political system, which she studied during a year spent at Georgetown University's School of Foreign Service in 1971-72, when her father was an executive director in the World Bank.[30] She attributes her return to the PRI National Executive Committee in 1992 under Colosio to this perceived expertise. In addition to her top party positions, she has been a longtime member of the Foreign Service, having served as ambassador to the United Nations and to Cuba under President Fox. Indeed, as she points out, she was the only member of the Mexican foreign service in 2007 to have been a party leader.[31]

Not all relevant career experiences are political or social. One of the dramatic changes in background experiences that can be strongly linked to the democratic opening is the rise in business backgrounds. Since the democratic transition began under Fox and Calderón, when approximately 6-7 percent of leading politicians came from business backgrounds, those figures doubled. Women politicians, although they have obtained MBAs at the same rate men have, rarely held management positions or owned their own companies in the private sector. In fact, only three women have done so, all since 1994. Thus, women are weakening this new development in Mexican politics since 2000, actually reducing the diversity that a successful business career might contribute in the political arena.

An increased presence of women among Mexico's top politicians can enhance the importance of certain noncareer characteristics, including the distribution of precareer credentials and experiences, which often influence career choices and emphasis. As I have suggested elsewhere in this work and in my previous explorations of political recruitment patterns, educational choices have played a crucial role in socializing and recruiting leading politicians.[32]

Three characteristics distinguish women's educational levels from men. First, men were better educated than women throughout all three periods (table 5.9). Many women in the predemocratic period passed through different types of educational experiences. By the Salinas presidency in 1988, women and men were graduating in nearly equal percentages from

30. She did not continue her studies there because her father insisted that she needed to complete her professional studies in Mexico. She later received a master's degree in political science from Stanford in 1977.

31. Personal communication, March 8, 2007.

32. Roderic Ai Camp, *Mexico's Leaders: Their Education and Recruitment* (Tucson: University of Arizona Press, 1980), and *The Making of a Government: Political Leaders in Modern Mexico* (Tucson: University of Arizona Press, 1984).

**Table 5.9.** Educational Attainments of Politicians by Gender

| Level of Education Completed | Women (%) | Men (%) |
|---|---|---|
| Elementary | 2.5 | 4.9 |
| Secondary | 8.3 | 4.4 |
| Normal | 14.2 | 3.6 |
| Preparatory | 8.3 | 6.5 |
| *Subtotal* | 33.3 | 19.4 |
| University | 28.9 | 46.7 |
| Postprofessional | 11.8 | 7.7 |
| MA | 15.2 | 11.9 |
| Ph.D. or LL.D. | 8.8 | 9.2 |
| M.D. | 2.0 | 5.1 |
| *Subtotal* | 37.8 | 33.9 |

*Source*: Mexican Political Biographies Project, 2009.

colleges and universities, and nearly equal numbers went on to graduate school. Thus, 90 percent of men and 82 percent of women completed college or higher levels of education. In the democratic consolidation period, the figures increase slightly, but college-educated men continued to maintain a 7–8 percent lead over women.

The second characteristic that stands out in these data is that women actually have achieved higher levels of graduate education than men. This is explained not by the assertion that women require higher educational credentials to obtain the same positions as men, but because as a group they are disproportionately younger than men, and both men and women in the younger generations have attended graduate school in equal numbers.

The third and most important finding, however, is that women were four times more likely than men to receive teaching certificates and to have taught in rural and urban elementary schools. Elsewhere in this book we have identified several important qualities attributable to politicians who emerged from the teaching profession. The increased educational attainments of women have been counterbalanced by a significant decrease in rural schoolteachers. In the 1900 generation, six out of ten female politicians (60 percent) were teachers, compared to only 6 percent of men. In the 1910 generation, more than a third of women still were teachers, and in the 1920s and 1930s generations, nearly a fourth continued to obtain this credential. Among the 1940s generation, there was a precipitous decline in this educational preparation to only 6 percent of women politicians

(1 percent for men). By 1960, elementary teaching certificates disappear altogether among all politicians.

From the standpoint of the democratic opening, an increase in the numbers of women has produced increased homogeneity in educational levels reached. The most important contribution to this level of educational homogeneity is the elimination of female rural elementary school teachers, who accounted for a fourth of all women politicians from working-class backgrounds. Thus, the more significant impact of this educational change is the further reduction in working-class backgrounds among all politicians and the social implications that it has for leadership recruitment and composition.

If we examine where women attended school, the increase in women produces educational differences that are much more important to leadership. At the preparatory school level, half as many women as men attended the National Preparatory School in the Federal District. The National Preparatory School was central to the education of many leading politicians and, similar to the National University, was critical as a focus of public sector recruitment. Women, on the other hand, were more diverse in their educational experiences, with larger numbers obtaining a preparatory education graduating from state public institutions and from private secular schools in the Federal District.

Women further add to the diversity of politicians' educational backgrounds in all eras through their degree choices. What stands out dramatically in table 5.10 is the overwhelmingly large percentage of women among politicians who have studied in nontraditional academic disciplines. A huge disparity exists between men and women who have pursued such degrees, and women were almost twice as likely to have graduated from such academic programs.[33] One would logically assume that this difference is once again explained in large part by the fact that women are a much younger cohort than men.

If we begin testing this assumption with the de la Madrid administration (1982–88), it becomes clear that women were 61 percent more likely to have studied nontraditional disciplines. Women who achieved top posts during the democratic transition from 1988 to 2000 opened that gap even further. After 2000, women were twice as likely to share the same types of degrees as men (38 to 19 percent) and in the Calderón administration

33. In part, this mirrors the distribution of all Mexican women graduates by profession. Women account for 60 percent of the degrees in the sciences and 33 percent in communications, the two most common fields in addition to education found in the Other category. Only 3 percent of all Mexican women graduated in engineering, 14 percent in law, and 13 percent in economics. Women generally have a greater presence in business and accounting programs, equaling 11 and 18 percent of all graduates, respectively. See Camp, "Women and Men, Men and Women," 172, table 11.1.

Table 5.10. Degree Choices of Politicians by Gender

| Degrees | Women (%) | Men (%) |
|---|---|---|
| Other | 42.9 | 14.8 |
| Law | 29.3 | 44.4 |
| Economics | 16.5 | 12.6 |
| Business administration and CPA | 6.0 | 5.5 |
| Medical | 3.0 | 6.9 |
| Architecture | 1.5 | 0.9 |
| Engineering | 0.8 | 11.8 |
| Agronomy | 0 | 3.0 |

Source: Mexican Political Biographies Project, 2009.

alone, nontraditional degrees account for half of women politicians' disciplinary choices.

Surprisingly, women help increase economics and economists in the backgrounds of recent politicians. They also contribute significantly to the decline in law graduates. The truly significant disparity between female and male educational choices lies with engineering, which has increased in importance in recent administrations. Although engineering can be considered one of the basic, traditional degrees obtained by male politicians since the 1930s, most of the degrees earned were in civil engineering.[34] Much more specialized engineering degrees can be found in the backgrounds of recent political figures, especially those serving as assistant secretaries in a number of federal agencies. Only one leading female politician obtained an engineering degree (in the Calderón administration), in contrast to more than one out of ten male peers.

Women's choice of disciplines is not the only source of diversity in politicians' educational backgrounds. They also attend different schools. Women were three times more likely to attend the Autonomous Technological University of Mexico (private), the Ibero-American University (Jesuit), the Technological Institute of Higher Studies of the East (Jesuit), and the Colegio de Mexico (elite public) than their male counterparts and were much less likely to have graduated from the National University. The social orientation and the values taught at the universities attended by women differ

34. To compare the changes occurring among top political leadership with the general population, see David E. Lorey, *The Rise of Professions in Twentieth-Century Mexico: University Graduates and Occupational Change since 1929*, 2nd ed. (Los Angles: University of California Press, 1994), and Peter S. Cleaves, *Professions and the State: The Mexican Case* (Tucson: University of Arizona Press, 1987).

widely, thus women add to the diversity of educational views and social-ization among politicians.[35] The same pattern continues in their graduate school choices. Women are less likely to have degrees from U.S. graduate schools than men, but to the same degree were more likely to have been a product of a European university. Again, the emphasis in both pedagogy and content between these two sets of graduate programs is substantial.

Finally, it is worth pointing out that women only infrequently are able to use higher education as a testing ground for their political skills. Manlio Fabio Beltrones, leader of the PRI delegation to the senate (2006–2012) and a leading politician from his party, indicates that his interest in a political career began during his days as a student activist at the National University, which was true of the majority of his generation.[36] One of the more common experiences Mexican politicians share from their school days is competing for leadership positions in student organizations. One in seven politicians has been a student leader in preparatory school or college compared to one in twenty-three women. This can be explained in part by choice of degree programs. Women tend not to study in highly politicized faculties, includ-ing law, which is also the case elsewhere in Latin America.[37]

An increasing influx of women resulting from the democratic reforms could have the potential for reinforcing or decreasing the prevailing ten-dency for large numbers of Mexican politicians to have relatives in public life. My expectation is that women would be less likely to have established kinship ties to other individuals in public life. In reality, female politicians are nearly as well connected as men to other relatives in public life.[38] If that were not the case, the pool of individuals would be broadened beyond those Mexicans who already have established personal ties to politics. Presently, at least a third of all politicians are known to have such kinship connections. In fact, if only politicians whose fathers or mothers served in a high-level political or military post are examined, women are nearly as likely as men to have been raised in a political nuclear family.

Nevertheless, two important differences in these informal characteris-tics exist between men and women. Among leading male politicians, more than one of ten was related to an important revolutionary or Porfirian fam-ily, suggesting a high degree of continuity among leaders over more than

35. For a discussion of these differences in Mexico and elsewhere in Latin America, see Daniel H. Levy's excellent *Higher Education and the State in Latin America: Private Challenges to Public Dominance* (Chicago: University of Chicago Press, 1986), 114–70.

36. Personal communication, May 14, 2008.

37. Chaney, "Women in Latin American Politics," 114.

38. In her study of the United States, Emmy Werner found that half of the women who had served in Congress had relatives in that same body. "Women in Congress, 1917–1964," *Western Political Quarterly* 19 (March 1966): 16–30.

a century. Women, on the other hand, were much less likely to have these historic family connections. Furthermore, when we attempt to explore the networking ties of politicians to cultural and economic elites, we find that men are twice as likely as women to have such ties. Thus, women can be viewed as more likely to be outside the existing system of elite leadership regardless of the potential for historic political connections or contemporary economic and intellectual connections.

## CONCLUSIONS

The democratic opening in Mexico produced a number of changing characteristics in prominent political leadership. One change is based on gender and is the result of an increasing percentage of women in national leadership positions. An important change alone can be attributed to the altered proportions of gender representation among Mexican politicians, and it is significant in terms of leadership characteristics to emphasize those qualities that women enhance, introduce, or reduce compared to the pre-democratic period. Changes should not be attributed solely to the potential differences in beliefs, behavior, and ideological preferences between women and men but also to differences in their demographic, educational, and career characteristics.[39]

Without developing a detailed analysis of the literature on the actual and real impact of female politicians on decision making, in a more fundamental way it is apparent that any increased presence of women in a democratic setting would have an impact on legislation because women share a different set of values in their expectations from and definitions of democracy.[40] Contrary to some conclusions from the survey literature on the importance of gender, gender-related issues are not the only variables that generate significant gender-related results.[41] In a recently published survey of Latin America, we concluded that

> when gender views of democracy are compared across cultures…based on procedural versus nonprocedural conceptualizations, women are more

39. Also cultural perceptions of women versus men, in terms of the language of politics, remain significant. For example, see Tania Rodríguez Mora, "Por que no es lo mismo decir gallo que gallina, discurso político y representaciones de género en la nueva democracia mexicana," *Andamios* 2, no. 3 (December 2005): 51–75.

40. For a detailed discussion of women in the policy-making process, see Victoria Rodríguez, *Women in Contemporary Mexican Politics* (Austin: University of Texas Press, 2003), 191.

41. Eliska Rendlová, "The Gender Paradox in Public Opinion Surveys," *Czech Sociological Review* 7, no. 2 (1999): 177.

likely than men to choose equality, progress, and respect and lawfulness over procedure regarding expectations of democracy, and women are more likely than men to choose fighting crime over procedure regarding the main task of democracy.[42]

There is no reason to believe that Mexican women leaders would not share these differences.[43]

Beyond differing attitudes and emphasis, what does the influx of women most emphasize? The most significant contribution women make in terms of altering career patterns among leading politicians is their significantly greater emphasis on legislative careers. Thus, allowing more women to reach the top in Mexico has increased legislative backgrounds among all politicians. Furthermore, as we demonstrated, it produced a fascinating general characteristic about democratic transitions and leadership: if change in the composition of leadership can be linked to democratic transformations, the most fundamental of those changes will occur in the legislative branch. In the longer term, if the executive branch increasingly draws on leaders with legislative experience, as is the case of Calderón, then alterations in the composition of the legislative branch will be transferred, in part, to the executive.

An increase in women politicians signifies a decrease in executive experience, both on the local level as mayors and on the state level as secretaries general and governors.[44] Women are more likely than men to have held elective office, which increases the importance of elective positions in the background of all politicians, but not the importance of elective executive positions. Gubernatorial office increasingly provides a jumping-off place to reach even more influential national, executive posts, and to compete for the presidency. Because few women have ever been elected governors, an increase in the presence of women in national leadership will actually decrease this type of career experience. Furthermore, the lack of gubernatorial experiences places future women politicians at a serious disadvantage

---

42. Roderic Ai Camp and Keith Yanner, "Democracy across Cultures: Does Gender Make a Difference?," in Joseph S. Tulchin and Meg Ruthenburg, eds., *Citizenship in Latin America* (Boulder, Colo.: Lynne Rienner, 2007), 163–64.

43. In fact, a case could be made that one explanation for union positions being found more commonly in the backgrounds of women politicians is that, based on the survey research conducted for the foregoing study, Mexican women are more interested in social justice issues than men.

44. Joe Foweraker, in his excellent presentation of important theses about women in political life, made the accurate point in 1998 that in Mexico "there is little possibility of creating an upward flow of recruitment from the municipalities and regions to the federal level." Instead, the municipality has been bypassed and women have relied on the state legislature and their respective local party apparatus to accomplish this feat. See his "Ten Theses on Women in Political Life of Latin America," in Victoria Rodríguez, ed., *Women's Participation in Mexican Political Life* (Boulder, Colo.: Westview Press, 1998), 76.

in achieving the visibility necessary to obtain certain other higher offices, including the presidency.

An increase in women politicians also has altered the preparation of PRI electoral candidates given the traditional PRI view that undervalued party experience as an important component of one's overall career. This bias among PRI women is also helpful in increasing their potential to achieve nominations as state legislative and congressional candidates, where links to parties are strongest. On the other hand, it remains to be seen if increased partisanship, measured by the percentage of women compared to men who were active party militants, is beneficial to democratic consolidation.

Finally, an increased presence of women in the last two administrations enhances the diversity of values learned in higher education because women come in greater numbers from nontraditional schools and private institutions than politicians in the past. On the other hand, because few individuals from working-class backgrounds graduate from these institutions, women today reinforce the increasing emphasis on middle-class origins among politicians, a pattern that has persisted across predemocratic, democratic transformational, and postdemocratic eras.

Whatever qualities women bring to national political leadership, are women less likely than men to continue a successful national career once they have achieved their first prestigious position? Surprisingly, the answer is yes and no. Among the small percentage of politicians in Mexico who have achieved three or more top positions in multiple administrations (13 percent), women have been equally successful compared with men. Only among those politicians who continue to a second post in a different administration are women a third less likely than men to obtain that second office. It is impossible to ascertain from this study whether a larger percentage of women than men, as some authors have suggested, decide to forgo a future career in politics after achieving initial success, or for the many reasons that have been mentioned in the present analysis, are denied the opportunities to succeed.

# 6

# The Rise and the Fall of
# the Economic Technocrats

One of the most striking changes in Mexican political leadership at the end of the twentieth century was the emergence of a new type of politician—the technocrat. I have extensively explored the arrival of this type of individual among Mexican politicians and their influence on economic policy making prior to the democratic period.[1] In this chapter, however, I analyze the effect of competitive electoral politics on the staying power of the technocrat to characterize the nature of complementary professional trends among several new generations of politicians, and to determine why they create new as well as respond to established structures that generate significant trends in leadership careers and recruitment. I make the case that three generations of technocrats have appeared on the Mexican scene in the 1940s, the 1980s, and the 2000s. Has democracy altered these longer term patterns, and if so, what trends does democracy introduce and why? Are these new characteristics likely to have staying power among Mexican politicians and, if so, among whom?

I have previously used a number of characteristics to describe Mexico's version of an economic technocrat. It is especially important to distinguish

1. See Roderic Ai Camp, "Tecnocracía, representación y crítica: México en los próximos seis años," in Comité Ejecutivo Nacional del PRI, ed., *Perspectivas del sistema político mexicano* (Mexico: PRI, 1982), 61–66; Roderic Ai Camp, "El tecnócrata en México," *Revista Mexicana de Sociología* 45 (April–June 1983): 579–99; Roderic Ai Camp, "The Technocrat in Mexico and the Survival of the Political System," *Latin American Research Review* 20, no. 1 (1985): 97–118; Roderic Ai Camp, "Technocracy a la Mexicana, Antecedent to Democracy," in Miguel A. Centeno and Patricio Silva, eds., *The Politics of Expertise in Latin America* (New York: St. Martin's Press, 1997), 196–21; Roderic Ai Camp, "The Time of the Technocrats and Deconstruction of the Revolution," in Michael C. Meyer and William H. Beezley, eds., *The Oxford History of Mexico* (New York: Oxford University Press, 2000), 609–36; and Roderic Ai Camp, *Mexico's Mandarins: Crafting a Power Elite for the Twenty-first Century* (Berkeley: University of California Press, 2002). Also see Sarah Babb, *Managing Mexico: Economists from Nationalism to Neoliberalism* (Princeton, N.J.: Princeton University Press, 2001); and Jonathan Schlefer, *Palace Politics: How the Ruling Party Brought Crisis to Mexico* (Austin: University of Texas Press, 2008).

the Mexican genre from their counterparts in Latin America.[2] By far the most distinguishing characteristic of the technocrat is an increased specialization in educational credentials, represented most clearly by the acquisition of disciplinary training in economics, an increase in the level of college education (typically graduate work at the master's or doctoral levels) and by advanced studies in the United States rather than in Mexico or Europe. There are other characteristics associated with these three qualities that are analyzed.[3]

Mexican politicians, as is also the case of national political figures in the United States, most typically have been lawyers.[4] Scholars have suggested in earlier studies of politicians generally that the practice and curriculum of law lent itself to political activities. Another way to examine the political benefits of a law degree is that lawyers who became public officials were essentially generalists with no specific knowledge stemming from their educational credentials to address narrow policy issues.[5] Therefore, if economists and other individuals with more specialized training were to replace the legal generalist as the typical politician, what does their presence represent in determining the composition of Mexican leadership?

An examination of all Mexican politicians' college degrees since the mid-1930s based solely on their date of birth, unencumbered by each president's individual choices that would skew their composition, suggests some important patterns. The oldest generations of Mexican politicians represent two important but distinctive patterns (table 6.1). First, the largest single group of politicians is composed of those without a university degree. The two earliest generations represent those Mexicans who, given their age, actually fought or could have participated in the Mexican Revolution of 1910. The next generation, born between 1900 and 1910, is a civilian generation whose influence is represented symbolically and realistically by President Miguel Alemán, the leading politician of that generation. More than any other Mexican politician in the twentieth century, Alemán represents a

2. For example, see Verónica Montecinos and John Markoff's excellent work "The Ubiquitous Rise of Economists," *Journal of Public Policy* 13, no. 1 (1993): 37–68 and "From the Power of Economic Ideas to the Power of Economists," in Miguel A. Centeno, ed., *The Other Mirror: Essays on Latin America* (Princeton, N.J.: Princeton University Press, 2001).

3. For important and valuable insights on the technocrat's role in China and Mexico, see He Li, "Technocrats and Democratic Transition: The Cases of China and Mexico," *Journal of International and Area Studies* 8, no. 2 (2001): 67–86.

4. Allan Kornberg and Norman Thomas, "The Political Socialization of National Legislative Elites in the United States and Canada," *Journal of Politics* 27 (November 1965): 770.

5. A famous Mexican politician who served in four cabinets anticipated this development when he told me in 1970 that economics would replace law as the preferred discipline of public figures in Mexico and Latin America because of the complexities of economic development and economic decision making. Personal interview with Antonio Carrillo Flores, secretary of foreign relations, January 25, 1970.

Table 6.1. Economics and Other Degrees in the Backgrounds of Mexican Politicians by Generation

| Generation | Economics | Law | Degree (%) None | Business | Others |
|---|---|---|---|---|---|
| Pre-1889 | 0.0 | 33.3 | 42.4 | 0.0 | 3.0 |
| 1890–99 | 0.7 | 32.2 | 44.6 | 1.0 | 5.9 |
| 1900–1909 | 1.9 | 44.4 | 28.5 | 1.1 | 8.9 |
| 1910–19 | 3.0 | 36.0 | 31.2 | 1.1 | 8.9 |
| 1920–29 | 7.7 | 35.6 | 22.0 | 2.5 | 9.3 |
| 1930–39 | 10.7 | 37.5 | 16.8 | 5.6 | 12.5 |
| 1940–49 | 17.9 | 28.5 | 8.8 | 9.2 | 20.4 |
| 1950–59 | 23.3 | 27.4 | 6.8 | 7.3 | 20.1 |
| 1960– | 19.4 | 32.1 | 9.7 | 10.4 | 19.4 |
| All generations | 10.1 | 34.1 | 21.7 | 4.4 | 12.8 |

*Source*: Mexican Political Biographies Project, 2009.

Others refers to degrees in the liberal arts and more recent specializations, such as communications, sciences, and mathematics. The traditional professional degrees of medicine, architecture, engineering, and agronomy are excluded from the table to highlight these patterns. They have varied little over time.

shift away from the self-made, often self-educated military officers whose prior achievements typically could be attributed to their performance on the battlefield.

The revolutionary officer's influence is illustrated dramatically by the presence of career army officers among national politicians in those two pre–twentieth-century generations. Career army officers account for three out of ten politicians in these two generations. Beginning with the 1900 generation, that figure drops precipitously to only one out of ten, continuing at 7 percent or lower over all remaining generations.[6]

No revolutionary general better represents the political success of the pre-1900 generation (other than Presidents Cárdenas and Avila Camacho) than Francisco J. Múgica, who was born in the modest community of

6. What is remarkable is that Alemán's generation marks such a sudden decline in career officers by two-thirds, basically setting the benchmark for all remaining administrations. Figures from the 1950s and 1960s generations are not representative because high-ranking officers who hold the positions of cabinet secretary, assistant secretary, oficial mayor, and chief of staff are in their late fifties or early sixties when they make two- or three-star rank, the norm for these posts. Depending how long they serve, generally 20 or so officers are represented in each generation of some 400 politicians. For more information about civil–military relations and the characteristics of military leadership, see Roderic Ai Camp, *The Mexican Military on the Democratic Stage* (Westport, Conn.: Praeger and the Center for Strategic and International Studies, 2005).

Tinguindín, Michoacán, in 1884, the son of a rural school teacher. After attending various elementary schools, he also studied in the Zamora seminary before becoming a school teacher, postal employee, and journalist. He joined Francisco I. Madero's forces on November 20, 1910, as a second lieutenant, and rose to chief of staff of General Lucio Blanco's forces by 1913.[7] By the end of 1914, he reached the rank of brigade general in the constitutionalist forces. He served as the chief of military operations in various states, including chief of military operations and governor of Tabasco in 1915–16, before being chosen as a deputy to the 1916–17 Constitutional Convention. He was given a number of military assignments in the 1920s and 1930s after having served as governor of Michoacán. Cárdenas, his longtime friend, appointed him as secretary of public works, a post he remained in from 1934 to 1939, when he resigned to compete for the presidency in 1940. He reached the rank of division general in the postrevolutionary army in 1939, and Avila Camacho appointed him as governor of Baja California del Sur in 1940.[8] Múgica became one of the last division generals to serve in a nonmilitary cabinet post.

These pre-1900 generations dominate leadership in the Cárdenas and Avila Camacho administrations, accounting for an overwhelming four-fifths and two-thirds of national leaders in those presidencies, respectively. The 1900 generation, as can be seen in the data presented in table 6.1, introduced a sweeping change in the educational preparation of national

---

7. Not all revolutionary officers from the provinces who achieved successful political careers were self-made men. A number of civilians and officers could trace their antecedents to relatives who were supporters of Benito Juárez. General Juan Barragán Rodríguez, a colleague of Múgica's who came from Río Verde, San Luis Potosí, was the great-grandson of Miguel Francisco Barragán, interim president of Mexico (1836), and the grandson of a constitutional deputy and governor of San Luis Potosí. His father was mayor of Ciudad del Maíz, were he was raised, and a rancher, who was a descendant of one of the largest landowners in San Luis Potosí, but not a supporter of Díaz. General Barragán attended the Scientific and Literary Institute of San Luis Potosí, and organized a strike with other students to support Madero. He left school as a fourth-year law student to support the revolution in 1913, and eventually became chief of staff to Venustiano Carranza until the president's murder in May 1920. He helped divide and return the first lands after the revolution with General Lucio Blanco in August 1913 in Los Borregos, Tamaulipas. General Barragán, in spite of his college education, was formed by his participation in the revolution, which took the life of his brother in 1916. Barragán was governor in 1917, served in the first session of congress, and then as a senator, and served twice more as a member of congress in the 1960s and 1970s. Personal communication to the author, April 3, 1974; *Hispano Americano*, October 7, 1974, 11; and Píndaro Urióstegui Miranda's interview, *Testimonios del proceso revolucionario de México* (Mexico: Agrin, 1970), 191–92.

8. Anna Ribera Carbó, *La patria ha podido ser flor: Francisco J. Múgica, una biografía política* (Mexico: INAH, 1999); Armando de María y Campos, *Múgica: Crónica biográfica* (Mexico: Compañía de Ediciones Populares, 1939); Albert L. Michaels, "The Mexican Election of 1940," Special Studies, Council on International Studies (Buffalo: State University of New York, 1971); and Mexican Political Biographies Project, 2009.

politicians, representing in part a decline in rural Mexicans entering their ranks. Those Mexicans from rural origins traditionally have had less access to formal education, especially university-level education. For example, half of all rural-born politicians through the 1910–19 generation did not graduate from college. By contrast, among these same generations who came from urban birthplaces, only one in four, or half as many, did not attend college. This significant geographic influence continues to the present, but it can also be associated with the disciplines that politicians from each setting chose to study. Proportionately, economists are more likely to come from urban rather than rural origins, and even as recently as the 1950s generation, more than twice as many could be found with urban than with rural backgrounds.

This rural impact explains why so many older Mexicans were rural elementary schoolteachers who graduated from rural normal schools in their respective states.[9] The 1900 generation represents an extraordinary 36 percent decline in non–college-educated politicians. Most of the decline in the noneducated politicians is taken up by college-educated lawyers who alone account for 44 percent of all prominent politicians, a figure equaled by non–college graduates in the previous generation (table 6.1).

There are three waves of technocrats among Mexican national leadership. Most analysts have only identified one, which appeared in Mexico and elsewhere in Latin America in the 1980s and 1990s. The first of these waves is represented by the Alemán generation and is discussed in greater detail in a subsequent chapter. The argument offered here is that Alemán and his cohorts represent the civilian, college-educated technocrat of the 1940s, establishing the basis for a new type of politician in Mexico. With the exception of the following generation (1910–19), and the present generation (1960+), the percentage of politicians without a college degree has declined steadily among all successive generations. The temporary surge in non–college-educated politicians in the 1910–19 generation can be explained by the actions of Adolfo Ruiz Cortines, the only president since 1946 without a college degree, who appointed larger numbers of individuals with similar credentials.[10]

---

9. Four percent of all national leaders were elementary school teachers. At least an equal number went on to complete college degrees, often in education. Mexican Political Biographies Project, 2009.

10. Ruiz Cortines completed primary school at La Pastora, Veracruz, and studied for four more years at the Instituto Veracruzano. A member of the 1890 generation (born in 1890), he did not serve in the military but was an aide to two major revolutionary generals, Alfredo Robles Domínguez and Heriberto Jara, during the revolution and was a member of President Venustiano Carranza's secret service in 1913. Roderic Ai Camp, Mexican Political Biographies, 1935–1993 (Austin: University of Texas Press, 1995), 628–29.

The Alemán administration is filled with a plethora of highly trained college graduates from his generation, many of whom were his co-students or professors at the National University and the National Preparatory School in the 1920s. The individual who best represents the first wave of the civilian technocrats coming to the forefront of Mexican politics from the 1900 generation is Ramón Beteta Quintana. Born in the Federal District in 1901, he attended the National Preparatory School and began his studies at the National School of Law in 1919.[11] But Beteta, similar to several other prominent figures from his generation, became interested in economics, a discipline Mexican universities did not offer until the 1930s.[12] Consequently, he left Mexico and attended the University of Texas at Austin for the next three years, where he obtained a degree in economics, the first Mexican cabinet secretary trained in this field.[13]

11. As Antonio Martínez Báez pointed out in correspondence with me and later expanded on in multiple interviews, the National Law School generation of 1921-25 compressed two generations together, that is, the 1921 class and the 1922 class, because of changes in the curriculum. Therefore, it brought together two distinguished sets of students who not only became friends but became a critical group of young professors of the Alemán generation. In addition to Beteta and Martínez Báez himself, who became Alemán's secretary of industry and commerce in 1948, they included Manuel Gual Vidal, his secretary of public education; Carlos Novoa, his director general of the Bank of Mexico; José de Jesús Castorena, governor of Guanajuato in 1947; Mariano Ramírez Vázquez, whom Alemán appointed to the supreme court in 1947; Eduardo Bustamante, assistant secretary of the treasury under Beteta; and Bernardo Iturriaga Alarcón, also assistant secretary of the treasury under Beteta. Personal correspondence to the author, September 22, 1972.

12. Two other notable figures in the world of public finance who pursued training abroad were Eduardo Villaseñor Angeles (1896), who studied at the University of London, held numerous financial posts in the 1920s and 1930s, and became assistant secretary of the treasury, 1938-40, and in 1940-46, director general of the Bank of Mexico (Federal Reserve). Personal interview with the author, June 27, 1975. The other individual is Daniel Cosío Villegas, a leading intellectual and historian, who also studied in England. He used his economics background to promote the publication of economics texts through the publicly funded Fondo de Cultura Económica, which he co-founded in 1934 with Villaseñor. Personal interview with the author, June 30, 1975. Interestingly, all of these individuals are connected to Manuel Gómez Morín, who taught Beteta and other members of the Alemán generation, and is credited with founding the Bank of Mexico in 1925. Gómez Morín also was acting secretary of the treasury, but he is best remembered for founding and serving as the first president of the PAN. Gómez Morín, like Beteta, studied in the United States, taking courses in economics at Columbia University in 1921. As Carlos Novoa indicated to me, he believed Gómez Morín "influenced his entire generation by his exemplary life and extraordinary talent that was dedicated fundamentally to the study of Mexico's finances." Novoa became president of the National Banking Commission in 1933, and co-founded the PAN with his mentor. Despite his connection with PAN, Alemán, as noted, still appointed him head of Mexico's federal reserve bank. Personal correspondence to the author, January 18, 1975.

13. The first student to graduate from the National School of Economics was Eduardo Hornedo Cubillas, December 21, 1934. The earliest graduate to become a prominent public figure was Sealtiel Alatriste Abrego, who graduated on December 20, 1938, having already graduated in the 1920s with a CPA degree. He became assistant secretary of government properties in 1959 and secretary general of the Mexican Social Security Institute in 1964. He

Beteta anticipated several of the qualities that characterize the two later technocratic waves, first by studying abroad in the United States in the 1920s, a rare occurrence in those years. Additionally, he obtained a degree in economics, completed a Ph.D. in the social sciences from the National University in 1934, and received the first doctorate in social sciences awarded in Mexico. He taught the Alemán generation at the National Preparatory School and for nearly two decades taught economics at the law school and the newly founded economics school.[14] As Hugo B. Margáin, Mexico's treasury secretary in the Echeverría administration, recalled, Beteta insisted to his students that they always keep in mind Mexico's problems when studying economics—especially agrarian issues and legal protections for workers.[15] Beteta's first post in government was as a legal consultant to the Agricultural Bank. After holding several other positions in the federal bureaucracy, he began serving in positions relevant to his background in economics: as a department head, division head, and official mayor of the industry and commerce secretariat, the key secretariat in employing the first generation of politician economists in Mexico.[16] He became a technical adviser to President Cárdenas in 1935,[17] and then assistant secretary of foreign relations for the remainder of his presidency.[18]

---

married the first female graduate, Estela Sanjines Villalva (1940). Two fellow students from his class also pursued successful political careers: Alfonso Pulido Islas and Hugo Rangel Couto. Alatriste also expressed a high opinion of Beteta, who was his professor. Personal communication from Sealtiel Alatriste, January 17, 1974.

14. Before it became a separate program, students interested in economics could take courses from the National School of Law. Beteta is remembered by a generation of Mexican public figures as one of their most influential professors. Not surprisingly, these same students ended up guiding Mexico's financial and economic agencies.

15. Personal communication from Hugo B. Margáin, October 19, 1973.

16. See Roderic Ai Camp, "The Middle-Level Technocrat in Mexico," *Journal of Developing Areas* (July 1972): 571–82, for a detailed description of its impact. The key figure in establishing the linkage between the secretariat of industry and commerce and economists was Gilberto Loyo, the agency's director from 1952 to 1958. Although trained as a lawyer at UNAM, Loyo studied and received a degree in economic statistics from the University of Rome in 1938 and, on his return to Mexico, became director of the national census. Beginning in 1936, he taught for thirty years at the National School of Economics, becoming the dean from 1944 to 1952, prior to becoming secretary. He was influenced by Manuel Gómez Morín at UNAM and was a friend of Ramón Beteta and Narciso Bassols at the university. Personal communication to the author, September 14, 1972. Ironically, industry and commerce's influence on economists' careers continued to grow due to the influence of Raúl Salinas Lozano, an early graduate of the National School of Economics in 1944 and secretary of this cabinet agency from 1958 to 1964. Salinas Lozano is the father of President Carlos Salinas Gortari, who contributed significantly to the preeminence of technocrats from the second wave in the 1980s and 1990s.

17. Beteta's older brother, General Ignacio M. Beteta Quintana, was Cardenas's chief of staff.

18. He served under Ezequiel Padilla, having been his private secretary and legal adviser in 1928–30 when Padilla was secretary of public education.

In 1940, he became assistant secretary of the treasury, serving under Eduardo Suárez, the influential treasury secretary under Cárdenas and Avila Camacho. Beteta resigned his position in 1945 to manage the presidential campaign of Alemán, his former student. The president rewarded him with the post of secretary of the treasury.[19]

The second and unexpected increase in the rise of non-college-educated politicians since the 1950s generation is a fascinating consequence of electoral competition and an altered pool from which those politicians have been selected. Interestingly, the National Action Party (PAN) as well as the Institutional Revolutionary Party (PRI) have significantly contributed to this pattern by selecting larger numbers of gubernatorial and congressional candidates who have strong roots in their states and local communities. In the past fifteen years, as the nomination processes have become more decentralized and competitive, individuals who are self-made businesspeople have increased their presence among successful gubernatorial candidates. These individuals are much more likely to lack a college degree, having pursued a business career instead. Consequently, the percentage of non-college graduates in the 1960s generation exceeds the two preceding generations.

The second wave of technocrats appears in the 1940s and 1950s generations. As the data presented in table 6.1 suggest, generalists (largely represented by lawyers) reach their high point in the 1900 generation, accounting for more than two-fifths of all politicians. Lawyers as a percentage of all politicians remain at a stable level for three more generations, accounting for more than a third.[20] Beginning with the 1940s generation, however,

19. As a professor, Beteta taught Antonio Armendáriz, assistant secretary of the treasury (1952–58), and Hugo B. Margáin, secretary of the treasury (1970–73). Both men have indicated through interviews with and correspondence to the author Beteta's impact on their intellectual ideas and economics training. Interestingly, Beteta's nephew, who obtained a master's degree in economics from the University of Wisconsin, held four successive critical posts in the public financial sector as a manager of the Bank of Mexico (Federal Reserve) (1960–63), director general of credit, secretariat of the treasury (1964–70), assistant secretary of the treasury (1970–75), and like his uncle, secretary of the treasury (1975–76). Mexican Political Biographies Project, 2009.

20. Part of the reason the National Law School remains a critical variable in the backgrounds of so many politicians is the multigenerational linkage provided by professors and students, which often became key mentoring relationships. Take the case of Francisco González de la Vega, a co-student with Ramón Beteta, who graduated from the National Preparatory School in 1920 and the National School of Law in 1923. González de la Vega began teaching in 1922, a year before he graduated, and was still teaching fifty years later when he corresponded with me. He pointed out that he had the good fortune of teaching four Mexican presidents: Miguel Alemán, Adolfo López Mateos, Gustavo Díaz Ordaz, and Luis Echeverría, three of them at the National School of Law. He served as assistant attorney general just seven years after he graduated and became attorney general under Alemán in 1946. He directed the tourism department under López Mateos, was appointed ambassador

there is a sharp decline in the percentage of politicians who are lawyers, reaching a figure for the first time below that of the pre-1889 generation. Lawyers born during the 1930s declined by 25 percent in the following generation. Simultaneously, economists, who have consistently increased their numbers among all politicians from the 1890s to 1950s generations, accounted for nearly a quarter of their peers among the 1950s generation, nearly equal to lawyers.

The 1940s and 1950s generations clearly represent the second, most famous technocratic wave, symbolized strongly by Presidents Salinas (1948) and Ernesto Zedillo (1951). Salinas most represents the rise of the economic technocrat, suggested by the data demonstrating that, measured by generation, economists increased by two-thirds from the 1930s to the 1940s generation and by nearly a third from the 1940s to the 1950s generation. Salinas is analogous to Alemán in providing the opportunity to many of his classmates and professors to achieve prominent posts in the government, both as a cabinet officer under Miguel de la Madrid (1982–88) and as his successor. In the same way that Alemán influenced the recruitment of a college-educated civilian generation from the National University from Mexico's law school, Salinas drew a large portion of his fellow economists from the National School of Economics, having been a member of the 1966–69 class. He is the first and only president of Mexico to have graduated from the National School of Economics. He is also likely to be the last president from that school, given the origins of recent politician economists. He might well be the last president who is an alumnus of the National University.

A key figure in encouraging and influencing the rise of the second technocratic wave represented by economists was President de la Madrid. De la Madrid was a lawyer, but his thesis from the National School of Law was on economic thought. An outstanding student, he spent a year at Harvard where he earned a master's in public administration in 1965. Shortly after his graduation from law school, he began working for the Bank of Mexico under his uncle, Ernesto Fernández Hurtado, the director general, but was recruited to this position by a former economics professor.[21] Every post de la Madrid held from 1960 until 1975, when he became assistant secretary

---

to Argentina under Díaz Ordaz, and became a special adviser to Echeverría. His father and brother Angel were graduates, and his mother ran a boarding house for students, which increased the brothers' contact with other leading figures of that generation. His brother became assistant attorney general in the 1930s, assistant secretary of the treasury under Beteta, and Alemán appointed him to the supreme court in 1952. González de la Vega's great-nephew became assistant attorney general in the 1990s. Personal communication to the author, August 8, 1972.

21. That professor was José Ricardo Zevada, a contemporary of Ramón Beteta, who served as director general of credit, secretary of the treasury (1934–36), and later as director

of the treasury, can be described as influential public financial positions. In 1979, he left his post as assistant secretary to become secretary of planning and budgeting, the federal agency that became most influential in determining federal financial allocations and therefore exercised broad policy influence.[22]

The careers of De la Madrid and Salinas in public financial agencies and their subsequent election as presidents reinforced the importance of the financial agencies during these years as the place to be for ambitious politicians.[23] Because incumbent presidents selected incoming presidential candidates from their cabinets, politicians whose goal was to become

general of the National Bank of Foreign Trade from 1952 to 1965. Personal interview with Miguel de la Madrid, February 17, 1991, and José Ricardo Zevada, May 23, 1978.

22. Four successive presidents were assistant secretaries or headed this cabinet department: José López Portillo, Miguel de la Madrid, Carlos Salinas, and Ernesto Zedillo. López Portillo also served as secretary of the treasury. Indeed, more top political figures in the study held positions in this agency at the director general level or higher than any other federal agency in the past thirty years. In fact, in Eduardo Torres Espinosa's outstanding study of this secretariat, the most comprehensive analysis of bureaucratic decision making in a single agency in recent decades, the author provides a complete list of officeholders, including a list from the 1970s and 1980s of "low-ranked personnel." If one examines that list alone, several dozen names of leading politicians appear, demonstrating its lasting influence career-wise into the 1990s and 2000s. Those names include Eloy Cantú Segovia, two-time member of congress and the senate, including the 2006–12 session, Marco Antonio Bernal Gutiérrez, senator and deputy and secretary general of National Federation of Popular Organizations, 2006; Marcelo Ebrard, governor of the Federal District; Gabino Fraga Mouret, three-time assistant secretary of federal cabinet agencies from 1982 to 1996; Dulce María Sauri Riancho, deputy, senator, governor of Yucatán, and president of PRI, 1999–2002; Jorge Salomón Azar, governor of Campeche; and Tomas J. Yarrington, governor of Tamaulipas, 1999–2005. Eduardo Torres Espinosa, *Bureaucracy and Politics in Mexico: The Case of the Secretariat of Programming and Budgeting* (Brookfield: Ashgate, 1999).

23. A revealing example of the importance of such career paths is illustrated from my own unique experience. In 1990, I published a scholarly article on the most successful career paths for future Mexican politicians in *Mexican Studies*. A few months later, a friend mailed me four articles from the front page of Mexico's then-leading newspaper, *Excélsior*, in which my entire article, without permission, appeared in two successive issues, accompanied by an intense critique of several of the conclusions. I wasn't able to determine why a complete version of a scholarly article would appear in this newspaper on such a prominent page. Years later, in a conversation with a Mexican politician, I discovered the explanation. Apparently, a prominent politician with presidential ambitions in 1994 did not fit the criteria I outlined in the essay. Consequently, in an effort to lend greater credibility to his own career path, his representatives persuaded *Excélsior* to run a series of articles, in which they attempted to delegitimize my conclusions. This experience suggests the degree to which younger politicians were paying attention to such career patterns, including a North American's scholarly description of them. The original essay was "Camarillas in Mexican Politics, the Case of the Salinas Cabinet," *Mexican Studies* (Winter 1990): 85–108. The articles were Aurora Berdejo A., "Frentes Políticos," *Excélsior*, June 30, 1990, 1A, 28A; Aurora Berdejo A., "Frentes Políticos, Roderic A. Camp e las 'camarillas' en la política," *Excélsior*, June 23, 1990, A1, A26; Margarita García Colín, "Frentes Políticos," *Excélsior*, June 24, 1990, A1, 30A; and Aurora Berdejo A., "Frentes Políticos, Descalifican Salinistas el análisis de Ai Camp," *Excélsior*, June 28, 1990, A1, A30.

president during the predemocratic period (pre-2000) would seek out those positions. All four presidents after 1976 had come from one of the two leading financial agencies.[24] Younger politicians increasingly were replicating the careers and credentials of these presidents, men who typically favored individuals with credentials approximating their own.

If we consider that Luis Donaldo Colosio, not Ernesto Zedillo, was Salinas's actual choice to succeed him, it is worth noting that Colosio was also an economist. Unlike Salinas and most other PRI politicians of his era, he graduated from a leading regional university, the Technological Institute of Higher Studies of Monterrey (ITESM), highly respected in Mexico for its economics program. He completed a master's degree in regional development and urban economics at the University of Pennsylvania and studied economics in their Ph.D. program without graduating. With the exception of one year, he worked in his mentor's programming and budgeting agency from 1979 to 1985. What distinguishes Colosio from both Salinas and Zedillo, however, is that he left the federal bureaucracy to become a member of congress from his home state of Sonora in 1985; three years later he became a senator. It is important to keep in mind that although he served in both houses of congress, he first became oficial mayor of the PRI National Executive Committee and then president of the party in 1988, which he resigned from to become Salinas's secretary of social development in 1992.

Colosio represented a fresh hybrid among PRI politicians during the democratic transition, combining economic training, technical expertise, and extensive study in the United States with two national elective offices and two influential national party positions. Salinas himself was not a popular nominee among the party rank and file. Technocrats were often vilified in the press publicly and privately among experienced party officials and elected politicians.[25] Colosio was the first PRI presidential candidate since Luis Echeverría in 1970 to hold a national party post,[26] and he was

24. Zedillo established himself in programming and budgeting, but his entire agency was subsumed within treasury in 1992 and disappeared. Salinas then made him secretary of public education. Colosio became the PRI candidate in 1994, a product of the new social development secretariat. Zedillo, therefore, was an accidental candidate, largely having had the field to himself because he was one of the few leading cabinet members eligible to replace Colosio, having resigned to direct his presidential campaign, thus meeting constitutional requirements of holding no public office for a specific period of time before becoming a presidential candidate.

25. When I accompanied Ernesto Zedillo on the campaign trail in 1994, after he replaced Colosio as the PRI nominee, party officials complained to me privately about Zedillo's lack of experience and stiffness in speaking at public forums typical of a Mexican presidential or congressional campaign.

26. Echeverría boasted extensive party experience due to his early political mentor having been president of the party. He served both as secretary of press and publicity under

the first since Gustavo Díaz Ordaz (1964–70) to have held national elective office. Had he been elected, it is likely he would have brought a pronounced shift among PRIistas in the value placed on elective and party posts, thus anticipating actual career changes that came about during the late 1990s and since 2000.

From an ideological and policy perspective, the second wave of technocrats, including Colosio, introduced an influential group of economists who were trained in the United States and therefore were significantly influenced by U.S. economic teaching from the Ivy League programs they attended, typically Harvard and Yale.[27] A unique linkage exists between economists, graduate work, and graduate work in the United States. Among all Mexican politicians in our study, 357 have studied in graduate programs in the United States. A fourth of all politicians in graduate programs have been economists, by far the most well-represented discipline or profession. Among economists, six out of ten studied in graduate programs, half of them in the United States. It is safe to conclude that more economist politicians sought advanced education in the United States than any other profession represented among politicians.

A high official of the Zedillo administration, Javier Treviño Cantu, a product of this second technocratic wave, describes it in the following terms:

> The "technocrats" formed during the governments of Miguel de la Madrid, Carlos Salinas de Gortari, and Ernesto Zedillo were a generation of young people who studied in the best universities of Mexico and the best universities of the United States. It was a meritorious system, with great discipline and great ability to fulfill government tasks. Tasks as complex as renegotiating the foreign debt or the negotiation of the North American Free Trade Agreement demonstrated to the world that Mexico relied on a most distinguished and prepared group of public functionaries.[28]

The second wave of technocrats, unlike the first, represents a dramatic shift in the importance of private versus public universities in the educational credentials of national politicians. The statistics in table 6.2 highlight the importance of the Autonomous Technological Institute of Mexico

---

Alemán and as oficial mayor of the National Executive Committee under Ruiz Cortines. Echeverría also represented the party in numerous regional capacities, including as president of the PRI in Guanajuato, which was not his home state. Camp, *Mexican Political Biographies*, 211.

27. See Camp, *Mexico's Mandarins*, 168–78, including letters from such former Ivy League economists to the author as R. S. Eckaus, January 29, 1997 and Franco Modigliani, January 22, 1997.

28. Personal communication from Javier Treviño Cantu, former oficial mayor of treasury and assistant secretary of foreign relations in the Zedillo government, December 27, 2007.

**Table 6.2.** Leading Universities Attended by Mexican Politicians Who Were Economists

| University Attended (Degrees Awarded) | % with Degrees in Economics |
|---|---|
| UNAM (1,151) | 12.9 (149) |
| ITAM (63) | 85.7 (54) |
| ITESM (67) | 29.9 (20) |
| University of Nuevo León (32) | 25.0 (8) |
| University of Guadalajara (80) | 11.3 (9) |
| National Polytechnic Institute (71) | 11.3 (8) |
| Ibero-American University (54) | 7.4 (4) |

*Source*: Mexican Political Biographies Project, 2009.

(ITAM) and ITESM, the two leading private universities with distinguished economics programs. The National Autonomous University of Mexico (UNAM) is responsible for the undergraduate education of nearly half of all college-educated national politicians, an extraordinary achievement in itself. But considering its size and the age of its program, it has produced only approximately half of the 295 politician economists. ITAM, a private school founded in the 1950s, has captured nearly a fifth of all politician economist in a short period of time and through a much smaller enroll-ment. Nearly nine out of ten of its graduates who have achieved national prominence in public life are economists. ITESM, a private, regional uni-versity, has graduated an equal number of politicians as ITAM generally, but fewer than a third were economists. The other leading universities graduating future politicians, three public and one private, have only pro-duced a handful of economists.[29]

The decline in the prominence of UNAM's economic curriculum among leaders in both the private and public sectors can be more clearly seen in the economics programs that have graduated politicians born in the 1950s and 1960s. In the 1950s generation, ITAM produced twenty-six economists, compared to only twenty-two from UNAM. In the 1960s generation, ITAM is responsible for fourteen economists, and UNAM only one. Expressed differently, among all the youngest national politicians born since 1960, regardless of discipline studied, ITAM has produced seventeen total gradu-ates compared to sixteen for UNAM!

29. Many of the most distinguished provincial universities, which boast a long and proud history of producing regional and national politicians, have not graduated a single promi-nent politician economist. They include the University of México, Toluca; the University of Oaxaca, Oaxaca; the University of Michoacán, Morelia, the University of Veracruz, Jalapa, the University of Guanajuato, Guanajuato, the University of Coahuila, Saltillo, University of Campeche, Campeche, University of Querétaro, Querétaro, and the University of Chihuahua, Chihuahua.

I believe a third wave of Mexican political technocratic leadership is now under way. It shares some of the technocratic features inherited from the economist technocrat and others from the earlier college-educated civilian version highlighted among the Alemán generation. A careful examination of these significant new trends based on disciplinary or professional backgrounds alone can be discerned in the figures presented in table 6.1.

There are four important percentages that stand out among the 1950s and 1960s generations. Despite the fact that Zedillo is the last economist president, economics reaches a peak in the credentials of 1950s generation, with nearly one out of four politicians having earned an undergraduate degree in this discipline. However, with the arrival of the post-1960s generation, we witness a decline in economists. It remains to be seen, once the 1960s or younger generations have contributed fully to public life, whether this pattern is sustained. Second and perhaps more telling is the decline in legal backgrounds among politicians born in the 1940s and 1950s, reaching the lowest point ever since the 1880s generation. But the 1960s generation again reflects an increase in lawyers, which appears to be stabilizing at about one in three political figures and continues to be the most widely shared professional background. The fact that Felipe Calderón (1961) is a law school graduate contributed to this revival and to some extent tempered public leadership's increasing reliance on economists.[30]

Perhaps the most interesting pattern about the third wave of political leadership, in terms of professional credentials, is the significant increase from the 1930s to the 1940s generations in the number of politicians who have deviated from the traditional occupations of law, engineering, and medicine and, in addition to economics, have chosen specializations that were rarely pursued by students with political interests.[31] In addition to

30. It is also valuable to point out that Calderón is an alumnus of the Free School of Law, a prestigious private law school whose last presidential graduate was Emilio Portes Gil (1928–30), who played an important role in its founding. Personal communication to the author and personal interview, August 1, 1974.

31. A perfect illustration of the importance of one of the other traditional degrees during the 1930s and 1940s is that of engineering. As José Hernández Terán pointed out to me in a letter, he pursued his studies at the Evening University Extension program at the National University, the National Preparatory School, and the National School of Engineering, graduating as a civil engineer in 1946. He became secretary of hydraulic resources from 1964 to 1970. During his middle school studies at the extension program, he met José López Portillo. At the National Preparatory School, he studied with Luis Enrique Bracamontes, secretary of public works under President Echeverría; Jesús Reyes Heroles, president of the CEN of the PRI and secretary general of the Social Security Institute under Echeverría; Ernesto Fernández Hurtado, director general of the Bank of Mexico (federal reserve) under Echeverría; and Echeverría himself. He attended the National School of Engineering with Leandro Rovirosa Wade, who replaced him as secretary of hydraulic resources under Echeverría in 1970; Manuel Franco López, secretary of national properties, 1966–70; Gilberto Valenzuela Esquerro, secretary of public works, 1964–70; Luis Enrique Bracamontes, secretary of public

the liberal arts discipline of political science, many students with political interests began graduating in such fields as communications, hard sciences, and computer science, reflecting skills demanded by an increasingly complex economy in Mexico. In this one generation between 1930 and 1940, those specific educational/professional backgrounds increased more than 60 percent, remaining consistently at a level of one-fifth of educational credentials, on par with economists, in the last three generations.

Just as we suggested the existence of a link between economists, graduate training, and advanced studies in the United States, the pattern repeats for those students in the third wave of specialists who are from the new disciplines that became important in the 1990s and 2000s. Half of the politicians with undergraduate degrees in these diverse specializations attended graduate programs, second in number only to economists, and nearly half of them studied in the United States—a number far greater than the percentage of economists who studied in the United States. In this sense, these collective specializations have replaced economics as the single most important emphasis of politicians who sought U.S. graduate education in recent years.

Finally, the number of politicians with degrees in business administration and accounting have increased significantly in the last four generations, beginning in the 1930s, when they more than doubled from the previous generation. Such politicians reached a high point in the 1960s generation. PAN traditionally recruited many of its leaders from business backgrounds, where these fields are most valued. Equally important, however, is the fact that PRI itself, especially in the 1990s and since the democratic opening of 2000, has also seen a significant increase in the number of politicians coming from business backgrounds, thus simultaneously contributing to its increased presence. Vicente Fox reinforced this trend personally and symbolically by becoming the first president of Mexico with a business administration degree and with a long career in business management posts in international and family-owned enterprises.[32]

---

works, 1970–76; and Rodolfo Félix Valdés and Fernando Espinosa, assistant secretary of public works, 1966–76 and 1964–66, respectively. He also studied under Javier Barros Sierra and Pedro Martínez Tornel, secretary of public works from 1958 to 1964 and 1945 to 1946, respectively, and Antonio Dovalí Jaime, assistant secretary of public works, 1949–52, and later director general of Pemex under Echeverría. These individuals account for an extraordinary group of influential political figures in public works, let alone the two cabinets of Gustavo Díaz Ordaz and Luis Echeverría. Personal communication, November 17, 1972.

32. Calderón's victory as the president of PAN in 1996 represented the victory of the ideologically driven traditionalists within the party who defeated the probusiness pragmatists then led by former governor Ernesto Ruffo Appel, the first victorious PAN candidate for governor in the twentieth century. *El Financiero*, April 15, 1996, 5; *Mexico Business*, May 1996, 10–12.

The third trend in technocratic leadership is characterized by a much more diversified set of qualities. Rather than focusing specifically on economists, it combines a wide range of recent specializations with business and economics backgrounds, while continuing the stable role of lawyers, who have been a significant presence in all three technocratic waves and all nine generations. President Calderón himself represents this hybrid background. Like De la Madrid, he graduated from law school; his law thesis was titled "Unconstitutionality of Mexico's External Debt, 1982–1986," demonstrating his early interest in economics. He followed up that interest by pursuing studies toward a master's degree in economics at ITAM, the most influential economics program among political figures of his generation. Similar to both de la Madrid and Salinas, he attended the John F. Kennedy School of Government at Harvard University, obtaining a master's degree in public administration in 2000.[33]

This recent wave of highly trained politicians can be differentiated from its predecessors in terms of educational credentials in several important ways. As can be seen just from the analysis of economists alone, the dominance of the National University has declined significantly in recent years to be replaced by the influence of private universities and public and private regional universities. The same pattern can be found in the graduate programs pursued by all future politicians, who have moved away from concentrating exclusively in U.S. Ivy League programs to attending numerous colleges and universities in the United States.

Furthermore, the presence of the PAN in the executive branch, and specifically PAN members in the Calderón administration, has increased the importance of European education, given the interest of a number of prominent, intellectually oriented PAN party leaders in historical and even religious training in Europe, especially Spain, France, and Italy. For example, the late Carlos Castillo Peraza, who was Calderón's political mentor and served on the National Executive Committee of PAN before becoming the party's president in 1993, was one of the few Mexican national politicians with a degree in philosophy. He spent four years in Switzerland in the 1970s studying Greek philosophy at University of Fribourg.[34]

33. *El Financiero*, April 15, 1996, 5; *Diccionario biográfico del gobierno mexicano* (Mexico: Presidencia de la República, 1992), 431; *Mexico Business*, May 1996, 10–12; Mexican Political Biographies Project, 2009.

34. Another interesting example is Fernando Estrada Sámano, the son of PAN founder Miguel Estrada Iturbide, who studied in Guadalajara at the Jesuit Technological Institute of Higher Studies of the West in classical letters in 1962, and later completed a Ph.D. at Gutenberg University, Germany, in 1978. He also graduated with a bachelor's degree in philosophy from Fordham University in New York and a master's in political science from Columbia University before becoming a college professor. He has served in a number of national party posts, twice in the congress, and was Fox's ambassador to the Vatican.

The contrary pattern among this new wave of politicians is the unexpected reversal of an increase among prominent figures without college-level studies. This figure has grown from a low of 7 percent in the 1950s to nearly 10 percent in the 1960s, surpassing percentages as far back as the 1940s. The reason is strongly related to the democratic opening, in which different types of politicians became candidates, most commonly among PAN and PRI gubernatorial and legislative candidates. This pattern is not associated with an increase in politicians from working-class backgrounds but is a reflection of the emphasis on successful businesspeople who pursued business opportunities rather than formal education at a young age. Fox himself is such a person, for although he has a business administration degree from the Jesuit Ibero-American University, he did not actually complete the degree until 1999, during his presidential campaign.[35]

A generational analysis of these distinct waves among leaders provides many significant insights into the educational, technocratic credentials of prominent national political leadership. To determine its precise relationship to the democratic and democratic transition periods, since multiple generations are represented in each presidential administration, it is necessary to break these patterns down according to individual presidential administrations to determine each president's and each chronological era's influence on these same patterns.

The Alemán administration highlights even more strongly the president's emphasis on college-educated collaborators, primarily lawyers. Two figures stand out among national figures who reached high office for the first time under Alemán. First, the percentage of college-educated politicians rose to over 70 percent, a figure that was not duplicated by any other administration from 1935 to 1964. It becomes clear that Alemán was well ahead of his time in promoting and recruiting several generations of highly educated national politicians. The sentiments that Javier Trevino Cantú used to describe the second technocratic wave could just as easily have been used by many of Alemán's appointees in contrasting themselves

---

*Diario de Yucatán*, September 10, 2000 and September 14, 2000; *Excélsior*, June 23, 1997; and www.castilloperaza.com.

35. The president is not unique in this regard. According to Salvador Malo, citing official national educational data, four out of ten college graduates in 2003 did not complete their degrees. See Salvador Malo, "La educación superior en el nuevo mileno: Una primera aproximación," *Este País*, April 2006, 2-23. Furthermore, when I examined all of the degrees awarded to economics graduates from the National University, I discovered dozens of prominent politicians who never completed their thesis, and therefore their degrees, in spite of having listed a completed degree on their official résumés and, more surprising, gone on for graduate degrees from the United States and Mexico. "Titulados Facultad de Economia, 1934-1999," www.herzog.economia.unam.mx, 2007. Fox was awarded his degree on March 25, 1999, with the defense of his thesis. *Diario del Sureste*, March 24, 1999.

and their preparation with the self-made revolutionary politicians who preceded them.[36]

The second figure that stands out in the Alemán administration is that half of all top members of his administration were lawyers. This figure has never been replicated in any other presidential administration. The second highest discipline represented among his cohort is engineering, but is only true of 7 percent of his colleagues. Thus Alemán can be said to have established the norm for most of the predemocratic era: civilian, college-educated, and lawyers.

An examination of the Salinas and Zedillo administrations, which I have designated as the chronological parameters of the democratic transition, corresponds closely with the characteristics used to describe the second, most well-known technocratic wave of leadership. The most notable quality is the peak reached among college-educated politicians, which tops out at 94 percent under Salinas, its highest level in all administrations. Second, lawyers decline to only one in three during the two transitional administrations but, as was true within the generational patterns, remains fairly in line with percentages found during last years of the predemocratic era, at least since the mid-1970s.

It is also the case that economists reached their highest representation in a presidential administration during the transition era, accounting for one in five politicians. Some analysts argue that the political failures of these economists may well have contributed to the acceleration of the democratic process.[37] What is equally important is that these two administrations anticipated the importance of the newer disciplines because politicians with these backgrounds, in percentages equal to economists, are as well represented from 1988 to 2000 as in the years following 2000.

In the democratic post-2000 era, a significant decline begins to occur among economist politicians, reaching a low under Calderón and corresponding to the levels under de la Madrid. Furthermore, although it is clearly apparent that both Zedillo and Fox are responsible for the increase in non-college-educated politicians after years of decline, Calderón reversed this trend, confirming that the third technocratic wave will likely be as well educated as the second one. Similarly to Salinas's administration,

---

36. Dr. Ignacio Chávez Sánchez, who was born in 1897 but was not part of Alemán's political group, made precisely this distinction for their generation when he was appointed president of the prestigious Colegio Nacional de San Nicolás (University of Michoacán) in Morelia in 1920 at the age of twenty-three. Chávez Sánchez was one of Mexico's most distinguished cardiologists, personal physician to presidents, and president of the National University, 1961–66. Personal interview, June 13, 1978.

37. For a careful explanation of this outcome, see Pamela Starr, "Monetary Mismanagement and Inadvertent Democratization in Technocratic Mexico," *Studies in Comparative International Development* 33, no. 4 (Winter 1999): 35–65.

engineering graduates, including chemical engineers, are more important in his administration. The postdemocratic administrations also are populated with a sizable representation of politicians from business administration and accounting programs, a pattern that Zedillo introduced.

The presidential breakdown of administrations into the democratic transition and democratic consolidation eras suggest that some patterns in the latter era are fundamentally achieved by the two previous administrations, which is true of newer specializations, whereas other patterns that clearly defined the transitional administrations, such as the pronounced role of economists, decline precipitously from Zedillo to Calderón. At least in terms of professional and educational backgrounds, the changes occurring from predemocratic to the postdemocratic periods are typically quite well defined, and less well-established trends that began in the transitional period either persist (such as the emphasis on newer specializations in the last four administrations) or are altered, such as the decline of economists, who are associated to some degree disparagingly with the ills of the Salinas administration and perhaps equally so with the initial economic crisis during the first weeks of the Zedillo administration.

Naturally, one of the most important influences that drives some of the changes brought about by democratization is party affiliation. As we have seen in chapter 3, PRI militants overwhelmingly dominated party militants among national political leadership until 2000. Therefore, in addition to examining the generational and presidential driven–patterns, what has been the role of party affiliation and militancy? When analyzed from this perspective, strikingly different patterns begin to emerge that can be linked to democratization or that cross the boundaries of changing political models.

PAN and the Party of the Democratic Revolution (PRD) members, given the percentages of their partisans who have reached prominent political positions, if they do indeed exercise an influence will largely do so, especially in the executive branch in the post-2000 period. For example, of the 292 PAN members in the data set, 150 of them, slightly more than half, served in both the PAN-controlled presidential administrations since 2000. In the case of PRD members, who number sixty-five, an even higher percentage is achieved because nearly seven out of ten can be found in those two administrations alone.

In a number of cases, a politician's party affiliation has a dramatic impact on their educational and professional credentials (see table 6.3). One would expect the figures for PRI members to be higher for law, the traditional profession, and for no college degrees, given the huge numbers of PRI members who have served in the pre-1988 administrations. What is most striking about these figures is the contribution of PRD politicians to

Table 6.3. Party Affiliation and Academic Backgrounds of Leading Politicians

| Party Affiliation | Economics | Law | Degree (%) | | |
| | | | None | Business | Others |
| --- | --- | --- | --- | --- | --- |
| None | 23.4 | 22.8 | 7.0 | 7.6 | 17.1 |
| PAN | 5.1 | 32.2 | 15.8 | 13.0 | 13.4 |
| PRD | 18.5 | 13.8 | 12.3 | 4.6 | 36.9 |
| PRI | 9.0 | 36.4 | 23.9 | 3.2 | 10.9 |

*Source*: Mexican Political Biographies Project, 2009.

Others refers to degrees in the liberal arts and more recent specializations, such as communications, sciences, and mathematics. The traditional professional degrees of medicine, architecture, engineering, and agronomy are excluded from the table to highlight these patterns. They have varied little over time.

the post-1988 trends in two ways. First, PRD members, regardless of age, have come from economist backgrounds in percentages unlike the other two parties. However, unlike the PAN and PRI economist politicians, most are graduates of the National University. Second, the newer disciplines are heavily represented among PRD members, but unlike the PAN and PRI products of these disciplines, they are largely confined to the social sciences rather than the more technical disciplines.

A second conclusion that can be reached from these data is that few members of PAN are economists. The explanation for the decline of economists among national politicians in the democratic period can be attributed largely to their exaggerated underrepresentation among PANistas. In fact, if the two postdemocratic presidential administrations did not have so many PRI members represented in their ranks, the actual decline in economists would be staggering. In effect, the sizable presence of PRI politicians in both Fox's and Calderon's administrations has allowed economists to continue their presence.

Finally, politicians unaffiliated with any party, third in numbers to PRI and PAN members, are actually those who are most likely to be or have been economists, suggesting the view that many economists are appointed due to their professional abilities and reputation rather than any party affiliation. This perception of unaffiliated party members is reinforced by the fact that none of the major parties' partisans are as well educated as the unaffiliated politicians, 93 percent of whom have college degrees.[38]

Mexican politicians who can be described as true party militants, having held state and national party positions, share a number of characteristics

38. The only party members who have a higher level of education are the seventeen members of the Convergencia and Green parties (PVEM).

that distinguish them from their nonmilitant peers. In chapter 3, I noted how they have pursued different careers from other national politicians and how the introduction of electoral competition since 1994 has highlighted the importance of party roots for all politicians. Furthermore, the careers of these politicians also are influenced by their early educational choices; in reverse, their educational choices may make them more or less likely to follow paths in their respective party apparatus as a means of achieving national political prominence. Compared to all party members, militants boast some different (and in some cases more exaggerated) background characteristics from the rest of their peers.

Overall, among the most active party members, those from the PRD and the small, leftist parties are the most out of sync in nearly all of their educational choices, undervaluing law even among those early Left leaders, which is not unexpected, given the inability of individuals sharing a leftist ideology to pursue their social and economic goals through a corrupt, powerless judicial system. PRD militants also are less likely to have obtained a college education, which in large part is a product[39] of their working-class socioeconomic backgrounds. As is the case of PRD members generally, militants also have diverse educational professional backgrounds (see table 6.4). Finally, PAN militants, even more so that PAN members, have rarely pursued college degrees in economics. This minuscule representation among economists can be explained by the structure of the political system in which preeminent PAN leadership largely came from party and elective national legislative careers, where law and other fields would be more valued because PAN activists rarely were employed in federal and state bureaucracies, institutions that seek out economists.

The policy-making impact of the three waves of leadership is most telling in the executive branch, especially before 2000, and can be understood more precisely when examining each generation of cabinet-level secretaries

---

39. Nydia Iglesias, an analyst for the National Bank of Mexico, provided an interesting comparison between Calderón's first cabinet and that of PRD governor of the Federal District, Marcelo Ebrard. These differences suggest what a PRD government might be like. The PRD as a party, and Ebrard as governor, have done more to promote gender equality than any other party or leader. Thus, his cabinet boasts 53 percent women, compared to the national cabinet of 21 percent women (in the nineteen official cabinet posts). This distribution alone would affect the composition of a PRD cabinet versus a PAN or PRI government. The Federal District cabinet is populated by 16 percent lawyers, 11 percent economists, and 74 percent other disciplines compared to 21, 26, and 53 percent, respectively, of the national cabinet. Equally interesting is that the educational origin of the Federal District cabinet is 32 percent UNAM, 37 percent other Mexico City institutions, and 31 percent provincial schools in contrast to only 11, 53, and 37 percent, respectively, nationally. A future PRD government would likely be much more partisan, with 69 percent of the Federal District cabinet affiliated with a political party. See Nydia Iglesias, "The New Cabinets," *Review of the Economic Situation in Mexico*, December 2000, 422–25.

Table 6.4. Party Militants and Academic Backgrounds of Leading Politicians

| Party | Economics | Law | Degree (%) None | Business | Others |
|---|---|---|---|---|---|
| PAN/PDM | 3.1 | 31.2 | 18.4 | 10.2 | 13.3 |
| PRD/Left | 12.2 | 20.1 | 31.1 | 1.8 | 22.6 |
| PRI | 10.6 | 42.3 | 22.7 | 2.9 | 9.6 |
| Total | 10.0 | 34.0 | 22.0 | 4.4 | 12.8 |

*Source*: Mexican Political Biographies Project, 2009.

Others refers to degrees in the liberal arts and more recent specializations, such as communications, sciences, and mathematics. The traditional professional degrees of medicine, architecture, engineering, and agronomy are excluded from the table to highlight these patterns. They have varied little over time.

Left = PSUM, PPS, PRT, PST, PCM, PT, and PP.

and director generals as well as their assistant secretaries. Because our sample of cabinet secretaries since 1935 is complete, the data on these patterns are definitive. Not surprisingly, cabinet secretaries are better educated, as measured by the percentage of college graduates, than any other group except supreme court justices, all of whom have law degrees.

Cabinet secretaries who were born in the first decade of the twentieth century, the preeminent generation of Miguel Alemán, and were overwhelmingly lawyers, more than half having completed a law degree. Despite the importance of law, economics graduates make their strongest mark on cabinet secretaries, reaching the levels economists represent among all politicians in the 1950s generation (table 6.1) and as early as the 1920s generation, the generation represented by Presidents Luis Echeverría Alvarez (1922) and José López Portillo (1920). By the 1950s generation, one of three Mexican cabinet secretaries was an economist. Their presence on the cabinet explains to a great extent why economists are viewed as so influential— these are the politicians most Mexicans read about in their newspapers or see on television. The other profession that is overrepresented among cabinet secretaries compared to all politicians is engineers, third only to law and economics. Finally, by the 1950s generation, a fifth of all cabinet secretaries were trained in the newer disciplines, suggesting the importance of that professional background in the democratic administrations.

Cabinet secretaries' own backgrounds are crucial for understanding these and other patterns. Just as presidents appoint cabinet secretaries, often in their own image, cabinet secretaries appoint assistant secretaries, oficial mayores, division heads, and department heads. These executive branch appointees often become the next generation of cabinet secretaries, thus repeating the pattern. Therefore, to anticipate the future trends, especially what might happen after Calderón, it is worth evaluating the credentials of assistant secretaries. Economists are more common among these politicians than among their more prominent bosses.

What is most significant about the data on assistant secretaries is the fact that among the youngest generation, born after 1960, more than two-fifths are economists, suggesting that instead of a decline in economists in these federal agencies, we may continue to see a strong, perhaps even increased presence. Assistant secretaries are even better educated than cabinet secretaries.

The extraordinary levels of education among assistant secretaries is a dramatic occurrence in Alemán's generation, in which 92 percent are college-educated compared to only 70 percent in the previous generation. By the 1920s and 1930s generations, 98 percent are college educated; by the following two generations, only 3 out of 257 assistant secretaries did not graduate from college.

Another prominent political position that may have some explanatory potential in predicting future trends is that of governor, given the fact, as suggested earlier, that five of the six presidential candidates from the three leading parties in 2000 and 2006 were former governors. Again, as is true of our data on cabinet secretaries, we have a nearly complete sample of the 534 politicians who have served as governors since 1935. The college backgrounds of two-thirds of all governors is fairly evenly divided between no degrees and law degrees. Governors with law degrees number the same as all other prominent politicians collectively (approximately a third). Governors' educational backgrounds demonstrate that it has been a post that was traditionally more accessible to less educated individuals and therefore to those who came from more modest socioeconomic circumstances since three out of ten did not complete a college degree.

Governors are significantly underrepresented among those educational credentials that define the two recent technocratic waves, given that only half as many governors as all other national politicians are economists by training or have business degrees. Equally important is the fact that a third fewer governors are as likely as their national political peers to have pursued recent professional specializations in college.

During the democratic era, the professional orientation of recent governors shifted significantly to the extent that they share much in common with other politicians in the Fox and Calderón administrations. Several patterns stand out. First, law continues to be the overwhelming choice of governors, increasing to two out of five individuals. Second, unlike their national peers, even younger governors from the democratic period have not pursued economics as an undergraduate professional degree. For example, in the Fox administration, 15 percent of prominent politicians were economists, compared to only 6 percent of governors. On the other hand, there are more governors with business administration degrees than among other politicians since 2000, and in the Fox administration 14 percent of all governors earned such degrees. Interestingly, governors continue to be less well educated than most other politicians, particularly since Calderón became president. Finally, they, too, have increased the newer specializations in their backgrounds, but not to the same level as all other politicians since 2000.

Finally, although I devoted chapter 5 to the role of women politicians in the three political eras, it is useful to identify how women have contributed to these trends either as politicians who emulated the most successful male figures or as individuals who established different, early patterns emulated by men. Naturally, women account for a tiny number of leading politicians in the older generations, represented for the first time in the Alemán generation. Only 18 women emerge from the ranks of the 744 politicians who were born between 1900 to 1920.

Women stand out from male politicians in the sheer numbers that succeeded without a college education, not surprising given the parental bias against women seeking higher education in the first half of the twentieth century.[40] Nevertheless, this distortion persists overwhelmingly among women born during the four generations from 1900 to 1939, more than half of whom claimed no college degrees. Among all women from all generations, one out of three did not graduate from a university. Generally, they were three to four generations behind males in their educational achievements. Not until the post-1960s generations do women equal men in their level of undergraduate training. (table 6.5)

A second distinct pattern among women is that they provide the leading edge in diversifying their professional choices and educational degrees away from traditional male choices. As the data in table 6.5 clearly demonstrate, women beginning in the 1920s generation begin to surpass men in pursuing atypical undergraduate programs, a choice made by nearly half of all women politicians by the 1960s. One out of four women politicians chose nontraditional degrees. Many women have pursued degrees in the social sciences. For example, Calderón's secretary of foreign relations, Patricia Espinosa Cantellano, completed her elementary and secondary education at the German School in Mexico City, a private institution

40. Martha Robles, an important intellectual born in 1948, described this pattern in detail in a lengthy letter. Her father, a prominent PAN politician, and her grandfather expressed strong traditional patterns toward women, whereas her mother refused to conform to those expectations. Martha was the only female among seventy-two grandchildren to graduate from college. Personal communication, June 4, 1978.

Table 6.5. Educational Choices of Politicians by Generation and Gender

| | Degree % | | | | | |
|---|---|---|---|---|---|---|
| | Economics | | None | | Others | |
| Generation | Women | Men | Women | Men | Women | Men |
| Pre-1889 | – | 0 | – | 42.4 | – | 3.0 |
| 1890-99 | – | 0.7 | – | 44.6 | – | 5.9 |
| 1900-1909 | 0 | 1.9 | 57.1 | 27.9 | 0 | 9.0 |
| 1910-19 | 0 | 3.0 | 72.7 | 29.9 | 9.1 | 8.9 |
| 1920-29 | 7.4 | 7.8 | 51.9 | 19.3 | 14.8 | 8.8 |
| 1930-39 | 2.4 | 11.7 | 56.1 | 12.3 | 17.1 | 12.0 |
| 1940-49 | 14.3 | 18.3 | 22.4 | 7.2 | 32.7 | 19.0 |
| 1950-59 | 18.9 | 23.9 | 18.9 | 5.0 | 39.6 | 17.2 |
| 1960- | 15.4 | 19.8 | 7.7 | 9.9 | 46.2 | 16.5 |
| All generations | 10.9 | 10.0 | 35.3 | 20.7 | 27.4 | 11.7 |

Source: Mexican Political Biographies Project, 2009.

Others refers to degrees in the liberal arts and more recent specializations, such as communications, sciences, and mathematics. The traditional professional degrees of medicine, architecture, engineering, and agronomy are excluded from the table to highlight these patterns. They have varied little over time.

popular among numerous recent politicians raised in the Federal District,[41] and then graduated from the Colegio de Mexico's prestigious international relations program in 1982. She did postgraduate work in international law at the Institute of Higher International Studies in Geneva and also spent a year studying German in Ahrensburg, Germany. She joined the Foreign Service in 1981, shortly before completing her undergraduate degree.[42]

Finally, women have not been far behind men in the percentages who have chosen to become economists. They began choosing this professional program at about the same time as men, and from the 1930s to the present, with the exception of one generation, they follow the same upward trend until the 1950s, declining slightly (as is true of men) after 1960. Because

41. The Colegio Alemán Alexander von Humboldt has produced numerous leading figures in the political and capitalist world, and its alumni family names read like a list of the power elite. It is extraordinary that at least three other cabinet members in the Calderón administration in addition to Espinosa Cantellano were graduates in the 1970s: Luis Téllez Kuenzler (1977), secretary of commerce; Agustín Carstens Carstens (1977), secretary of the treasury; and Jesús F. Reyes Heroles (1971), director general of Pemex. Oscar de Buen Richkarday, assistant secretary of commerce, also was a graduate. Intellectuals are equally well represented, including Federico Reyes Heroles (1974), brother of Jesús. Both were the children of Jesús Reyes Heroles, prominent intellectual and secretary of government.

42. Los Angeles Times, November 28, 2006; www.presidencia.gob.mx, 2008.

women are latecomers to national politics, and because economics becomes available at about the same time they entered the political world, the percentage of women politicians who have been economists is actually slightly higher than for men.

## CONCLUSIONS

The traditional view of Mexican leadership suggests that only one significant shift in the professional training and education credentials has occurred in the second half of the twentieth century. A comprehensive examination of prominent politicians since the mid-1930s suggests otherwise. Indeed, we can identify and describe three distinct waves of leadership based on these credentials. These three waves are important because they help explain transformations to the political system and are products of those very transformations.

How are these broad shifts in background credentials tied to democratic political developments in Mexico? The first wave, which I argued is closely associated with President Miguel Alemán's generation, produced a dramatic change in leadership in the 1940s and 1950s. This wave, as described, is most remarkable for a change in two qualities characterizing national leadership: a significant decline in career military politicians and a concomitant increase in civilian leadership as well as an equally significant increase in college-educated leaders. These patterns reflect important underlying shifts about political behavior.

In the broadest sense, a movement away from determining leadership on the basis of who exerts the greatest control over the means of violence to an emphasis on controlling political institutions through nonviolent means, such as an all-encompassing, monopolizing political party, might be viewed as a shift from an authoritarian system controlled by actors with specially earned skills on the battlefield or in military academies to a less authoritarian system open to a larger pool of competitors whose political skills are largely nonviolent. Critically, it also shifts the task of political recruitment away from military academies, from military service, and from battlefield experiences during the revolution and subsequent revolts in the 1920s. In particular, public universities and preparatory schools in the capital overwhelmingly replace these former military sources of recruitment and socialization.

The second, well-known wave of change in educational and professional credentials is symbolized by President Carlos Salinas. It is equally dramatic in its consequences, but boasts different characteristics and produces different results. The generations born in the 1940s and 1950s who come to political fruition in the late 1980s and 1990s, also are civilian (almost exclusively) and college-educated. They differ significantly from the Alemán generation in that their educational choices shift from the generalist (typified by lawyers) to specialists (typified by economists) and from Mexican public institutions to Mexican and U.S. private institutions. In making such educational choices, these leaders increased the emphasis on economics as a professional preparation and on a narrower range of federal economic agencies as the source of leadership. This narrowing, resulting from the fact that economically trained politicians obtained the most influential political positions, including that of president, strongly exacerbated political elite divisions. This occurred especially among those politicians who wanted a stronger voice in the decision-making process, and among those whose backgrounds, with little emphasis on economics, placed them in the predemocratic period political institutions exercising the least influence on policy, specifically the legislative branch, gubernatorial leadership, and the political party. These politicians from the incumbent party became increasingly alienated from their peers.[43] Opposition party leadership from the Left and the PAN, especially beginning with the 1988 presidential election, further increased the pressures on the technocratic wing of government leadership. These divisions contributed significantly to the democratic transition from 1988 to 2000, generating conditions that were conducive to the democratic transformation in 2000.

Finally, a third wave in politicians' educational and professional credentials can be discerned. As is the case of the two preceding waves, it also builds on qualities that characterize each preceding wave. Again, however, there are important distinctions. First and foremost, the opposition parties, especially the PAN, contribute significantly to its overriding qualities. These parties did not affect the characteristics that highlighted the two previous waves. Second, the structuring of the opposition parties' roles prior to the 1990s notably influenced the qualities of their leaders, many of whom achieved top positions after 2000. Third, electoral competition requires skills that are different from those of bureaucratic managers, permitting a reversal in nearly a century of increasing levels of education among Mexican national leaders. Fourth, the presence of PANistas, the new incumbent party from 2000 to 2012, reduces the impact of U.S. graduate programs and reintroduces a somewhat traditional emphasis from an earlier era on European graduate studies. Fifth, a pattern of increasing

---

43. For an analysis of this consequence as it contributed to the development of the Democratic current and eventually the PRD and Cárdenas's opposition candidacy for the presidency in 1988, see Kathleen Bruhn, *Taking on Goliath: The Emergence of a New Left Party and the Struggle for Democracy in Mexico* (University Park: Pennsylvania University Press, 1997), 84–85.

specialization continues, reflecting the increasing complexity of Mexico's economy and decision-making institutions. In this case, however, the specialization is not concentrated in one profession (economics) but is spread among a large number of disciplines, many of which are sought after by the private and social sectors, as business backgrounds and nongovernmental organizational backgrounds appear more frequently in the resumes of prominent public servants.[44] Thus, one can make the argument that in many ways democracy opened up leadership pools to a more diverse group while continuing a focus on specialization.

44. For the importance of nongovernmental organizational backgrounds in future politicians and the impact of such leaders on Mexican parties, see the excellent essay by S. Ilgu Ozler, "Out of the Plaza and into the Office: Social Movement Leaders in the PRD," *Mexican Studies* 25, no. 1 (Winter 2009): 125–54.

# 7

# Political Institutionalization and Public Policy

## The Impact of the Alemán Generation

Throughout this book I note the importance of specific generations when identifying important shifts in leadership characteristics, formal and informal alike. Among all of these generations, one contributed most significantly to the development of Mexico's political leadership model in the predemocratic era—that of Miguel Alemán. This generation would stand alone if only because Alemán and his collaborators began the era of civilian governance, ending the domination of revolutionary veterans over the presidency.[1] However, Alemán's collaborators define and mold many patterns that generate long-term consequences for political elite recruitment, composition, socialization, and public policy orientations. John W. Sherman, a leading historian of Mexico, concurs with this assessment in terms of policy directions and new elite alliances, boldly stating that "Alemán is arguably the most important president in 20th-century Mexican history....Social scientists have given Lázaro Cárdenas disproportionate attention for crafting a political coalition under the auspices of his Party of the Mexican Revolution in 1938, but the real genius of modern Mexican political life was Alemán."[2]

This chapter examines closely the intertwining of their socialization and career experiences, identifying long-term patterns that made a major imprint on the Mexican political model. To provide more precision in the analysis of this generation, which as noted was largely born in the first decade of the twentieth century, we examine three university generations

1. President Emilio Portes Gil, the interim president congress appointed from 1928 to 1930 after president-elect Alvaro Obregón's assassination, was the only exception to this military leadership from 1920 to 1946.
2. "The Mexican 'Miracle' and Its Collapse," in Michael C. Meyer and William H. Beezley, eds., *The Oxford History of Mexico* (New York: Oxford University Press, 2000), 576. For more details of what Stephen R. Niblo labels "Alemán's counterrevolution," see his *Mexico in the 1940s: Modernity, Politics and Corruption* (Wilmington: SR Books, 1999), 160ff.

that include and overlap Alemán's own university generation. As noted previously, Alemán graduated from the National School of Law in 1929, and he and his fellow graduates are incorporated in the 1926–30 school generation. Both he and his closest collaborators have identified the previous school generation, that of 1921–25, as the source of numerous close friendships, many of them mentoring relationships stemming from the fact that significant numbers of this previous class were young professors of the 1926–30 graduating classes.[3] Finally, I also analyze the 1931–35 university generations, because so many of these students overlapped with Alemán's class and in some cases were taught by his generation, either in the National Preparatory School and at the National University, or in public universities in the provinces.[4]

It can be argued that the Alemán generation established the following characteristics of Mexico's political model during much of the second half of the twentieth century. First, that Mexican universities, specifically the National University and National Preparatory School, would become the dominant source of political elite training, socialization, and recruitment for most of the twentieth century. Second, that the experiences of this generation as children of the revolution reinforced a strong sense of unity among their members and a strong desire for peaceful change. Third, that their views of the revolution and violence increased their orientation toward reinforcing civilian control, represented by increasing the influence of the executive branch, emphasizing national bureaucratic careers as the source of Mexico's most successful political leaders and stressing pragmatism rather than ideology in their decision making. Fourth, their involvement as students in José Vasconcelos's opposition campaign for the presidency in 1929 furthered their desire to strengthen civilian control of the government and to subordinate the armed forces to civilian leadership. Fifth, the importance of civilian control was represented by the extraordinary growth in lawyers and legal careers in the backgrounds of national politicians.[5] Sixth,

3. Roderic Ai Camp, "Education and Political Recruitment in Mexico: The Alemán Generation," *Journal of Inter-American Studies and World Affairs* 8 (August 1976): 295–321.

4. Roderic Ai Camp, *Mexico's Leaders: Their Education and Recruitment* (Tucson: University of Arizona Press, 1980), table 6.5, "Students and Professors of the 'Alemán Generation' Who Followed Public Careers," 139ff. It is important to point out that Alemán not only became friends with students from overlapping generations but also knew students from many other professional programs, including medicine and engineering. As José Hernández Terán, secretary of hydraulic resources in Díaz Ordaz's administration pointed out, "there were about 600 students altogether during his generation. As a student he knew many different students of various generations quite intimately. There were many cases of co-students helping each other in their professional careers." As noted earlier, many of his professors also were appointed to cabinet posts. Personal interview, Mexico City, July 28, 1974.

5. For the implications of the shifts to and from lawyers, see Peter S. Cleaves's interesting analysis in *Professions and the State: The Mexican Case* (Tucson: University of Arizona Press,

and finally, as suggested previously, the Alemán (not the Salinas) generation represents the first technocratic wave among national political leadership. As the firsthand testimony of many members of the Alemán generation to the author suggested, their exposure to the revolution and their educational experiences were critical to their formation and their decision to enter public life. The first of these shared experiences, as suggested earlier, contributed to their sense of unity. Their shared university experiences, and for many the risks they shared in the Vasconcelos campaign, strongly supported this view.[6] Indeed, for many members of this generation, the Vasconcelos campaign became a forerunner of Alemán's campaign in 1946 when interpreted as opposition to the armed forces' control over the Mexican government.[7] As one member of their generation expressed it, the

politization of the students was in response to the circumstances of the country beginning to evolve politically, based on the Constitution of 1917, as a representative democracy, of federal character, respecting state sovereignty and autonomy theoretically. In reality, we were living in a military dictatorship of the victorious caudillos of the Revolution. The contrast between constitutional theory, doctrinairely speaking, and the reality, consisted of fictitious elections but an authentic military dictatorship, determined that *Vasconcelismo* headed a movement that repudiated the military and supported a civil ideal. I wish to say that the historic moment was to liquidate the revolutionary caudillos and begin to give truth to the political constitution of the United Mexican States of February 5, 1917.[8]

A fourth of the three university generations identified with Alemán were student activists. No combined group of university generations among all Mexican politicians since 1920 achieved that level of student activism.[9] Most student activists and leaders came from the provinces, not Mexico City.[10] Even more important than their activism generally was their direct

1987). For society generally, see David Lorey, *The Rise of the Professions in Twentieth-Century Mexico: University Graduates and Occupational Change since 1929* (Los Angeles: UCLA Latin American Center Publications, 1994).

6. Roderic Ai Camp, "La campaña presidencial de 1929 y el liderazgo político en México," *Historia Mexicana* 27 (Fall 1977): 231–59.

7. Interestingly, the only dissenting voice from this view among the numerous political and intellectual figures I interviewed who were actual participants and observers of this campaign was Daniel Cosío Villegas, one of Mexico's most distinguished historians. He believed the campaign was focused on a single issue, that Mexicans were tired of presidents who all came from the northern states, the so-called Sonora dynasty. Personal interview, June 30, 1975.

8. Personal communication from Ricardo Rivera Pérez, November 21, 1975. Rivera also recalled Vasconcelos commenting in his sociology class that "Mexicans lived in a fictitious democracy," and that he "ran for president in order to protect the real democracy."

9. Mexican Political Biographies Project, 2009.

10. The Federal District was hugely underrepresented compared with all other regions. Mexican Political Biography Project, 2009.

involvement in the 1929 presidential campaign.[11] It is crucial to remember that the 1929 campaign was the first presidential race presided over by the official party, the National Revolutionary Party (PNR), the antecedent of the Institutional Revolutionary Party (PRI). The election was held to replace President Emilio Portes Gil, who was selected by congress to become the interim president in 1928 after General Alvaro Obregón was elected in the contentious 1928 presidential race and was assassinated before taking office.[12]

Formal student leaders from student societies affiliated with provincial universities joined students from similar organizations in the Federal District. Because they represented multiple generations of students, the campaign provided an additional vehicle for bridging more than one generation.[13] Most important, it established a connection between two future presidents, Miguel Alemán and Adolfo López Mateos, and many of their key collaborators.[14]

11. For an outstanding analysis of the antecedent student movements from 1910 through 1917, see Javier Garciadiego Dantan, "Movimientos estudiantiles durante la Revolución mexicana," in Jaime E. Rodríguez, ed., *The Revolutionary Process in Mexico: Essays on Political and Social Change, 1880-1940* (Los Angeles: UCLA Latin American Program, 1990), 115–60.

12. The most comprehensive account of this campaign is John Skirius's excellent analysis, *José Vasconcelos y la cruzada de 1929* (Mexico: Siglo XXI, 1978).

13. Efraín Brito Rosado, a leader of the Vasconcelos movement, describes the phenomenon: "During my life in the National Autonomous University of Mexico, I had friendships and acquaintances with numerous students who later occupied distinguished positions in Mexico's public life. These students were from diverse academic classes and diverse disciplines, but because of my situation as a leader and president of the Federation of University Students, I had contact with them. Miguel Alemán and Adolfo López Mateos, later presidents of the republic. Antonio Carrillo Flores who later occupied among other positions, secretary of the treasury, foreign relations, and director of the National Finance Bank, Octavio Sentíes, actual head [1974] of the Department of the Federal District; there are many more, professors as well as students from my era, who were and continue being my friends." Another student leader from the provinces, Roberto Mantilla Molina, who was treasurer of the Student Society of the preparatory school of the University of Veracruz in Jalapa, came to know López Mateos when Vasconcelos visited Veracruz. Sentíes was head of preparatory school's news department for the student newspaper *El Eco Estudiantil*, which he later directed.

14. For example, Benito Coquet Lagunes, a strike leader for the autonomy movement at the National University, who eventual graduated from the University of Veracruz in 1935, became oficial mayor of government under Alemán, secretary of the presidency under Adolfo Ruiz Cortines, and director general of social security under López Mateos. Salvador Azuela, son of the novelist, also participated in the university autonomy movement and joined the Vasconcelos campaign as an orator. He attended law school with Alemán and was a personal friend of López Mateos. His brother, Mariano, became a Supreme Court justice under Alemán, and his nephew served as president of the supreme court under Fox and Calderón. Mexican Political Biographies Project, 2009. Even future founders of PAN were notable in the campaign, including Daniel Kuri Breña, who became the first president of the Mexico Autonomous Institute of Technology (ITAM) in 1946 and whose son-in-law served as assistant secretary of government for legislative affairs in the Fox administration. *Diccionario Porrúa* (Mexico: Porrúa, 1995), 1938. Finally, Manuel Moreno Sánchez, who graduated in

The campaign also brought together numerous prominent professors who were linked to many students. No individual appears more frequently in the recollections of those future leaders who actively participated in the movement than Manuel Gómez Morín, co-founder of the National Action Party (PAN) and the intellectual and political mentor of dozens of leading political figures.[15] Many of these activists suffered persecution and imprisonment.[16] It is also clear that a number of veterans of the 1929 campaign, even though they pursued successful public careers, also had a tendency to involve themselves in opposition campaigns in later years.[17]

A leading professor of Miguel Alemán's classmates, a member of the earlier graduating classes in the early 1920s, Francisco González de la Vega became the attorney general of Mexico in 1946. He studied under Vasconcelos, and they became friends. He joined Vasconcelos's campaign as a propagandist and recalled an intense interest among students in debate and oratory during those generations. He confirmed the more widespread interest in student politics compared to later generations he himself taught at the National School of Law.[18]

For other professors from this generation, Vasconcelos's presidential campaign became their sole experience with Mexican politics. Ignacio Chávez Sánchez, the president of the National University from 1961 to 1966 and the leading cardiologist of his generation, described Vasconcelos as the "apostle of his generation," and a "very impulsive man with a volcanic personality." His educational work for Chávez and numerous other students was an inspiration, influencing Chávez's values. Ironically, Chávez was the personal physician to former president Calles. Despite the fact that Chávez

1932, was a campaign orator for Vasconcelos and a close friend of López Mateos. President López Mateos rewarded him with a senate seat, and he became president of the senate, 1958–64, and was considered by some observers as an early precandidate for the PRI presidential nomination in 1964. Moreno Sánchez maintained his maverick status, becoming the presidential candidate of the short-lived Social Democratic Party in 1982, and supported the "Democratic Current" in the PRI in 1986 and Cuauhtémoc Cárdenas for president in 1988.

15. I am deeply indebted to Manuel Ulloa Ortiz, a disciple of Gómez Morín, graduate of the 1932 law class, and a prominent Catholic student leader, who later served as treasurer of PAN, for his extraordinary seventeen-page, single-spaced letter outlining in detail the history of the Vasconcelos movement.

16. Personal communication from Salvador Azuela, July 10, 1974.

17. Another member of the earlier university generation, Octavio Véjar Vázquez, who became attorney general of the Federal District and secretary of public education under President Avila Camacho, who joined the military justice system but campaigned for Vasconcelos, founded the National Independent Democratic Party in 1944 and became president of the Popular Party in 1949–52. Other leading professors, who were among the most prominent intellectuals in the twentieth century, including Daniel Cosío Villegas and Samuel Ramos, collaborated with Vasconcelos and directed his publication, *Antorcha*, when he left the country in 1929. Mexican Political Biographies Project, 2009.

18. Personal interview, July 23, 1974.

campaigned openly for Vasconcelos, Calles never said anything to him during the campaign and later said he respected him for not abandoning his personal political philosophy to keep his clients.[19]

In addition to those students who held leadership posts in formal student organizations, other students developed lasting friendships, adding to the cohesion of this generation, through their participation in preparatory and university publications. This experience had the added advantage of giving cohesion to a future generation of Mexico's most prominent intellectuals. This was a particularly important vehicle because Alemán himself directed the student magazine *Eureka* in the National Preparatory School, financed by his allowance.[20] Manuel R. Palacios, another student supporter of Vasconcelos who worked with the president on this student publication, recalls the magazine's editors: Adolfo Zamora, later director of the National Mortgage and Public Works Bank; Antonio Ortiz Mena, director general of the Mexican Institute of Social Security and secretary of the treasury; and Gabriel Ramos Millán, president of the National Corn Commission.[21]

One additional event that brought together leaders of the formal university organizations and individual students across various disciplines was a student strike in the early months of 1929 against the president of the National University, who wanted to impose a new system of exams.[22] The student opposition culminated in President Portes Gil granting the university autonomy later that year.[23] Students from this generation are in agreement that no cause and effect existed between motivations for participating in the student strike at the National University and the Vasconcelos campaign.[24] Nevertheless, many students who were active in this movement joined the Vasconcelos presidential campaign, indicative of their political

19. Personal interview, August 15, 1974. Also see his autobiographical comments about Vasconcelos in his "Discurso pronunciado en la ceremonia conmemorativa del xxv aniversario de la fundación de El Colegio Nacional," *Memoria, El Colegio Nacional* 6, nos. 203 (1967–68): 249–56.

20. Personal interview with Adolfo Zamora, July 24, 1974.

21. Personal communication to the author, February 1, 1973.

22. Letter from Ricardo Rivera Pérez Campos, director of the National Preparatory School, 1944–45, November 21, 1975.

23. As indicated earlier in the book, Portes Gil himself, and several collaborators in his administration, opposed the appointment of the law school dean by a university president with government approval when they were students and consequently founded the Free School of Law. Thus, he personally believed that the university should be self-governing. Letter from Eduardo Bustamante, December 16, 1975. Donald Mabry concurred with this view (see note 24).

24. For more details about the movement and its link to other student university strikes and to the Vasconcelos campaign, see Donald Mabry's comments in *The Mexican University and the State: Student Conflicts, 1910–1971* (College Station: Texas A&M Press, 1982), 273.

interest generally and their commitment to pursue political careers after 1929, despite Vasconcelos's defeat.[25]

Student support for Vasconcelos is linked to the broader issue of anti-reelectionism, a principle that is one of the foundations of Francisco Madero's movement in 1910. Palacios describes their ideals in support of Vasconcelos's candidacy as "anti-reelectionist, enemies of the dictatorship and nationalistic."[26] Many students who supported Vasconcelos already had participated in the more dangerous campaign against Obregón in 1927. When it became apparent that General Alvaro Obregón would run for the presidency a second time in 1928, a number of students supported other candidates in 1927, and several, along with the candidates themselves, were brutally murdered. Alemán supported Generals Arnulfo R. Gómez and Francisco R. Serrano, who were executed, whereas others, such as Manuel R. Palacios, campaigned for Gilberto Valenzuela, a prominent civilian lawyer and politician. Efraín Brito Rosado, who also campaigned for these two men, argues that he was involved in both campaigns for the same reason, to achieve honest elections, a political motto of Madero's campaign.[27] Unlike many other student veterans of both campaigns, Brito Rosado continued his opposition to the government party, supporting General Juan Andrew Almazán against Avila Camacho in 1940.[28]

The depth of the support for Vasconcelos among students increased dramatically when supporters of the official party's candidate, Pascual Ortiz Rubio, attacked Vasconcelos's activists early in the campaign, killing a popular student leader and producing a general reaction against the PNR. The students' critical attitudes toward the PNR exerted a significant impact on public opinion.[29] This opinion lasted after the campaign because the PNR absorbed all the local political groups, which for many years had maintained individuals whom the students considered unprepared and corrupt in popularly elected public positions. The long-term impact of Mexican dissatisfaction with the PNR culminated in the creation of the PAN, which

25. Personal communication from Antonio Carrillo Flores, companion of Alemán at the National Preparatory School and the National School of Laws.

26. Manuel R. Palacios, personal communication.

27. Personal interview, August 11, 1974. He later supported Miguel Alemán because he would become the first civilian president.

28. Brito Rosado spent many periods in jail for his continued opposition between 1927 and 1940. Other students who were involved in the 1927 campaigns included Braulio Maldonado, who was elected federal deputy in 1946 and again in 1952 before Alemán left office. He became the first governor of Baja California after statehood in 1953. *Proceso*, December 15, 1986, 11–13; and Mexican Political Biographies Project, 2009.

29. Personal communication from Salvador Aceves, student supporter of the Vasconcelos campaign, and secretary of health under President Díaz Ordaz, January 29, 1976.

played a crucial role in the 1939 presidential campaign.[30] Alemán, in spite of being viewed as the civilian candidate of the PNR in 1946, never generated the same level of student and professor participation as Vasconcelos because both Vasconcelos supporters and civilian supporters within the PNR remained unsure whether the military would be eliminated from government leadership.[31]

Nevertheless, their participation in the Vasconcelos campaign paved the way for these future politicians to support Lázaro Cárdenas in his break with Calles in June 1935. They threw their support to Cárdenas because they viewed Calles as responsible for Vasconcelos's defeat. If one also views Cárdenas as a dissenter and reformer within the Calles-dominated system from 1928 to 1934, then it is logical that he would attract young people who would view him as a leader of the internal opposition, but also someone to whom they could give their support and who could affect their future political ambitions.

Alemán himself provides a personal variable that affects his strong personal sentiments in favor of the antireelectionist sentiment behind Vasconcelos. In early March 1929, General José Gonzalo Escobar led the last of the major rebellions by officers and army troops against the government. Alemán's father, a former revolutionary general who supported Madero, Carranza, and Obregón, opposed the constitutional reforms allowing for the reelection of President Obregón, joined the rebellion in Veracruz, and was killed on March 19.[32] Alemán not only carried this family tragedy with him but was placed in great personal danger by his father's participation and was saved from a possible similar fate by obtaining safe conduct. As Alemán noted, "My father was the person who most influenced my ideas. In my home, as a child, I heard the propaganda of Flores Magón, and others, which circulated in tiny pamphlets or booklets."[33]

30. For the linkage between the Vasconcelos campaign and the founding of PAN, see Donald J. Mabry, *Mexico's Acción Nacional: A Catholic Alternative to Revolution* (Syracuse, N.Y.: Syracuse University Press, 1973), 22–23.

31. Personal communication from Eduardo Bustamante, assistant secretary of the treasury under Alemán and secretary of national properties under López Mateos, December 16, 1975.

32. For a complete accounting of these events and their chronology to the Vasconcelos movement which both preceded and followed the rebellion, see John W. F. Dulles's revealing account, based on numerous interviews and documentary sources. *Yesterday in Mexico: A Chronicle of the Revolution, 1919-1936* (Austin: University of Texas Press, 1961), 414ff.

33. Personal interview with Miguel Alemán, October 27, 1976. Specifically, he noted that because of his father, "I feared for my life, and finally, I was able to join some regular government troops in Tampico [commanded by a friend of his father's] who gave me a safe conduct back to Mexico City where I re-entered the National Preparatory School and completed my studies."

Many observers have wondered why so many of these talented students who were devoted supporters of Vasconcelos so easily transferred their loyalty to the very party and leadership they opposed in 1929. Obviously, any young adult interested in a successful political career could ascertain by 1946 that he or she would have to become associated with the antecedent parties of the PRI. But Julián Garza Tijerina, a career military medical officer who fought in various battles in the 1920s and held several positions on the National Executive Committee of the PNR in 1933 (shortly after its founding), offers a frank opinion about the campaign's long-term impact on their careers. He noted shortly before his death that the "huge student impact in favor of Vasconcelos was due to his being a cultured, courageous, and bright opponent with many roots among the students for his brilliant work as secretary of education; Vasconcelos in that time did not attack the revolution but its leaders." Those students, after his "political defeat and the candidate's voluntary exile, were insulted together with all of his supporters, called cowards for not taking up arms; the students that participated with Vasconcelos at the end of his career were dispersed to all parts of the country distanced from politics, completely disillusioned with their activity and their candidate."[34]

Antonio Armendáriz, Alemán's companion at the preparatory and law schools, further explains why they joined the government party. He argued that they were disillusioned after 1929, not because of Vasconcelos's ideas but because of the circumstances in which the campaign occurred. Therefore, "we had the opportunity to control the political apparatus of Mexico, but we lost—so then we had to learn how to win."[35] He believed this loss became a prod that prompted many of these young students and intellectuals to go into political life and become extremely capable politicians who did know how to win. He was convinced that many of them wanted to take the revolutionary ideas of the 1920s and permeate government with them.

It is important to note, however, that three-quarters of the collaborators during Alemán's presidential administration were not active members of the Mexican Revolutionary Party (PRM) or the PRI. The majority of his collaborators were not partisan politicians who sought to use the party as a vehicle for advancing their public careers but instead were chosen by successive presidents and their collaborators for influential posts in the executive branch. Suggestive of this orientation is the fact that among Alemán's own university generation, only 5 percent ever held a post in the PRI or

34. Personal communication, January 12, 1976, forwarded to the author by his son, Luis Garza Alejandro.
35. Personal interview, June 24, 1975.

Table 7.1.  Educational Experiences of the Alemán Generation

| | Institution Attended (%) | |
| --- | --- | --- |
| Generations | National Preparatory School | National University |
| 1921-25 | 37 | 53 |
| 1926-30 | 54 | 56 |
| 1931-35 | 42 | 59 |

Source: Mexican Political Biographies Project, 2009.

its antecedents, the lowest figure until the 1986-90 university generation. Even when we broaden political activism to include party activists generally, only 15 percent fall into that category, the smallest figure until the 1991-95 generation.[36]

The potential for the shared impact of educational experiences can be demonstrated by data from Alemán's generations. Of the preparatory education received by Alemán's university generation (1926-30), an extraordinary 54 percent attended his alma mater. Attendance at the National Preparatory School accounted for 37 percent of the previous generation and 46 percent of the following generation. No generation of national political leaders has attained that level of concentration at a single school before or since (table 7.1). A similar pattern emerges for graduates of the National University, who accounted for over half of all three school generations representing the Alemán generation.[37]

Even more important to the evolution of Mexico's political system, Alemán's preference for civilian, university-educated leadership marked a significant departure in the importance of presidential university generations being represented during a president's own administration. As the data in table 7.2 illustrate, in both the Alemán and in the Zedillo presidencies, one out of every five prominent politicians came from the president's own university generation.

We have noted that more than half of Alemán's most well-represented university generations, including his own, were graduates of the National University and the National Preparatory School. Alemán's generation reinforced this pattern in the long run by increasing the percentages of

36. Mexican Political Biography Project, 2009.
37. It deserves to be mentioned that among the first generation, many of whom taught Alemán's own class, and introduced notable public figures to the importance of economics, 7 percent attended undergraduate school in the United States or Europe. That figure has never been equaled since the 1921-25 generation.

Table 7.2.  Presidential University Generations and National Leadership

| Presidential University Generation | Collaborators from Presidential University Generation (%) |
| --- | --- |
| Alemán 1926–30 | 20 |
| López Mateos 1931–35 | 16 |
| Díaz Ordaz 1931–35 | 14 |
| Echeverría 1941–45 | 13 |
| López Portillo 1941–45 | 13 |
| De la Madrid 1951–55 | 14 |
| Salinas 1966–70 | 15 |
| Zedillo 1971–75 | 19 |
| Fox 1961–65 | 13 |
| Calderón 1981–85 | 13 |

Source: Mexican Political Biographies Project, 2009.

politicians who taught in preparatory schools or colleges, especially at the president's alma maters. Among his three university generations, six out of ten individuals were preparatory and college teachers, an increase of 18 percent over the entire 1910–20 decade. More than a third of his college generation taught at the National University, a pattern that continued until the university classes of the 1960s.

Alemán established the beginnings of a technocratic leadership, a generation of politicians who represented early characteristics of the later waves of technocratic politicians under Salinas and since 2006. This early technocratic generation, as is the case of its more recent counterparts, is characterized by their high level of formal education. Seventy percent of Alemán's political collaborators during his administration boasted college degrees. No other presidential administration achieved that level of education from 1935 to 1964, again demonstrating the value Alemán placed on his educated colleagues. Furthermore, 92 percent of the assistant secretaries he and his cabinet members appointed during his six years in office, many of whom became future cabinet secretaries, were college graduates.[38] By stressing educational credentials, Alemán also anticipated

38. Alemán's administration could not have been well represented by economists because most formally trained economists in Mexican public life did not graduate until the late 1930s and early 1940s, after the National School of Economics was founded, noted earlier. However, Antonio Martínez Báez, a companion of Alemán who became his secretary of industry and commerce in 1948, was the first secretary of that ministry to use numerous economists. He argued that the coordination of economic planning in the government was developed by economists from the Bank of Mexico, the National Finance Bank, the Foreign Trade Bank, and his ministry. He described the entrance of economists in Alemán's administration as massive, noting they were invited by lawyers who were in a position to make

two additional characteristics of future political leadership: an increasing emphasis on middle-class social backgrounds and on national bureaucratic careers. Despite the fact that a fourth of Alemán's friends from his student days were from modest social circumstances, during his administration 69 percent of the officeholders came from middle-class families, the highest level achieved by any administration until 1970. College graduates were more strongly valued in the executive and judicial branches than within the party bureaucracy and the legislative branches. Thus his generation, and their disciples, entrenched themselves in politics largely through successful bureaucratic careers, establishing that path as the one of follow until the 1990s.

The Alemán generations were also notable for the emphasis they gave to legal training. Lawyers have always exercised a disproportionate role in Mexican public life, and with the exception of career military officers during certain periods of the Porfiriato, lawyers have been a well-represented profession. Among college-educated politicians, no university generation before or since has been so overrepresented by lawyers than Alemán's own university generation from 1926 to 1930. Sixty-eight percent of his classmates graduated from law school. Immediately before and after, about half of the college graduates who were prominent politicians became lawyers, declining from 1941–45 generation through the 1980s generations.

These figures have been translated into a special emphasis of the Alemán generation in public careers: positions in the judicial branch. Since the 1920 university generations, only a small number of successful politicians have largely followed judicial careers, and even fewer achieved the post at the pinnacle of that career—that of Supreme Court justice. Among all politicians, fewer than one of twenty ever held a local judgeship, even though lawyers are overrepresented among top public figures generally. The three university generations associated with Alemán represent a nearly 200 percent increase in that average figure, and again, no university generation since has come anywhere close to that figure of one in seven politicians. For anyone valuing a judicial career, an important step up that ladder is to become a state supreme court judge, a position achieved by approximately 3 percent of leading politicians. Among Alemán's generations, the figures are four times as common. Finally, twice as many politicians among Alemán's groups became ministers of the supreme court as the average for all other university generations.[39]

---

39. Mexican Political Biographies Project, 2009.

The multiple experiences led to behaviors that influenced political careers and the locus of political decision making in Mexico prior to 1970. These experiences also contributed to certain preferences in policy orientations, many of which influenced later administrations. As I argued in my earlier work on the socialization of Mexican political figures, I do not suggest that the Alemán generation "agreed on ideological means as a result of these shared experiences; rather they gradually developed an elite culture characterized by certain unwritten rules or beliefs. Among these beliefs was *one* agreed upon means: orderly transition without large-scale violence."[40] The closed nature of Mexico's political system, especially prior to 1970, the fact that mentors and socializers often were the same individual, that success within the political and other elite sectors typically required active networking, and that the Alemán generation specifically shared common socialization experiences all contributed to the perpetuation of these beliefs and patterns. These conditions reinforced the ability of the Alemán generation to create informal rules of behavior that became ingrained in the political system and influenced political leadership and institutions for generations.[41]

All of the foregoing implications of the socialization of Mexican political leaders are important to understanding the political system they produced prior to 1988. But the most provocative implication would be to determine the relationship between what political leaders believe and value, and what they actually do in public life. The difficulties in establishing such a relationship are overwhelming and obvious. Not only does the pragmatic nature of public life as a profession make such a relationship highly tenuous, but there are so many other intervening variables that it would be impossible to attribute individual policy decisions solely to the beliefs of the decision maker. For example, "intervening between initial political socialization and incumbent behavior are political experiences that condition subsequent behavior irrespective of factors associated with initial socialization. These experiences interrupt the career sequence and retard or even reverse patterns formed during earlier stages."[42] These intervening experiences, even though political leaders themselves believe their preadult socialization processes have been more important, may indeed take precedence.

There are also a number of structural limitations on the impact of beliefs and values on elite decision making. Foremost in the Mexican political system prior to 2000 was the centralized and personal nature of decision

40. Roderic Ai Camp, *The Making of a Government: Political Leaders in Modern Mexico* (Tucson: University of Arizona Press, 1984), 153.

41. Camp, *Making of a Government*, 154.

42. Kenneth Prewitt, Heinz Eulau, and Betty H. Zisk, "Political Socialization and Political Roles," *Public Opinion Quarterly* 30 (Winter 1966–67): 579.

making in Mexico, in which broad policy decisions were made in the name of the president.[43] It is therefore difficult to attribute many policies to individual cabinet members. However, a few available case studies and numerous memoirs show that policy makers made numerous decisions within boundaries set forth by individual presidents from 1946 to 1970 and even persuaded the president to support their own views.[44] Although political leaders can and do implement policies they believe in, others have been stymied in their efforts:

> I had a clear idea of what I wanted to do as assistant secretary, but the secretary was corrupt and uninterested in the problems. I resigned four times but the president would not accept my resignation. It was a frustrating experience; the secretary only wanted to be president and devoted all of his efforts to accomplishing this goal.

> When I was head of tourism my main goal was to bring in more tourists. That was predefined as my mission. I believe I did contribute to this goal by removing many of the obstacles in the way of such growth. Mexico's change in this area, in a symbolic way, was represented by my becoming head of the World Tourism Organization. My mission was already defined for me, so it was difficult to have a personal impact on policy.

> I became a member of the advisory board under President Cárdenas to develop some new ideas. One of the other members was Alejandro Carrillo Marcor, the governor of Sonora [1975-79]. One of the little known ideas which we proposed was the division of the country into six sections, each of which would contain a regional university supported by the federal government to help eliminate the dominance of the National University. But this was a difficult time for Cárdenas and it would have fueled opposition which had developed in relation to other problems.

These personal experiences of Mexican decision makers illustrate that predefined boundaries, the personal ambitions of superiors, and

---

43. For a detailed assessment of how this relationship worked between treasury secretaries and presidents, also based on extensive interviews, see Jonathan Schlefer's engaging account, *Palace Politics: How the Ruling Party Brought Crisis to Mexico* (Austin: University of Texas Press, 2008), 99.

44. For examples from 1946 to 1970, see Susan K. Purcell, *The Mexican Profit-Sharing Decision: Politics in an Authoritarian Regime* (Berkeley: University of California Press, 1975); Roderic Ai Camp, *The Role of Economists in Policy-Making: A Comparative Study of Mexico and the United States* (Tucson: University of Arizona Press, 1977); and Guy Benveniste, *Bureaucracy and National Planning: A Sociological Case Study in Mexico* (New York: Praeger, 1970). For decisions taken from 1970 to 2000, see John Bailey, *Governing Mexico: The Statecraft of Crisis Management* (New York: St. Martin's, 1988); Enrique Krauze, *Mexico: Biography of Power* (New York: HarperCollins, 1997); Eduardo Torres Espinosa, *Bureaucracy and Politics in Mexico* (Brookfield: Ashgate, 1999); and Sidney Weintraub, *Financial Decision-Making in Mexico: To Bet a Nation* (Pittsburgh: University of Pittsburgh Press, 2000).

the political implications of a policy can all be influential in altering or eliminating a policy.[45] Furthermore, political leaders hoping for higher offices often temper their own beliefs or policy goals to improve their political situation. In a political culture where personalism was rampant, innovative policies were not in vogue. Daniel Cosío Villegas described the Mexican political leader of this era in the apt analogy of a man in the water, a man who works at floating and not swimming, because his goal is not to govern but to continue in office.[46]

In spite of the many reasons political leaders might not be able to implement policies, and in spite of the other variables that would affect policies they do implement, a broad overview of policy direction in Mexico from 1946 to 1970 would at least suggest significant areas of discrepancy between what political leaders believe and what they have advocated and implemented in office. The following analysis attempts to briefly describe the direction of government policy since 1946 and relate to it the beliefs of Mexican leaders during those years. Antonio Carrillo Flores, Alemán's classmate who directed the National Finance Bank during his friend's administration and became Ruiz Cortines's treasury secretary from 1952 to 1958, noted that the 1929 depression produced a major impact on the lives of their generation. He argues that economic development and social justice were the basic goals of his generation, and those ideological controversies, such as Marxism, were never of great importance to their group because they were pragmatically oriented to solving the country's economic problems, rather than concerning themselves with dogmatic, ideological solutions.[47]

The economic policy that best reflects the general emphasis of the post-1946 regimes in Mexico is that of industrialization. The shift toward modernization through industrialization took place during Avila Camacho's presidency from 1940 to 1946.[48] As one author suggested, the official economic policy of the Mexican government from 1940 was based on the belief

---

45. Several other studies have commented on the influence of the structure and culture of the political system and its relationship to belief patterns of elites and decision making. See Erwin C. Hargrove, "Values and Change: A Comparison of Young Elites in England and America," *Political Studies* 17 (September 1969): 343; and Jeffrey A. Hart, "Cognitive Maps of Three Latin American Policy Makers," *World Politics* 30, no. 1 (1977): 115–40.

46. *Memorias* (Mexico: Joaquin Mortiz, 1976), 247; for an excellent scholarly analysis of the influence of personalism on middle-level decision making, see Merilee Grindle, "Patrons and Clients in the Bureaucracy: Career Networks in Mexico," *Latin American Research Review* 12, no. 1 (1977): 42.

47. Personal interview, June 26, 1975.

48. John H. Kautsky, *Patterns of Modernizing Revolutions: Mexico and the Soviet Union*, Sage Professional Papers in Comparative Politics, vol. 5 (Beverly Hills, Calif.: Sage Publications, 1975), 32.

that industrialization and capital formation were imperative.[49] The decision to emphasize industrialization led to other policies that complemented or were interdependent with the main thrust of economic policy. Under Alemán, Mexican officials realized that to accomplish industrial development, the nation had to obtain the confidence of foreign investors. This did not mean they would give up their nationalism; rather, they hoped in the long run to improve national strength as a result of foreign investment.[50] Furthermore, the government encouraged industrialization through tax incentives and financial policy, channeling funds into this area through loans from government banks and international organizations at lower interest rates than those found in the private sector.[51] This policy meant that other alternative areas were neglected; in fact, close to 30 percent of all public investment since 1940 occurred in the industrial sector.[52] It also meant that the concern of policy makers for agrarian reform shifted from the land distribution policies of the Cárdenas era to an emphasis on the industrialization of agriculture. Edward J. Williams explains: "It did this for the reason that larger production units supposedly changed after 1940 because the 'idea of bigness' also applied to the *campo*. Large scale farming, in short, seems more respectable and 'modern' with all its paraphernalia of sophisticated machinery, efficient methods and smoothly devised division of labor."[53]

We must not conclude, however, that industrialization, because it neglected social benefits to the masses, deprived the average Mexican of an increase in his standard of living. It is true that the political leaders who governed Mexico from 1946 to 1970, with the exception of the Adolfo López Mateos's administration (1958-64), did neglect overt social benefits in favor of public policies that contributed to industrialization. On the other hand, one prominent scholar has concluded on the basis of statistical evidence that Mexico experienced its most rapid social change for the masses between 1940 and 1960, rather than under such presidents as Lázaro Cárdenas.[54]

49. Ruben Vargas Austin, "The Development of Economic Policy in Mexico with Special Reference to Economic Doctrines," unpublished Ph.D. dissertation, Iowa State University, 1958, 76-77.

50. Vargas Austin, "The Development of Economic Policy in Mexico," 304.

51. Leopoldo Solís, "Mexican Economic Policy in the Post-War Period: The Views of Mexican Economists," *American Economic Review* 61 (June 1971): supplement, 5.

52. Roger D. Hansen, *The Politics of Mexican Development* (Baltimore, Md.: Johns Hopkins University Press, 1971), 45.

53. "Mutation in the Mexican Revolution: Industrialism, Nationalism and Centralism," *Secolas Annals* (March 1976): 38.

54. James Wilkie, *The Mexican Revolution: Federal Expenditure and Social Change since 1910* (Berkeley: University of California Press, 1970), 277. Wilkie's poverty index, used as a basis for this assessment, has come under some criticism. Although I agree with the criticism that several of the variables are not useful in his index, it does not change the direction of his

Several of the political leaders interviewed in our study had minor or major roles in the decision to industrialize. One of them, Javier Gaxiola, played an important part in the transitional regime of Manuel Avila Camacho as his secretary of economy (later industry and commerce). He felt that several policies he implemented as secretary were a reflection of his beliefs, especially those dealing with the marginal intervention of the government in the area of prices, the protection of new industries during World War II, the establishment of a national advisory board for tariffs, the creation of Conasupo, and the formulation of the structure for the Federal Electric Commission.[55] Another leader, involved in a more recent stage of this process, believed that he, along with several colleagues, through his position in the public investment department of the Secretariat of the Presidency, influenced government policy in regard to the basic criteria for deciding the priorities for federal investment.[56]

The policy of industrialization chosen by Mexican political leaders does not conflict with the beliefs of those leaders since 1946. Industrialization might be defined as a policy goal of these leaders, but it can be described more accurately as a method for achieving social justice, which Mexicans viewed as including peace and an improved standard of living for all citizens. Even when thought of as a means, industrialization can be seen to have encouraged an emphasis on two additional elements prominent in the ideologies of professors and political leaders: nationalism and statism. Edward J. Williams describes how these elements became a part of that goal:

> The present situation in Mexico is essentially explained as a matter of choice. That is, the Mexican elites chose to be where they are because they

findings for the other variables. His findings are also supported by several Mexican studies. For these and for an exchange of views, see the following: Ignacio Aguilar Alvarez, Arturo Lamadrid Ibarra, and Martín Luis Guzmán Ferrer, "Desarrollo socio-económico comparativo de las entidades del país, 1940–70," *Comercio Exterior* 22 (March 1972); Luis Unikel and Edmundo Victoria, "Medición de algunos aspectos del desarrollo socio-económico de las entidades federativas de México, 1940–1960," *Demografía y Economía* 4 (1970); Paul Lamartine Yates, *El desarrollo regional de México* (Mexico: Banco de México, 1961); Roderic Ai Camp, "A Reexamination of Political Leadership and Allocation of Federal Revenues in Mexico, 1934–1973," *Journal of Developing Areas* 10 (January 1976): 193–212; Felix G. Boni and Mitchell A. Seligson, "Applying Quantitative Techniques to Quantitative History: Poverty and Federal Expenditures in Mexico," *Latin American Research Review* 8 (Summer 1973): 105–10; David Barkin, "Public Expenditures and Social Change in Mexico: A Methodological Critique," *Journal of Latin American Studies* 4 (May 1972): 105–12; and Thomas E. Skidmore and Peter H. Smith, "Notes on Quantitative History: Federal Expenditure and Social Change in Mexico since 1910," *Latin American Research Review* 5 (Spring 1970): 71–85.

55. Personal interviews with F. Javier Gaxiola, June 25, 1975, and October 22, 1976. For more details, see his *Memorias* (Mexico: Editorial Porrúa, 1975).

56. Personal interview with Roberto Robles Martinez, October 29, 1976.

committed themselves to a headlong decision to industrialization. Once that decision was made, the other elements of the syndrome (nationalism and centralization of power) were defined and evolved to contribute to that primary goal. It is incontestable that industrialization has been the driving force of the Mexican dream in recent years.[57]

Industrialization could not have been accomplished without state intervention, a concept that had considerable acceptance in Mexico. Historically, the country was conditioned to governmental intervention through the Church, Crown, and eventually the state in the nation's economic activity.[58] Later, in the 1917 constitution, a document from which many Mexican leaders received their economic, social, and political beliefs, the state was identified as responsible for bringing about structural changes.[59] One perceptive critical scholar explains the political rationale for strong state control and intervention:

> In sum, the Constitution of 1917, which outlines the essential features of the new State, is clear testimony to the contradictions which the political-military-bureaucracy—its creator—had to deal with. So, in some parts of the Constitution we observe the classic precepts of liberalism, in others they are denied. In the same way, the equal rights of all citizens are recognized, as well as class antagonism. And it is precisely to prevent this irreconcilable antagonism from destroying society in a senseless war that the intervention of an "impartial arbiter" is proposed, a power apparently rising above the fundamental classes of society which is in charge of regulating the dispute. This "arbiter" is the State, and, in the beginning, more than the State—which has not been consolidated: the ruling political-military bureaucracy.[60]

Mexican political leaders used state intervention to promote industrialization. The high point of state activity in promoting industrialization in Mexican economic life involving the Alemán generation occurred from 1946 to 1958.[61] During this period, the government attempted to stimulate private investment in the developmental process. One former cabinet secretary under Alemán believed he carried out just such a policy: "I think very definitely that my policies reflected my attitudes and that they benefited Mexico. When I was in the ministry, we tried to create a policy of stimulating Mexican investment in those areas which were lacking domestic

---

57. Williams, "Mutation in the Mexican Revolution," 39.
58. Vargas Austin, "The Development of Economic Policy in Mexico," 299.
59. Solís, "Mexican Economic Policy in the Post-War Period," 54.
60. Juan Felipe Leal, "The Mexican State: 1915–1975, A Historical Interpretation," *Latin American Perspectives* 2 (Summer 1975): 56. Also see Vargas Austin for a complementary interpretation, 159.
61. Wilkie, *The Mexican Revolution*, 278.

capital. I believe this was a crucial policy and that it reflects our ideology as students."[62]

Others saw their roles as using the powers of the state for the protection, development, and expansion of natural resources in Mexico.[63] Víctor Manuel Villaseñor, a Marxist political activist for many years, combined his ideological beliefs and his personal goals to persuade Alemán to allow him to direct one of the new state enterprises—the making of railroad cars in Mexico. In directing this industry, Villaseñor hoped to use his position to prove that the state was equally capable (or more so) than the private sector of successfully operating a large factory.[64] Another public official saw his contributions to the policy of state intervention in nonideological terms. He believed that the principles he learned as a student guided him as assistant secretary of national properties in restructuring and organizing a department for controlling all of the federal decentralized agencies in Mexico.[65]

The role of the state and the goal of industrialization during this era complemented a universal desire among all political leaders: that of nationalism. Although it can be argued that Mexico's industrialization was imitative of the United States and other Western European countries, it can also be viewed in a nationalistic light. In the latter sense, Mexicans hoped to give their nation the industrial strength to provide a basis for growth and political independence from other powers. As Leopoldo Solís, the coordinator for economic planning in the Secretariat of the Presidency and for many years assistant director general of the Bank of Mexico (Mexico's Federal Reserve) suggested, government economic ideology comprises "all social groups and acquires a definite form—national interest, national unity, general submission to the state, xenophobia, and the casting into oblivion of the class struggle."[66] Nationalism as an element of industrialization and state intervention affected two areas: foreign investment and the protection of new industries and natural resources essential

---

62. Personal interview, October 29, 1976.

63. Personal interview with Antonio Martínez Báez, June 27, 1975. As indicated previously, Martínez Báez was in the generation before Alemán at the National School of Law and taught in his last year of law school.

64. Personal interview, Mexico City, June 26, 1975; and his *Memorias de hombre de izquierda*, vol. 2 (Mexico: Editorial Grijalbo, 1976), 194ff. Villaseñor became friends with Alemán at the National School of Law, finishing his degree at UNAM during the last two years of Alemán's program.

65. Personal interview with Sealtiel Alatriste, June 24, 1975. Alatriste supported Alemán for the presidency in 1946, after he was recruited by his former economics professor, Mario Sousa, who became Alemán's head of the cabinet-level Department of Agrarian Affairs and Colonization, 1946–52. Alatriste was awarded the post of treasurer of the Federal District for his support.

66. Solís, "Mexican Economic Policy in the Post-War Period," 59.

to industrialization. Two of our respondents commented on their efforts in this regard:

> Everything I did as assistant secretary of industry and commerce was to transform imported North American goods into Mexican produced goods.[67]

> When I was in the commission of mining I helped develop what I consider to be my most important efforts in the nationalization of the mining industry, a goal which definitely reflects my philosophy. I think our efforts to bring together private resources, the government and foreign capital in the same industry were also important.[68]

Although nationalistic sentiments seemed strong in the ideological beliefs of all respondents interviewed, the actual results of the post-1946 policies have been criticized by many Mexicans as detrimental to nationalism. A critical view suggests that the political leaders of this period went overboard to attract needed foreign capital, thereby establishing a firm base for foreign economic dominance to the detriment of domestic capital investment.[69] Economic statistics partly substantiate this pattern, showing direct foreign investment (compared to private investment) accounting for only 14.5 percent of the total prior to Alemán's administration, but reaching 25.5 percent in 1952 and increasing to 40.7 percent by 1958.[70] The statistics also show that from 1959 to 1967, the figures dropped below 1940 levels to 9 percent. It is therefore difficult to suggest the nationalistic achievements of the post-1946 regimes, because the statistics can be used to support opposing views of its influence through 1970 depending largely on where you start measuring its influence or your personal interpretation.[71]

It is obvious that Mexico's economy is interdependent with that of the United States. It would be nearly impossible for this not to be so, and such a relationship was established long before the post-1946 era. Furthermore, the Mexican government slowly nationalized basic industries and natural resources, the number of decentralized government enterprises increased

67. Personal interview with Hugo B. Margáin, March 14, 1977. Margáin was a disciple in his economic thought of Ramón Beteta. Margáin himself followed in the footsteps of his mentor, becoming Luis Echeverría's first treasury secretary, 1970–73.

68. Personal interview with Luis de la Peña Porth, October 27, 1976. He later became assistant secretary of national properties in the Echeverría administration.

69. A dissertation by Peter R. Sugges Jr. might have revealed some attitudes of Mexican political elites about multinational companies, but unfortunately Mexicans did not respond. See "Beliefs about the Multinational Enterprise: A Factor Analytic Study of British, Canadian, French, and Mexican Elites," unpublished Ph.D. dissertation, New York University, 1976.

70. José Luis Ceceña, *México en la orbita imperial* (Mexico: Ediciones "El Caballito," 1975), 144.

71. For an excellent discussion of the paradox of economic nationalism and economic dependence see Clark W. Reynolds, *The Mexican Economy: Twentieth-Century Structure and Growth* (New Haven, Conn.: Yale University Press, 1970), 350.

substantially, and domestic industries and business were taken over by the public sector, reaching an apex under José López Portillo in 1982, when he nationalized the Mexican banking system.

The eclectic approach of Mexican leaders in solving their problems, and the combination of nationalism and state control over large areas of the economy, had important political and social implications for Mexico. As a leading economist pointed out prior to 1970, "Nationalism, in the wake of patriotism and the Mexican identity, made it more and more difficult to pass judgment on political centralism, paternalism and economic policy; in effect, the public sector is immune from independent criticism."[72]

In the political sphere, nationalism was turned into a concept supportive of national unity, but a unity achieved at the loss of some liberties and the freedom to criticize effectively government policies. As has been made clear in the previous section, Mexican political leaders placed a high value on unity and on political liberty, and although the two beliefs are neither necessarily mutually exclusive nor contradictory, in the Mexican context, they emerged as such. Alemán himself stressed the fact that as students, they had "a strong belief in the principle of democracy and the necessity of its growth in Mexico."[73]

In the contest between political liberty and unity, the former lost out. The explanation for this is twofold. First, although the revolution was fought in part for the principles of political liberty, the violence, instability, and suffering produced by the revolution affected the middle and lower middle classes and their children, the future political leaders of Mexico, who could see a future for Mexico only if peace and order under the guise of unity were retained. Enrique Beltrán Castillo, who grew up in the same decade as Alemán and overlapped with him at the National Preparatory School and the National University, recalled that many of his friends lost close relatives in the revolution. He remembered 1915 in Mexico City as a year of hunger and starvation for most Mexicans. They always talked about these subjects as students, and many of their fellow students had participated in the revolution or witnessed it personally. He carried a pistol at the age of fifteen, and he did not remove it until 1923, when he went to the United States. He remarked that he felt rather naked when he took it off, but this was the kind of environment in which they

72. Solís, "Mexican Economic Policy in the Post-War Period," 60. Solís later became assistant secretary of trade and coordinator of President Miguel de la Madrid's economic advisers. He served as an influential mentor to President Salinas' closest economic collaborators.

73. Personal interview, October 27, 1976. Ironically, in 1976 Alemán argued that "Above all, the most important principle which needs to be maintained and achieved in any solution to our problems is to develop democratic principles and to develop individual freedoms. We must continue to grow in this area so that our solutions are justified."

had lived during these years.[74] Salvador Azuela, the son of the famous revolutionary novelist, argued that his personal experiences, even more so than those of Beltrán, influenced his formation. He noted numerous disruptions and deprivations as a consequence of his father's participation in the revolution. His class attendance was disrupted by the pressing priorities of providing the necessities to his family to survive.[75]

Therefore, as suggested both by the respondents and by Mexican scholars, unity was a universally held belief born of this political generation's violent experiences, which produced the extraordinary level of deaths.[76] It is also accurate to conclude that political liberalism, when viewed as effective suffrage and other political freedoms, retrogressed under Alemán, reflecting its subservience to political unity.[77]

The second reason unity superseded the growth of political liberties is the natural self-interest on the part of politicians. Kenneth Coleman suggests why this is the case: "when one has built a career in no small part on the ability to foster public acquiescence in the belief that national unity itself is ill-served by the existence of opposition, it is not to be expected that one will discard this belief when put to the test by the growth of real opposition."[78] It is difficult, therefore, for a politician to take the initiative to change a political system that has provided his livelihood and offered his country some growth and orderly change, or for him to persuade others to support changes when some leaders attempt new policies. "The system has become an acceptable tradition to many and the politician is himself part of that political culture."[79] It could be argued that in their desire to gain control over the political system, prodded by their failure to defeat the beginnings of such a system in 1929, they resisted relinquishing control over a system they had both captured and molded.

74. Personal interview, August 13, 1974. Beltrán, a zoologist, became assistant secretary of agriculture from 1958 to 1964.

75. Letter to the author, July 10, 1974.

76. Luis Medina, "Orígen y circunstancia de la idea de unidad nacional," in Centro de Estudios Internacionales, La vida política de México (Mexico: El Colegio de México, 1974), 7–32.

77. Frank Brandenburg, The Making of Modern Mexico (Englewood Cliffs, N.J.: Prentice Hall, 1965), 103, and Sergio Aguayo Quezada, La charola, una historia de los servicios de inteligencia en México (Mexico: Grijalbo, 2001), 61ff.

78. Kenneth M. Coleman, "Diffuse Support in Mexico: The Potential for Crisis," Sage Professional Papers in Comparative Politics, vol. 5 (Beverly Hills, Calif.: Sage Publications, 1976), 9.

79. This reaction is perfectly illustrated by the severe criticisms that most PRI leaders directed toward President Ernesto Zedillo, who attempted to reduce presidential dominance and open up the PRI itself to internal competition. The fact that PRI traditionalists remained in control of the party itself until Roberto Madrazo's overwhelming loss in the 2006 presidential election demonstrates the persistence of these values.

Mexican political leaders did not entirely lose their beliefs in political liberties, and some even believed in the 1970s that they deserved a higher priority than national unity. As most political leaders suggested in response to the question concerning Mexico's readiness for increased participation, the masses required further civic education. From 1946 to 1970, unity—both in practice and in the beliefs of Mexican political leaders—took precedence over the development and exercise of political liberties. But nationalism, industrialization, and unity were achieved at the price of deemphasizing immediate social benefits. "Buttressed by the centralization of power, nationalism-cum-industrialization contributed to legitimizing mal-distribution of wealth and the lack of social services. It justified budgets bloated with expenditures for expensive infra-structural projects and for the importation of costly machinery rather than wage hikes for the poor."[80]

One of the universal beliefs among Mexican political leaders, particularly encouraged through the teachings and writings of Antonio Caso, a popular and influential professor of the Alemán and later generations, was humanism, the concern for the human qualities in government policy. During the 1930s in the field of law, Mexican jurists accepted public utility as the prevailing legal principle, a principle that argues that law must be based on communal interests.[81] Yet despite the emphasis on humanism in the socialization process and the emphasis placed on this value by political leaders, the policies of the regimes from 1946 to 1958 did not stress direct social benefits. Instead, Alemán undertook indirect social programs, which James Wilkie argues did not sacrifice the masses (as critics have suggested) but provided the base for social advance with "too little direct attention to the people."[82] As Solís concludes, with statistical support, the role of the public sector in the distribution of income in Mexico in the 1940s and 1950s was not significant.[83]

An emphasis on social programs, such as public education, welfare benefits, and increases in workers salaries, did not take place until 1958, when Adolfo López Mateos became president.[84] Although some of the political leaders in our sample collaborated with his administration, the majority held their positions under the other three administrations prior to 1958.

80. Williams, "Mutation in the Mexican Revolution," 38–39.
81. Albert Louis Michaels, "Mexican Politics and Nationalism from Calles to Cárdenas," Ph.D. dissertation, University of Pennsylvania, 1966, 218.
82. Wilkie, The Mexican Revolution, 283.
83. Solís, "Mexican Economic Policy in the Post-War Period," 7. For example, salaries and wages represented 29.3 percent of total income in 1940, but only 23.8 percent in 1950, 6.
84. For comments on this trend, see Kautsky, Patterns of Modernizing Revolutions, 33; Solís, "Mexican Economic Policy in the Post-War Period," 60; and Wilkie, The Mexican Revolution, 278.

However, the general direction of policy did not always reflect attempted policies or programs actually implemented by these men. The following quotations from Mexican political leaders suggest their successes and failures in two policy areas with direct social implications: education and personal income taxes.

> I became a member of the advisory committee on schools. I suggested a campaign against illiteracy, a program of which I always have been proud. The first year this campaign was highly successful, but each year thereafter, the teachers who were doing the work in a disinterested way after their regular teaching became unenthusiastic. The program died because of a lack of funds to pay instructors. People will not sacrifice forever.[85]

> The reform of secondary education was one of the most important contributions I made as director general of that program in the Secretariat of Public Education. I wanted to change secondary education and give it a coherent organization so that a student who left secondary and did not go on for further schooling would be prepared at a certain level and could make a good living. This was the essence of my reforms. I was very much influenced in my own experiences by Edward Herriott, the great French leader, who did the same thing in his country.[86]

> When I was assistant secretary of treasury, I created, for the first time, an income tax list. I was personally doubtful about the results of our reform and if they would work. I had many talks with the U.S. Assistant Secretary of Treasury, who argued that it would be very difficult to keep track of the incomes of these people. Still, I was strongly committed to implementing the reforms. Alemán, who was facing many problems, decided not to continue our reforms. When he notified us of this, I told him I wanted to resign. I was really interested in seeing these reforms continue. The tax law was not a problem, but enforcing it and deciding what amount of revenues the government needed were. I had an obsession with these reforms so I left.[87]

> When I became assistant secretary of income for the Secretariat of the Treasury I wanted to revise all of the laws to make them much more humanistic and to make the system more progressive. I advocated reform of the

85. Personal interview with Ernesto Enríquez Coyro, October 26, 1976. Enríquez Coyro served as oficial mayor of public education under Avila Camacho, assistant director general of the Mexican Institute of Social Security under Ruiz Cortines, and assistant secretary of public education under López Mateos.

86. Personal interview with Antonio Armendáriz, June 24, 1975. Armendáriz, who was a disciple of Manuel Gómez Morín, later served as assistant secretary of the treasury, 1952–58, and director general of the National Bank of Foreign Trade, 1965–70.

87. Personal interview with Eduardo Bustamante, Mexico City, October 2, 1976. Bustamante resigned in 1949, having served under his classmate Ramón Beteta. Also a disciple of Manuel Gómez Morín, he, too, overlapped with Alemán at the law school, becoming Adolfo López Mateos's secretary of national properties, 1958–64.

income tax law. I was also responsible for a law known as El Padron Federal de Causantes, which is something like a tax list of possible persons owing taxes to the federal government. I believe that the teachings of my professors Miguel Palacios Macedo and Ramón Beteta, exercised an important impact on my revision of these two laws.[88]

Other leaders interviewed were instrumental in implementing policies affecting social security benefits for workers, designing banking institutions to create funds for small businessmen and for housing projects, and formulating public health programs. Several of these leaders, in implementing or attempting to implement social policies, did so because these goals were established in the 1917 constitution. Hugo Margáin, as assistant secretary of industry and later secretary of the treasury, believes two programs he helped formulate—the Profit Sharing Plan and the workers housing program through the government agency known as INFONAVIT—reflected constitutional principles and the influence of that document on him and his generation.[89]

Perhaps the area in which social benefits were most neglected was land reform. It should be remembered that land reform was a concept stressed by many of the influential professors under who these political leaders studied. Initially, the principal goal of the agrarian reform program was social justice, but, as Leopoldo Solís suggests, although it attempted to redistribute wealth, income, and power to the masses of peasants, in absolute terms its impact was quite small. The reason for this failure is that the agrarian program lacked definition, planning, and an economic criterion.[90] During the years 1946 to 1970, most of the efforts of the government were directed toward irrigation projects and the providing of credit for middle-size and large industrialized farms. In this, and in other areas, political leaders did not fulfill the value they placed on humanism; like political liberty, it lost out to statism, nationalism, and industrialization. Perhaps humanism, at least in the sense of increased social equality, is impossible to achieve during the process of dynamic economic growth and industrialization. John Kautsky suggests such an incompatibility in arguing that "industrialization, while overcoming some of the inequalities of traditional societies, introduces some new inequalities of its own."[91]

88. Personal interview with Antonio Armendáriz, 1975.

89. For details about his role in the Profit Sharing program, see Susan K. Purcell, *The Mexican Profit-Sharing Decision: Politics in an Authoritarian Regime* (Berkeley: University of California Press, 1975). In an interview, he told the author that he and Ernesto Fernández Hurtado, director of the Bank of Mexico, suggested INFONAVIT to the president. March 14, 1977. See Nancy Robinson, *The Politics of Low Income Housing in México: A Case Study of INFONAVIT, the Workers' Housing Fund* (Stanford, Calif.: Stanford University Press, 1980).

90. Solís, "Mexican Economic Policy in the Post-War Period," 7, 11, 16.

91. Kautsy, *Patterns of Modernizing Revolutions,* 36.

There may be many other variables that explain why these political leaders placed less stress on political liberties and social justice in the concrete implementation of policies. One reason may be that most ideological tenets were only loosely adhered to.[92] The postrevolutionary generation, as will be remembered, placed a high value on pragmatism and concrete achievements. Pragmatism itself was an influential part of the ideological beliefs of Mexican leaders, but it does not have the same social and political implications as do political liberties. In discussing his generation, Antonio Carrillo Flores made numerous comments relevant to this point:

> The philosophy of my generation was to form an elite which was well prepared to govern, rather than to use the resources indiscriminately on the masses.... Most all of my generation were romantic supporters of the Vasconcelos movement, but in reality they looked to the governmental machinery to make their ideas reach fruition. In this respect we were a mediocre generation because we did not talk about great ideas; rather we worked with the practical.[93]

This generation, and those who followed, did stress a *pragmatic* approach to problem solving, and this word constantly reappears in conversations with political leaders about policy making. In a revealing statement about Mexican financial planning, Hugo B. Margáin comments on its influence:

> The Constitution of 1917 is the basis for formulating our policy goals, but the lines are not well delineated. In Mexico, we have discovered certain means to achieve our goals. For example, we have developed a pattern in the finance ministry: one-third of the budget goes to productive sectors, one-third to salaries, and one-third to social programs. This is a rough rule, but within this rule we use pragmatic and intuitive approaches. We have to think of the concrete problems.[94]

One member of Alemán's generation argues frankly that the downside to this pragmatic approach is that it tempered the possibility of leading figures of this generation achieving major or significant contributions. Adolfo Zamora believes that they were a talented group of public servants who could be most praised for serving but not for their creativity or initiating innovative policy solutions to developmental problems. He also believed

92. Mexicans aren't unique in this regard. See William Quandt, *Revolution and Political Leadership: Algeria, 1954-1968* (Cambridge, Mass.: MIT Press, 1969), 267, for a similar emphasis among Algerian postrevolutionary leaders.

93. Personal interview, June 26, 1975. Carrillo Flores was only twenty when he graduated with Alemán at the National School of Law. He became director general of the National Finance Bank under Alemán, secretary of treasury under Ruiz Cortines, ambassador to the United States under López Mateos, and secretary of foreign relations under Díaz Ordaz, the most successful public figure after Alemán himself.

94. Personal interview, March 14, 1977.

that members of this generation contributed to the evolving principle of Mexican politics in placing personal interest above public service.[95]

Of the five major tenets Mexican political leaders describe themselves as holding, three have characterized Mexican policies since 1946: political order and unity, state intervention in the economy, and pragmatic decision making. The fourth tenet, nationalism, has been reflected in many policy decisions but less so in others. The last of these beliefs, the concept of political liberty, has been almost totally neglected, although participation did increase in the 1950s with women's suffrage, and an abortive attempt was made in the mid-1960s to provide for democratic competition in the selection of precandidates within the official party at the local level, but substantial electoral fraud continued.[96] As I have argued, it is apparent that their desire for unity, peace, and continuity exceeded their youthful commitment to liberty. Their failure also might be explained in part by the fact that the political leaders we have examined concentrated their efforts in administrative and economic cabinet and executive branch positions rather than in those party positions or political agencies most responsible for such changes on the ground. Nevertheless, presidents and their secretaries of government clearly determined the boundaries of political liberty and effective suffrage during these formative years.

It was intimated at the beginning of this section that solid evidence could not be produced to suggest that socialization experiences, reflected in the beliefs and values of Mexican political leaders, were responsible for government policies during the years covered by our study. It can be argued, however, that this brief examination of the policy directions of these governments, as a whole mirrors the major beliefs of Mexico's political leadership from the Alemán generation, with the exception of political liberty.

In the first section of this chapter and elsewhere in this book I have argued that the Alemán generation significantly altered the composition of Mexico's political leadership and therefore the importance of institutions which determined that leadership. In drawing comparisons between the democratic administrations since 2000, in contrast to the transition administrations from 1988–2000 and the predemocratic administrations from 1934 to 1988, we noted significant changes among the composition of leadership during those periods. If we compare the impact of the Alemán

95. Personal interview, July 24, 1974.

96. For an analysis of these changes, see Ward Morton, *Woman Suffrage in Mexico* (Gainesville: University of Florida Press, 1962); Antonio Ugalde, *Power and Conflict in a Mexican Community: A Study of Political Integration* (Albuquerque: University of New Mexico Press, 1970); Richard R. Fagen and William S. Tuohy, *Politics and Privilege in a Mexican City* (Stanford, Calif.: Stanford University Press, 1972); and Kenneth F. Johnson, *Mexican Democracy: A Critical View* (Boston: Allyn and Bacon, 1971).

administration on various characteristics of Mexican leadership with that of the Fox administration, which represents the first postdemocratic regime, it becomes apparent the extent to which the presidency of Alemán introduced significant alterations, even though they occurred within the nondemocratic PRI-controlled era.

A central feature of the Alemán administration was the significant increase in college-educated civilians, especially the role of Mexico's National University in producing those graduates (table 7.3). Non–college graduates declined from the Cárdenas and Avila Camacho administrations (1934–46) by 18 percent. During the Fox administration, the percentage of non–college graduates also continued to decline, but in smaller percentages. What is most significant about the Alemán administration is the dramatic increase in college graduates specifically from the National University. Of the more than 250 members of his administration, half graduated from that single institution, representing an increase of more than 50 percent

**Table 7.3.** The Degree of Changes in the Composition of the Alemán Administration Compared to the First Democratic Administration

| Variables | Pre-Alemán | Alemán | % Change | Democratic Transition | Fox | % Change |
|---|---|---|---|---|---|---|
| College teaching | 37 | 44 | 19+ | 59 | 50 | –15 |
| UNAM only | 40 | 64 | 60+ | 46 | 33 | –28 |
| Graduated UNAM[a] | 32 | 49 | 53+ | 45 | 28 | –38 |
| Graduated UNAM[b] | 51 | 68 | 33+ | 49 | 30 | –39 |
| Non-college graduates | 38 | 31 | –18 | 35 | 31 | –11 |
| Law graduates | 41 | 50 | 22+ | 10 | 9 | 10+ |
| Gubernatorial career | 43 | 33 | –33 | 14 | 12 | –4 |
| Father in politics | 10 | 12 | 20+ | 17 | 12 | –29 |
| Middle-class parents | 63 | 69 | 10+ | 81 | 84 | 4+ |
| Related elite families[c] | 20 | 16 | –20 | 7 | 5 | –29 |

*Source*: Mexican Political Biographies Project, 2009.

a. Among all members of the administration.
b. College graduates only.
c. Prominent Porfirian or revolutionary families.

over the prior two administrations. Among college graduates alone more than two-thirds were alumni, an increase of one-third.

As noted repeatedly in the analysis of the interrelationships among members of the Alemán administration, professors played a crucial role in these networking relationships. Nearly half of all top political figures in his government had prior experience with college teaching. Two-fifths of his colleagues taught at the National University, a dramatic increase of 60 percent over the prior governments. Finally, college graduates with law degrees increased significantly (by a fifth) under Alemán. With the arrival of an opposition government in 2000, Fox also brought a change to the distribution of lawyers versus other professions, notably economists. This reversal in favor of lawyers, however, is far less significant under Fox than what occurred under Alemán.

If the extent of the changed nature of these variables in the Fox administration is examined, for reasons explained elsewhere, after reaching an apex during the last years of PRI governance, both college teaching and graduating from the leading public institutions have declined in national politicians' credentials. The extent of these declines from the democratic transition administrations to that of Fox, with the exception of UNAM graduates among all college graduates, represents a significant change but less so than the changes witnessed between the Alemán administration and that of his immediate predecessors (table 7.3).

Finally, it would be fair to say that Alemán and Fox expanded the pool of politicians among a different group of individuals. If we measure this by the degree to which their respective political collaborators were related to prominent revolutionary and Porfirian families, both administrations are characterized by a definite decline in politicians boasting such family ties. What is surprising about the Alemán cohort is that it represents a substantial increase in politicians whose fathers were in politics. In contrast, given the fact that many of Fox's collaborators held office for the first time, his administration represents an expected but equally substantial decline in such parental political involvement (table 7.3).

# 8

# Is One Career More Democratic Than Another?

Any attempt to analyze the composition of national political leadership must consider politicians collectively and separately. We have examined a number of different variables that revealed fascinating differences among Mexican politicians as well as differences resulting from Mexico's democratic transition. As noted in the case of women and party militants, politicians whose careers focused on the legislative branch were affected most strongly by democratic reforms. If we separate all leading politicians into three broad career categories—executive, legislative, and judicial—what patterns occur? Do they correspond to our specific conclusions about women and militants? Are other career paths generally more strongly affected by democratic change? What explains those differences?

One of the most interesting and significant patterns affecting Mexican politics over the past century is the impact of regionalism. Imbalances among regions produced major political consequences in Mexican leadership in the 1920s and 1930s. Given the manner in which legislative seats are distributed, one would expect a strong link between the percentages of Mexicans born in those regions and the percentages of elected, legislative officials. Furthermore, because members of congress have been more strongly represented among all leading politicians than any other political office, congressional representation among these elites should help skew these geographic percentages to correspond more closely to the regional birthplaces of all Mexicans.

In fact, if we examine the most prominent political leaders, the distribution of the population by region is not necessarily a useful predictor of the distribution of prominent political leadership. Indeed, only in the case of two regions can we argue that all leading politicians are representative of the general Mexican population: the North, which accounted for 15 percent of Mexico's population in 1950, and the Gulf, which represented 12 percent (table 8.1). In the remaining four regions we can distinguish two significant patterns among prominent public figures. Most important is that the

Table 8.1. Regional Backgrounds of Leading Mexican Politicians

| | Region of Birth (%) | | | | | | | |
|---|---|---|---|---|---|---|---|---|
| Position | Federal District | East Central | West | North | South | Gulf | West Central | Foreign |
| *Legislative* | | | | | | | | |
| Senator | 8.2 | 17.7 | 19.6 | 17.7 | 10.8 | 12.7 | 12.7 | 0.05 |
| Deputy | 12.1 | 15.9 | 17.9 | 15.9 | 10.5 | 12.5 | 14.7 | 0.4 |
| Deputy twice | 13.5 | 15.0 | 20.3 | 15.3 | 10.4 | 10.9 | 14.5 | 0.002 |
| *All Politicians* | | | | | | | | |
| 1920 Census | 6.3 | 20.0 | 15.8 | 12.0 | 13.7 | 12.7 | 19.5 | – |
| 1950 Census | 12.0 | 18.0 | 14.0 | 15.0 | 13.0 | 12.0 | 17.0 | – |
| All politicians | 23.0 | 13.2 | 15.2 | 15.0 | 8.4 | 11.9 | 12.2 | 1.1 |
| *Executive* | | | | | | | | |
| Secretary | 33.0 | 8.5 | 11.2 | 14.0 | 6.2 | 12.8 | 13.0 | 1.4 |
| Assist. secretary | 40.3 | 8.5 | 9.2 | 14.6 | 4.9 | 9.7 | 10.6 | 2.2 |
| Oficial mayor | 28.6 | 11.4 | 13.0 | 14.6 | 6.0 | 12.1 | 12.7 | 1.6 |
| *Judicial* | | | | | | | | |
| Supreme court | 20.6 | 12.3 | 11.0 | 7.7 | 14.2 | 14.8 | 19.4 | 0 |

*Source*: Mexican Political Biographies Project, 2009.

Federal District as a birthplace of leading politicians is highly overrepresented: nearly twice as many politicians come from this location compared
to the general population who reside there. Those figures are even more
skewed if we compare them to the 6 percent of Mexicans residing in the
capital in 1920, the closest median date of birth for all political leaders in
the sample. Consequently, the other three geographic regions, the South,
West Central, and East Central, are significantly underrepresented in the
backgrounds of prominent politicians, with the South, Mexico's poorest
region, the most underrepresented.

If the total sample of politicians is separated into career categories,
do these career preferences produce significant differences in their geographic origins? We discover significant disparities in the regional distribution of leading politicians according to the career paths they have pursued.
These differences are important to identify and explain. In the first place,
as expected, the assertion that politicians following legislative careers in
the Chamber of Deputies are more representative of the general population's birthplaces than the figures for all leading political figures combined
is accurate. Compared to all politicians, members of congress are nearly
half as likely to have come from the Federal District as all other politicians
in percentages precisely equal to the general population. Once again, the

South and the West Central regions are underrepresented among members of congress, but not at the same level as among all elite politicians.
However, similar to all politicians, the North and the Gulf are represented
at levels approximating the general population.

In addition to the huge difference in their numbers from those of all
leading politicians from the Federal District, members of congress are better represented in the West. The most likely explanation for this overrepresentation is that the National Action Party (PAN) has achieve greater
success in that region, and it has increased its presence dramatically in
the legislative branch, thus affecting those numbers from the West most
strongly in that career track. This is also confirmed among members of
congress who served two or more times in the lower legislative body (qualifying them for inclusion among prominent national politicians), who contributed even more to the West's overrepresentation.

As we move up the legislative ladder to the senate, it is apparent that
differences exist between senators and members of congress. Fewer senators are from the Federal District than any other important national position only because the Federal District, although one of the most populous
regions in Mexico, is represented by only four senators, the same number
as all other individual states. Therefore, each region, made up of multiple
states, automatically draws on a pool of many more senators than does the
Federal District. Senators from the West also are strongly overrepresented,
and once again they are underrepresented in the South.

If we contrast the distribution of leading politicians between those holding national legislative versus executive posts, prominent distinctions in
the distribution of regional backgrounds readily appear. The two clearest
patterns found among all politicians takes on added importance when we
confine the sample to the executive branch. A third of cabinet secretaries compared to a fourth of all politicians come from the Federal District.
Cabinet secretaries are two and a half times more likely to have been born
in the Federal District than all other Mexicans. Given their importance
in choosing subordinates, creating national political networks (*camarillas*),
and forming that tiny pool of potential presidential candidates before 2000,
these figures are that much more significant.

When we compare the cabinet's bias toward the Federal District with the
subcabinet, the distortion becomes even greater. Two-fifths of all assistant
secretaries come from Mexico City. This is truly extraordinary. Assistant
secretaries are almost twice as likely to come from the capital compared
with all other leading politicians, nearly two and a half times that of the
general population. Individuals who become assistant secretaries have a
strong chance of moving up the ladder to a cabinet post. One-fifth of assistant secretaries eventually join the cabinet, accounting for one-third of all

cabinet secretaries. Thus, the background and career characteristics of assistant secretaries can impact the composition of cabinet secretaries.

An interesting example of an assistant secretary who bridges the democratic transition and democratic periods is the career of Luis Téllez Kuenzler. Born in the Federal District in 1958, the son of a civil engineer, Téllez is the nephew of María Emilia Téllez Benoit, the first female assistant secretary of foreign relations, and the grandson of Manuel C. Téllez, secretary of government and foreign relations in the 1930s. Téllez attended the Autonomous Technological Institute of Mexico, where he studied economics, and he simultaneously studied law at the National School of Law. He became a student of Pedro Aspe and Guillermo Ortiz Martínez, sequential secretaries of the treasury under Salinas and Zedillo, both of whom were assistant secretaries born in the Federal District and are excellent examples of the assistant secretary–to-secretary pattern from the 1940s generation.[1] Téllez became an analyst at treasury under his mentor, Pedro Aspe, and then received a scholarship to complete a Ph.D. in economics at Massachusetts Institute of Technology from 1982 to 1986, Aspe's alma mater.[2] Returning to Mexico, he served in several positions in treasury and programming and budgeting under Aspe before becoming assistant secretary of planning in the agricultural ministry in 1991. When Zedillo ran for the presidency, he became the coordinator of the candidate's advisers, rising to his chief of staff when Zedillo took office. In mid-term, Zedillo appointed him secretary of energy. During the Fox presidency, Téllez became vice president and CEO of DESC, a leading manufacturing firm. In 2006, Felipe Calderón appointed him secretary of commerce.[3]

The huge percentage of assistant secretaries from a single region, more than double that of any other region, causes other regions to be significantly underrepresented in their backgrounds. The South is by far the most distorted of these underrepresented regions because one in eight Mexicans was born there in the 1950s, compared to only one in twenty assistant secretaries.

---

1. Guillermo Ortiz Martínez's career, similar to that of Téllez, spans the democratic transition and democratic eras. He served as assistant secretary of the Treasury from 1988 to 1994, secretary of communications briefly in December 1994 under Zedillo, when the president appointed him as secretary of the treasury January 1, 1994, until he left that post in 1998 to become the first director of Mexico's Federal Reserve to serve under a tenure system that did not coincide with each incoming presidency. Reappointed under Fox in 2004, his term ended in 2010. Ortiz Martínez is the disciple of another influential assistant secretary, referred to in previous chapters: economist Leopoldo Solís.

2. Aspe worked on his Ph.D. at MIT from 1974 to 1978.

3. *Diario de Yucatán*, March 28, 2001, November 21, 2006; *Diccionario biográfico del gobierno mexicano* (Mexico: Presidencia de la República, 1992), 365.

The third ranked position in the executive branch, that of oficial mayor, is more of a political management than a policy appointment and represents, in contrast to the assistant secretary, a broader geographic constituency, as does the cabinet secretary. Interestingly, within the executive branch, the more political the appointment, the more balanced the regional distribution.

If we compare the regional origins of the executive with the legislative leadership, two important patterns are consistent across these careers: the North has most consistently maintained its actual percentage distribution according to the general population's birthplaces, whereas the South has been underrepresented significantly in every career category. Why is this the case?

What is fascinating about these two patterns is their linkage to historically established patterns of leadership in the prerevolutionary and revolutionary periods. The presence of the South in politicians' backgrounds has never exceeded that of the general population except in Porfirio Díaz's second and third terms, not surprising given the fact that the general himself came from Oaxaca, a key state located in this region, and under Abelardo Rodríguez's short administration (1932–34) immediately prior to Lázaro Cárdenas. Of all the regions in Mexico, the South is the poorest economically, the most ethnically diverse, and characterized by a high percentage of indigenous residents.[4] Even though it has accounted for approximately 13 percent of the Mexican population during the decades we examine, a much smaller percentage of those residents would have opportunities to access higher political office based on language, culture, education, and social networks.

The consistency of the North is equally interesting but for different reasons. Many ambitious generals and politicians after the 1910 revolution were disgruntled with the dominant role played by northern revolutionaries and politicians. For example, Francisco I. Madero, Venustiano Carranza, Alvaro Obregón, and Plutarco Elías Calles were all born in northern Mexico in the states of Coahuila and Sonora, giving rise to such labels as the Sonoran Dynasty to describe Mexico's national leadership after 1920.[5] Most students of Mexican politics are unaware that this northern dominance began long before the revolution, beginning with Díaz's 1901 administration, in which the North accounted for a fourth of prominent first-time

---

4. For example, nearly two and a half million residents of Oaxaca, Guerrero, and Chiapas speak indigenous languages, they rank highest in illiteracy at approximately 20 percent of their populations, and they rank lowest in level of education completed, approximately 6.5 grades compared to 10.2 in the Federal District.

5. For its importance, see Elisa Servín, Leticia Reina, John Tutino, eds., *Cycles of Conflict, Centuries of Change: Crisis, Reform, and Revolution in Mexico* (Durham, N.C.: Duke University Press, 2007).

national politicians. The northern region actually reached its apex in politicians' birthplaces in Díaz's final term, before the revolution.[6] Only since Cárdenas's administration have their numbers moderated, eventually averaging the same percentage as the general population from that region.

The public career that deviates the most in geographic origins from the norm is that of supreme court justice. Justices, a large percentage of whom have pursued long-standing legal careers through local, state, and federal judgeships, are strongly overrepresented in two regions that are underrepresented among legislative and executive branch politicians.[7] Interestingly, justices originating from the West Central region are almost equal in numbers to those from the Federal District and are more than half as likely to come from the West Central states as all other politicians. Even more surprising is the fact that the South receives its due representation for the only time among prominent politicians, with 14 percent of justices coming from this region. Finally, justices are the only Mexican national public figures underrepresented in the North, accounting for only slightly more than half as many as northern politicians from other career tracks.

Two possible complementary explanations may be relevant. Given the socioeconomic disadvantages of the South, individuals coming from states with the least influence may have sought opportunities to pursue careers more frequently in the least competitive branch of government, the branch exercising the least political and policy influence. Ambitious politicians from the North, given their economic and educational advantages, were more likely than their southern peers to follow executive and legislative branch careers.

Finally, an argument can be made that both the Federal District's overrepresentation among the birthplaces of all politicians and executive branch figures and the North's consistent representation since the 1930s can be explained by these regions' superior economic achievements. Both produced comparatively larger middle-income populations who, over time, dominated the socioeconomic backgrounds of political leadership.

Does democratic reform alter the geographic distribution of prominent political leadership specifically according to their careers? To sharpen any such changes, I compare leaders in the three branches of government from the predemocratic period (1935–88) to the democratic consolidation era (2000–2009) (table 8.2). These comparisons reveal several major trends,

    6. See Roderic Ai Camp, *Political Recruitment across Two Centuries: Mexico, 1884–1991* (Austin: University of Texas Press, 1995), 167, table 6.5.
    7. Based on an analysis of the online biographies of all supreme court justices since 1917, many of which appear in the *Directorio biográfico del poder judicial federal*, 2 vols. (Mexico: Suprema Corte de Justicia, 1989). The Mexican Political Biographies Project provides data that confirm 36 percent of justices were local judges, 21 percent served in the state's highest court, and 20 percent were Federal District superior court judges.

Table 8.2.  Regional Backgrounds of Leading Predemocratic Mexican Politicians

| | | | | Region of Birth (%) | | | | |
|---|---|---|---|---|---|---|---|---|
| Position | Federal District | East Central | West | North | South | Gulf | West Central | Foreign |
| *Legislative only* | | | | | | | | |
| Senators | | | | | | | | |
| Democratic | 17.9 | 14.1 | 19.6 | 16.8 | 9.2 | 10.9 | 11.4 | 0 |
| Predemocratic | 10.1 | 18.2 | 19.5 | 16.2 | 10.8 | 12.0 | 13.2 | 0 |
| Deputies | | | | | | | | |
| Democratic | 18.0 | 12.4 | 17.4 | 14.3 | 9.9 | 12.4 | 15.5 | 0 |
| Predemocratic | 10.7 | 16.5 | 21.4 | 14.2 | 10.7 | 12.6 | 13.9 | 0.003 |
| *All politicians* | | | | | | | | |
| 1920 Census | 6.3 | 20.0 | 15.8 | 12.0 | 13.7 | 12.7 | 19.5 | – |
| 1950 Census | 12.0 | 18.0 | 14.0 | 15.0 | 13.0 | 12.0 | 17.0 | – |
| All politicians | 23.0 | 13.2 | 15.2 | 15.0 | 8.4 | 11.9 | 12.2 | 1.1 |
| *Judicial only* | | | | | | | | |
| Justices | | | | | | | | |
| Democratic | 50.0 | 0 | 0 | 0 | 20.0 | 0 | 30.0 | 0 |
| Predemocratic | 12.9 | 19.4 | 10.8 | 7.5 | 17.2 | 11.8 | 20.4 | |
| *Executive only* | | | | | | | | |
| Cabinet | | | | | | | | |
| Democratic | 48.2 | 3.6 | 8.9 | 9.8 | 4.5 | 8.0 | 14.3 | 2.7 |
| Predemocratic | 23.4 | 11.4 | 12.9 | 15.1 | 7.5 | 16.2 | 12.9 | 0.005 |
| Asst. secretary | | | | | | | | |
| Democratic | 45.2 | 5.4 | 5.9 | 16.1 | 5.4 | 9.6 | 9.1 | 0.03 |
| Predemocratic | 30.0 | 10.8 | 10.5 | 14.6 | 6.7 | 13.1 | 12.1 | 2.2 |

*Source*: Mexican Political Biographies Project, 2009.

contradicting commonsense expectations about what consequences greater electoral competition might be expected to produce.

If we examine those members of congress who have served in the lower chamber two or more times, we discover a significant increase in the percentage of national leaders who come from the Federal District, even though the number of congressional districts in the Federal District actually declined in the 1990s as more Mexicans began to reside in the populous neighboring state of México.[8] Prior to 1988, the Federal District was slightly underrepresented among politicians who pursued legislative careers.

Since the 2000 benchmark election, nearly a fifth of all repeating members of congress were born in the capital. A substantial decline in

8. By 2006, the state of México accounted for 14,227,630 residents compared to only 8,222,349 in the Federal District. See data in Sergio Aguayo Quezada, *El almanaque mexicano, 2008* (Mexico: Aguilar, 2008), 252.

the East Central region in the backgrounds of these leaders accounts for a large part of the increase in politicians from Mexico City. Thus, as far as the long-term trend suggesting Mexico City–born politicians' increased presence among elites, democracy further enhanced the pattern. Among senators, the percentage from the Federal District is equal to that of deputies, and the percentage increase from the pre- to the postdemocratic period has been equally dramatic. Senators also have witnessed a substantial decline in East Central backgrounds between these two periods.

Just as striking as the increased legislative emphasis on the Federal District as a result of democratization is the same pattern among cabinet secretaries. Cabinet secretaries from the nation's capital after 2000 increased by two-thirds. The South has been underrepresented in all periods, but it reaches its lowest level among cabinet secretaries appointed since the inauguration of President Fox—about one-third of what it should be compared to general population figures. Even more remarkable is the dramatic decline in East Central regional birthplaces among cabinet members to an unheard-of low of 4 percent. The East Central region is the most populous in Mexico as of 1950, accounting for approximately 18 percent of the population. Given the fact that nearly one out of two cabinet members from the democratic period were born in the Federal District, all other regions are underrepresented.

Democratic change at the highest levels of Mexican political leadership has greatly exacerbated some existing trends, producing far greater geographic inequality than at any time under the semi-authoritarian, Institutional Revolutionary Party (PRI)-controlled era. Those inequalities are duplicated at the next level of executive branch influence among assistant secretaries. Assistant secretaries also at nearly the same levels come disproportionately from the capital, seriously underrepresenting the East Central, West, and South regions compared to the predemocratic administrations. Because a large percentage of assistant secretaries become cabinet secretaries, as I pointed out, the next generation of cabinet secretaries after 2012 is likely to reproduce these same geographic distortions among top executive branch politicians.

Finally, an examination of supreme court justices, the most influential members of the judicial branch, suggests a relatively balanced representation in their geographic backgrounds compared to the other two branches of government. Firm conclusions from the data on postdemocratic justices should not be drawn given the fact that the sample, although complete, is too small (11) across the number of regions we are comparing to make accurate predictions. These numbers are explained by the reality that Fox and Calderón have not been given the opportunity to appoint large numbers of justices since they serve for up to fifteen years or to their retirement age (sixty-five), whichever comes first.

In my earlier work on presidential recruitment under the PRI-dominated era, I discovered some evidence of presidents increasing the number of appointees from their home state, the result of early networking taking place between a president and friends in those locales.[9] Doing so naturally might increase the percentage of politicians from specific regions. Nevertheless, the two democratically elected presidents are not from the capital, yet that locale has achieved its highest level of representation under their administrations. Ironically, geographically speaking, Mexico's political leadership has become more geographically centralized under a decentralizing political model while having become more geographically decentralized under a highly centralized model.

Geographic biases in leadership can also be measured by the size of one's birthplace. Mexico has changed significantly over the twentieth century from a predominantly rural to an urban population. Despite the dramatic level of urbanization that has taken place, well over half the Mexican population through 1950 were living in communities of fewer than 2,500 people.[10] The access of rural Mexicans to national political office has declined significantly over time. In both the judicial and executive branches, even with the advent of electoral democracy, the dominance of urban birthplaces in politicians' backgrounds continues unabated, accounting for 90 and 92 percent, respectively, of supreme court justices and cabinet secretaries and assistant secretaries. As suggested in my analysis of demographic variables, the only channel most rural Mexicans can seriously pursue for political advancement is through congress. Since 2000, it is not surprising that a fifth of all congressional deputies continue to come from small Mexican villages.

Significant political change, both peaceful and violent, is often associated with generational change in leadership. This relationship definitely occurred during and after Mexico's 1910 revolution, in many African countries achieving independence in the mid-twentieth century, and even periodically in the United States without altering the political model, such as a generation of World War II veterans taking over national leadership in the 1950s. A generation may initiate institutional change as a means of

9. Roderic Ai Camp, "A Re-examination of Political Leadership and Allocation of Federal Revenues in Mexico, 1934–1973," *Journal of Developing Areas* 10 (January 1976): 193–213.

10. James W. Wilkie, *The Mexican Revolution: Federal Expenditure and Social Change since 1910* (Berkeley: University of California Press, 1970) reported that 57.4 percent in 1950 and 49.3 percent in 1960 were rural residents (218). These two decades account for most of the top leaders after 2000, suggesting the extreme degree to which rural backgrounds are underrepresented in the political leadership.

**Table 8.3.** Generations, Administrations, and Democracy: First-time Officeholders by Democratic Period

| Generations | Predemocratic (%) | Democratic Transition (%) | Postdemocratic (%) |
|---|---|---|---|
| Pre-1989 | 100.0 | 0 | 0 |
| 1890–99 | 100.0 | 0 | 0 |
| 1900–1909 | 100.0 | 0 | 0 |
| 1910–19 | 99.0 | 1.0 | 0 |
| 1920–29 | 94.4 | 5.2 | 0.4 |
| 1930–39 | 77.2 | 18.5 | 4.3 |
| 1940–49 | 31.6 | 44.8 | 23.6 |
| 1950–59 | 8.8 | 42.8 | 48.1 |
| 1960 | 0 | 15.7 | 84.3 |

*Source*: Mexican Political Biographies Project, 2009.

achieving access to political power, which is true of Mexico's revolutionary generation.

Is Mexico's transformation to an electoral democracy the product of generational change? Which generations dominated the three phases of Mexican leadership we have identified since the 1930s? The data in table 8.3 suggest several important generational shifts. Political leaders born before 1939 overwhelmingly dominated leadership positions before 1988. In the brief transition period from 1988 to 2000, 79 percent of politicians come only from the 1940s and 1950s generations. It has even been argued that these generations, which dominated Zedillo's administration, contributed to the PRI's loss of the presidency as a result of its errors in judgment and its generational biases.[11] Since 2000, the 1950s and 1960s have produced seven out of ten leading politicians. In essence, therefore, the 1950s generation becomes the bridge between the transition period and the democratic period, particularly between the Zedillo and Fox administrations. Clearly, the presence of the 1960s generation is overwhelmingly a democratic phenomenon.

An influential source of leaders comes from the legislative branch—nearly half of all top political figures have served in congress. Three legislative sessions, the 1991–94, 1994–97, and 1997-2000, anticipated the generational distribution found in the democratic period. Among their members, two-thirds of top legislators from the first session and more than 90 percent of their peers from the following two sessions, held influential posts in the Fox and Calderón administrations. Congressional backgrounds are important in understanding

11. See Rogelio Hernández Rodríguez, "Ernesto Zedillo: La presidencia contenida," *Foro Internacional* 43, no. 1 (January–March 2003): 39–70.

Table 8.4.  Representation of the 1950s and 1960s Generations
by Party among Leading Mexican Deputies, 1988–2000

| | 1950s and 1960s Generations by Party Affiliation (%) | | |
|---|---|---|---|
| Legislative Session | PAN | PRD | PRI |
| 1988–91 | 61 | 70 | 34 |
| 1991–94 | 51 | 50 | 43 |
| 1994–97 | 58 | 91 | 63 |
| 1997–2000 | 78 | 80 | 44 |

*Source*: Mexican Political Biographies Project, 2009.

leadership trends because they tend to be younger in composition, largely because of the higher percentage of PAN and Party of the Democratic Revolution (PRD) members who served in that body than in the past.

For example, more than half of the leading members of congress during these three sessions came from the 1950s and 1960s generations. If we examine the generational distribution according to party affiliation and expand it to include all four legislative sessions during the transitional period, we discover just how significant the PAN and PRD deputies are in introducing the decisive, younger democratic generations (table 8.4).

Equally interesting in terms of predicting the future impact of these generations is their distribution among all members of congress, not just the select group who achieve prominence in the political system. For example, the survey research firm Consulta Mitofsky completed a comprehensive analysis of 485 of the 500 members of congress during the 2003–2006 (fifty-ninth legislative session).[12] They reported several findings that are relevant to these highlighted generational patterns. The average age during the fifty-ninth legislative session was forty-five years old. A fourth of the members were younger than thirty-nine, all of whom were born after 1960, and more than a fourth were over fifty-one.

All deputies, however, are not equal when it comes to these generational distributions. In the first place, 200 seats (40 percent) in congress are determined by proportional representation. Most of the deputies older than fifty-one arrived in congress through these seats, designated by their respective party leadership. The overall distribution by party affiliation replicates the general patterns in table 8.3, but PAN members are by far the youngest, accounting for 46 percent of all deputies under thirty-nine years of age, compared to 24 and 21 percent among PRI and PRD members.

12. "Perfil de los diputados federales LIX legislatura," July 2004.

PRI, in contrast to the PAN and PRD, accounts for 43 percent of the forty- to fifty-year-old age group, and 56 percent of all legislators over fifty-one. In the 2006–2009 legislative session, exactly half of all PAN deputies were under the age of thirty-nine, and only a fifth were over fifty.

PRI, whose leadership dominated both the predemocratic and democratic transition periods, is an older leadership characterized by much slower generational change in favor of the youngest generations, which have recently entered Mexican public life. This is apparent among PRI members in the legislative branch immediately prior to the change in the political model.[13] It becomes equally apparent when comparing members of the two former opposition parties and independents with PRI members of the two administrations after 2000 (table 8.4). Non-PRI members of the democratic administrations are 40 percent or more likely to come from these two youngest generations. It is fair to describe these two age cohorts as the Democratic Generation.

Does generational change occur more rapidly among certain political institutions? It can be argued that among all leading politicians in this study, the lower house of congress serves as a leading edge in identifying the importance of younger generations and when its leaders are likely to shift their dominant generational origin. If a representative post for each of the three branches of government is selected, how do they compare by generations? Our expectation would be that supreme court justices in the democratic period, given their fixed and longer tenures, would be composed of the oldest generations. Members of the executive branch, because they are appointed by or through the influence of the incoming president, provide the greatest opportunity for shifting generational backgrounds suddenly, especially in a case where the incoming president, such as Felipe Calderón, himself represents the youngest generation (1960+) (see table 8.5).

The data in table 8.6 suggest that our speculation about the judicial branch as the slowest source of generational change is correct. They are more unlikely than other career tracks to produce public figures from the Democratic Generations. What is more surprising, however, is that little distinction occurs between members of the legislative and executive branches regardless of the position examined. These figures demonstrate that party affiliation or no affiliation are more significant in signaling a politician's

---

13. For example, in their examination of PANista senators from the 1994–2000 legislative sessions compared to those elected in the 2000–2003 session, Víctor Alarcón Olguín and Claudia Jiménez González also discovered the importance of the 1950s and 1960s generation, although they used different dates that do not allow us to draw precise comparisons. See their "Carreras legislativas en el Senado de la República: 1994–2006, el caso del Partido Acción Nacional," in *Los partidos en el Congreso de la Unión: La representación parlamentaria después de la alternancia* (Mexico: UNAM, 2006).

**Table 8.5.** Representation of the 1950s and 1960s Generations in Top Mexican Leadership by Party

| | 1950s and 1960s Generations by Party Affiliation (%) | | | |
| Administration | Independent | PAN | PRD | PRI |
| --- | --- | --- | --- | --- |
| Fox 2000–2006 | 67 | 59 | 89 | 47 |
| Calderón 2006–2012 | 84 | 83 | 80 | 60 |
| Combined 2000–2012 | 72 | 71 | 85 | 51 |

*Source*: Mexican Political Biographies Project, 2009.

**Table 8.6.** Representation of Democratic Generations among the Branches of Government since 2000

| Branch of Government | 1950s and 1960s Generations (%) |
| --- | --- |
| *Executive* | |
| Cabinet secretary | 63.4 |
| Assistant secretary | 61.1 |
| *Legislative* | |
| Deputies | 63.0 |
| Repeating deputies | 66.5 |
| *Judicial* | |
| Supreme court | 54.5 |

*Source*: Mexican Political Biographies Project, 2009.

date of birth than their career position. A dramatic increase in the importance of these two generations occurs between Fox and Calderón—from little more than half to three-quarters—but little difference is present from one career pattern to the next.

Politicians' origins, as we have discovered previously, extend well beyond empirical demographic, geographic, or generational variables to include familial origins. In addition to the traditional socioeconomic background variable, family history can explain the ability of politicians to improve their politically beneficial networking ties. They demonstrate the political system's flexibility in allowing entry to "politically contaminated" families unofficially banned from political office, especially shortly after a violent clash. It can also suggest the degree of continuity among previous generations of political elites in spite of such dramatic political upheavals.

We have four variables that allow us to test some aspects of these informal background qualities shared by Mexican politicians: the degree of

involvement of their fathers or mothers in political life; their connection
to extended political families through siblings, uncles, grandparents, and
so on; their ties to prominent Porfirian or revolutionary families from the
nineteenth and early decades of the twentieth centuries; and their familial
networking links to economic and intellectual elites.

The data presented in table 8.7 suggest a significant pattern in familial
ties among politicians. The most influential pattern occurs in the executive
branch at the highest level. Approximately one in seven leading politicians,
regardless of the career path they have taken, are known to be the children
of another prominent political figure. What is even more striking, however,
is that nearly half of Mexico's cabinet secretaries are known to be related
through close family kinship ties to other politicians. One in ten cabinet
secretaries are known to be related to Mexico's leading capitalists and cultural elites. Finally, one in seven cabinet secretaries has family ties to an
important revolutionary figure, typically a high ranking officer who fought
in the revolution. Perhaps more surprising is that more than one in twenty
actually were related to one of Mexico's influential Porfirian families.[14]

A fascinating example of the family linkages from the contemporary
period, which extended two generations to the revolutionary period, can
be found in the experiences of the Labra and Manjarrez families. Pelagio
C. Manjarrez, a railroad worker, composer, poet, journalist, and social
organizer, was born in Tochimilco, Puebla, in 1886, the oldest of five children. His brother Froylan became a distinguished constitutional deputy
in 1916–17 and governor of Puebla. His brother David lost his life helping

14. These ties are so extensive among a number of influential families that they are
often related to both distinguished Porfirian and revolutionary figures. For example, César
Sepúlveda Gutiérrez, a leading lawyer, dean of the National School of Law, ambassador to
Germany, and his brother, Bernardo, a distinguished physician and member of the prestigious National College, are the sons of Ricardo A. Sepúlveda, a merchant and industrialist
who made a fortune in Monterrey. César describes his father as follows: "He was a pure
liberal, those who were called 'Chicanos' or 'Jacobins.' He was deeply anti-imperialist, he
believed in Juárez and his ideas. He was one of the first to launch the revolution on April 2,
1907, the first blow from Monterrey. As a classmate of Emilio Madero, Lorenzo Hernández,
Rafael Hernández, Lorenzo Aguilar and others, in 1910, he formed the San Luis Rifle
company. Much later, when Emilio Madero joined Villa, my father was on the staff of the
Zaragoza Brigade, in the finance section, given his banking experience since he was one
of the founders of the Mercantile Bank of Monterrey. He viewed the Porfiriato as a sick-
ness, a decadence of the country, and opposed the lack of political liberties and the tremendous social inequalities. He was of the opinion that Díaz, since 1884, had betrayed the
reform and the 1857 Constitution." Two of César Sepúlveda's nephews, Bernardo and Jaime
Sepúlveda Amor, achieved prominent positions in public life as secretary of foreign relations
and assistant secretary of health, respectively. Their mother, Margarita Amor Schmidtlein,
was related to a prominent landed Porfirian family whose antecedents extended back to the
military physician who accompanied Maximilian to Mexico. Their great aunt, Guadalupe
Teresa (Pita) Amor, was a noted poet who modeled for Diego Rivera. Personal communication, August 7, 1974.

Table 8.7. Politics as a Family Tradition among Mexican Politicians

| Branch of Government | Family Connections (%) | | | | |
|---|---|---|---|---|---|
| | Father a Politician | Nuclear Family | Porfirian Family Ties | Revolutionary Family Ties | Other Elites |
| *Executive* | | | | | |
| Cabinet secretary | 15 | 47 | 6 | 13 | 12 |
| Assistant secretary | 16 | 37 | 4 | 5 | 8 |
| *Legislative* | | | | | |
| Deputies | 13 | 35 | 3 | 5 | 4 |
| Repeating deputies | 13 | 35 | 2 | 3 | 3 |
| *Judicial* | | | | | |
| Supreme court | 15 | 45 | 9 | 3 | 10 |

*Source*: Mexican Political Biographies Project, 2009.

Categories: father or mother a national or high-level state public figure; related through nuclear family, including in-laws, to other national or high-level state public figures; related through parents, in-laws, or siblings to prominent Porfirian and revolutionary families; related through parents, in-laws, or siblings to economic and intellectual elites.

peasants obtain land. His sister María Luisa, a teacher and prorevolutionary, married Gilberto Bosques, a member of congress, who served on the National Executive Committee of the Mexican Revolutionary Party and became ambassador to Cuba. Known as the "Schindler of Mexico," he helped bring hundreds of refugees from the Spanish Civil War to Mexico.

Pelagio fought in the revolution alongside Colonel Porfirio del Castillo and traveled as the auditor of the Mexico–Puebla railroad. When Zapatistas dynamited his train and captured all aboard, he was recognized by a wrangler on his father's farm and rescued from immediate execution. In 1923, he and his brother, then governor of Puebla, supported the De la Huerta rebellion and had to flee when the rebellion failed. They were captured by General Juan Andrew Almazán, a family friend, and, on direct orders from President Obregón, were ordered to be shot. Not wanting to execute the brothers, Almazán decided to send them to the capital. Once again, through the sympathetic assistance of train employees, Pelagio escaped and found refuge locally, while his brothers fled to Veracruz.

Pelagio's son, Luis Cruz Manjarrez, became a local deputy, member of congress, and senator from Puebla. He married the daughter of General Maximiliano Avila Camacho, President Avila Camacho's brother and the influential political boss of Puebla. He worked with his father in developing journalism in Puebla. Luis's daughter, María Cristina, married Wenceslao Labra García, a dominant figure in México state politics, having served as governor in the late 1930s and as a senator and a member of congress. Their son, Pelagio's grandson, Armando Labra Manjarrez, became assistant secretary of political development in 2000, the third generation to hold prominent public office.[15]

The second pattern that stands out in table 8.7 is the importance of these same linkages among supreme court justices. Similar to cabinet secretaries, nearly half were known to be related to other prominent politicians. Again, they are strongly linked through kinship ties to other leading elites. The most remarkable figure that distinguishes supreme court justices from all other leading politicians is that nearly one in ten were known to be related to Porfirian families, more than any other type of prominent national public figure.

Why have supreme court judges, measured by continuity between economic and political elites from the prerevolutionary period with the postrevolutionary period, been most likely to represent these linkages? Several variables appear to play a role. First, it is the only career pursued at the national level that requires a college degree. Thus, there exists a social barrier that in the past favored the children and grandchildren of middle- or upper-class Mexicans. Perhaps the most interesting example of a justice with extensive ties to wealthy, influential Mexicans is the family of Xavier Icaza y López Negrete, appointed to the court by Lázaro Cárdenas. In addition to his legal career, he was a major figure in the Estridentist literary movement and the author of numerous novels, poetry collections, and books on social and political issues. Icaza y López Negrete's grandparents owned one of the largest haciendas in the state of Durango, where he was born. Pancho Villa, a leading figure in the 1910 revolution, worked on one of their ranches.[16] His mother, Dolores López-Negrete, was related to one of the most influential families during the Porfiriato, the leading member of which was Pablo Martínez del Río, who served in the chamber of deputies under Porfirio Díaz from 1894 to 1907, amassing a huge fortune as a landowner in Durango while representing major railroad and mining interests.[17] Martínez del Río's

15. Personal communication from Alejandro Manjarrez, July 18, 2008.

16. Manuel Mestre Ghigliazza, *Efemérides biográficas* (Mexico: Antigua Librería Robredo, 1945), 6, 229.

17. Interestingly, he obtained his position as a federal deputy through his childhood friend, Adelaida Pani de Darqui, who asked Porfirio Díaz's wife if Pablo could occupy the post on the condition that his salary go to Adelaida after her husband died. He became friends with José Limantour, Díaz's treasury secretary and the most recognized symbol of the *científico* faction of the Porfirian leadership, while serving on the Railroad Commission. Ramón Puente, *La dictadura, la revolución y sus hombres* (Mexico, 1938), 109-12.

son Pablo was considered to be one of Mexico's leading intellectuals in the first half of the twentieth century. López y Negrete's mother was also the aunt of Mexico's most famous international actress in the 1940s and 1950s, Dolores del Río (real name was Dolores Martínez Asúnsolo y López Negrete).[18] After graduating from the Free Law School in Mexico City, Icaza y López Negrete began to practice law in 1917 with Carlos Díaz Dufoo, a leading antirevolutionary, intellectual, and federal deputy from 1900 to 1912. López Negrete's daughter, Ana María, married Ramón Xirau, another leading intellectual and dramatist in the second half of the twentieth century.

Second, the legal educational credential is the most traditional degree found among all generations of Mexican politicians, whether they served in the Porfiriato, the revolutionary period, or since 1920. Finally, a number of cases exist where presidents have given special recognition to supreme court justices whose families have long histories of public service in the judicial branch.[19]

For example, Ezequiel Burguete Farrera, who was appointed justice of the supreme court in 1966, was the grandson of an extremely wealthy landholding family in Chiapas during the Porfiriato. His father, who served in the state superior court of justice in 1916, retired as a federal circuit court judge.[20] The frequent pattern of individuals following in the footsteps of their fathers and grandfathers as lawyers and judges continues to the present. Mariano Azuela Guitrón, president of the supreme court from 2002 to 2007 and one of the few justices to be reappointed after the new legislation governing supreme court justices was introduced in 1995, is the son of Mariano Azuela Rivera, a justice from 1951 to 1972 (although not a member of the PRI) and the grandson of Mexico's distinguished revolutionary novelist Mariano Azuela. His sister, María Antonieta, is a federal circuit court judge.[21]

Finally, the data in table 8.7 also suggest that leading politicians with the fewest ties to other politicians, other elites, and historically

18. See www.estaciongomezpalacio.galeon.com, 2000; www.estrada.bz, 2008.

19. When José Castro Estrada retired from the court in 1967, during the administration of Gustavo Díaz Ordaz, the president wrote him a letter and brought up the fact that his grandfather had been a justice of the supreme court. Personal interview, August 4, 1974.

20. Personal interview, July 29, 1974, and Richard Benjamin, *A Rich Land, a Poor People: Politics and Society in Modern Chiapas* (Albuquerque: University of New Mexico Press, 1989), 134.

21. Personal interview, Mariano Azuela Rivera, May 31, 1978. Azuela Guitrón's uncle, Salvador Azuela Rivera, was a prominent historian and intellectual who supported José Vasconcelos's opposition presidential campaign in 1929 and General Juan Almazán's opposition campaign in 1940. He was a close personal friend of Cárdenas and President Adolfo López Mateos. Personal interview, June 26, 1975.

important figures opposed to or in support of the revolution served in the legislative branch. Surprisingly, public figures who served two or more times in congress were the least likely to have these extended kinship relationships. If one considers individuals without such links as broadening the pool from which Mexico's political leadership emerges, then members of congress and those who have emphasized legislative careers are the most accessible to those Mexicans providing fresh blood to that pool.

As Mexico shifted to an open electoral process, did these new administrations alter the level of politicians' family ties after 2000? The comparative data in table 8.8 from the Fox and Calderón administrations suggest some significant changes in the traditional patterns favoring a different and broader group of political actors. The most surprising change across all categories occurs among cabinet secretaries, representing a significant decline in family ties by up to a third to more than half. Such a dramatic decline illustrates the argument raised earlier that presidents can produce the most immediate change in the composition of the executive branch through their cabinet appointments. Among assistant secretaries, the change is much less dramatic and is only significant in their kinship links to important Porfirian and revolutionary families.

Table 8.8. Democratic Politics as a Mexican Family Tradition, 2000–2009

| Branch of Government | Family Connections (%) | | | | |
|---|---|---|---|---|---|
| | Father a Politician | Nuclear Family | Porfirian Family Ties | Revolutionary Family Ties | Other Elites |
| *Executive* | | | | | |
| Cabinet secretary | 10 | 28 | 4 | 5 | 9 |
| Assistant secretary | 15 | 33 | 2 | 2 | 7 |
| *Legislative* | | | | | |
| Deputies | 12 | 32 | 1 | 2 | 3 |
| Repeating deputies | 11 | 29 | 1 | 1 | 2 |
| *Judicial* | | | | | |
| Supreme court | 36 | 45 | 0 | 0 | 27 |

*Source*: Mexican Political Biographies Project, 2009.

Categories: father or mother a national or high-level state public figure; related through nuclear family, including in-laws, to other national or high-level state public figures; related through parents, in-laws, or siblings to prominent Porfirian and revolutionary families; related through parents, in-laws, or siblings to economic and intellectual elites.

In the legislative branch, declines in all five categories among repeating members of congress are present, but these are less extreme than those found among cabinet members. What is important to emphasize, however, is that the declines are significant in terms of historical family ties, for example, the number of all deputies who were related to prominent revolutionary figures dropped from 5 to 1 percent. This pattern reinforces the conclusion that members of congress during the democratic era continue to have the least family baggage when it comes to political, economic, and intellectual relationships.

Finally, the figures among supreme court justices illustrate some significant differences between the pre- and post-2000 administrations. Although recent appointees increasingly appear to be the sons and daughters of public figures and have the highest level of ties to other elites of any branch before or after the 2000 presidential election, the small numbers, although complete, give less confidence to establishing a trend.

The composition of political leadership can be altered in more formal ways by their educational backgrounds. Educational credentials are significant in assessing political leadership for several reasons. The level of education achieved by national leaders suggests an informal requirement for achieving a certain type of position. Politicians who have pursued different career tracks to reach the most influential positions have confronted different educational barriers. As the educational credentials increased in importance at the end of the twentieth century, they limited access to politics to fewer and fewer Mexicans.

In addition to the level of education, significant differences in career tracks occurred in the educational disciplines most commonly represented among leading public figures. Changes in disciplinary backgrounds are often indicative of changing directions in public policies and in the expertise valued by incumbent public figures who are in a position to recruit disciples to public office. Finally, where a politician obtains his education, from private, religious, and public institutions in Mexico and graduate or undergraduate work abroad in the United States or Europe, significantly affects individual and collective values and intellectual orientations, which impact public policy directions.

If we examine the educational patterns of all politicians for the past eighty years, we can detect three general patterns (table 8.9). The judicial branch, in certain respects, is the most well-educated career track because a law degree is required to become a supreme court justice, therefore, no justice is without a college degree. On the other hand, if we focus on the educational achievements of politicians beyond their undergraduate professional training, it is apparent that the executive branch has produced the most highly educated public figures measured by the percentage who have

Table 8.9. Education and Political Careers of Mexican Politicians

| Branch of Government | Level of Education Achieved (%) | | | | |
| --- | --- | --- | --- | --- | --- |
| | Normal | Preparatory | University | MA | Ph.D. |
| *Executive* | | | | | |
| Cabinet secretary | 7 | 5 | 43 | 28 | 18 |
| Assistant secretary | 3 | 2 | 39 | 32 | 24 |
| *Legislative* | | | | | |
| Deputies | 19 | 8 | 48 | 16 | 9 |
| Repeating deputies | 23 | 13 | 45 | 12 | 7 |
| *Judicial* | | | | | |
| Supreme court | 0 | 0 | 74 | 9 | 17 |

*Source*: Mexican Political Biographies Project, 2009.

Normal includes elementary and secondary only; MA includes postprofessional and master's degree; Ph.D. includes M.D., LL.D, and Ph.D.

obtained significant postgraduate training, master's degrees or doctorates. More than four out of ten cabinet secretaries in Mexico have graduate studies or degrees, and one in five has earned a Ph.D. Assistant secretaries are even better educated than their bosses: nearly six out of ten boast graduate studies and a fourth have completed doctorates.

If one thinks of increased educational attainments as a barrier to numerous Mexicans, it is politicians in the legislative branch, similar to the findings of their broader distribution of socioeconomic backgrounds, who are more likely to be non-college graduates. Over time, nearly three in ten deputies never obtained a college degree, and one in five never went beyond a secondary or normal education. This greater degree of openness in educational requirements continues to be true among federal deputies. For example, among the 485 of 500 deputies surveyed by Consulta Mitofsky in 2004, 17 percent of the PAN, 58 percent of PRI, and 25 percent of PRD deputies reported they had not completed preparatory studies.[22] It is also important to point out that those national politicians who have chosen the legislative branch as their focus for national leadership, having served as a member of congress two or more times, were even more likely to have done so without obtaining a college degree.

22. "Perfil de los diputados federales LIX legislatura," July 2004.

In the first legislative session under President Calderón (2006-2009), *El Universal*, one of Mexico's leading newspapers, ran an article indicating that 142 deputies and senators (1 in 5) had no college degree, and 13 had not even completed the sixth grade. The newspaper reported that the National University of Mexico signed an agreement with the Chamber of Deputies in 2007 to assist legislators in completing their preparatory or university education.[23]

To what extent has a change in Mexico's political model altered this significant feature of politicians' credentials? Furthermore, has democratic change produced a more homogeneous leadership or broadened their educational backgrounds? A truly dramatic change in the level of education among different national politicians has taken place between those serving prior to and after 2000. The most striking change overall is the increase in postgraduate education among all politicians representing all branches of government. Naturally, the educational levels of national politicians has increased over time. Nevertheless, the figures are dramatic in certain categories. For example, supreme court justices with only law degrees are no longer typical in Mexico; instead, the figures are completely reversed from justices prior to 2000, with three-quarters having obtained postgraduate education, typically with an M.A. in law or an LL.D. (table 8.10).

Among prominent federal deputies, although the numbers are not as large as can be found among all members in recent legislative sessions, 10-15 percent of prominent members of congress have obtained their posts without a college degree. In the democratic era, many of these individuals are self-made businessmen who have obtained elective office and earned a reputation and prestige because of their business acumen and community leadership skills rather than through formal educational credentials.[24] Others, from modest circumstances, have used careers in public life at the local level to achieve the recognition necessary to rise up the national political ladder. Josefina Cota Cota represents this latter type of politician. She was raised in a peasant family in the tiny community of San Juan de los Planes, near La Paz, Baja California del Sur, in the 1950s and 1960s. She attended high school in Comondú and became an organizer in the local women's peasant union. After winning a seat on the city council of

---

23. Selene Avila, "Una de cada 5 legisladores no terminó la licenciatura," *El Universal*, April 9, 2007. The article includes an interesting discussion about the importance of access to the chamber based on educational backgrounds as well as suggestions for improving the academic preparation of legislators.

24. For an excellent analysis of how this involvement came about within the PAN in the 1980s and 1990s, see Yemille Mizrahi, "Entrepreneurs in the Opposition, Modes of Political Participation in Chihuahua," in Victoria Rodríguez and Peter Ward, eds., *Opposition Government in Mexico* (Albuquerque: University of New Mexico Press, 1995), 81–96.

**Table 8.10.** Education and Political Careers under a Democracy, 2000–2009

| Branch of Government | Level of Education Achieved (%) | | | | |
|---|---|---|---|---|---|
| | Normal | Preparatory | University | MA | Ph.D. |
| *Executive* | | | | | |
| Cabinet secretary | 0 | 5 | 21 | 54 | 21 |
| Assistant secretary | 0 | 3 | 27 | 45 | 24 |
| *Legislative* | | | | | |
| Deputies | 5 | 6 | 47 | 35 | 9 |
| Repeating deputies | 7 | 6 | 47 | 32 | 8 |
| *Judicial* | | | | | |
| Supreme court | 0 | 0 | 27 | 64 | 9 |

*Source*: Mexican Political Biographies Project, 2009.

Normal includes elementary and secondary only; MA includes postprofessional and master's degree; and Ph.D. includes M.D., LL.D, and Ph.D.

Comondú in 1983, she won a seat in the state legislature, representing the fourth district. A decade later she reached the post of secretary general of the League of Peasant Communities and Unions, and the PRD selected her as an alternate senator from 1997 to 2000. She worked in the state government during the first half of the Fox administration, winning an election as an alternate member of congress from the first congressional district in 2003, but she replaced the deputy a year later. In the 2006 elections, she received her party's nomination for one of the senate seats and was elected to the senate.[25]

The executive branch, however, has continued to eliminate nearly any possibility for a Mexican with political ambitions who is not a college graduate to serve in the cabinet or subcabinet since 2000. The small number of secretaries and assistant secretaries who previously achieved such national prominence without a college education has dropped in half since 2000, and 94 percent have graduated from college. Since Vicente Fox took office, three-quarters of Mexico's top government decision makers have gone on to graduate school, representing a 63 percent increase from the predemocratic era.

25. See www.senado.gob.mx, 2008; Jorge V. Alcocer, ed., *Directorio Congreso mexicano, lx legislatura, 2006-2009* (Mexico: Nuevo Horizonte Editores, 2007), 32.

Table 8.11. College Degrees of Leading Mexican Politicians

| Branch of Government | Discipline (%) | | | | | |
|---|---|---|---|---|---|---|
| | Law | Economics | Medical | Engineering | Business | Other |
| *Executive* | | | | | | |
| All cabinet secretaries | 40 | 17 | 6 | 15 | 5 | 17 |
| Democratic secretaries | 25 | 21 | 3 | 15 | 10 | 25 |
| All assistant secretaries | 32 | 20 | 8 | 15 | 6 | 19 |
| Democratic assist. secy. | 25 | 30 | 3 | 11 | 7 | 24 |
| *Legislative* | | | | | | |
| All deputies | 50 | 11 | 4 | 9 | 6 | 20 |
| All PAN deputies | 38 | 5 | 7 | 15 | 17 | 19 |
| Democratic deputies | 37 | 13 | 3 | 11 | 10 | 29 |
| *Judicial* | | | | | | |
| Supreme court[a] | 100 | 0 | 0 | 0 | 0 | 0 |

*Source*: Mexican Political Biographies Project, 2009.

a. Three supreme court justices also have degrees in other fields.

Changes in disciplinary backgrounds occur more slowly than the level of educational attainment itself among politicians. The disciplinary backgrounds of Mexican politicians are linked more strongly to certain career choices (table 8.11). Law, as we have explained previously, is the most common and traditional degree found in politicians' credentials. Law has declined as a degree and a profession among recent politicians, whereas other professions have increased their presence.[26] Part of this change among democratic politicians is attributable to PAN's presence, which has increased the number of politicians with engineering and especially business administration and accounting backgrounds.[27] PRD politicians,

26. Graduates in 2002-2003 in Mexico accounted for the following percentages in the leading disciplines, differing considerably from the disciplinary backgrounds of recent politicians: business administration and accounting, 18 percent, engineering, 12 percent, law, 11 percent, computer systems, 10 percent, graphic design, 4 percent, and medicine, 4 percent. Only 1 percent of recent graduates majored in economics! See Salvador Malo, "La educación superior en el nuevo milenio: Una primera aproximación," *Este País*, April 2006, 9.

27. For example, among all PAN deputies in the 2006-2009 legislative session, forty-five were engineers, including electronics, communications, telecommunications, geology,

on the other hand, have enhanced the growing presence of economists in government.

Economics, which began a rapid rise during the 1988-2000 transition years, established a significant niche in educational preparation in the executive branch among assistant secretaries, accounting for three out of ten individuals, the largest percentage of any profession or degree among all public figures. Given the different distribution of college degree fields in the backgrounds of members of congress from those in the executive branch, congressional politicians would likely find it more difficult to pursue successful careers as assistant secretaries because they do not have the preferred university credentials.

Perhaps the most important component of politicians' educational credentials is where they attend school. The type and location of schools politicians attend is significant in Mexican politics for two reasons: the formation of their political and social values and their intimate networking with peers and mentors, critical to a successful career in public and intellectual life. Some politicians have made such contacts with their peers in elementary and high school. For example, presidents Luis Echeverría and José López Portillo, who followed each other in office, attended the Benito Juárez Elementary School in the Colonia del Valle in Mexico City, and eventually attended the National School of Law together, traveling as students on a formative trip to South America in 1941.[28]

The most important precollege experience universally among politicians, however, is among those who attended preparatory school, the academic track that typically qualifies a student for admission to college. There exist several important types of preparatory schools in Mexico. Most important have been the National Preparatory School and what might be described as their provincial counterparts. These schools are associated with the leading public state universities that typically evolved from literary and scientific institutions established by liberal educational reformers in the second half of the nineteenth century, many in prestigious institutions whose origins extended back to the colonial period.[29] A select group of politicians attended private secular schools in both the Federal District and important provincial cities, typically the state capitals. An equal number

---

industrial, chemical, electrical, computing, and food. See www.148.245.48.180, September 13, 2006.

28. Personal interview with José López Portillo, February 19, 1991.

29. For a brief discussion of its evolution, see Mal Leicester, *Education, Culture and Values: Pupils, Schools and Teacher Education* (London: Routledge, 2000), 48. For a superb analysis of the establishment and impact of the National Preparatory School, see Charles A. Hale, *The Transformation of Liberalism in Late Nineteenth-Century Mexico* (Princeton, N.J.: Princeton University Press, 1989).

Table 8.12. Preparatory Schools Attended by Leading Mexican Politicians

| Preparatory School | Branch of Government (%) | | | |
|---|---|---|---|---|
| | Executive | | Legislative | Judicial |
| | Secretary | Assistant Secretary | Deputies | Supreme Court |
| Public state | 22 | 25 | 26 | 34 |
| Private D.F. | 4 | 5 | 1 | 4 |
| Religious D.F. | 7 | 8 | 4 | 5 |
| Religious state | 3 | 2 | 2 | 1 |
| Private state | 2 | 3 | 2 | 3 |
| Military | 10 | 10 | 5 | 5 |
| Foreign | 4 | 4 | 2 | 3 |
| ENP | 33 | 31 | 19 | 41 |
| None | 16 | 14 | 39 | 3 |

*Source*: Mexican Political Biographies Project, 2009.

attended religiously operated preparatory schools in the Federal District and in provincial cities. Finally, especially in the predemocratic period, sizable numbers of leading politicians were graduates of the Heroic Military College, the military's equivalent of a preparatory education.[30]

The attendance data in table 8.12 suggest several major differences on the basis of career tracks alone. As one would expect, more members of congress have not attended any preparatory institution compared to attending any institution. Furthermore, we would not expect attendance at Mexico City institutions to be high because federal legislators are distributed among all thirty-two states and the Federal District. Nevertheless, surprisingly, a fifth of all leading members of congress are products of the National Preparatory School (ENP). This can be explained by the fact that regardless of their birthplaces, politically ambitious students since the nineteenth century have sought to be educated in this school.[31]

During the revolution, including the 1920s, when some provincial institutions were closed, top students were able to obtain state scholarships to go to Mexico City schools. What is also surprising is that the number of

30. Juan N. Chávarri, *El Heroico Colegio Militar en la historia de México* (Mexico: Libro-Mex, 1960).

31. Camp, *Political Recruitment across Two Centuries*, 89. "Out of a population of millions, only several hundred students had the opportunity to attend this institution in the last third of the nineteenth century. Of their numbers, a disproportionate percentage accounted for Mexico's future political and intellectual leadership." This conclusion was based on my analysis of the official registration records of the school at the National University of Mexico archives in Mexico City.

legislative leaders who are products of provincial public schools are equal to their peers in the executive branch. Even though state preparatory schools have been central to political recruitment within those states, given the centralized nature of the political system prior to 2000, the ENP has even drawn heavily among future members of congress.

A second distinctive pattern that emerges in the preparatory education of politicians by branch of government is the significant difference that occurs among all three branches in their level of religiously oriented schooling. One in ten members of the executive branch has received such an education from prestigious religiously operated schools, typically in the Federal District. The most important of these schools for Mexican politicians have been (1) the Centro Universitario Mexicano (CUM), a Brothers of Mary school whose graduates included Porfirio Muñoz Ledo, a founder of the PRD and president of both the PRD (1993–96) and the PRI (1975–76); Manuel Bartlett, secretary of government under Miguel de la Madrid; and Miguel Mancera, head of Mexico's Federal Reserve under three presidents; (2) Colegio Cristóbal Colón (de la Salle Christian Brothers), which includes Miguel de la Madrid among its alumni; and (3) Colegio Francés Morelos (the antecedent of CUM), which graduated President Echeverría.[32] There have been several important politicians, not just from the PAN, who also initially attended seminary schools. These schools frequently provided the best education for rural Mexicans in the early part of the twentieth century.[33]

If we examine the legislative and judicial branches, however, it is apparent that only half as many of these individuals (compared to executive branch politicians) have attended religious schools. The explanation for this is twofold. Among deputies, generally lower socioeconomic backgrounds explains lower attendance at such schools. Among future judges, given the extreme constitutional restrictions on religious institutions from 1917 to 1992, some of which remain in effect, a religious education may have deterred some future public figures from pursuing judicial careers where church–state legal conflicts likely would emerge.

Finally, two additional educational patterns develop that distinguish career tracks pursued by Mexican politicians. First, nearly one third of the leaders of the executive branch agencies are products of a single nationally funded institution, the National Preparatory School, which has contributed significantly to elite leadership in the country since its founding

---

32. For more details on their importance, see Roderic Ai Camp, *Crossing Swords: Politics and Religion in Mexico* (New York: Oxford University Press, 1997), 208–209.

33. Such experiences resulted in important personal ties between leading politicians, several of whom became governors, and bishops, who were co-students at local seminaries.

in the nineteenth century. Among supreme court justices, the National Preparatory School alone accounts for two-fifths of their preparatory education. Second, those Mexican public figures who have experienced the extreme socialization experiences of attending a military academy, which is far more significant professionally than any substantive technical or military training, are twice as likely (one in ten) to be found in the executive rather than the legislative or judicial branch.[34]

Mexican politicians who have completed university studies also are influenced by some of the same private-public or religious-secular patterns occurring at the preparatory levels. University attendance only increases the socialization distortions between the executive and judicial versus the legislative branches. The National University (UNAM) domination is extreme, accounting for the higher education of half of all secretaries and assistant secretaries in the executive branch and two-thirds of all supreme court justices.[35] Two conditions contribute to this pattern. First, as I discovered earlier, a large percentage of assistant secretaries and justices were born and raised in the capital. This gave them easy access not only to the National Preparatory School but to its logical university counterpart, the National University. Second, those provincial students fortunate enough to attend the National Preparatory School also are more likely to continue their education at the National University, due in no small part to the networks between preparatory school teachers and students and their peers at the National University. Indeed, 85 percent of politicians who attended the National Preparatory School went on to UNAM, compared to only a third of those who attended state public institutions.

Politicians who are from the provinces have succeeded in obtaining the most influential government posts, but they are more likely to pursue successful careers in the legislative and judicial branches in equal numbers. Few public school university graduates from cities outside the capital ever become cabinet-level agency heads. Politicians who have graduated from private universities, an increasingly significant presence among all public figures, are much more likely to have obtained positions as assistant secretaries. Nearly a fifth of these officeholders are private university graduates.

Finally, no supreme court justices have ever studied abroad at the undergraduate level, making them the least cosmopolitan of all leading

---

34. For evidence of this, see William S. Ackroyd, "Military Professionalism, Education, and Political Behavior in Mexico," *Armed Forces and Society* 18, no. 1 (Fall 1991): 81–96; and Serge Guimond, "Encounter and Metamorphosis: The Impact on Professional Values," *Applied Psychology: An International Review* 44, no. 3 (1995): 251–75.

35. In 2002–2003, the National University accounted for 14 percent of all students enrolled in a university program.

politicians. Of all branches of government, they almost exclusively have graduated from public universities in the capital or states (see table 8.13). They are also the only group of leading politicians who have graduated in large numbers from a single leading state public university: the University of Guadalajara in Jalisco. One-third of public university graduates on the supreme court from provincial universities were alumni of this college.

To what extent has the democratic opening altered the university experiences of Mexican politicians? In the executive branch, a significant shift occurred away from the National University in favor of private and religious institutions. The figures for secretaries and assistant secretaries in the democratic period graduating from such institutions essentially doubled compared to those figures for all cabinet secretaries and assistant secretaries and tripled among secretaries graduating only from secular private institutions. Secular and religious private institutions combined accounted for the university experiences of one-third of leading politicians since 2000.

Even more remarkable is the shift in favor of private education among Fox's and Calderon's supreme court justices. A third of their judicial appointees, compared to less than one in twenty from previous administrations, were private school graduates. The judicial branch can be distinguished from its sister branches by the fact that in addition to the extraordinary increase in private school graduates, explained by a decline in UNAM and military academy graduates, state public university graduates increased threefold. If we lump all of the publicly funded institutions together, 96 percent of all supreme court justices have emerged from public university backgrounds compared to only six out of ten since 2000.

**Table 8.13.** Universities Attended by Leading Mexican Politicians

|  | Branch of Government (%) | | | |
| --- | --- | --- | --- | --- |
|  | Executive | | Legislative | Judicial |
| University | Secretary | Assistant Secretary | Deputies | Supreme Court |
| Public state | 13 | 18 | 29 | 28 |
| Private | 9 | 13 | 7 | 4 |
| Religious | 3 | 4 | 3 | 1 |
| Military | 6 | 5 | 2 | 1 |
| Foreign | 3 | 3 | 1 | 0 |
| UNAM | 54 | 52 | 32 | 67 |
| None | 12 | 5 | 26 | 0 |

*Source*: Mexican Political Biographies Project, 2009.

A complementary change that also accompanies the radical decline in national university graduates, especially in the executive and judicial branches, is an important reversal of a longtime trend characterizing the predemocratic period, in which politicians from public state institutions decreased significantly while those from institutions in the Federal District increased. After 2000, a dramatic increase occurs in the importance of public provincial universities among political leaders in the executive and legislative branches. Again, the presence of PAN helps explain the decline in politician graduates from UNAM because only one in ten PANistas in the Calderón administration lists that institution as their alma mater. Both PAN and especially PRD members are especially well represented among provincial public institutions, which explains those institutions' increasing numbers. The significant decline in non-college-educated politicians since 2000 also can be attributed to both PAN and PRD members, who are more typically college graduates than their PRI peers.

The democratic opening has introduced a significant change in the values and orientations learned by politicians through their university experiences.[36] This condition is the result of the growing influence of private institutions, which had little impact in the predemocratic period. Its presence before 2000 was largely felt during the democratic transition since 1988, with the exception of graduates from the Free Law School.[37] In the transition period, secular institutions, especially the Autonomous Technological Institute of Mexico (ITAM) and the Monterrey Institute of Higher Studies, increased their presence in politicians' backgrounds as economics became a more frequent disciplinary choice.[38] By 2000, not only did those institutions produce increasing numbers of graduates (for example, ITAM alone accounted for half of the private university experiences of assistant secre-

36. Daniel Levy's excellent chapter, "Private-Public Distinctiveness: Mexico," provides a detailed exploration of the differences between private and public educational institutions, including many of the distinctions I have alluded to. *Higher Education and the State in Latin America: Private Challenges to Public Dominance* (Chicago: University of Chicago Press, 1986), 114–70.

37. Calderón is not the first president who graduated from this institution. Emilio Portes Gil, who appointed his law school professor, Julio García, to the supreme court, as mentioned previously, was a proud student founder of the Free Law School in 1912. Two fellow students included Ezequiel Padilla, secretary of foreign relations, 1940–45, an independent presidential candidate, 1945–46, who served as Portes Gil's attorney general and secretary of public education, and Enrique Medina, whom he also appointed as attorney general during his administration. Personal communication, October 20, 1972.

38. As Sarah Babb has pointed out, the first private economics program in Mexico was founded for ideological, not practical reasons.(73). For insight into how this shift took place and its impact on government economic leadership, see her fascinating account in chapters 6 and 7 of *Managing Mexico: Economists from Nationalism to Liberalism* (Princeton, N.J.: Princeton University Press, 2001), 137–98.

taries since 2000) but they were complemented by private religious universities, of which the most influential has been the Jesuit Ibero-American University in Mexico City.

The most important explanation for the increase in private university degrees among politicians across all three branches is the presence of PAN members in Mexico's leadership. For example, in the Calderón administration, 21 percent of PANistas were private university graduates. In addition, another 15 percent were products of private religious schools. In contrast, only 10 percent of PRI politicians attended similar private institutions, and the PRD did not produce a single private or religious university graduate.

The increasing diversity in politicians' university backgrounds and intellectual formation is a product of this opening, resulting in a greater balance between public and private educational experiences among political elites (table 8.14). On the other hand, the decreasing emphasis on working-class socioeconomic backgrounds among politicians since 2000 is also linked to that very diversity given the unequal access of those Mexicans to private universities, which only rarely offer scholarships to such students.

The educational socialization of Mexican politicians occurs not only at the undergraduate but also at the graduate level. It further contributes to the complexity of experiences because, unlike Mexican politicians' undergraduate education, which rarely occurs abroad, huge numbers of public figures completed postgraduate studies in the United States and Europe. This graduate trend began to accelerate in the 1980s, represented by José López Portillo's studies in Chile, and, more important, by Miguel de la Madrid's master's in public administration from Harvard University.

**Table 8.14.** Universities Attended by Leading Mexican Democratic Politicians, 2000–2009

| | Branch of Government (%) | | | |
|---|---|---|---|---|
| | Executive | | Legislative | Judicial |
| University | Secretary | Assistant Secretary | Deputies | Supreme Court |
| Public state | 23 | 26 | 48 | 9 |
| Private | 29 | 25 | 8 | 36 |
| Religious | 6 | 8 | 10 | 0 |
| Military | 7 | 4 | 0.002 | 9 |
| Foreign | 4 | 4 | 2 | 0 |
| UNAM | 28 | 30 | 26 | 45 |
| None | 3 | 3 | 7 | 0 |

*Source*: Mexican Political Biographics Project, 2009.

Has democratization altered these graduate experiences among politicians since 1988, and how have they differed across the branches of government? It is apparent from the data in table 8.15 that the increase in graduate training is not just a general chronological phenomenon but has been affected specifically by the composition of leadership since the democratic opening in 2000. Among all three career tracks pursued by politicians, the most universal pattern is a significant increase in postgraduate studies generally, as well as from just the 1988-2000 period to after 2000. The one exception is assistant secretaries, who have remained among the best educated group since 1988, but boast no increase in their graduate training. The second pattern, which is universally shared among all politicians regardless of career track is an increase—significantly among legislators and supreme court justices—in graduate training only in Mexico. Two out of every ten politicians have pursued advanced studies in Mexico.

The most interesting change that has taken place is the decline among politicians who have attended graduate school in Europe (the numbers from Latin America are quite small) in the executive and legislative branches. Whereas politicians who studied in Europe at the graduate level increased significantly from 1988 to 2000, they have decreased equally significantly since 2000 with the exception of supreme court justices. Again, because the

Table 8.15. Graduate School Trends of Politicians since the Democratic Transition

| | Location of Graduate Training (%) | | | |
| --- | --- | --- | --- | --- |
| Government Branch | United States | Europe/ Latin America | Mexico | None |
| *Legislative* | | | | |
| All deputies | 5 | 6 | 11 | 79 |
| Democratic transition | 6 | 11 | 13 | 69 |
| Democratic era | 7 | 8 | 24 | 60 |
| *Executive* | | | | |
| All secretaries | 20 | 12 | 13 | 56 |
| Democratic transition | 24 | 21 | 15 | 40 |
| Democratic era | 37 | 14 | 18 | 30 |
| All assistant secretaries | 24 | 13 | 15 | 48 |
| Democratic transition | 29 | 18 | 18 | 36 |
| Democratic era | 31 | 12 | 21 | 36 |
| *Judicial* | | | | |
| All supreme court justices | 2 | 11 | 17 | 74 |
| Democratic transition | 4 | 19 | 21 | 56 |
| Democratic era | 0 | 36 | 36 | 27 |

*Source*: Mexican Political Biographies Project, 2009.

number of judicial appointees since 2000 are quite small, one should not give too much significance to those figures. If these recent justices do represent any trend, having graduate studies is the most significant change, increasing from one-fourth of all justices since 1935 to slightly more than half in 1988 to three-quarters since 2000.

Finally, in the executive branch, among cabinet secretaries, a dramatic increase has occurred in the percentage of prominent public figures who have pursued graduate work in the United States, continuing and increasing significantly a trend begun in the Salinas and Zedillo era from one-fourth to one-third of all cabinet members. Since the advent of the democratic period in 2000, cabinet secretaries have surpassed assistant secretaries in achieving some postgraduate studies.

The diversity in the composition of political leadership can also be measured by comparing changes that occur in some career experiences over time with those changes that have occurred since 2000. Certain experiences have traditionally been important to leading Mexican politicians. One of the most important and universally present experiences that politicians across all career tracks share is having been a student leader. The fact that one in six of all top politicians are known to have been actively involved in student politics as leaders in secondary, preparatory, and college institutions suggest the importance of an early start in initiating a political career, and many politicians' early ambition and interest in politics.[39]

What is striking about the data in table 8.15 is the equally dramatic decline in student political experiences (by nearly half or more) among all politicians regardless of the public career track they pursued. The significant decline in this early experience suggests the depoliticization of student experiences, which can be explained by the increase in the numbers of private and religious university graduates, where the university environment

---

39. Student activism leading to prominence in national politics has a long and glorious history in Mexico. Emilio Portes Gil, president of Mexico from 1928 to 1930, explains what happened when he was a fourth-year law student at the National School of Law in 1912. "The dean of the school, Luis Cabrera, issued some disciplinary regulations which provoked general discontent that produced a strike. [My] fellow leaders of that movement included other fourth-year law students, Ezequiel Padilla, Luis and Vicente MacGregor, Manuel Herrera y Lazo, and José María Gurría Urgell. They had various interviews with the dean who didn't accept their proposals or withdraw the regulations, which he considered beneficial to the school's development. Then it occurred to them to speak to President Francisco I. Madero. The interview was cordial and he explained to us that the government would have to support the dean because he considered his regulations adequate and fair. Given this situation, they went to see President Madero to express their desire to found a Free Law School. The president was in agreement with their proposals, indicating to us that it was time for the private sector to fund professional schools. He named a committee of the most prestigious lawyers in the profession, who offered to help us achieve our goal. The Escuela Libre de Derecho opened its doors in July of 1912." Personal communication, October 20, 1972.

is rarely politicized. Thus recent politicians are obtaining their early political experiences from other venues, primarily through the auspices of their
respective party organizations and youth wings, but not on campus.

A second important change that has occurred in a less widely shared
career experience among politicians is an equally important decline among
those who were *agentes del ministerio público*, investigative agents employed
by the public prosecutors in each judicial district. It has often been the first
public job recent law graduates traditionally have taken. Other than judgeships at the local and state level, it is the most common post found in the
backgrounds of supreme court justices. Among politicians in the executive and legislative branches, approximately one in twenty also worked as
agents. Since 2000, however, those numbers have dropped in half and for
justices have gone from one-fifth to none. Again, although the sample for
justices is small, the change is extreme. It is obvious from the decline in
the other two branches that employment as a federal agent is no longer an
attractive starting point for a lifetime career in public service, including in
the justice system.

Given the corporate structure of political life prior to 2000, when nearly
all unions were affiliated in some way with the governing party, it is not
surprising that many influential politicians were union leaders at the
state, regional, or national levels. Union leaders have been most successful in translating their skills to careers in the legislative branch, especially
as members of congress. One in six deputies were important union officials. Although the number was much smaller in the executive branch,
many cabinet secretaries counted such union experiences in their backgrounds. Since 2000, union posts in the backgrounds of politicians serving
in the executive branch have nearly disappeared, appearing among secretaries and assistant secretaries only 1 percent of the time. This decline
is explained not only by the presence of PAN militants in the executive
branch but also by the fact that Fox and Calderón appointed PRI officials
who were less partisan, lacking attachments to labor unions.[40]

It is also important to note that even in the legislative branch, members
of congress since the democratic era were much less likely to have union
credentials than has been the case previously (table 8.16). Only 1 PAN
member of the 229 individuals who are leading members of the legislative
branch has ever been associated with a union organization. Among PRD
deputies, one in ten shares a union background; among PRI, one in five.

---

40. Steve Wuhs cites the following figures for PAN deputies who were union leaders
in the 2000–2003 legislative session (1.9 percent) and PRD deputies (6.5 percent). See his
*Savage Democracy: Institutional Change and Party Development in Mexico* (University Park:
Pennsylvania State University Press, 2008), 111.

**Table 8.16.** Career Experiences of Mexican Politicians

|                        |                  | Career Experience (%) |                 |                            |          |                     |
| ---------------------- | ---------------- | --------------------- | --------------- | -------------------------- | -------- | ------------------- |
| Government Branch      | Federal Agent    | Student Leader        | Union Leader    | Professional Organization  | Military | Business Manager    |
| *Legislative*          |                  |                       |                 |                            |          |                     |
| All deputies           | 5                | 16                    | 17              | 3                          | 5        | 4                   |
| Democratic era         | 2                | 8                     | 11              | 0.4                        | 1        | 9                   |
| *Executive*            |                  |                       |                 |                            |          |                     |
| All secretaries        | 6                | 17                    | 7               | 1                          | 11       | 13                  |
| Democratic era         | 4                | 8                     | 1               | 0                          | 8        | 21                  |
| All assistant          | 4                | 10                    | 4               | 1                          | 6        | 8                   |
| secretaries            |                  |                       |                 |                            |          |                     |
| Democratic era         | 2                | 4                     | 1               | 0                          | 4        | 9                   |
| *Judicial*             |                  |                       |                 |                            |          |                     |
| All justices           | 22               | 16                    | 0               | 1                          | 3        | 3                   |
| Democratic era         | 0                | 9                     | 0               | 0                          | 9        | 9                   |

*Source*: Mexican Political Biographies Project, 2009.

Military = career military with rank of colonel or higher; Business Manager = owner or top manager of large firm or corporation; Professional Organization = national or regional leaders of the National Federation of Popular Organizations.

Even the Left has produced nearly one in five deputies who were former union leaders. Given these figures among all deputies, the decline since 2000 is substantial and goes well beyond the lone effect of PAN's increased presence.

Career military officers, as we have suggested in previous chapters, played a critical role in Mexico's political leadership. In recent years, in the executive branch, career officers have been largely confined to the national defense and navy secretariats, although several have served as attorney general and assistant attorney general since 2000. What is most important to point out is that in the legislative branch career officers have almost disappeared, accounting for only 1 percent of leading members of congress since 2000. Among the eleven justices, only one served in the military.

However, midway into the Calderón administration, there appears to be a growing trend in retired or active-duty military personnel being appointed to security positions at the state level because of the extraordinarily high incidence of drug-related violence and organized crime, including dramatic increases in murder and kidnapping rates. This pattern in 2008–2009 was highlighted by the appointment of Division General Javier del Real Magallanes as the assistant secretary of police strategy and intelligence in Mexico's national Public Security agency. General del Real Magallanes resigned his post as commander of the Fourth Military Region in Monterrey, Nuevo León. Del Real Magallanes is a graduate of the army's Higher War College and holds a master's degree in higher command and national security from the Center for Advanced Naval Studies. He directed the military's elite National Defense College and headed the intelligence section of the general staff in the early 1990s. He earned a reputation in leading the fight against drug traffickers and will be in charge of implementing the government's new federal police model.[41]

Of all the prior activities we have identified, only one, involvement in the private sector, has actually increased the diversity of background experiences among top public figures. Politicians who have achieved top posts since 2000 are much more likely to have been successful businessmen, owning their own firms or serving in top management posts in large corporations. Cabinet secretaries signal this important change, where one in five now originate in the private sector, an increase of some 60 percent. An even more dramatic increase has occurred among members of congress, among whom former successful businesspeople have more than doubled.[42]

No recent Mexican politician better reflects that quality than Fernando Canales Clariond, who governed his home state of Nuevo León from 1997 to 2003 before becoming Fox's secretary of economic development, and when Calderón resigned to run for the presidency, his energy secretary. A native of the state capital and northern industrial center, Monterrey, Canales Clariond grew up in the heart of a prominent industrialist family. His cousin, Ernesto Canales Salinas, was for many years the general counsel to the ALFA Group, one of Mexico's largest and most powerful holding groups. His maternal uncle is Eugenio Clariond Garza, the CEO of IMSA from 1947 to 1986, a leading industrial firm, whose son Eugenio Clariond Reyes bought Probursa and became president of the elite capitalist business group the Mexican Council of Businessmen in 1998.[43] Another cousin, Benjamín Clariond Reyes, is his business partner and served as interim governor immediately before him. His brother Marcelo was director of finances at IMSA. Canales Clariond was one of the few prominent businessmen

41. *Por Esto*, December 5, 2008; www.sedena.gob.mx, 2000, 2003; *La Jornada*, December 4, 2008; *Diario de Yucatán*, December 4, 2008.

42. In a study conducted by Kathleen Bruhn and Kenneth Greene of congressional candidates in 2006, 11 percent of PAN and 4 percent of PRD candidates owned firms with more than twenty employees, and 25 and 29 percent managed firms of more than ten employees. Draft tabulations of survey between June 6 and June 30, 2006.

43. Fewer than forty leading capitalists, many of whom are related to each other, belong to this organization. To be invited as a member requires a unanimous vote of all other members. See Ben Ross Schneider, "Why Is Mexican Business so Organized?" *Latin American Research Review* 37, no. 1 (2002): 77–118.

connected to the capitalist class in Mexico—having been assistant director general of IMSA Group for thirty-two years and vice president of the board of directors—to join an opposition party in 1978, long before PAN became a successful opponent in the electoral arena. He ran for a seat in congress from the first congressional district, winning one of the few majority districts from the PRI in 1979. In the 1980s, he became a member of the PAN National Council and later of the National Executive Committee. He joined Manuel Clouthier's alternative cabinet as secretary of government properties, a position that brought him in contact with numerous future leading PAN political figures, including Vicente Fox. Before his election as governor, he presided over the PAN state party organization.[44]

## CONCLUSIONS

Of the many striking findings in this chapter, one stands out. The democratic era has unleashed changes in leadership composition that has led to leading Mexican politicians being less representative of the general population than at any time during the semi-authoritarian period prior to 2000. This finding, which applies to the geographic origins of top politicians, dispels the notion that democratic models, in all respects, are more representative than centralized, authoritarian models.

Over time, we found that politicians consistently came from only two regions in numbers equivalent to the percentage of the Mexican population living in those locales. Two geographic distortions in particular stand out in their backgrounds: the significant underrepresentation of the South in the executive branch, and the extraordinary overrepresentation of the Federal District, especially among assistant secretaries. Democracy and the opening of the political system to other parties have increased the number of legislative elite and cabinet secretaries born in the capital, which seems counterintuitive to our expectations.

I offered a number of potential explanations for many of these patterns. Perhaps the most comprehensive explanation is that the structure of the PAN as the new incumbent party since 2000 was deeply influenced by the PRI's dominance and the evolution of the one-party system. We have noted elsewhere, for example, how the most influential politicians in the legislative branch were products of the proportional representation system, a system that is not geographically representative in its selection process. In other words, some of the centralized features of the pre-2000 political model significantly flavored the PAN leadership and recruitment model,

44. *Excélsior*, June 8, 1997, A1; *Excélsior*, June 2, 1997; www.elector.com.mx.

which centered on the national party bureaucracy, including the necessity in the early days to send out national party activists to direct the party's development in states other than the representative's home state. Rather than decentralizing the geographic biases introduced by the PRI, PAN, and PRD, which since its founding has been highly successful in Mexico City, have exacerbated these differences.

The exploration of extensive kinship ties among politicians is another even more significant measure of a political system's openness. One can assume that these figures overall are underreported, given the difficulty of identifying familial linkages extending across generations among Mexican politicians. The fact that nearly half of all cabinet secretaries, Mexico's most influential policy makers, are known to have been related to other politicians, is remarkable. Unlike the case of geographical representation, the democratic opening has produced a major decline in these numbers. Cabinet secretaries since 2000 are much more likely to have come from families with no political connections, and therefore, the pool from which appointees are drawn, in terms of those linkages, are different today than they were prior to 2000.

It may well be that when a significant change in a political model occurs, the narrowing quality characterizing the familial pool from which leading politicians emerge in a long-standing political system will reproduce itself over time in a newly minted political model, but drawn from a different set of families. In other words, it takes a certain amount of time for a new leadership to establish itself and for its familial networks to dominate and produce a new generation of politicians.

The examination of educational credentials of leading politicians suggest three broad trends: the increasing postgraduate education among all government career tracks, the rise of economics as a discipline specifically among assistant secretaries in the executive branch, and the extraordinary dominance of a publicly funded Mexico City institution, the National University, graduating half of the assistant secretaries and cabinet secretaries and two-thirds of Mexico's supreme court justices. Furthermore, public university graduates from the provinces rarely have gone on to become cabinet members.

The democratic era has influenced significantly the educational credentials of Mexico's politicians. It reversed provincial public institutions' lower visibility by dramatically increasing the presence of state colleges and universities among leaders in the executive and legislative branches. The increased presence of state institutions is an important change because provincial public education is less homogeneous than national public education, retaining the importance of regional perspectives toward numerous issues distinct from Mexico City's vision, similarly flavored by the Beltway phenomenon alluded to in describing Washington, D.C.'s mentality.

The increasing prominence of state public university training is linked to the increasing importance of local politics and legislative careers as mayors and state legislators. As Joy Langston correctly asserts in her analysis of the PRI, "The consequences of political competition on legislative recruitment mean state politics has become an important arena for ambitious politicians who used to travel to Mexico City to further their careers."[45]

In combination with this dramatic democratic shift from national to state public institution graduates is the equally significant alteration in private university experiences, both secular and religious, in the backgrounds of Mexican politicians. From a socialization perspective, more diversity exists since 2000 in politicians' educational backgrounds, affecting their ideological orientations as well as the way they perceive public policy solutions.

Finally, two important changes stand out in politicians' prior career experiences. One of the most interesting of those changes involves the level of experience politicians share as student leaders. Traditionally, many politicians began their careers as student activists, indicating the politicized environment of public institutions, especially the National Preparatory School and the National University, where student strikes often led to national political conflicts, including the infamous 1968 student strike and subsequent massacre in Tlatelolco square, which produced far-reaching social and political changes with consequences for democratization.[46] The percentage of politicians since 2000 who were student leaders has declined significantly, a reflection of the less politicized religious and private schools from which democratic politicians increasingly are graduating.

Ironically, this decreasing partisan experience at a young age has not been translated into decreasing partisanship among politicians since 2000. As discovered in the analysis of party militants over time, the percentage of militants has actually increased in recent years, and of course, those militants are more evenly divided among the three major parties. To illustrate, in their interviews with congressional candidates in 2006, Kate Bruhn and Kenneth Greene found that 99 percent of PAN candidates favored private investment in the electric industry, compared to 30 percent of their PRD counterparts. Or on the highly controversial social issue of abortion,

45. Joy Langston, "The Changing Party of the Institutional Revolution: Electoral Competition and Decentralized Candidate Selection," *Party Politics* 12, no. 3 (2006): 409.

46. Imanol Ordorika, "The Limits of University Autonomy: Power and Politics at the Universidad Nacional Autónomo de México," *Higher Education* 46, no. 3 (October 2003): 361–88, for the event, and Roderic Ai Camp, "Political Modernization in Mexico: Through a Looking Glass," in Jaime Rodríguez, ed., *Political Evolution in Mexico* (Wilmington: Scholarly Resources, 1993), 211–28, for the consequences.

44 percent of PAN members thought it should be illegal, in contrast to only 8 percent of PRD candidates. Interestingly, the authors concluded in another essay that "polarization is limited to the political elite and does not feed off of deep political divisions in the electorate. This finding implies that despite the important transition from authoritarian dominant party rule under the PRI to fully competitive democratic electoral politics by 2000, Mexico had not undergone a major partisan realignment."[47]

47. Kathleen Bruhn and Kenneth F. Greene, "Elite Polarization Meets Mass Moderation in Mexico's 2006 Elections," *PS: Political Science and Politics* 40 (January 2007): 36.

# 9

## Violence and Democracy

### Which Produces Change?

Surely one of the most interesting theoretical debates in the history of violent political change is the question scholars and citizens alike have asked
long after a historical event has occurred: could the societal and political
changes produced by widespread violence have ensued peacefully at less
cost to a society? The present analysis cannot answer that broader question. Nor does it reexplore whether the Mexican Revolution of 1910 can
be classified as a social revolution, a highly contentious issue among leading historians.[1] What it can suggest in focusing on the narrower scope of
prominent political leaders is the extent to which violence versus peaceful
change alters the leadership's composition. Does a violent change in the
political system produce deeper alterations in Mexican leadership than
peaceful, democratic change; how do these opposing forms of change differ from each other; and what consequences ensue for politicians?[2]

In establishing a valid comparison between the two types of change in
Mexico we can use, when appropriate, three different variables. First, we
can test these changes from a generational perspective. We have already
established in the case of Mexico's democratic leadership (covering
the period from 2000 to 2009) that the dominant generation consists of
politicians born in the decade of the 1950s. This group alone accounts for
45 percent of those first-time officeholders. For purposes of the analysis,
this group can be called the Democratic Generation. Nearly 100 years earlier the dominant revolutionary generation that represented the administrations from 1920 to 1928 (Alvaro Obregón and Plutarco Elías Calles)

1. For an excellent discussion of some of these opposing views, see Paul J. Vanderwood,
"Explaining the Mexican Revolution," in Jaime Rodríguez, ed., *The Revolutionary Process in
Mexico: Essays on Political and Social Change, 1880-1940* (Los Angeles: UCLA Latin American
Center, 1990), 97–114, and Alan Knight, "Revolutionary Project, Recalcitrant People: Mexico,
1910-1940," in Rodríguez, ed., *The Revolutionary Process in Mexico*, 227–66.
2. Surprisingly, I have not encountered any empirical evidence comparing revolutionary
and democratic elites in other societal settings.

was born in the 1880s. It, too, accounts for 45 percent of their comparable officeholders, and will be labeled the Revolutionary Generation.

The second measure we can use, relying on those same representative administrations from the two periods, are first-time officeholders. First-time officeholders represent a clearer picture of brand-new top political figures chosen by respective presidents and their closest collaborators undiluted by repeating politicians from prior administrations, who typically come from older, less representative generations. Finally, our third measure, which may reveal patterns different from first-time officeholders, often moderating sharper differences highlighted among newly arrived officeholders, is that of all top officials in a given administration or administrations, in this case the Obregón–Calles and Fox–Calderón presidencies. In using this last variable, it is worth keeping in mind that the data only incorporate the first three years of the Calderón presidency.

A number of fascinating patterns already raised in the analysis of democratic versus predemocratic leadership can be addressed. Intuitively, social scientists would expect violent change to produce stronger and deeper shifts in the types of leaders who emerge, and therefore equally pronounced alterations in their background characteristics and credentials. One of the most interesting sets of background characteristics are politicians' geographic and social origins. The distribution of these characteristics can generate long-term consequences on the stability of and access to political leadership.

An exploration of the generational, geographic distribution of Mexican politicians suggests a unique finding when comparing the Revolutionary Generation to the Democratic Generation. One of those background variables is the changing pattern in the percentage of politicians who come from rural settings. In Mexico, no consistent pattern emerged in the prerevolutionary period other than politicians from urban communities being overwhelmingly overrepresented. Somewhere between 36 to 46 percent of the preceding generations came from rural backgrounds. If we compare the 1880s generation (table 9.1) with the preceding generation, the percentage of rural-born politicians grows 12 percent. What is important to note is that in the next generation born in the 1890s, the percentage of rural born politicians declines once again, falling to a level lower even than the 1870s generation.

Interestingly, the Democratic Generation follows the same pattern in that we discover a completely unexpected increase in rural backgrounds among national politicians beginning with the Fox administration. What is more astounding is that the increase in rural-born politicians after 2000 is 20 percent more than in the preceding 1940s generation, exceeding the level of change (12 percent) revolutionary violence produced. Again, in the 1960s

**Table 9.1.** Geographic Origins of the Revolutionary and
Democratic Politicians

|  | Geographic Birthplace (%) | | |
| --- | --- | --- | --- |
| Generation | Rural | Percentage Increase | Urban |
| Revolutionary (1880s) | 52 | 12 | 48 |
| Democratic (1950s) | 17 | 20 | 83 |

*Source*: Mexican Political Biographies Project, 2009 and
Mexican Political Biographies Project, 1995.

Percentage increase refers to the increase in rural origins
from the prior generation, 1870–79 for the Revolutionary
group and the 1940–49 for the Democratic group.

generation, at least through 2009, rural-born politicians have followed the
general longitudinal, historical pattern, declining below the 1940s level.

What explains the sharp upward spike in rural birthplaces in these two
generations? In the Revolutionary Generation, a number of characteristics
play a role, and I turn to several of these shortly. As we learned in my earlier study of nineteenth-century political recruitment, the Revolutionary
Generation was made up of two quite distinct groups of politicians: those
who fought in the violent phase of the revolution as members of guerrilla
groups or the constitutional forces, and those who never participated in
combat.[3] These groups come from entirely different social classes.

The Revolutionary Generation who were combat veterans accounts for
80 percent of those politicians whose fathers were peasants or laborers.
"Indeed, the children of laborers, peasants, and small farmers are the only
individuals to have overwhelmingly fought for the revolutionaries. Only a
minority of the children of the other occupational groups participated in the
Revolution."[4] Expressed differently, two-thirds of all politicians from this
generation whose origins were working class fought in the revolution.[5]

---

3. For interesting comparisons with other elites' experiences in combat, see Thomas H.
Rigby, *Political Elites in the USSR: Central Leaders and Local Cadres from Lenin to Gorbachev*
(Brookfield, U.K.: Gower, 1990), 183.

4. Roderic Ai Camp, *Political Recruitment across Two Centuries: Mexico, 1884–1991*
(Austin: University of Texas Press, 1995), 70.

5. Comparisons with other revolutionary leaders can be found in Harold D. Lasswell
and Daniel Lerner, eds., *World Revolutionary Elites: Studies in Coercive Ideological Movements*
(Cambridge, Mass.: MIT Press, 1965).

The revolution provided numerous opportunities for working-class Mexicans, especially those from rural settings, to side with political change.[6] This is a pattern that has occurred in other countries experiencing violent change.[7] In Mexico, this geographic reversal was short-lived among leaders in the 1920s. It also appears to be equally short-lived in the 2000s. The explanation for the surge in rural birthplaces today is quite different from that in the early twentieth century. Again, it is related to social class origins but also to important institutional differences.

The democratic opening, as we discovered previously, has allowed more politicians from modest backgrounds an opportunity to achieve prominent public office, typically through the legislative branch. The introduction of democracy, initially the product of electoral competition, relies heavily on the legislative branch. This branch, which increased the representation of political parties other than the Institutional Revolutionary Party (PRI), opened the door somewhat wider, from 2000 to 2009, for rural Mexicans, many of whom were from modest circumstances.

In the chapter on demographic characteristics, I analyzed the importance of regionalism and the patterns emerging in the broad geographic representation of regions among politicians over time. What is immediately apparent in the data presented in table 9.2 is that democratic change again is as dramatic as violent change in the shift it produces in the provincial distribution of leading politicians. In fact, overall, it produces more extreme changes from the past than the era of violence in the geographic backgrounds of politicians.

The single most important regional shift occurs in the Federal District. Porfirio Díaz, over the length of the Porfiriato, developed a leadership that was disproportionately overrepresented by the Federal District. Less than 5 percent of the Mexican population resided in the Federal District in 1910, at the end of his administration, yet over the entire life of his regime, from 1885 to 1911, 14 percent of his collaborators, three times the population even at that late date, claimed it as their place of birth.

When the victorious revolutionaries consolidated their power in 1920, only 5 percent of their members, equal to the actual population in 1910, originated from the Federal District, representing a dramatic decline in Federal District birthplaces by nearly two-thirds, the largest single change up or down in regional birthplaces among revolutionary leadership.[8] The

6. Judith Adler Hellman, *Mexico in Crisis* (New York: Holmes and Meier, 1978), 15.

7. For a discussion of these varied experiences, see Carl Leiden and Karl M. Schmitt, eds., *The Politics of Violence: Revolution in the Modern World* (Englewood Cliffs, N.J.: Prentice Hall, 1968).

8. An examination of all leading politicians in these two administrations reveals an even smaller figure for individuals from the capital: slightly fewer than 4 percent.

Table 9.2. Regional Backgrounds of Revolutionary and Democratic Politicians

| | | | | Region of Birth (%) | | | | |
|---|---|---|---|---|---|---|---|---|
| Generation | Federal District | East Central | West | North | South | Gulf | West Central | Foreign |
| Revolutionary | 5 | 14 | 19 | 20 | 13 | 17 | 12 | 1 |
| Change | -64 | 17+ | -58 | 5+ | 18+ | -11 | 9+ | 0 |
| Prerevolutionary | 14 | 12 | 12 | 19 | 11 | 19 | 11 | 1 |
| Democratic | 31 | 9 | 17 | 19 | 6 | 11 | 12 | 1 |
| Change | 72+ | -40 | 13+ | 27+ | -40 | -27 | -25 | |
| Predemocratic | 18 | 15 | 15 | 15 | 10 | 15 | 16 | 1 |

Source: Mexican Political Biographies Project, 2009 and Mexican Political Biographies Project, 1995.

Prerevolutionary refers to the 1885-1911 administrations; predemocratic refers to the 1935 to 1988 administrations.

same explanations that applied to the increase in rural backgrounds are relevant to the decrease in politicians born in the highly urbanized Federal District. Revolutionaries typically came from the provinces, and the non-combatant politicians from larger cities and the capital. The increasing importance of the National Preparatory School as a centralized educational funnel also was advantageously located for Mexico City residents who could attend without living with relatives or in boardinghouses, typical of provincial students.[9]

When we shift our attention to Mexico's democratic leadership, an equally dramatic alteration in regional representation in the Federal District is apparent, but in the opposite direction. Politicians born in the capital instead increased 72 percent from the predemocratic to the democratic era, again accounting for the largest geographic shift in the contemporary period. One would expect this figure to increase over time, but not so dramatically given the population that lived there between 1940 and 1950: approximately one in ten Mexicans. The Federal District's overwhelming dominance was reinforced by the growing presence of recruiting institutions located in the capital, including civil educational and military academies, recent private secular and religious universities, the National Action

9. Octavio González Cárdenas, Los cien años de la Escuela Nacional Preparatoria (Mexico: Porrúa, 1972). According to students who attended the National Preparatory School and the Law School, students from the provinces easily outnumbered those from Mexico City, suggesting just how influential these schools were in bringing together young adults from all over Mexico. Letter from Hugo Pedro González Lugo, member of the 1928-32 generation, who became governor of Tamaulipas in 1945, August 15, 1974.

Party's (PAN) national party bureaucracy, and PAN's distorted legislative representation in the capital, exacerbating the existing gradual upward trend of Federal District birthplaces.[10]

The other major regional shift in the Revolutionary Generation takes place among politicians from the West. This largely can be explained by the fact that similar to the North, a disproportionate percentage of revolutionary veterans emanate from those states, creating an important foothold in the Obregón and Calles administrations. An excellent example of a westerner (especially Sinaloa and Jalisco) who rose to the top during the revolutionary era was Angel Flores, the illegitimate son of a small farmer from the village of San Pedro, near Culiacán, Sinaloa. He worked as an agricultural laborer and on the docks of Mazatlán as a stevedore. He joined Madero's forces in 1910 and later signed on with the constitutionalist forces under General Ramón F. Iturbe, eventually rising in 1920 to division general and commander of the First Division of the North East. During the revolution he became interim governor and military commander of his home state, and in 1920, he served four years as the constitutional governor. In 1924, he opposed Calles as a presidential candidate, obtaining the second largest number of votes cast. He left public life in 1926, poor and despondent, and died from apparent poisoning in that same year.[11]

The additional significant alternations in regional patterns during the democratic era were most strongly represented in the East Central and South regions. Neither the Party of the Democratic Revolution (PRD) nor especially the PAN have been well represented in these regions. Thus the decline in the PRI's political fortunes, especially among voters in the South in 2006, contributed to the serious underrepresentation of these regions since 2000. The PRD's success among voters in the South in 2006 may help alter this pattern in the future, but it is too soon to measure

10. It is worth noting that some important revolutionaries, especially military physicians, influenced the next generation (1900-1920) in the classroom, in the case of doctors, at the Military Medical School. For example, Dr. Julian Garza Tijerina, who was born in General Bravo, Nuevo León, in 1900, graduated from the Military Medical School in 1925 and participated in combat attached to a cavalry regiment in the late 1920s, a medical task he described as difficult. He notes that his most influential professors, all of whom supported Madero during the revolution, were General Francisco Castillo Nájera, who became ambassador to the United States under Cárdenas and secretary of foreign relations under Avila Camacho; Colonel Donato Moreno, who became governor of Zacatecas in 1920; and Colonel Francisco Reyes, who became a member of congress, 1918-20. Dr. Garza Tijerina was elected senator under Cárdenas and served on the National Executive Committee of the PNR in 1933. Letter to the author, January 22, 1974, and August 22, 1974.

11. Amado González Dávila, *Diccionario geográfico, histórico, biográfico y estadístico del estado de Sinaloa* (Culiacán, 1959), 212-13; *Quién es quién en la nomenclatura de la ciudad de México* (Mexico: Costa Amic, 1971), 208; and Roderic Ai Camp, *Mexican Political Biographies, 1885-1934* (Austin: University of Texas Press, 1991), 84-85.

**Table 9.3.** Socioeconomic Backgrounds of Revolutionary and Democratic Politicians

|  | Parents' Socioeconomic Status (%) | | |
| --- | --- | --- | --- |
| Generation | Working | Middle | Upper |
| Revolutionary | 24 | 67 | 8 |
| Change | 41+ | 56+ | –80 |
| Prerevolutionary | 17 | 43 | 40 |
| Democratic | 14 | 86 | —[a] |
| Change | –50 | 19+ | |
| Predemocratic | 28 | 72 | — |

*Source*: Mexican Political Biographies Project, 2009, and Mexican Political Biographies Project, 1995.

Prerevolutionary refers to the 1885–1911 administrations; predemocratic refers to the 1935–88 administrations.

a. Less than 5 percent of all leadership, democratic and predemocratic, have come from wealthy families and are combined with the middle-class category. In 1895, they accounted for 1.5 percent of the general population. In 1950, 1.7 percent, and in 1990, 6.8 percent.

any impact on prominent national political leadership in the Calderón administration.[12]

The most interesting variable historians have examined in the scholarship on revolutions and violent change is the degree to which these upheavals alter the social origins of a country's leadership.[13] There is no question in the conclusions from the historical literature on Mexico that given the social composition of those who fought the revolution, combined with their rural origins, that postrevolutionary leadership would better represent the working classes, including peasants, than the preceding, nonrevolutionary governments. What is shocking about the data in table 9.3 is that the revolution only modestly opens up leadership positions to working-class Mexicans.

The explanation for this modest increase becomes quite clear when we examine revolutionary leaders from 1914 to 1920, before that leadership becomes consolidated. Two-fifths of prominent politicians emerge from

12. In the July 2009 congressional elections, the PRI swept all the congressional districts in Oaxaca, captured seven out of nine in Guerrero, and won four out of twelve in Chiapas. Thus, it is unlikely that PRD, which won only five seats of the twenty-nine in the South, will significantly increase its presence in that region.

13. William B. Quandt, *Revolution and Political Leadership: Algeria, 1954–1968* (Cambridge, Mass.: MIT Press, 1969), provides comparative insights into this issue for Algeria.

working-class families, the highest level ever of working-class representation in politicians' backgrounds from 1885 to the present with the exception of Lázaro Cárdenas's administration, which equally well represents this social class. To express this explanation more bluntly, working-class revolutionaries were far more successful and prominent in fighting the revolution and achieving office before institutional consolidation occurred, but much less successful in obtaining posts in the governance structure after the violent phase ended. They also disproportionately were associated with some of the more radical revolutionary factions, the very groups that lost out in the struggles between Emiliano Zapata and Pancho Villa versus Alvaro Obregón and Venustiano Carranza. Gertrudis G. Sánchez was such a figure. The son of peasants, his father died when he was four years old. He had to abandon his elementary schooling for economic reasons, but his aunt taught him, and he completed the sixth grade. He moved to the Agua Nueva Hacienda in Coahuila, where he continued working as an agricultural laborer. He supported Madero's Plan of San Luis Potosí. In 1913, he joined Villa's forces and commanded the rurales against Victoriano Huerta's forces. He became governor and military commander of Michoacán from 1914 to 1915, and after joining the Constitutionalists was killed by Zapatista troops in 1915.[14]

Interestingly, in contrast to the leadership found during the 1914–20 period, leaders under Madero, who personally came from a wealthy landowning family in Coahuila, largely originate from the middle and upper classes. Only 7 percent of the politicians during his administration were from modest backgrounds, one-third of the number during the Porfiriato.

In contrast to the Revolutionary Generation, the Democratic Generation produced a more dramatic alteration in politicians' working-class backgrounds, but in the opposite direction. Politicians from modest social origins declined by a whopping 50 percent after 2000 compared to their predemocratic peers.

The truly astounding alteration in revolutionary leadership is reflected in the data on upper-class (not working-class) politicians. The revolution, instead of opening the door to working-class Mexicans, closed the door significantly to upper-class Mexicans, the majority of whom would not have expressed prorevolutionary sympathies or have participated in the combat phase of the revolution. Politicians from such families declined by four-fifths after 1920.

14. Jesús Romero Flores, *Diccionario michoacano de historia y geografía* (Morelia, 1960), 399–400; Alberto Moviedo Mota, *El trágico fin del general Gertrudis G. Sánchez* (Morelia, 1939); Alan Knight, *The Mexican Revolution: Counter-Revolution and Reconstruction* (Lincoln: University of Nebraska Press, 1990), 44ff.; and Mexican Political Biographies Project, 1995.

Nevertheless, some individuals with prominent family pedigrees did achieve influential political posts in the postrevolutionary era. Antonio Ancona Albertos, whose distinguished family heritage extended back to the 1600s in Yucatán, was a member of the Revolutionary Generation born in Mérida. He was the son of an influential lawyer, politician, journalist, novelist, and intellectual, who became the constitutional governor of Yucatán under Benito Juárez in 1875 and later served as a Supreme Court justice in the 1890s. Antonio graduated from the Literary Institute of Yucatán (founded by his father) and pursued an active career as a journalist, writing for *El Peninsular*, a newspaper published by José María Pino Suárez, later Mexico's vice president under Madero. Ancona Albertos co-founded the Anti-reelectionist Party in Yucatán and became Pino Suárez's private secretary in 1911, when Pino Suárez became governor. After Pino Suárez and Madero were murdered by Victoriano Huerta in 1913, he fled into exile to Cuba and then to the United States, returning to Mexico in 1914 to join the Constitutionalists in Hermosillo, Sonora. He was elected as a member of congress from the first district of Yucatán, in 1917, after also representing the state in the Constitutional Convention of 1916, later serving as a senator from 1918 to 1924. He briefly served as interim governor of his home state in 1920, and Calles appointed him governor of Quintana Roo in 1926.[15]

Finally, both the Democratic and Revolutionary Generations produced positive increases in middle-class politicians who filled the vacuum from the decline in working and wealthy family backgrounds during their respective eras. The increase, of course, was more dramatic during the revolutionary era because the decrease in politicians from well-off circumstances was much sharper.

Family circumstances is only one social variable that deserves attention. The other, more informal characteristic found among political leaders is the familial presence in politics, affecting the breadth of the pool from which they are recruited. In other words, how widespread is upward mobility in political life for those who are not related to family members previously having held important political offices? Given the role of kinship ties in Mexican politics since the Porfiriato, family political ties become a crucial variable in measuring the degree of change within the political leadership (see table 9.4).

15. His grandfather was *regidor* Juan Ramón de Ancona y Cepeda. Juan Alvarez Coral, *Galería de gobernadores de Quintana Roo* (Mexico: Gobierno de Quintana Roo, 1972), 103–4; José María Valdés Acosta, *A través de las centurias* (Mérida, 1931), 2, 52–53, 56–57; Jesús Romero Flores, *Maestros y amigos* (Mexico: Costa Amic, 1971), 52–58; Lázaro Pavía, *Apuntes biográficos de los miembros más distinguidos del poder judicial* (Mexico: Barroso, 1893), 48–59; and Mexican Political Biographies Project, 2009.

**Table 9.4.** Political Families of Revolutionary and
Democratic Politicians

| Generation | Father Held Influential Political or Military Post (%) |
|---|---|
| Revolutionary | 10 |
| Change | –58 |
| Prerevolutionary | 24 |
| Democratic | 9 |
| Change | –40 |
| Predemocratic | 15 |

*Source*: Mexican Political Biographies Project, 2009, and
Mexican Political Biographies Project, 1995.

Prerevolutionary refers to the 1885–1911 administrations;
predemocratic refers to the 1935–88 administrations.

The comparative data on kinship ties, testing the openness of the pool
from which future politicians are recruited, further reinforces the finding that nonviolent, democratic change can alter similar characteristics as
deeply as violent change in the composition of leaders. Again, one might
expect far greater levels of decline in political families, measured by the
degree to which their father or mother held an influential political or military post, in the revolutionary era. In the prerevolutionary era, at least one
in four politicians came from a "political family." That figure declined by
58 percent during the 1920–28 administrations. That prerevolutionary figure is not equaled in subsequent administrations.

Interestingly, the democratic generation produces a similar down-
ward trajectory in political families, from 15 to 9 percent, declining by
40 percent. One would expect a democratic opening also to introduce
fresh political blood, but not nearly to the same degree as would occur
under violent change, especially since the ideological extremes characterizing a violent transition tend to be more radical. The Fox administration
produced the smallest group of leaders (8 percent) whose parents were
influential officeholders since Pascual Ortiz Rubio's brief administration
from 1930 to 1932.

If we expand the definition of a political family beyond the confines
of a parent to members of the nuclear family, kinship linkages become
more widespread.[16] In both the shift from a prerevolutionary to a

16. Kimberly L. Casey, "Political Families in American Electoral Politics," paper presented
at the annual meeting of the Western Political Science Association, San Diego, California,

Table 9.5. Political Families of Revolutionary and Democratic
Politicians

| Generation | Relative Held Influential Political or Military Post (%) |
|---|---|
| Revolutionary | 26 |
| Change | -30 |
| Prerevolutionary | 37 |
| Democratic | 27 |
| Change | -33 |
| Predemocratic | 40 |

Source: Mexican Political Biographies Project, 2009, and Mexican
Political Biographies Project, 1995.

Prerevolutionary refers to the 1885–1911 administrations; predemocratic refers to the 1935–88 administrations. Relative refers to
siblings, grandparents, in-laws, aunts, and uncles.

postrevolutionary era and a predemocratic to a democratic era, one would
expect these kinship networks to decline. That is indeed the case, as the
data in table 9.5 suggest. Two notable conclusions can be reached in comparing the data from the two eras. First, little change has taken place
in the level of family political connections in the 1880s and early 1900s
compared to those from the 1930s through the 1980s. Second, peaceful
change produced a slightly greater decline in the presence of family political ties compared to the pattern found in the postviolent 1920s, again
suggesting the ability of a democratic opening to compete with the consequences of violent change in numerous measures of political leadership
characteristics.

Regardless of whether change is peaceful or violent, it can also alter
politicians' formal credentials, including schooling, nonpublic careers, and
career tracks in public life, all of which impact institutions influencing
leadership composition, often over long periods. The comparison in educational achievements between the prerevolutionary and revolutionary leadership clearly suggests that violent change creates severe consequences
on leaders' formal credentials, specifically educational achievements (see
table 9.6).

This impact can be explained in several ways. My earlier work on all
aspects of political recruitment suggests that leaders, similar to nonleaders,

December 11, 2008, www.allacademic.com/meta/p238293_index.html. Casey argues, using
a similar expanded definition, that in American politics, contrary to the conclusions of some
classic works, political families have not declined precipitously in recent years.

**Table 9.6.** Educational Credentials of Revolutionary and Democratic Politicians

| | Level of Education Achieved (%) | | | |
| --- | --- | --- | --- | --- |
| Generation | Primary/Normal | Preparatory | University | Postgraduate |
| Revolutionary | 36 | 13 | 38 | 13 |
| Change | 112+ | 0 | −39 | 63+ |
| Prerevolutionary | 17 | 13 | 62 | 8 |
| Democratic | 3 | 5 | 39 | 53 |
| Change | −84 | −29 | −19 | 104+ |
| Predemocratic | 19 | 7 | 48 | 26 |

*Source*: Mexican Political Biographies Project, 2009, and Mexican Political Biographies Project, 1995.

Prerevolutionary refers to the 1885–1911 administrations; predemocratic refers to the 1935–88 administrations.

tend to prefer individuals who share similar credentials when they are choosing disciples to promote up the political ladder.[17] The combat phase of the revolution, as I suggested, opened the doors to many capable individuals who made their mark on the battlefield, not in public office, and therefore achieved positions in the military that gave them access to political office. For example, a huge percentage of governors in the 1920s were former military commanders, continuing a tradition from the previous decade in which many governors were simultaneously commander of military operations and governor.[18]

This type of revolutionary leader, often from humble backgrounds and rural origins, had little access to formal schooling, either by virtue of its geographic availability or the resources available to him to attend school instead of working and contributing to his family's survival. The percentage of leaders in the 1920s who never went beyond a secondary education jumps well over 100 percent from the prerevolutionary leadership. A third of Mexico's revolutionary leadership obtained little formal education. These figures are complemented by a substantial decline in college graduates, from 70 percent prior to 1911 to only half of all politicians after 1920.[19]

17. Roderic Ai Camp, *Mexico's Mandarins: Crafting a Power Elite for the Twenty-first Century* (Berkeley: University of California Press, 2002), 18–19.

18. Roderic Ai Camp, *Mexico's Military on the Democratic Stage* (Westport, Conn.: Praeger Security International and CSIS, 2005), 238–39.

19. Some college graduates or students enrolled in college became active participants in the revolution. For example, students from the normal schools and from the National

The career of Jesús Agustín Castro Rivera, a revolutionary general born on the Eureka Ranch near Ciudad Lerdo, Durango, in 1887, reflects the background typical of so many of his comrades in arms. He attended elementary school but had to leave for economic reasons. On November 20, 1910, abandoning his position as a streetcar conductor at the age of twenty-three, he led 127 men in opposition to the Díaz regime. He later joined the forces of General Pablo González, supporting both Francisco I. Madero and Venustiano Carranza. He rose through the ranks in the constitutional army, and eventually became military commander of Tlaxcala, Puebla, and Veracruz, serving as governor and commander of military operations in Chiapas, 1914–15, and in Oaxaca, 1915–16. He became assistant secretary of war during Carranza's presidency. In 1920, he was elected governor of his home state. He retired from public life in 1928 after serving in the senate, but he eventually returned to active duty, commanded numerous military zones in the 1930s, and served as Cárdenas's secretary of national defense at the end of his administration. In 1946, he accepted the presidential nomination of the National Constitutional Party.[20]

What does this dramatic shift in educational attainment mean for the two groups of leaders? It demonstrates that under Porfirio Díaz, educational credentials increased persistently from his 1885 administration to his 1910 administration, with college graduates rising from a little more than half in his first administration to four-fifths in his last administration. Such an increase suggests not only the value that politicians began placing on university training but the importance such a preference gave to educational institutions in recruiting and socializing future top public servants.

Mexico's revolution devalued those credentials by comparison and shifted the importance of influential institutions away from higher education.[21] The revolutionary experience extended its influence to some

---

School of Agriculture were especially important. Marte R. Gómez Segura, who enrolled in that college in 1909, joined the revolution in 1914, and supported Emiliano Zapata, who collaborated closely with several teachers, too. He noted that many of his classmates made the same decision. His father, a graduate of the Military College, died in the fighting in 1913, and his mother was a schoolteacher. Just six years after he completed his degree in 1917, he became dean of the school. In 1928, Portes Gil appointed him assistant secretary of agriculture, a position he left to represent his home state in the senate. He then became secretary of the treasury in 1934, governor of Tamaulipas in 1936, and secretary of agriculture. He was considered an early potential candidate for president in 1946. Letter to the author, September 11, 1973.

20. *New York Times*, January 28, 1946, 9; José María Dávila, *El ejército de la revolución* (Mexico: Slyse, 1938), 81–82; *Diario de Yucatán*, January 24, 1939, 1; *World Biography*, 1948, 1029; Mexican Political Biographies Project, 2009.

21. However, it should be remembered that an important group of revolutionaries did come out of college settings. This was true, for example, of the National School of Medicine in Mexico City. Dr. Ramiro Tamez, who grew up in General Terán, Nuevo León, was in his third

members of the next generation (1900-1920) who were children during the violent phase and experienced consequences of the upheaval as family members, not combatants.[22] To some extent, the armed forces replaced academia as an institutional source of future politicians. Yet most of the combat veterans who served in the 1920s administrations and were products of the 1880-89 generation were not members of a fully institutionalized military, but rather the constitutional forces, which did not have its own professional institutions or highly organized structure.

The democratic generation also introduces its changes to formal educational credentials. Perhaps the most astonishing pattern historically is that a comparison of the two periods demonstrates to some extent how slowly institutional changes occur given the fact that college educated politicians are not restored to their prerevolutionary levels until the end of the predemocratic era, seventy years after the revolution began.

The Democratic Generation produced the strongest shift away from a sizable percentage of non-college graduates, reducing their numbers significantly. However, this is a long-term decline characterizing recent, predemocratic administrations. What the democratic administrations truly accentuate educationally is the huge upsurge in postgraduate training. The increase in graduate education is as dramatic among the democratic

---

year of medical school when the revolution broke out. He left school in 1911 to participate in the revolution with his closest friends, including Salvador Aguirre, who was the cousin of General Eugenio Aguirre Benavides, a revolutionary who supported Francisco Madero in 1910, and became one of the principal officers under General Francisco Villa in 1913-14. Tamez and his fellow students, including Dr. Francisco Castillo y Nájera, became members of the medical service under General Aguirre Benavides, who later served as assistant secretary of war in the 1914-15 convention government. Tamez later became the interim governor of Nuevo León in 1922-23 and senator in 1940-46, while Castillo y Nájera rose to the rank of division general and served for ten years as ambassador to the United States under presidents Cárdenas and Avila Camacho before being appointed secretary of foreign relations in 1945. Personal letter from Dr. Ramiro Tamez, February 26, 1974.

22. For example, Salvador Azuela, son of the most widely read novelist of the Mexican Revolution, was born in 1902, became a student leader in José Vasconcelos's 1929 opposition presidential campaign, and was part of the Alemán generation and a personal friend of Adolfo López Mateos. He argued that in spite of his attendance at the National Preparatory School and the National School of Law, "the factors which had the most influence in my educational formation...emerged more from life than from school because I had to suffer bitter days in the Revolutionary era, while a child and adolescent, because of my father, Dr. Mariano Azuela, author of the novel *The Underdogs*, participation in that historical episode. Because of this, during the first years of high school, my attendance at classes wasn't normal due to the urgent family necessities of subsistence and the anomalies derived from the revolutionary struggle." He goes on to mention that after being expelled from the National Preparatory School in 1923, he spent four years in Michoacán, were he came to know well General Cárdenas and, to a lesser extent, General Francisco Múgica. Because of his father, he counted many friends who were prominent in the revolution, including General Antonio I. Villarreal and Antonio Díaz Soto y Gama, a prominent leader of the agrarian movement. Personal communication, July 10, 1974.

generation as is the decrease in college-educated politicians from the revolutionary generation.

What is interesting about the comparison between the two generations is that violence produced a change in credentials that reversed a firmly established pattern, that is, an increase in the level of education. To reestablish the prior trend required decades, thus leaving open an opportunity for other credentials to replace the previous educational credentials, and perhaps more important, the possibility of different institutions to provide those same credentials.

Career experiences define the trajectories of future politicians and influences their skills and behavior. Similar to educational experiences, they emphasize institutional settings that affect leadership recruitment and socialization. An examination of these background experiences further reveals the impact of violent versus peaceful change.

One of the fascinating findings which stands out in the career data presented in table 9.7 is the major increase in local, elective experience shared by both the revolutionary and democratic generations. One of the significant complaints early revolutionaries dwelled on was the lack of municipal autonomy and local rights.[23] The Porfiriato increased the centralization of political control at the center and devalued local, elective experiences. Typically, local bosses or governors controlled the choices for those positions. In the transitional years from 1911 to 1920, many revolutionaries and their sympathizers pursued local political careers, thus providing a grassroots base for pursuing state and national political pathways.

The Democratic Generation, as seen in the earlier analysis of the importance of local elective office, also gave rise to a truly dramatic increase (170 percent) in just two local offices (mayor and local deputy) in politicians' backgrounds. What was perceived as a democratic change through violence in 1920 mirrors a democratic change through institutional reforms in 2000. Yet remarkably, although the results were the same in both periods, democratic change produced a much larger shift.[24] The Democratic Generation, especially PAN members of that generation, share similar experiences with their revolutionary precursors in that the engine for democratic change crystallized in local communities and states, transforming Mexican electoral politics in less than a decade in the 1990s

An illustrative example of such a PAN career is that of Ramón Galindo Noriega, born in Ciudad Juárez, Chihuahua, in 1955, who graduated

---

23. See, for example, Michael Meyer's biography of Pascual Orozco, who made local autonomy a central issue of his opposition. *Mexican Rebel: Pascual Orozco and the Mexican Revolution, 1910-1915* (Lincoln: University of Nebraska Press, 1967).

24. These results would even be more dramatic had I incorporated syndic among the local offices for the predemocratic and democratic generations.

**Table 9.7.** Career Experiences of Revolutionary and Democratic Politicians

| | Type of Experience (%) | | | |
| --- | --- | --- | --- | --- |
| Generation | Local | Governor | Military | Business |
| Revolutionary | 43 | 38 | 47 | 6 |
| Change | 48+ | 3+ | 15+ | -71 |
| Prerevolutionary | 29 | 37 | 41 | 21 |
| Democratic | 46 | 8 | 4 | 12 |
| Change | 170+ | -68 | -67 | 140+ |
| Predemocratic | 17 | 25 | 12 | 5 |

*Source*: Mexican Political Biographies Project, 2009, and Mexican Political Biographies Project, 1995.

Prerevolutionary refers to the 1885–1911 administrations; predemocratic refers to the 1935–88 administrations. Local refers to mayor, local deputy, and syndic for the revolutionary and prerevolutionary generations, but only to mayor and local deputy for the democratic/predemocratic generations.

from the Technical Institute of Ciudad Juárez in 1977. While still in middle school, he joined the PAN in 1970. An independent businessman, he founded numerous companies and directed various departments in several major beer companies. In 1989, he won a seat in the state legislature of Chihuahua. After leaving the legislature, he became director general of social development in Ciudad Juárez from 1992 to 1995. He joined the PAN state party committee in 1992 and successfully ran for mayor of Ciudad Juárez in 1995. He failed to win the governorship of his home state as the PAN candidate in 1998, but he represented PAN in the fifty-ninth legislative session (2003–6) and was elected senator in 2006, becoming chair of the municipal development committee.[25]

A second major conclusion that can be reached from the prior career experiences of the two generations is that once again the shifts in career patterns that characterized democratic change are far more dramatic overall than those produced by violence. This is completely unexpected. In all four categories, the differences between the predemocratic and democratic generations are huge. With the revolutionary and prerevolutionary generations the differences are noteworthy largely for the shifting levels of experiences in local politics and business management and ownership.

25. See www.senado.gob.mx, 2007; www.diputados.gob.mx, 2003–2006, 2008; hacienda-muncipal.org, 2008; Jorge V. Alcocer, ed., *Directorio Congreso mexicano, LX legislatura, 2006–2009* (Mexico: Nuevo Horizonte Editores, 2007), 67–68; and Mexican Political Biographies Project, 2009.

The other category that demonstrates a dramatic change in both the revolutionary and democratic generations, but in the opposite direction, is in the presence of business backgrounds. The historical literature, incorporating excellent studies of regional politics, makes clear the deep integration between Mexico's leading capitalists and political leadership in the nineteenth century.[26] The rhetoric of the revolution directed against many business interests, including against those capitalists controlling railroads, mining, and large landholdings, and the fact that numerous local revolutionaries seized private property, reflected popular attitudes shared by many Mexicans. Thus, it is not surprising that so few revolutionary politicians after 1920 claimed management-level experience or ownership of major firms.

In contrast to the reversal of fortunes among business leaders with political ambitions, the success of democratic electoral politics, especially the rise of PAN, for the first time since 1910 reintroduces the influence of business careers directly in the composition of national leadership. The 140 percent increase in politicians with private sector career credentials reflects changing attitudes toward incorporating individuals with business experiences in politics, especially among mayors and governors, and even more symbolically in the national executive branch, represented by President Fox. Electoral politics dramatically accomplished that higher level of increase more quickly than violence was able to accomplish its decrease eighty years earlier.

The presence of military careers in the backgrounds of the prerevolutionary and revolutionary politicians largely remains unchanged. What is shared by both groups is the large percentage of individuals who were career military officers. They also were typically combat veterans from different historical events. Later generations in the prerevolutionary era also were products of a more institutionalized military, including graduating from a national military academy. Most revolutionary officers from the 1880s generation were not military school graduates or products of an institutional background, but emerged from the Constitutionalist forces. In short, military politicians, represented by Porfirio Díaz from 1885 to

26. For example, see Mark Wasserman's excellent study, *Capitalists, Caciques, and Revolution: The Native Elite and Foreign Enterprise in Chihuahua, Mexico, 1854-1911* (Chapel Hill: University of North Carolina Press, 1984). For economic ties at the national level, see Stephen Haber, *Industry and Underdevelopment: The Industrialization of Mexico, 1890-1940* (Stanford, Calif.: Stanford University Press, 1989), 63ff. The most comprehensive examination can be found in Armando Razo, *Social Foundations of Limited Dictatorship: Networks and Private Protection during Mexico's Early Industrialization* (Stanford, Calif.: Stanford University Press, 2008). For extensive details on the political and economic elite, see Jacqueline Ann Rice's outstanding Ph.D. dissertation, "The Porfirian Political Elite: Life Patterns of the Delegates to the 1892 Unión Liberal Convention," UCLA, 1979.

1911, and by generals Alvaro Obregón and Plutarco Elías Calles from 1920 to 1928, controlled Mexico's political system, establishing the armed forces' dominance over civilian politics.

The significant decline of a military presence in the composition of political leadership from the predemocratic to the democratic era is not the result of democratic change but represents a firm but gradual decline in politicians' military experience, especially after 1976. Essentially, in the democratic era, career officers are only found in the national defense and naval ministries, and occasionally rarely in the office of the attorney general and Mexico's public security agency.[27]

Perhaps the most surprising pattern is the decline in governors among leading national politicians. It is possible to make the argument that as the number of positions in the legislative and executive branch increased and the number of governors remained static, fewer individuals in percentage terms entering elite political circles would have the opportunity to serve. In reality, however, if we only measure the percentage of cabinet members who previously have served as governors, who have remained fairly stable in numbers in recent years, the decrease is real. In the predemocratic era, governors accounted for exactly a fifth of all cabinet secretaries. That figure declined to only 14 percent in the democratic transition and to only 10 percent since 2000. In the first three years of Calderón's administration, only one in twenty governors reached cabinet rank.

The level of gubernatorial experience remained unchanged between the prerevolutionary and revolutionary eras. Why is this not the case in the democratic era? If any change were to occur, one might expect there to be an increased presence of gubernatorial service in the backgrounds of prominent politicians. This is especially true, as I noted earlier, given the fact that five out of six leading presidential candidates in the last two presidential elections were governors. Governors are not likely to achieve national prominence without moving to the national political arena. We have examples of governors using their respective political party presidency as a vehicle for achieving that recognition, such as Roberto Madrazo in the PRI, who then became the party's 2006 candidate, but this is uncommon. Some governors also can use the legislative branch as their avenue to national influence, typically through the senate, especially as legislative leaders.

27. For example, Javier del Real Magallanes became the first active-duty general since 2000 to hold a post of assistant secretary or higher in the executive branch when he was appointed as the new assistant secretary of police strategy and intelligence in the secretariat of public security in 2008. The most recent general besides Del Real Magallanes to hold a cabinet post outside of defense and navy was Fox's first attorney general, Rafael Macedo de la Concha, appointed in 2000.

An excellent example of such a career pattern is that followed by Manlio Fabio Beltrones Rivera, who grew up in Villa Juárez, Sonora, in the 1950s and studied economics at the National University in Mexico City, graduating in 1974. One of his professors introduced him to Fernando Gutiérrez Barrios, a major figure in Mexican politics in the 1970s and 1980s, who served consecutively in the secretariat of government for many years and has long been identified as one of the *hombres del sistema*. Beltrones became his assistant and then private secretary. He was also deeply influenced by the secretary of government in that era, Jesús Reyes Heroles, who represented the PRI's liberal wing, favoring political reforms to the system.[28] Beltrones left the federal government to become a member of congress from his home state in 1982–85, returning to Sonora to serve as secretary general of the state government. He than ran for senator and, after serving briefly, became assistant secretary of government under Gutiérrez Barrios. Three years later he ran for and was elected governor of Sonora. After 2000, he again became a member of congress, secretary general of the Federation of Popular Organizations, the most influential professional federation affiliated with the PRI, and senator again, serving as the leader of the PRI delegation, 2006–12.[29]

The most common channel through which former governors travel to obtain national prominence, despite Beltrones's highly successful career in the legislative branch, is the cabinet. The most successful governor since 2000 in translating his state career into national prominence is Alberto Cárdenas Jiménez, who grew up on his father's wheat ranch in Zapotlán el Grande in the politically influential western state of Jalisco. He completed his preparatory schooling and engineering degree at the Regional Technical University in Ciudad Guzmán, Jalisco, before pursuing a doctorate at the Polytechnic University of Madrid, after which he taught and held administrative posts at his alma mater. Like many members of PAN, he began his public career locally, serving as secretary of studies on the city council of Ciudad Guzmán. Following this experience, he was elected mayor of the same community, after which he joined PAN, becoming a member of the state committee. A year later he ran for governor on the PAN ticket, becoming the first opposition candidate to win a gubernatorial election in his home state. Fox appointed him secretary of the environment in 2003. He resigned in 2005 to compete for the PAN presidential nomination, which he lost to Calderón, who after winning the election appointed

28. Personal communication, May 14, 2008.

29. *El Nacional*, October 23, 1991, 11; *La Jornada*, July 15, 2006, 1; *Proceso*, March 11, 1991, 17; *Diccionario biográfico del gobierno mexicano* (Mexico: Secretaria de la Presidencia, 1989), 52; and Mexican Political Biographies Project, 2009.

Cárdenas his secretary of agriculture, one of the very few individuals to hold two cabinet posts in both democratic administrations.[30]

## CONCLUSIONS

A comparison between two decisive generations in Mexican politics, the historic Revolutionary Generation and the recent Democratic Generation, strongly suggests that among the many variables that characterize credentials and career patterns of leading Mexican politicians, those produced by peaceful, democratic change can be as deep and broad (or more so) than those produced by violent change. Interestingly, the pace of the change, as far as the composition of political leadership, is not necessarily accelerated by violence. In fact, as we have shown, in some cases violence produces no change in some of these patterns, or at best incremental change, just as one might expect of peaceful change.

These findings, which I believe are unique in the literature, can contribute to the way we view the short- and long-term impact of violent change on a political model in contrast to a peaceful alternative. Obviously, given the ideological orientations of many revolutions, certain changes that impact structural features and the direction of those changes are shared by violent upheavals across different societies. Nevertheless, what is interesting in comparing these two processes of change in Mexico is that in many cases certain credentials are altered slowly despite their violent origin, such as the rise of college-educated leadership before the Revolution of 1910, and the restoration of a similarly educated leadership after 1920.

A possible explanation for why violent change may produce patterns that are narrower or not as deep as those generated by peaceful change is the extent to which a population, specifically certain components of that population, have been reduced by the extensive loss of life, by the forced emigration of hundreds of thousands of Mexicans, and by the unborn children from both of these categories. Thus, what has been labeled by some as "vacancies created by death," produce long-term, generational consequences that show up in the postrevolutionary administrations and beyond. For example, many of the individuals who fled Mexico were themselves well educated and, given their social circumstances, likely would have had an effect on the percentage of well-educated children of their generation. Or, as I have demonstrated, if most of the combat leadership

---

30. See www.pan.org.mx, 2007; Alejandro Envila Fisher, *Cien nombres de la transición mexicano* (Mexico: Grupo ERA, 2000), 69–71; and Mexican Political Biographies Project, 2009.

came from rural, humble backgrounds, they were less likely to survive the revolution than their middle-class generational peers. If Robert McCaa's figures, mentioned in the introduction, are correct, and a combination of unborn children, emigrants, and actual deaths totaled 2 million people out of 15 million Mexicans, the impact of eliminating 13 percent of the population in one decade would be devastating.[31]

Finally, even when we examine specific leadership characteristics that these two broad types of change introduced, their results may be unexpected. For example, we would expect violent change to open the doors to a new generation of rural-born leaders from modest social backgrounds. Democracy, however, impacts more strongly on this shift than its violent counterpart. The actual change in the working-class backgrounds of Mexican leadership after 1920 is relatively modest compared to the more dynamic increase in middle-class politicians and the truly dramatic decrease in politicians from wealthy circumstances.

31. Robert McCaa, "Missing Millions: The Demographic Costs of the Mexican Revolution," *Mexican Studies/Estudios Mexicanos* 19, no. 2 (Summer 2003): 367–400.

# 10

# Governors: National Democrats of the Future?

Since 2000, at least two convincing arguments can be made for why Mexican governors might dominate future national political leadership. During the transition to democracy in the 1980s and 1990s, mayors and governors were the first sources of elective executive leadership to provide opposition victories and accomplish a change in political fortunes in less than a decade, rapidly transferring control into the hands of non–Institutional Revolutionary Party (PRI) leadership over half the population.[1] I have made the point repeatedly that much of the impetus for democratic change came from provincial leadership, beginning at the state level in 1989 with the victorious election of a PAN governor in the northern border state of Baja California, long an opposition stronghold.[2] This pattern also occurred elsewhere in Latin America, for example, in Brazil, although different variables played a role in determining the importance of regional politics.[3]

The second convincing argument is that the first democratic president, Vicente Fox, achieved national recognition from his position as governor

---

1. On the other hand, for the contradictions that emerge at the local level as a result of a narrowly defined "electoral democracy," see John Stolle-McAllister, "What *Does* Democracy Look Like? Local Movements Challenge the Mexican Transition," *Latin American Perspectives* 32, no. 4 (July 2005): 15–35.

2. Rogelio Hernández Rodríguez agrees with the argument that local party structures have been reinforced by the strengthening of governors' autonomy in Mexico. He provides the best analysis of the evolution of the governors' role during the transition period, providing insights into the differences between PRI and PAN officeholders. See his "The Renovation of Old Institutions: State Governors and the Political Transition in Mexico," *Latin American Politics and Society* 45, no. 4 (Winter 2003): 115, and his more in-depth analysis of these changes in *El centro dividido, la nueva autonomía de los gobernadores* (Mexico: El Colegio de México, 2008), the most comprehensive study to date of gubernatorial decision-making. For a similar view, see Rafael Morales Ramírez, "El Regreso de los gobernadores," *Este País* (February–March 2004): 39–43.

3. Timothy J. Power and Marília G. Mochel, "Political Recruitment in an Executive-Centric System: Presidents, Ministers, and Governors in Brazil," in Peter M. Siavelis and Scott Morgenstern, eds., *Pathways to Power: Political Recruitment and Candidate Selection in Latin America* (University Park: Pennsylvania State University, 2008), 230.

of Guanajuato. His two opponents for the presidency, Francisco Labastida Ochoa of the PRI and Cuauhtémoc Cárdenas of the Party of the Democratic Revolution (PRD), were also former governors, the first time in recent Mexican political history that the presidential candidates from the three leading parties had held that post.[4] The importance of the gubernatorial post as a vehicle for achieving national political stature continued in the 2006 race when two of the three candidates once again recently held this office.[5]

Did Calderón's victory as the only leading nongubernatorial candidate restore the importance of the national executive branch as the dominant actor in the political careers of ambitious politicians, or does his public career, representing a party, legislative, and executive hybrid, suggest a new direction in democratic politics?[6]

If we consider regional representation important in the backgrounds of Mexican national politicians and a feature of democratic politics, governors play an important role in moderating significant regional biases shared by members of the executive and judicial branches. In the prior analysis of regional backgrounds, I emphasized the extraordinary bias of the Federal District in the birthplaces of national politicians from these two branches of government. Furthermore, we noted that this distortion continues through the democratic era among cabinet secretaries, assistant secretaries, and supreme court justices. The data presented in table 10.1

4. Since 1934, only three PRI presidents were previously governors: Lázaro Cárdenas from Michoacán, Miguel Alemán from Veracruz, and Adolfo Ruiz Cortines from Veracruz. All were nominated by the PRI when they were serving in their predecessors' cabinets— Cárdenas as defense secretary and Alemán and Ruiz Cortines as government secretary. In 1994, Zedillo came from the cabinet; Cuauhtémoc Cárdenas, the PRD candidate, had served as governor of his home state Michoacán in the 1980s; and Diego Fernández de Cevallos, the PAN candidate, came directly from congress. Fernández de Cevallos shared several characteristics in common with Felipe Calderón, having grown up in a PAN family whose father was a founder of the party in 1939. Fernández de Cevallos began speaking at rallies when he was only eleven. Similar to Calderón, his experience was in the legislative branch and heavily in the party as a member of the national council and the National Executive Committee. Unlike Calderón, given the PRI's monopoly until 2000, he did not have the opportunity to serve in the executive branch. *Líderes* 6, 1994, 65–71; www.senado.gob.mx, 2003; *Diccionario biográfico del gobierno mexicano* (Mexico: Presidencia de la República, 1992), 458–59; *El Financiero Internacional*, October 18–24, 1993, 20; and Mexican Political Biographies Project, 2009.

5. This can be seen symbolically by the fact that immediately following the 2006 presidential election, a small group of governors were already well recognized by the public at large. They were Enrique Peña Nieto, México (61 percent), Marcelo Ebrard, Federal District (42 percent), Mario Marín Torres, Puebla (39 percent), and Lázaro Cárdenas Batel (29 percent). Three years before his election, only 26 percent of Mexicans recognized the name of Felipe Calderón. Consulta Mitofsky, "En busca de líderes; los gobernadores," http://72.52.156.225, 2006.

6. Some commentators recently have argued that governors are the newly independent political elite in Mexico, collectively exercising more influence than the last two presidents. See René Avilés Fabila, "La elite del poder en México," *Excélsior*, March 1, 2009.

Table 10.1.  Regional Backgrounds of Governors, 1935–2009

| Era | Selected Regions (%) | | |
|---|---|---|---|
| | Federal District | East Central | West |
| Predemocratic | 3 | 21 | 19 |
| Democratic transition | 8 | 18 | 20 |
| Democratic | 3 | 11 | 34 |
| All governors (all eras) | 3 | 20 | 20 |
| All other politicians | 27 | 12 | 14 |

*Source*: Mexican Political Biographies Project, 2009.

clearly demonstrate some significant differences among prominent politicians who were governors compared to all other politicians, as well as equally important differences among the three political eras. Clearly the most dramatic difference is that nine times as many politicians as governors come from the Federal District.

The number of individuals who were governors and were born in the Federal District more than doubled during the democratic transition. The percentage of governors in the political elite since 2000 born in the Federal District has returned to predemocratic levels. The increase in the percentage of governors from the capital during the transition years can be explained by the fact that since the mid-1970s, politically ambitious Mexicans born in the Federal District but with family roots in the provinces, especially if they were the children of politicians, returned to their "home" states to establish legal residency to become eligible to run for the governorship. This pattern was reinforced by the fact that the PRI gubernatorial nominees were determined in large part by the national leadership, including the president, which gave politicians residing in the capital a distinct advantage.[7] Recently, however, with the advent of competitive state elections, local roots and local constituencies became critical for electoral success, thus favoring all candidates with well-established trajectories in state politics.[8]

7. For evidence of this see my detailed analysis of governors from the 1930s through the 1970s, Roderic Ai Camp, "Mexican Governors since Cárdenas: Education and Career Contacts," *Journal of Inter-American Studies and World Affairs* 16, no. 4 (November 1974): 454–81.

8. In his excellent analysis of PRI gubernatorial candidates in the 1990s, Christopher Díaz discovered an interesting pattern. He found that among the competing candidates for the PRI nomination, as electoral competition increased during this transitional period,

The other significant change between the predemocratic and transitional eras compared to the democratic era is in the number of governors from the West who have become prominent political figures. The West consists of seven states: Baja California del Sur, Sinaloa, Nayarit, Jalisco, Colima, Durango, and Aguascalientes. In the 2000 presidential election, the National Action Party (PAN) carried four of those seven states, including Jalisco, the most populous and politically important state in the West. PAN boasts a long and illustrious history in Jalisco, a state that has produced significant opposition to the central government since the Cristero rebellion of 1926.[9] Of the governors represented in President Calderón's administration, 43 percent are from the West. The two most recent governors of Jalisco—Francisco Ramírez Acuña, who served as his first secretary

---

PRI candidates were less likely to have careers centered in Mexico City. On the other hand, when he compared winners and losers among the PRI competitors for the gubernatorial nomination, contrary to expectations, the losers were more likely to have stronger local grassroots careers. See his "Electoral Competition in Mexico and Career Trajectories of PRI Gubernatorial Candidates, 1991-2001," *Politics & Policy* 33, no. 1 (March 2005): 44.

9. A number of PRI politicians from Jalisco share ideological roots and experiences with early PANista members. Among the most prominent is one of Mexico's leading novelists, Agustín Yáñez, who became governor of Jalisco from 1953 to 1958, and served as secretary of public education from 1964 to 1970. One of his biographers has argued that he was a Cristero, or at the very least pro-Cristero. When he saw that he had no future in that movement because of religious persecution and the position of President Calles, he went to Mexico City, like other intellectuals, to be discovered. See Roderic Ai Camp, "Un intelectual e la política Mexicana: Agustín Yáñez," *Relaciones* 2 (Summer 1981): 137-62, and "An Intellectual in Mexican Politics: The Case of Agustín Yáñez," *Mester* 12 (May 1983): 3-17. However, his personal secretary, Raúl Cardiel Reyes, is emphatic that he never had any direct ties to the Cristeros, and such a connection is untrue. He did, however, attend the seminary in Guadalajara, but abandoned studies toward the priesthood in his second year. Personal communication, September 9, 1980. Personal interview, Agustín Yáñez, August 22, 1978, and Alfonso Rangel Guerra, "Agustín Yáñez y su obra," in Agustín Yáñez, *Obras escogidas* (Mexico: Aguilar, 1968), 125-54. Another observer of Yáñez, Emmanuel Palacios, describes him as being affected by Catholic issues, but that he was inclined toward liberal ideas and was not a Cristero. Personal communication, September 20, 1980. The most successful open Cristero, however, was Antonio Gómez Robledo, who also came from Guadalajara, and as a career foreign service officer eventually became ambassador to Italy and ambassador emeritus in 1993. He was awarded the National Prize in letters in 1976, and was invited to become one of the elite members of the National College, Mexico's most prestigious intellectual organization, in 1960. He became a member of the Jesuit order in 1923 and left the order in 1925, joining the Cristeros with his father under Anacleto González Flores. Both he and his father were saved from a firing squad by his uncle, a member of the senate and a former constitutional deputy. He became president of the Nacional Union of Catholic Students after leaving the Cristeros, an organization that produced many future PANistas. *Hispano Americano*, February 22, 1971, 31; *Excélsior*, November 29, 1974; www.colegionacional.org, 2007; www.juridicas,unam. mx, 2008; www.omnibiography.com/bios, 2008; www.jalisco.gob.mx, 2007; and Mexican Political Biographies Project, 2009. For the influence of the National Catholic Party in Jalisco in the preceding decade, see Jennie Purnell's helpful account, *Popular Movements and State Formation in Revolutionary Mexico: The Agraristas and the Cristeros of Michoacán* (Durham, N.C.: Duke University Press, 1999), 56ff.

of government, and Alberto Cárdenas Jiménez, who became Fox's secretary of environment before being appointed by Calderón as secretary of agriculture, livestock, and rural development—illustrate the West's importance.[10]

Finally, the other important regional pattern that shows up in the data in table 10.1 is the major decline in the representation of the East Central states, consisting of Hidalgo, Puebla, Querétaro, San Luis Potosí, Tlaxcala, and Zacatecas. During the PRI-dominated eras, a fifth of all governors came from this region. That figure has declined by nearly half since 2000. These states, with the exception of San Luis Potosí, have been among Mexico's lowest income states and also have been PRI strongholds for many years. The opposition victories since 2000, including both the PAN and the PRD, have deprived these states of their traditional importance as a path for governors who have achieved national political prominence.

In the same way that governors have contributed to decreasing the bias favoring the Federal District among all prominent politicians, they also have produced an important reversal in the declining rate of rural birthplaces. As the data in table 10.2 illustrate, rural birthplaces have declined significantly among governors from 1935 to 1988, as is the case among all politicians. This is to be expected as Mexico increased its level of urbanization. What the data do not reveal is that all other politicians typically have been much more likely than governors to have been born in urban communities. Therefore, rural-born Mexicans were more likely to pursue a gubernatorial path as a channel into national political prominence than channels offered through other career paths, such as the federal bureaucracy. It was not until Zedillo became president in 1994 that rural-born governors were fewer in number than were all other politicians.

What is remarkable is the huge increase of rural backgrounds among governors who served in the democratic administrations since they more than doubled their numbers from the preceding democratic transition. Because a third of recent governors came from rural origins, the governorship once again provided opportunities for politically ambitious individuals

10. Both men had lengthy political careers at the state and local level. Ramírez Acuña was a member of the city council of Zapopan, twice a state legislator, and mayor of Guadalajara before becoming governor; Cárdenas Jiménez was secretary of studies for the city council of Ciudad Guzmán and mayor of Ciudad Guzmán prior to winning the governorship. He was elected senator from Jalisco in 2006. *Quehacerpolitico*, December 10, 2006; Alejandro Envila Fisher, *Cien nombres de la transición mexicana* (Mexico: Grupo ERA, 2000), 69–71; www. pan.org.mx, 2007; *Diario de Yucatán*, November 28, 2006; and Mexican Political Biographies Project, 2009. The first PAN candidate to run for governor of Jalisco was Jaime Robles León Martín del Campo, co-founder of PAN in 1939, and federal deputy from the third Jalisco congressional district, 1949–52. He opposed Yáñez in the 1952–53 gubernatorial race. His daughter, Martha Robles, is a distinguished intellectual and author. Personal communication from Martha Robles, June 4, 1980.

**Table 10.2.** Geographic Origins of Governors, 1935–2009

| Era | Rural Birthplace (%) |
|-----|----------------------|
| Predemocratic | 46 |
| Democratic transition | 16 |
| Democratic period | 34 |

*Source*: Mexican Political Biographies Project, 2009.

from smaller communities to achieve recognition and reach national political prominence.

All the major parties have contributed to this increase by emphasizing involvement in local elective offices and local party organizations. The PRI has followed suit in an attempt to make their gubernatorial candidates stronger among the electorate, linking them to grassroots politics and party experiences. The PRI's willingness to emulate PAN choices has reinforced certain credentials that distinguish the new generation of governors from past governors. In fact, among governors born in the 1950s and 1960s, the PRI-affiliated politicians come from rural backgrounds in numbers greater than the PAN or PRD. Under the Calderón administration, 43 percent of governors were born in villages and small rural communities.

José Guadalupe Osuna Millán, elected governor of Baja California in 2007, typifies this recent pattern. He was born in the village of Aguacaliente de Gárate in the mid-1950s. He was one of ten children of an agricultural laborer. His father moved to Baja California when Osuna Millán was a child, and when he turned sixteen he began working in a *maquiladora* (assembly plant) in Tijuana, where he met his wife. Hoping to improve himself, he attended night school at the University of Baja California to study economics. After graduating, he traveled to Mexico City to complete a master's degree in economics with many fellow students from modest backgrounds at the National Polytechnic Institute, a university founded during the Cárdenas presidency to educate working-class students. Returning to Baja California, he taught at his alma mater and became the assistant director of academic programs. Osuna Millán held a series of state public works posts before being elected mayor of Tijuana in 1995, followed by a stint as a member of congress from his home congressional district in 2003–2006.[11]

I cited the case of two governors from Jalisco represented in the Calderón administration as having held local political office. To what extent has such a linkage between local and state political experience characterized

11. See www.bajacalifornia.gob.mx, 2008; www.signonsandiego.com, August 7, 2007.

Table 10.3. Local Elective Career Experiences of Governors, 1935–2009

|                      | Position Held (%) | |
| Era                  | Mayor | State Legislator |
| -------------------- | ----- | ---------------- |
| Predemocratic        | 17    | 15               |
| Democratic transition| 39    | 16               |
| Democratic period    | 51    | 37               |

Source: Mexican Political Biographies Project, 2009.

governors over time, and how has this been altered with the introduction of a competitive electoral model? The data in table 10.3 demonstrate just how clearly the career experiences of governors have changed.

The most pronounced change from the predemocratic to the democratic transitional period beginning in 1988 is the more than twofold increase in the number of governors who previously were mayors. Caroline Beer found evidence of this trend earlier when controlling for the level of competition in state elections, arguing that "case study data combined with a statistical analysis of data from all of the governors from 1970 to 1998 suggest that states with more competitive elections are more likely to elect candidates with careers rooted in the state than candidates who parachute in from Mexico City."[12] By the end of the Zedillo administration, two-fifths of all governors had been elected mayor of their hometowns. This position became an increasingly critical channel for a politician hoping to achieve a gubernatorial office as well as pursue a national career.[13]

Since 2000, governors who first held elective office as mayors increased by nearly a third to half of all governors. This increase, occurring in a brief, nine-year period, suggests just how important most political parties have considered such experiences as crucial to nominating a candidate. Voters, in turn, have assessed numerous recent gubernatorial candidates on the basis of their impressions of an individual's performance governing local communities. Given that half of all recent governors served as mayors, their specific presence in the national executive and legislative branches has contributed to the increasing percentage of all leading national politicians who have held local elective office.

12. Caroline Beer, *Electoral Competition and Institutional Change in Mexico* (Notre Dame: University of Notre Dame Press, 2003), 116.
13. For a detailed examination of recent governors' political networks and prior positions, see David Pérez Calleja's useful work on Aguascalientes, *Aguascalientes, la sucesión 2004, alternancia o continuidad?* (Mexico: Talleres Gráficos de La Universal, 2004).

Governors who served in the state legislature did not follow the same pattern as those who previously were mayors. Essentially, no increase occurred in governors (table 10.3) with this career experience between the predemocratic and democratic transition eras. In fact, under Luis Echeverría's administration, only a minuscule 8 percent of politicians who were governors had served previously in the state legislature. Under Zedillo, the figures for governors declined further to zero.

The sudden and dramatic increase of governors who previously served in their state legislatures in the administrations after 2000 is therefore particularly notable. The figure since 2000 is nearly two-fifths of all governors—more than double that of their peers in the two previous political eras. How can such an extraordinary increase be explained? In the analysis of the importance of local officeholding in the careers of all prominent politicians, we discovered the importance of the state legislature as a vehicle for PAN politicians to obtain political experience before climbing the national ladder. PAN governors are more than half again as likely as all governors to have held a post in the state legislature. Thus, the dramatic increase in this experience in the backgrounds of governors is largely due to the increased proportion of PAN governors overall since 2000.[14]

Héctor Terán Terán was a PAN governor who contributed personally to this transitional pattern of emphasizing state legislative experiences among all governors. Terán was born in the rural community of Moctezuma, Sonora, in 1931. From a modest family, he began working as a child while attending public school in Agua Prieta. He then moved to Monterrey, Nuevo León, where he was able to attend preparatory school and ultimately earned a business administration degree from the recently opened Monterrey Technical Institute of Higher Studies. As a student, he joined the PAN youth sector, serving as the publicity secretary for this group in Monterrey. As was true of so many future politicians in Baja California, he moved to the state to seek greater economic opportunities. He was persecuted and imprisoned for his opposition activities in PAN, similar to his notable political mentor, Salvador Rosas Magallón.[15]

Terán ran for every conceivable office on the PAN ticket, including city council member, mayor of Mexicali, federal deputy, and senator, all without

14. Interestingly, this argument does not apply to PRD governors. No governor in our study from the PRD is known to have served in their respective state legislature.

15. Salvador Rosas Magallón was a political legend in Baja California, viewed locally as the people's lawyer. He twice ran for governor of Baja California, and the second time Terán directed his gubernatorial campaign in 1971. He twice was a candidate for PAN's presidential nomination in 1963 and 1975. Similar to Terán, he twice chaired the state party organization, later winning a seat in congress before becoming a member of the PAN National Executive Committee. Had Terán won the governorship in 1977, Rosas Magallón would have become the state's attorney general. Personal communication from Salvador Rosas Magallón, n.d.; *Por qué*, October 4, 1968, 5.

success, in the 1960s and 1970s. When he ran for the state legislature in 1980, he became the first member of PAN in Baja California history to win a seat. Halfway through his term, he competed for PAN's presidential nomination as a leading candidate in 1981, ultimately losing to Pablo Emilio Madero Belden.[16] That seat and his constant activities in the local and national PAN organization, including two stints as state party chairman in the 1970s, provided him with the opportunity to become his party's candidate for congress from the Mexicali district, a seat he won in 1985. After his victory in the congressional race, he tried for the senate once again, becoming the first member of PAN from Baja California to win a seat there in 1991. Before completing his term, he won the governorship in 1995.[17]

Education was one of the most influential credentials among politicians examined previously because it often determined who and where political recruitment occurred and nonfamilial socialization affecting politicians' economic and social values. As one might expect given the increased importance of local political ties, governors, as members of the nationally prominent political elite, contributed to the important decline in graduates from the National University of Mexico. In the past, nearly a third of governors went to Mexico City for their university education. There they often met mentors, fellow students, and professors who achieved highly successful political careers, using their influence to nominate their closest friends as gubernatorial candidates.

No president did this more frequently and could be said to have established a long-term trend in the source of university education among future Mexican governors than Miguel Alemán.[18] Alemán ensured that six of his companions from the National University became state governors during his administration: Angel Carvajal Bernal of Veracruz, Oscar Soto Máynes of Chihuahua, Raúl López Sánchez of Coahuila, Alfonso García González of Baja California, José de Jesús Castorena of Guanajuato, and Horacio Terán Zozaya of Tamaulipas.[19] Five of these individuals were co-students with Alemán, and one was his professor.[20]

16. Madero Belden won 66 percent of the vote among PAN delegates against Terán and Luis Castañeda. *Hispano Americano*, October 5, 1981, 9, and *La Nación*, September 16, 1981.

17. *Proceso*, October 12, 1998; *La Nación*, September 16, 1981; *Hispano Americano*, June 6, 1983, 32–33; *Diccionario biográfico del gobierno mexicano*, 587; and Mexican Political Biographies Project, 2009.

18. Ironically, by imposing a number of governors, including several of his UNAM classmates over popular protests, Alemán anticipated the increasing objections of local citizens by many decades. Such protests ultimately led to governors who were products of the local environment, not Mexico City.

19. Roderic Ai Camp, "Education and Political Recruitment in Mexico: The Alemán Generation," *Journal of Interamerican Studies and World Affairs* 18, no. 3 (August 1976): 304.

20. Other fellow students of Miguel Alemán also became governors, but under different presidents. For example, Dr. Luciano Huerta Sánchez, who attended the National Preparatory School in the famous 1920–24 generation, indicated his friendship with the

The most successful politician among this group of governors was Angel Carvajal Bernal, who, like Alemán, was a native of Veracruz. He and the president both attended the National Preparatory School from 1920 to 1924 before enrolling in the National School of Law. Both men graduated one year early in 1928. Carvajal pursued a career in higher education and in the federal bureaucracy, where he became chief of auxiliary agents in the criminal division of the attorney general's office. Remarkably, eight years after graduating from law school, he became assistant attorney general of Mexico, and briefly, in 1944, a supreme court justice before returning to his home state to serve as secretary general of government under Adolfo Ruiz Cortines. When Alemán appointed Ruiz Cortines to his cabinet, Carvajal replaced him as governor, a position he held until 1951, when Alemán appointed him as secretary of government properties. He later served Ruiz Cortines as secretary of government and then remained in public life as a supreme court justice until 1972.[21]

As noted previously, the dominance of the National University declined, replaced by other Mexico City universities, especially private institutions, and by state public and private institutions. The decline of the National University in the educational backgrounds of governors, however, has been quite recent. During the last three presidential administrations (1970–88) prior to the transition period, half of all governors were still graduates of the national university, most from the law school. Under Salinas, himself an alumnus, only one-fifth of governors were alumni of the National University.

The decline in governors who were National University (UNAM) graduates deepened after 2000, when only 7 percent of the governors who served in the Fox administration were products of that institution. Recent national politicians who were governors are important in determining the wider distribution of university backgrounds among public leadership, especially in increasing the number of prominent figures who come from provincial institutions.

The decentralization of university education among governors away from the capital and from UNAM specifically is complemented by a reversal in governors who were college educated. Only under Salinas did all politicians

president in correspondence to me when he was governor of Tlaxcala in 1972. Personal communication, July 10, 1972.

21. *Hispano Americano*, August 10, 1951, 14; *Diario de Yucatán*, December 2, 1952, 1; *Hispano Americano*, December 5, 1952, 9; *La Jornada*, January 28, 1985. Carvajal was one of the front runners for the PRI presidential nomination in 1958 but lost to López Mateos. Many analysts and Carvajal himself believe he lost because he would have been the third president in a row from Veracruz. Personal interview, October 25, 1976. Letter from co-student Adolfo Zamora, March 12, 1973.

who were governors receive college degrees. Recent governors contribute to the importance of other institutions in playing an influential role in recruiting future public figures. Not only have governors reduced the importance of higher education overall in the credentials of national leadership, they have also altered the disciplinary educational patterns found among other politicians or in prior generations of politicians and governors.

In the predemocratic era, few governors who were college graduates were economists, and almost none had completed a degree in business administration or accounting. This pattern changed significantly after 1988, when governors began to emulate the university patterns of executive branch politicians, who increasingly were attending undergraduate economics and business programs. A sixfold increase in economics graduates and a twelvefold increase in business graduates occurred among governors during the democratic transition compared to the predemocratic era (table 10.4).

In the democratic era, both PAN and PRI governors continued the importance of business administration degrees in their educational choices, and many came from solid business backgrounds. Again, PAN has not produced many economists among their gubernatorial candidates; consequently, economic degrees have declined as part of the credentials among governors, as well as among prominent national politicians.

Governors are distinctive from all other prominent politicians in their higher education, especially when comparisons are drawn with the graduate training of Mexican politicians. As noted earlier, a huge increase has taken place in the graduate training of leading Mexican politicians in recent decades. In the democratic period alone, over 70 percent of cabinet secretaries and assistant secretaries achieved master's and doctoral degrees. In contrast, less than a fourth of governors since 2000 boast graduate training. Even among members of congress, who are the least well educated of prominent national politicians, more than two-fifths have achieved a graduate degree.

Table 10.4. Educational Backgrounds of Governors, 1935–2009

| Era | Educational Credential (%) | | | |
| --- | --- | --- | --- | --- |
| | UNAM Graduate | No Degree | Economics | Business |
| Predemocratic | 35 | 36 | 4 | 1 |
| Democratic transition | 29 | 2 | 24 | 12 |
| Democratic period | 12 | 9 | 9 | 14 |

Source: Mexican Political Biographies Project, 2009.

Governors, as can be seen from the data in table 10.5, emulated the generally increasing educational trends among other prominent politicians from the predemocratic period to the transitional administrations. They were not as well educated as executive branch politicians, nevertheless those with graduate degrees increased fourfold from 1935 to 1988 to 1988 to 2000, an extraordinary change. The advent of democracy, however, has reversed that trend among governors, whose graduate school backgrounds declined by more than half after 2000.

The decline in the importance of graduate training among recent governors is a reflection of the decentralization of the nomination process; the reliance on local party leaders and state politicians, including incumbent governors, to influence the process; and different nonpublic careers, including the private sector. Recent governors, as suggested, are selected on the basis of credentials other than their level of education and where they received that education.

The source of governors' postgraduate education is equally revealing. The trend among leading national politicians, which reached its apex in the Salinas and Zedillo administrations, was to attend U.S. universities, especially Ivy League schools such as Harvard, Yale, and MIT. Governors did not attend Ivy League schools at the same levels as other prominent politicians, but they doubled their attendance at institutions in the United States from the predemocratic to the democratic transition period. Again, as is the case of their level of graduate training, governors in the democratic period have decreased their attendance at U.S. institutions by more than half.

The dramatic increase in graduate degrees among governors from the predemocratic to the democratic transition era is represented overwhelmingly by increases in attendance at Mexican and European graduate programs, not schools found in the United States. Attendance at the former graduate programs sets governors apart from executive branch politicians historically and recently. Essentially, nine out of ten governors who attended a graduate program did so in Europe or Mexico. These graduate

Table 10.5. Graduate Education of Governors, 1935–2009

| Era | Graduate Education (%) | | | |
| --- | --- | --- | --- | --- |
|  | Graduate Degree | United States | Mexico Only | Europe |
| Predemocratic | 12 | 4 | 3 | 5 |
| Democratic transition | 49 | 8 | 27 | 14 |
| Democratic period | 23 | 3 | 11 | 9 |

Source: Mexican Political Biographies Project, 2009.

programs often provide a different emphasis in their respective disciplines, and few contemporary governors would come in contact with future influential Mexican politicians in the executive branch while studying abroad, specifically in the United States.

A number of recent governors who fit this description have completed their doctorates and have gone on to make academia their career. These governors, similar to individuals who pursued careers in the private sector, established scholarly and administrative reputations at state universities. Presidents and administrators of local and regional universities are highly respected in Mexico and are automatically assigned influential roles in their communities. One of the most successful examples of such a career is that of the former PAN governor of Jalisco Alberto Cárdenas Jiménez, who grew up on a wheat ranch in Zapotlán el Grande. After attending a religious elementary school and a public secondary school, he completed his academic preparatory education at the Regional Technical University of Ciudad Guzmán. He continued his college education there, graduating with a degree in electrical engineering. Cárdenas Jiménez then went to Madrid, where he attended the Graduate School of Technical Engineering at the Polytechnic University, receiving a master's degree in industrial organization. He completed his Ph.D. in 1983 with a dissertation on socioeconomic planning of medium-size cities, a subject he could put to good use as a local politician. He returned to his alma mater and taught various subjects in finance, administration, and industrial engineering, becoming coordinator of the electrical engineering program. Eventually, he was appointed director of graduate studies. He became mayor of Ciudad Guzmán in 1992, and shortly thereafter was elected governor in 1995.[22]

One of the expected changes among governors since the advent of the democratic era is the increasing importance of party militancy and leadership of local and state party organizations. If the grassroots connections are indeed more important in advancing one's career, what role has party activities played in the career trajectories of Mexican governors? The level of partisanship among all governors differs substantially. A rule of thumb is that the more intense a party's struggle for representation, the higher the level of partisanship among nominal members.

The highest level of party militancy among governors is claimed by the PAN with three-quarters of its governors having held party posts, followed by the PRD, with 60 percent of its governors serving in comparable posts. PRI governors have been the least militant of the three leading party

22. See www.pan.org.mx, 2008; Fisher, *Cien nombres de la transición mexicana*, 69–71; and Rafael Pérez Franco, *Quiénes son el PAN* (Mexico: Fundación Rafael Preciado, 2007), 58–59.

Table 10.6. Partisan Activism of Governors, 1935–2009

| Era | Party Militancy among Governors (%) | | | |
| --- | --- | --- | --- | --- |
| | None | PAN/Right | PRD/Left | PRI |
| Predemocratic | 53 | – | – | 45 |
| Democratic transition | 29 | 60 | 67 | 80 |
| Democratic period | 51 | 89 | 50 | 57 |
| All governors | 51 | 75 | 60 | 48 |
| All politicians | 60 | 85 | 97 | 33 |

Source: Mexican Political Biographies Project, 2009.

affiliations, with slightly less than half experiencing such levels of party activism (table 10.6). Again, I argue that PRI's long-term lower levels of party militancy can be explained by the way in which governors for much of the period under study were designated in Mexico City from the top down.[23]

The most notable pattern appearing in the data on party activism among governors in table 10.6 is the significant increase in partisanship during the democratic transition. Earlier, we noted the remarkable finding that half of Mexico's politicians since the 1930s were not active partisans of their respective parties. This characteristic is equally true of governors. This nonpartisan pattern changes dramatically during the democratic transition, when the percentage of nonmilitants declined almost by half, and partisan politicians accounted for seven out of ten governors. As electoral competition for governorships increased after 1989, party organizations at both the state and national level became increasingly influential as the PRI joined the PAN and PRD in performing the actual functions of a political party in a democracy.

Even in the pretransition era some PRI members before PAN and PRD won their first gubernatorial elections attributed their nomination and election as gubernatorial candidates to their party activities, in spite of being personal friends of the president in whose administration they were nominated and elected. Guillermo Jiménez Morales, who governed Puebla from 1981 to 1987, shortly before the democratic transition began, is a classic example of such a governor. Jiménez Morales argues that politics was in his blood, and that by the age of six, when he was in elementary school,

23. For a thorough discussion of how scholars of various political systems have analyzed the role of parties in the designation of candidates, see Peter M. Siavelis and Scott Morgenstern, "Political Recruitment and Candidate Selection in Latin America: A Framework for Analysis," in Siavelis and Morgenstern, eds., *Pathways to Power*, 14–17.

he used to say to his classmates and to the teacher that "when he became governor, he would do this and that." He attributes his strong, early interest in politics to growing up in a political family. His father was mayor of Huauchinango, his hometown, and later became president of the PRI in the Federal District and a member of congress. When Jiménez Morales graduated from the National University like most of his PRI peers in that period, he returned home to become vice chairman of the Puebla state party organization, his first political office. He obtained this post, as he openly admitted, because the state party chairman was a relative. Fifteen years later he was elected to congress from the Huauchinango district, and within three weeks he became chairman of the state PRI. He recalls the importance of that post in giving him an opportunity to travel far and wide in Puebla, making dozens of political contacts and talking to ordinary citizens. He served as a general delegate of the PRI's National Executive Committee to numerous states before representing Puebla again in congress and then being nominated for governor.

In spite of becoming friends with President José López Portillo as his student at the National School of Law, he did not attribute his nomination to presidential influence, pointing out that other leading candidates for the nomination were even closer friends of the president.[24] After completing his term as governor, he became president of the party in the Federal District, the most influential regional party position in Mexico, and was elected to congress for a third time, becoming the party's national secretary of political action for three years.[25]

When comparing the data on party militancy between governors in the democratic transitional period with that of the democratic era since 2000, we are struck by another dramatic shift that reflects a reversal in the highest levels of party militancy in the transitional period, declining back to comparable levels found in the predemocratic era. The only difference is that the PAN and PRI are largely responsible for governors' militancy, rather than solely the PRI, as was true in both the predemocratic and democratic transition years. This significant change is remarkable because it contradicts the intuitive expectation that stronger party involvement would characterize greater numbers of winning gubernatorial candidates

24. He also became a friend of future president Miguel de la Madrid at the Cristóbal Colón secondary school in Mexico City in the late 1940s. *Almanaque de Puebla* (Mexico: Almanaque de México, 1981–82), 25.

25. Jiménez Morales went on to serve in Salinas's cabinet as secretary of fisheries, and in Zedillo's presidency as ambassador to the Vatican and then assistant secretary of religious affairs in the secretariat of government. *Diccionario biográfico del gobierno mexicano*, 195–96; Blanca Lilia Ibarra Cadena, "Gobernador no pone gobernador: Guillermo Jiménez Morales," *Periódico Digital de Puebla, Oaxaca y Tlaxcala*, May 27, 2008; and Mexican Political Biographies Project, 2009.

since 2000 compared to governors prior to 1988. Joy Langston found that among PRI and PAN candidates for certain types of congressional and senatorial candidates (plurality seats), "party loyalists" were much more likely to prevail.[26] Those findings jibe with my own data on the actual deputies and senators who qualify for inclusion as the most successful national politicians. The question remains: why do high levels of party activism appear to be present among certain types of political career positions but not among all governors?

In my earliest study of governors during the depths of a centralized political model, one could not predict which of many variables determined the selection of PRI's gubernatorial candidates, who of course actually became governors. Many variables played a role, including party activism, local officeholding, friendship with national political actors, friendship with incumbent governors, and social-economic factors characterizing a particular state. For example, in an attempt to pick successful candidates who appeal to state electorates, local party leadership and incumbent governors may push for individuals who have distinguished themselves in other ways, including having been a successful professional person or university administrator, or even more likely, a local businessman who served on municipal commissions and was a visible presence in the community.

Governors, as is the case of all leading politicians, bring their own set of experiences to their successful political careers. If we first examine their nongovernmental careers, we might learn how governors differ from other prominent figures and how their presence in Mexican leadership alters these prior career experiences. The previous examination of the three branches of government suggested that national politicians with early experiences as student politicians, experiences that often whetted their appetite for public life, suggested that it was equally common to politicians from all walks of life. Nearly one in six politicians shared this early experience. Among college-educated politicians, this figure exceeded more than one in four. As noted from the data, however, the percentage of politicians since 2000 who shared student leadership posts declined significantly, at least by half in the legislative and executive branches.

It is interesting to point out that governors during the predemocratic period were even more likely to have led student organizations in their youth. In fact, a fifth of all governors shared in this experience. Similar to all other politicians, the presence of a student organization post in one's background declined precipitously beginning with the democratic transition. What is revealed in the comparative data between all politicians and

26. Joy Langston, "Legislative Recruitment in Mexico," in Siavelis and Morgenstern, eds., *Pathways to Power*, 147–63.

governors alone is that the decline is even more dramatic among nongovernors, and governors in the democratic period have revived the importance of this experience in their backgrounds, even though the percentages are much lower than was true in the pre-1988 period.

Governors, therefore, contribute significantly to the revival of such an experience among future prominent leaders. I believe the explanation for why governors are more likely to have been student leaders than any other group we have analyzed is that they are among the recent groups to have benefited most from the decentralization of college education, thereby increasing their potential among dozens of state universities to hold such student organizational posts, rather than competing against each other in two or three huge universities in Mexico City. This student leadership experience remains important because student organizations are often linked to national political organizations, especially their youth divisions. The party youth groups serve as a recruiting vehicle for identifying and tapping politically interested and talented young people from preparatory and university campuses.

Many politicians in the predemocratic era reached the ranks of political leadership through their performance in affiliated organizations, notably labor and peasant organizations. Rising up through union organizations typically led to important posts in the legislative branch and to some extent to PRI national party executive posts. In the executive branch, we detect a huge decline in union leadership posts in the backgrounds of assistant secretaries and secretaries in the democratic era. By contrast, one in ten members of congress continues to have successful union careers. Governors in the predemocratic era were second only to members of congress in having union leadership posts in their backgrounds. By the transition years, those numbers declined to half, and by the democratic era, none were former union leaders. These figures are comparable for their national executive peers, of whom only 1 percent were former union leaders.

Where governors most stand out among nongovernment career experiences compared to other leading national politicians is the percentage who pursued important, successful careers in the private sector. The figures in table 10.7 demonstrate conclusively that the argument suggesting governors increasingly were coming from business backgrounds is indeed the case. What is striking about the figures for business managers is that governors in the predemocratic era only were a third as likely as all other politicians to have emerged from the private sector, an experience on average shared by one in twenty leading politicians.[27] Whereas the percentage

27. Although only a small group of prominent politicians who were governors came from business backgrounds in the predemocratic era, they share numerous career

**Table 10.7.** Nongovernmental Career Experiences of Mexican Governors, 1935–2009

| | Position Held (%) | | |
|---|---|---|---|
| Era | Student Leader | Union Leader | Business Manager |
| *Governors* | | | |
| Predemocratic | 20 | 12 | 4 |
| Democratic transition | 6 | 6 | 16 |
| Democratic period | 9 | 0 | 20 |
| *All politicians* | | | |
| Predemocratic | 14 | 15 | 6 |
| Democratic transition | 3 | 3 | 5 |
| Democratic period | 4 | 5 | 12 |

*Source*: Mexican Political Biographies Project, 2009.

Student leader = leader of any preparatory school or university student organization; union leader = secretary general of a state or national union; business manager = owner or top manager of a large firm or corporation.

of business backgrounds found among all politicians remains static from the predemocratic through the democratic transition, among governors it increases an incredible 300 percent.

The dramatic increase from 1988 to 2000, when the first opposition governor was elected, demonstrates clearly how rapidly winning PAN governors increased the presence of business experience and also how the PRI jumped on the bandwagon to select an increasing number of their candidates from similar backgrounds. Since 2000, prominent national figures who are governors are much more likely than other politicians to have been successful businessmen.

---

characteristics with contemporary governors with such origins. Nazario S. Ortiz Garza, who had to abandon his high school studies after the first year for financial reasons, began working at age fourteen in 1907. By the age of twenty, he started his own business. He joined the revolution in 1915 as a civilian, becoming the purveyor of military trains in Chihuahua City in 1917. His first involvement in politics was as a failed candidate for city council of Torreon, Coahuila. Yet he indicated to me that from the time of this experience, "he had in his mind the desire to become governor of [his] state." He eventually became a member of the city council, then mayor, then a state legislator, then mayor again, and governor, after which he served as senator under Cárdenas and as secretary of agriculture and livestock. During this time, "in a word, I devoted myself to" these businesses. He eventually founded and directed numerous successful grape growing ranches and companies. Personal communication, August 12, 1974.

Governors traditionally have experienced high levels of militancy within their respective political parties. PRI governors similar to PRI members of congress often have pursued repeated posts within their party bureaucracies. Approximately a third of all leading governors and half the leading members of congress can claim such party posts in the predemocratic period (table 10.8). In contrast, those politicians who followed federal bureaucratic career paths were slightly less likely in the predemocratic period to have held posts in the PRI. As parties increased their importance in the electoral arena, actually competing for votes to elect their candidates, the importance of those party experiences significantly increased among PRI governors. The figures for PAN and PRD governors do not represent an increase from the predemocratic to the democratic transitional period, but an initial starting point from 1988 for the two opposition parties to actually occupy gubernatorial seats. However, as the data demonstrate in table 10.8, in the democratic era fewer politicians from all other career paths, with the exception of the PRI, held party positions. The PRI increased its party officeholding dramatically since 2000. As the parties nominated different types of candidates for all elective offices, those individuals winning gubernatorial posts were less likely to share these militant party experiences.

Governors also bring additional public career experiences to the pool of prominent national public figures. The data in table 10.9 reinforce a major finding we have alluded to earlier—governors, who are elected executive officials, typically have held elective office much more frequently than

Table 10.8. Political Party Experiences of Mexican Governors, 1935–2009

| Era | Party Position Held by Governors (%) | | |
|---|---|---|---|
| | PRI | PAN | PRD |
| *Governors* | | | |
| Predemocratic | 34 | – | – |
| Democratic transition | 69 | 70 | 67 |
| Democratic period | 57 | 56 | 50 |
| *All politicians* | | | |
| Predemocratic | 27 | 89 | 100 |
| Democratic transition | 33 | 86 | 100 |
| Democratic period | 60 | 71 | 47 |

*Source*: Mexican Political Biographies Project, 2009.

All figures are based on the percentages of officeholders who were members of the three leading parties.

Table 10.9.  Public Careers of Mexican Governors, 1935–2009

| | | | Oficial | Secretary | |
| Era | Deputy | Senator | Mayor | General | Mayor |
| --- | --- | --- | --- | --- | --- |
| *Governors* | | | | | |
| Predemocratic | 50 | 39 | 14 | 15 | 17 |
| Democratic transition | 69 | 41 | 2 | 20 | 39 |
| Democratic period | 43 | 66 | 0 | 16 | 50 |
| *All politicians* | | | | | |
| Predemocratic | 56 | 25 | 6 | 7 | 6 |
| Democratic transition | 55 | 27 | 16 | 4 | 9 |
| Democratic period | 36 | 30 | 13 | 3 | 16 |

*Position Held (%)* spans the Deputy through Mayor columns.

*Source*: Mexican Political Biographies Project, 2009.

many other prominent leaders in the executive and judicial branches. With the exception of having served in the congress, traditionally governors were much more likely than their peers to have held national and local elective office. Even in the predemocratic period, governors were more than twice as likely as all other politicians to have served as mayors. Although a remarkable increase in the presence of mayors in the backgrounds of all politicians has occurred, more than doubling from the predemocratic to the democratic era, even more dramatic is the fact that now half of all governors have been mayors compared to only one-sixth of their peers prior to 1988. Once again, we see how this career shift begins to occur, significantly so, during the 1988–2000 transition to democracy.

Another major difference in governors' public careers from other prominent figures is the percentage who have served in the senate. Among all politicians, 25–30 percent have been senators. Among governors, however, two-fifths were senators in the predemocratic and transitional eras, increasing by more than half to two-thirds since 2000.

Bureaucratic posts, national or regional, are not as common in the backgrounds of Mexican governors compared to other national politicians. A distinct difference is apparent in the bureaucratic careers of governors and other politicians in the predemocratic period. More than twice as many governors served in cabinet agencies as oficiales mayores, the third-ranked post in Mexico's national executive branch agencies. Such bureaucratic experiences have disappeared among governors in recent years and more than doubled among other politicians. The figures for governors suggest how centralized decision making linked national bureaucratic careers to PRI designations of gubernatorial candidates, all of whom won office until 1989. As the nomination process decentralized and other variables became influential, such national career visibility was no longer critical.

Finally, career experiences in the state bureaucracy, illustrated by politicians who have served as lieutenant governors (secretary general), an appointed post in Mexico, suggests a significant decline to 3 percent (or lower) of politicians.[28] Yet five times as many governors who form the elite political pool continue to list this post on their résumés. Again, governors, regardless of whether the position is elective or appointed, bring a greater emphasis on state and local officeholding as a whole, and with a few exceptions, have contributed significantly to increasing such experiences during the democratic transition and after.

Finally, have the informal credentials that governors bring to the table changed since the predemocratic days, and to what extent do these politicians differ from other national elites? Some striking patterns which differentiate governors from other politicians appear in the data presented in table 10.10. The most important difference between governors and all other leading politicians is their level of family political activity. Nearly half of all governors in the predemocratic era were known to have close family members in public life compared to more than a third of other politicians. Figures for both groups declined as the democratic transformation began, suggesting an increasing pool of new blood during the 1990s. Since 2000, this family political connection continued to decline to only a fourth among all politicians. In contrast to the general pattern, however, governors with such connections were on the upswing.

What explains the significant deviation between governors and other political figures? Although Mexico has a long history of political families, I believe that pattern in Mexican politics traditionally has been more deeply

---

28. Serving as a lieutenant governor also led to many other careers in national politics. One of the most interesting and forthright politicians I came to know in Mexico was Manuel Hinojosa Ortiz, who grew up in a middle-class provincial family with strong Catholic values, in the village of Parangaricutiro, in the first decade after the 1910 revolution. He worked as a lawyer for the Department of Agrarian Affairs (DAAC) in the 1930s and 1940s, and became lieutenant governor of Aguascalientes under Jesús Rodríguez Flores in 1944, a former miner he met in DAAC. In 1948, he became director of the PRI legal department, leaving the following year to coordinate the gubernatorial campaign of Dámaso Cárdenas (the former president's brother) in Michoacán. When Cárdenas became governor, he appointed Hinojosa Ortiz as lieutenant governor, a post he left to become a member of congress from the sixth district of Michoacán in 1952. A year later he resigned to become assistant secretary of forestry resources of the secretariat of agriculture and livestock. He finished his public career as senator from his home state. Personal communications, August 13, 1974, and January 28, 1974, and personal interviews.

Table 10.10. Social Networks of Mexican Governors, 1935–2009

| Era | Social Networks (%) | | | | | |
|---|---|---|---|---|---|---|
| | Relative Public Life | Parent Held Post | Working-Class Parents | Porfirian Family Ties | Revolutionary Family Ties | Other Elite Ties |
| *Governors* | | | | | | |
| Predemocratic | 48 | 16 | 39 | 3 | 11 | 7 |
| Democratic transition | 35 | 24 | 20 | 0 | 6 | 4 |
| Democratic period | 43 | 14 | 17 | 0 | 6 | 9 |
| *All politicians* | | | | | | |
| Predemocratic | 38 | 14 | 24 | 6 | 4 | 9 |
| Democratic transition | 31 | 11 | 15 | 1 | 3 | 5 |
| Democratic period | 26 | 9 | 16 | 11 | 2 | 3 |

*Source*: Mexican Political Biographies Project, 2009.

Other Elite Ties = related to members of Mexico's intellectual and economic elite; Revolutionary Family Ties = related to important revolutionary family; Porfirian Family Ties = related to important Porfirian family; Parent Held Post = parent held high-level positions in government or the military; Relative Public Life = in-laws, spouse, uncles/aunts, nephews/nieces held public office.

ingrained in local politics, confirmed in the historical analysis of mayors and regional politics. It is easier for families to compete for positions through prominent state offices than to enter into the fierce competition for national positions with peers from all other states. The dip in governors with such links during the democratic transition can be explained by the fact that a new crop of opposition party governors achieved office, most of whom in the 1990s were unconnected to established political families because such families were the bailiwick of the PRI. Once achieving success in obtaining the governorship, these individuals from the former opposition parties, similar to their PRI antecedents, begin generating their own more extensive links to successful family members in other state and national political offices, thus increasing the percentages after 2000.

Amalia García Medina, elected governor of Zacatecas from the PRD in 2004, is a politician whose career reflects multiple family connections in politics. Born in the capital of Zacatecas in 1951, she is the granddaughter of Ursulo A. García, a schoolteacher, revolutionary, and member of congress who opposed the reelection of Alvaro Obregón as president in 1929, and daughter of Francisco Espartaco García Estrada, who served as the PRI governor of Zacatecas in the 1950s. As a student, Amalia joined the Mexican Communist Party and was active in Zacatecas and Puebla, as was her father in the 1960s, which exiled him from the PRI establishment. She became a member of the party's national committee. Years later she ran unsuccessfully for congress on the Unified Socialist Party of Mexico ticket, after co-founding the party in 1981. In 1987, she co-founded the Mexican Socialist Party, winning a plurinominal seat in congress in the 1988 elections. She left congress and won a seat in the Federal District Assembly (state legislature) as a member of the PRD, which she had joined in 1989, serving on the party's first national council.[29] She held a series of national party posts and, after winning a senate seat in 1997, became president of the party's National Executive Committee two years later. Her sister became mayor of Guadalupe, Zacatecas, during this period; her daughter ran as a PRD candidate for congress in 2000; and her son-in-law became secretary of international affairs on the PRD National Executive Committee during her presidency.[30]

A much smaller number of politicians, governors included, were the children of politicians. As other politicians have joined the pool of prominent public figures beginning in the democratic transition, those individuals with politically prominent fathers have declined. In the case of governors, however, those with politically influential parents increased significantly and briefly during the transition, returning to pretransition levels after 2000. The longer term pattern that can be perceived with politically active fathers or mothers is that governors are much more likely than other important political figures to have such a parent, again because of the importance of extended families in regional politics.

The figures on family networking through parents or other relatives is all the more striking among governors because they gave greater representation to working-class families in their backgrounds during the predemocratic and transitional eras in comparison to all other politicians. Today, social class differences no longer exist between governors and other political figures.

If we extend the analysis of social networks beyond the immediate family to multigenerational ties extending back to the nineteenth century, as well as to two other influential leadership groups, intellectual and economic elites, some important differences are revealed. Mexican governors personally have been much more strongly connected to the revolution. Why should this be the case? Governors themselves were more likely than

---

29. For many years her father was a friend of Cuauhtémoc Cárdenas, one of the primary founders of the PRD, which partly explains why she shifted to the PRD after the 1988 elections.

30. *Diario de Yucatán*, April 2, 2000; www.diputados.gob.mx, 2003; *Proceso*, October 17, 1999; *Diccionario biográfico del gobierno mexicano*, 614; and Mexican Political Biographies Project, 2009.

any other set of politicians after 1935 to have fought in the revolution and therefore to have been related to other individuals (especially parents or siblings) who also were active and often prominent participants. Moreover, at the provincial level, where the fighting actually took place, one's revolutionary reputation (or lack of it) would be far more valued, especially from the 1930s through the 1950s, as a legitimating badge for political office.[31] Even as such historic family ties grow more distant, governors are still more than twice as likely to have been related to prominent revolutionaries, and therefore enhance the presence of that special family linkage among all other politicians.

In contrast to governors' more common ties to revolutionaries, those politicians who were not governors were far more likely to be related to prominent families associated with Porfirio Díaz's reign. Incredibly, these even more historic associations doubled from the predemocratic to the democratic era.[32] This can be explained by two conditions. First, as the historical distance has grown, being related to a prominent Porfirian family is no longer a black mark against someone with political ambitions. Second, the opening of the political leadership pool, especially to PAN and other right-of-center parties such as the Mexican Democratic Party, has increased the potential for families with the appropriate social backgrounds to have such kinship ties.

Finally, and quite surprisingly, politicians' ties with two important elite groups reflect two notable patterns. Among all politicians these links have declined precipitously. There are a number of explanations for why such

31. For a numerous insights into the characteristics and roles of governors in the 1930s and 1940s, see the excellent collection of case studies and William H. Beezley's introductory chapter, "The Role of State Governors in the Mexican Revolution," in Jurgen Buchenau and William H. Beezley, eds., *State Governors in the Mexican Revolution, 1910-1952* (Lanham, Md.: Rowman and Littlefield, 2009), 1–19.

32. Outstanding examples of this include Santiago Creel Miranda, a leading precandidate for the PAN presidential nomination in 2006, who served as secretary of government in the Fox cabinet. Creel is the grandson of Enrique C. Creel, secretary of foreign relations in the last Díaz cabinet, governor of Chihuahua from 1904 to 1911, and the largest single landholder in Mexico at the time of the revolution. Creel leads the PAN delegation in the senate, 2006-2012. His uncle, Enrique Creel Luján, was the treasurer of PAN from 1959 to 1975. Other recent politicians with such historic ties include Demetrio Sodi de la Tijera, an independent senator during the Fox administration, whose grandfather and uncle Demetrio Sodi Candiani and Carlos Sodi Candiani were from prominent landholding families. His grandfather was the last minister of justice in the Díaz cabinet in 1911, and previously had been a supreme court justice since 1906. His uncle was a senator under Díaz. Irma Pía González Luna Corvera, the assistant secretary for media regulations in the ministry of government in 2008, was the granddaughter of Dr. Aureliano Urrutia, a brilliant surgeon who became Victoriano Huerta's secretary of government in his second cabinet. He refused to accept an amnesty offered by presidents Emilio Portes Gil and Lázaro Cárdenas. See Roderic Ai Camp, *Mexican Political Biographies, 1884-1934* (Austin: University of Texas Press, 1991), for details about their relatives' careers.

linkages were historically more common. One is that intellectuals and economic elites shared institutional backgrounds with PRI politicians. For example, in the 1920s and 1930s, many economic elites graduated from UNAM with their political counterparts.[33] Among intellectuals and politicians, that was the case from the 1920s through the 1950s.[34] As the institutional experiences broadened and decentralized, so did the points of contact, increasing the difficulty of establishing such social associations.

One would expect governors to have had fewer contacts with other national elites, and that is the case in the two earlier eras, even though the overall differences between governors and nongovernors is not large. What is surprising, on the other hand, is that since 2000, governors are three times as likely as all other politicians to share such contacts. It is difficult to explain this. One possible contributor to this increase is the fact that a number of recent governors, beginning in the 1990s, from all parties, are themselves prominent businessmen and therefore are related directly or indirectly through their spouses to leading members of the private sector.

José Eduardo Bours Castelo, the PRI governor of Sonora from 2003 to 2009, perfectly illustrates this new private sector career experience, demonstrating how PRI also has joined the bandwagon initiated by PAN.[35]

33. Personal interview with Jorge Sánchez Mejorada, May 15, 1985, and Carlos E. Represas, March 3, 1986. Sánchez Mejorada, who directed two of the leading businessmen's organizations in Mexico in the 1970s, graduated from UNAM in chemical engineering in 1948. However, his middle and high school training was at a Mary Brothers School. The classic example from the 1930s is that of Juan Sánchez Navarro, an original member of the Mexican Council of Businessmen and president of Cevecería Modelo. He graduated from the National School of Law in 1939. He attended law school with Hugo B. Margaín, who became treasury secretary. One of the most influential classes in terms of this overlap is the 1939–44 generation. Carlos E. Represas, who graduated from the National School of Economics in 1967, also a member of the Mexican Council of Businessmen and president of Nestlé of Mexico, was the last major capitalist to study at UNAM. See Roderic Ai Camp, *Mexico's Mandarins: Crafting a Power Elite for the Twenty-first Century* (Berkeley: University of California Press, 2002), 85. For the consequences of ties between capitalists and politicians from this era, see Roderic Ai Camp, *Entrepreneurs and Politics in Twentieth-Century Mexico* (New York: Oxford University Press, 1989), 94ff.

34. For extensive evidence of this, see Roderic Ai Camp, *Intellectuals and the State in Twentieth-Century Mexico* (Austin: University of Texas Press, 1985), 104ff., which cites numerous interviews and correspondence from leading Mexican intellectuals.

35. It is worth pointing out that the credit is often given to Vicente Fox as the PANista who generated PAN's emphasis on prominent entrepreneurs. But the individual who really began this trend and initiated Fox and many other leading politicians' careers in PANista politics during the democratic transition was Manuel J. Clouthier, the party's presidential candidate in 1988, who represented a powerful group of ranchers and produce growers in Sinaloa, and who eventually became president of the most activist national independent business organization, Coparmex, in 1978–80 and (similar to Robinson Bours) president of the CCE. Before becoming the presidential candidate, he ran without success as a candidate for mayor, congress, and governor. He came from two generations of influential landowners. His daughter, Tatiana, served in the forty-ninth legislative session, 2003–2006, as an independent. *Expansión*, April 13, 1994, 39–40.

His father, Javier Robinson Bours Almada, came from an entrepreneurial family. His grandfather, Alfonso Robinson Bours Monteverde, was the Ford distributor for Ciudad Obregón in Sonora. Four of his uncles were co-founders of Bachoco, which became Industrias Bachoco. One of the four uncles, Enrique, then president of Bachoco, was invited to join the elite Mexican Council of Businessmen in 1987. His father, who had a taste for politics, became mayor of Cajeme, Sonora, in the 1960s, followed by a term in congress.[36] José Eduardo's brother succeeded his uncle as the next CEO of Bachoco. José Eduardo was himself a director of Bachoco from 1980 to 1992 and briefly served as director general and president of the Board of Del Monte produce from 1994 to 1996, before becoming president of the most important peak business interest group, the Coordinating Council of Businessmen (CCE) in 1996. He left the presidency to coordinate the finances for PRI presidential candidate Francisco Labastida in 1999–2000 and was elected senator from Sonora in 2000, becoming chairman of the senate economic development committee. He served in the senate until his election as governor.[37]

## CONCLUSIONS

The most important conclusion we can reach about governors and prominent politicians who were also governors is that they have contributed significantly, in many ways, to diversifying the composition of Mexico's national political elite. It is equally important to highlight the fact that governors have distinguished themselves from other politicians before and after the democratic transition. In short, they have played this role for many decades.

If we examine their noncareer differences from all other politicians, their contribution to geographic diversity among leading politicians is significant given the overwhelming percentages of individuals from the executive and judicial branches born and raised in the Federal District. Without their presence among prominent political leaders, this distortion favorable to the capital would be even more exaggerated because nine times as many politicians as governors came originally from Mexico City. Governors also have contributed to a significant change from the predemocratic to the democratic era as far as the regional distribution of leading politicians is concerned. The two major regional patterns that governors helped alter

36. His brother Ricardo held the same post from 2000 to 2003.

37. *Expansión*, April 22, 1998, 39–40; www.sonora.gob.mx, 2008; *Quién es quién en el Congreso, lviii legislatura 2000–2003* (Mexico: IETD, 2002), 365; Mexican Political Biographies Project, 2009.

were an increase in politicians from the West since 2000, and a decrease in those from the East Central region. Given the control of a new party, the PAN, over the national executive branch and its regional strengths, not only do we witness changing regional distributions in the future, but a longer term trend may be a decline in the Federal District's distorted representation, accounting for the birthplace of a fourth of all leading politicians.

A surprising increase in governors from rural communities and villages has occurred in combination with governors' more diverse regional distribution. Governors from the democratic era actually have reversed this decline from the predemocratic to the democratic transition period. On the national scene, politicians who were governors are more likely to represent rural interests, having shared those interests growing up in such provincial communities. Again, by slowing down the trend toward increasing urban experiences among all politicians, governors have helped make national politicians more representative of all Mexicans regardless of their place of origin.

Throughout this work I have stressed the growing importance of local political careers in the selection process of future national politicians. One position that stands out in the backgrounds of politicians is that of mayor. Among governors it has been even more dominant. A career experience more pronounced than that of mayor among governors was that of state legislator. One of the explanations for this dramatic increase from both the predemocratic and democratic transition periods to the democratic period is that PAN members used state legislative posts as their initial means of electoral success. The dramatic upsurge in governors who were state legislators is due to an influx of PAN governors. The linkage between local elective office, local party leadership, and gubernatorial elections has proved to be strong, marking an important departure representing the decentralization of the gubernatorial nominating process.

One of the informal credentials governors bring to the table is their differing educational experiences, whether we are describing disciplinary interests or educational locations. This difference is no better illustrated than in the pattern of graduate-level education. Governors not only have gone against the grain of increasing levels of education beyond their undergraduate degrees, but in where they have obtained such training. Both characteristics suggest two important conclusions. First, these patterns are linked to the changing decentralization of political decision making where governors have been selected on the basis of other variables, some of which are not shared by the typical executive branch politician. Second, once again governors have increased the diversification among national politicians, in this case in their education. They have attended a much broader range of Mexican universities, and if they study abroad, they are much more likely to attend European than U.S. programs. Therefore, their training and the socializing experiences are far more national and European-centric than American.

Among the nonpolitical career and party experiences that governors contribute to leading politicians are the numbers who have pursued successful business careers locally, regionally, and nationally. Although .a generally increasing trend in Mexican politicians who come from private sector backgrounds has taken place, the increase among governors with business backgrounds has been phenomenal. As already noted, from the predemocratic to the democratic transition period alone, governors with business backgrounds increased an incredible 300 percent. More than any other single variable, this pattern reinforces the importance of a different type of politician emerging at the state level, reflecting a changing attitude among voters who perceive successful businessmen to have as much or more merit as a potential candidate as popular public figures. Although the PAN pioneered this shift, the PRI rapidly joined this dramatic trend through its own nomination process.

Finally, governors can be distinguished from other politicians in the importance of informal family ties. Surprisingly, governors were much more likely to have come from or been related to politically active families, thus increasing the importance of social networking. Despite the fact that overall such family ties have declined among leading Mexican politicians, especially during the years of the democratic transition when the pool of politicians was at its freshest level, governors have retained the strongest level of such kinship ties, bringing them back to a level nearly equal to the predemocratic period. These changing patterns in social ties demonstrate that competitive electoral politics does indeed bring in fresh blood to the pool of future politicians, but in a relatively short period of time (just twelve years) those new politicians rapidly began to establish their own family connections and linkages to other political actors, thus emulating the traditional social network patterns found in predemocratic Mexico.[38]

38. See George W. Grayson, "They're 'Off and Running': The July 4, 2010 Mexican Gubernatorial Elections: A Preliminary Assessment," unpublished paper, May 20, 2010, for how these and other gubernatorial characteristics are likely to effect the outcome of state elections.

# 11

# Themes on Mexican Leadership and Democracy

Throughout this work I have identified numerous findings revealed from an original data set and the accumulated information from four decades of research, interviews, and correspondence with Mexico's national political leaders. Major findings have been discussed in the concluding section of each chapter. In summing up the conclusions from the whole book, it seems appropriate to identify briefly a select group of themes that cross the boundaries of the individual chapters and in many cases also have potential implications for understanding the relationship between democracy and leadership elsewhere.

My commentary here on those broader consequences is speculative in tone, having already provided empirical as well as qualitative evidence. The first major theme emerging from the analysis is that political reforms that impact the electoral process can have long-standing and unintended consequences on characteristics of political leadership, on the gatekeepers of that leadership, and on the homogeneity of leadership under a democratic electoral model. When the incumbent party, the Institutional Revolutionary Party (PRI), made a decision in the 1960s to alter the distribution of seats in the legislative branch, adding 31 to 40 party positions in the Chamber of Deputies, it did so to remove pressure from the opposition parties, allowing them a guaranteed amount of representation in national offices. Furthermore, it made this decision to suggest at least symbolically to the public and its critics that Mexico boasted a "democratic polity" that allowed for opposition representation in national institutions. In fact, of course, none of the partisan members from other parties held offices in the federal executive or judicial branches, nor as the most influential regional actors, state governors. Moreover, given the formula created for the selection of these new "party" deputies, an analysis reveals that the smallest, least threatening parties from the Left were overrepresented, and that the National Action Party (PAN), the only party able to obtain a sizable opposition vote and therefore the only possible threat, was underrepresented.

What the PRI's leadership failed to anticipate, with serious long-term consequences, is how those decisions affected the opposition parties' designation of legislative candidates in both houses of congress and their own designations. As demonstrated, for many years after this change was instituted, the party deputy system produced most of the opposition deputies. This system relied almost exclusively on the party's national leadership to designate the list of individuals from which these deputies were selected after the congressional elections. That law, and subsequent legislation that ultimately added 200 deputies and altered the formulas for their distribution, accounted for 40 percent of the total membership in the lower chamber and eventually a doubling of senate representation.[1]

The plurinominal system became a structure that reinforced national party control while seriously weakening local and state party leadership. That structure produced two long-term consequences. First, it delayed a major change usually attributed to increased electoral participation: the increasing importance of grassroots political organizations and leadership. Indeed, as pointed out previously, national party leadership continues to make such plurinominal selections. Second, such a structure, now firmly ingrained despite democratic, electoral change, has produced a bifurcated leadership in the legislative branch. Again, as demonstrated empirically, a broad division exists between party deputies and district deputies, whose background characteristics are different, ranging from the average age they represent and the level of their insider status within their respective parties.

These two differences alone have contributed to serious policy consequences, readily illustrated during the Fox presidency, where PAN insiders versus PAN outsiders (the latter represented by Fox himself) often disagreed among themselves within the Chamber of Deputies, as well as with the executive branch. Partisanship alone does not explain all the difficulties in overcoming obstacles to major legislative proposals, but internal differences within the PAN added to these hurdles. PAN leadership realized the extent of this problem by 2006, when Calderón, a classic party insider, having been president of his party and heavily involved in the party bureaucracy for years, attempted to rectify and moderate these internal differences in the composition of PAN deputies and executive branch leadership, promoting individuals who previously served on the party's National Executive Committee and in the Chamber of Deputies.

1. The senate originally had sixty-four senators, two from each state and the Federal District. More recent legislation added thirty-two plurinominal senators who are chosen from their party's list, and thirty-two additional senators who are chosen from the party that receives the second highest vote, which to some extent is a variation of the plurinominal system.

A second theme that emerges from this work is that the peculiarities of a legislative system, particularly in the way it is structured, can unquestionably slow down the processes that democratic electoral change typically engenders. One of the issues addressed in the findings is the changing pool from which political leaders are recruited. The legislative branch in Mexico exercises a critical and overwhelming influence in the process of renewing and altering national political leadership. Of the nearly 3,000 individuals analyzed in this study, half served in the national legislative branch, a position held more frequently than any other post among the most influential Mexican politicians in the past eight decades.

It can be argued that the legislative recruitment process has produced and continued a more partisan leadership. Such a partisanship pattern is to be expected in a democratic system, as the parties themselves take on new and important roles in determining leadership through electoral processes. Nevertheless, this particular national political structure is responsible for the presence of an older generation who are heavily dependent on their linkages to national party leadership rather than to grassroots support. Expressed differently, Mexico's legislative system is perpetuating a percentage of the leadership who otherwise would not likely be serving in national, politically influential positions.

The renovation effect of competitive electoral democracy in Mexico is limited by a legislative nomination process for a certain type of deputy and senator. All of the numerous changes that democratic politics has introduced in the backgrounds and recruitment institutions of a post-2000 leadership is significantly moderated by this one prevailing plurinominal structure. Thus, most of the changes identified throughout this book attributed to democracy would be deeper and more extensive if Mexico's peculiar legislative pattern were not in place.

Such a conclusion naturally leads to a third theme, strongly linked to perhaps the most surprising finding in the book. Democratic change, measured by numerous background variables of leading politicians, can be extraordinarily radical in scope. I had no expectation that in a short period of years (less than a decade), a peaceful, democratic change would produce consequences among politicians as extensive as violent change.

The methodology of political change consequently becomes an interesting vehicle for analyzing alterations in political leadership. Both forms of change favor different skills or qualities among future political leaders, qualities that can detract or enhance their abilities to succeed in a more orderly, institutional political setting. For example, an analysis of postrevolutionary leadership in the 1920s demonstrates major differences between those who fought in the violent phase of Mexico's political development from 1910 to 1920, compared to those who achieved success in the more stable, institutional phase. This finding suggests that violence, as a form of change, produces two different types of leaders: the first type was short-lived but necessary for the success of the violence politically, and the second type was long-lived, establishing a pattern of leadership for decades after.

In contrast, democratic leadership produces no such dramatic division. The extensive data that allowed me to compare the democratic transitional period from 1988 to 2000 revealed that in many cases, an increasing competitiveness in the electoral process initiated background patterns that continued and expanded in the post-2000 era. In other words, democratic change has the advantage of continuity, and even though certain background qualities are altered significantly (often more so than those produced by violent change), there exists a certain incremental quality in which postdemocratic change builds on transitional democratic change. That fact alone explains why conflict, when it spills over into violence, would be less likely to occur during a peaceful than in a violent transition, where the generation that has been most successful in accomplishing the violent change is largely shut out of the leadership posts.

A fourth, fascinating theme having implications for Mexico and other countries is the degree to which institutions play an important role in the backgrounds of political leadership, particularly in their credentials and their recruitment. Two patterns emerge from the longitudinal data on national leadership. The first pattern is associated with violent versus peaceful change. Interestingly, of all the changes introduced by the revolutionary decade, contrary to what might be expected, an institutional change—that of level of education—is altered in a radical way. Beginning in the 1880s, after long periods of civil violence, political leadership increasingly boasted higher levels of formal education, including college degrees.[2] Mexico's violent decade in the 1910s eliminated the overwhelming presence of college-educated and professional politicians. The decline itself is not surprising considering the altered social origins of the leadership, characterized by the dramatic decrease of upper-class politicians. What is important to emphasize is the number of decades it took the country to recover to a level of educated politicians found at the end of the nineteenth century.

A countervailing theme about institutions is their persistence in nonviolent periods over time, an especially interesting pattern given the informal role of what ordinarily would be considered nonpolitical institutions on political recruitment, socialization, and mentoring. The

---

2. It reached 91 percent in Díaz's 1901–1905 administration. A similar level of college-educated politicians was not achieved until Carlos Salinas's presidency, 1988–94.

overwhelming influence of educational institutions on Mexican national leadership for decades, whether recruitment patterns were centralized in the capital or were increasingly decentralized to different geographic locales, is noteworthy. Educational institutions deserve a reexamination for the informal role they have played in political recruitment. They do not operate solely as an independent actor, a conclusion in evidence from my prior research in the 1970s and 1980s, but, more important, as a substitute for the role scholars might assign parties to play at the regional and national levels.

Did the weak role of political parties and the devalued experience of politicians as active militants result from the importance of public school networking that occurred among educated politicians, who were among the most successful individuals to establish themselves in political offices after 1920? Many of the inadequacies and peculiarities of the PRI and its antecedents can be attributed to the nondemocratic functions of a political party, and therefore can be explained by the semi-authoritarian setting of Mexican politics. This is the usual explanation scholars offer for the PRI's truncated functions, as a party that served to maintain itself in power rather than compete against credible opponents to gain power. Furthermore, a close examination of partisanship under the PRI, contrary to what most observers have implied, surprisingly demonstrated that more than half of Mexico's political leadership were not party militants.

Analysts of other democratic political settings point to parties, especially to local and regional party organizations, as a place where individuals sharing future ambitions as successful national political figures would network and develop political skills. In Mexico, even though many universities suffered temporary closures during the second decade of the twentieth century, both state and national universities continued to function throughout the 1920s, long before the first major national party was formed in 1929. This gave those institutions a generous head start on parties. The only other continuous party operating in the Mexican setting for more than half a century was the PAN, founded in 1939. In Mexico, as illustrated by the Alemán generation, the National Preparatory School and the National Autonomous University of Mexico (UNAM) served as substitute institutions in carrying out many of these informal functions.[3] Many future politicians and presidents from Miguel Alemán to Carlos Salinas became student leaders in their preparatory schools or at the university. They earned reputations as skillful leaders before they experienced initial, lowly posts in the federal bureaucracy.

3. They played a similar role in the Porfiriato and in the governments from 1910 to 1914.

The case can be made that selected universities, initially public in origin, provided a broader umbrella than did the "official" party in the performance of the leadership experiences and training. Although I am not suggesting that the parties, even in their early years, did not produce some of their own potential future "graduates" for influential national posts, as demonstrated elsewhere in the book, such party graduates were exceptional, not typical. Indeed, not one of the individuals I interviewed from the Alemán generation mentioned the party as formative in their public careers.

Each of the preceding themes focuses on institutions, political and nonpolitical alike, that have exercised an influence before, during, and after a democratic transition. The findings in this study also confirm a fifth theme, the importance of noninstitutional background variables that can be as significant on the composition of Mexican leadership as institutional variables. The most far-reaching informal variable that can be examined concretely in politicians' backgrounds is social networking. There is no question that politicians have relied on social networking to acquire and ensure the appropriate contacts to enhance their upwardly mobile careers. What is exceptional about Mexico (and most other countries compared to the United States) is the extent of these ties, where they occur, and their importance from one generation to the next.

Theorists often associate transparency and accountability with democratic governance. To a certain extent, voting forces a certain level of these two qualities on those politicians who are selected through a competitive electoral process. Meritorious achievements also are important in determining national political leadership, especially among individuals who become assistant secretaries and secretaries in the most specialized or technical of cabinet-level agencies.

In spite of these important influences, produced by perceptions of a politician's career experiences and accomplishments, noninstitutional relationships based on familial linkages are extensive in Mexico, potentially exerting greater influence on selections of leaders than those experiences or credentials that are publicly visible and concrete. Such family linkages, the most difficult to determine of all leadership background variables examined in this study, persist across time and political models. Democratic politics has by no means eliminated kinship ties among Mexican politicians, opening the door to an even broader and new pool of recruits. Instead, a natural decline occurred when electoral democracy opened the door to greater numbers of opposition politicians, the majority of whom could not claim family connections with a prior generation of politicians during the PRI-dominated era. Yet once the door opened to opposition politicians, especially from the PAN, kinship ties increased among the youngest generations, following a well-established pattern established previously by PRI politicians.

Although we think of democratic politics, when replacing a semi-authoritarian political model, as increasing the diversity of backgrounds among politicians, that outcome is inconsistent, suggesting a sixth theme. For example, one of the most interesting changes in career experiences is the dramatic increase in politicians who count successful private sector experiences in their backgrounds. Mexico, for most of the twentieth century, claimed only a handful of influential politicians who were successful entrepreneurs, although a small minority of successful politicians did achieve similar notoriety in business after leaving public life. A fascinating component of this change is that it became nearly universal, that is, it was emulated among members of the PRI who recognized that individuals who presented strong private sector credentials made successful candidates for political office.

Accompanying this particular shift in career backgrounds is an equally interesting change in kinship ties, suggesting just how long it can take for an altered pool of potential political leaders to appear on the scene and produce new familial ties. In the case of the PAN, a number of prominent figures are known to have personal ties to influential families strongly associated with the Porfiriato, families that as a result of the revolution and the ideology imposed by the postrevolutionary leadership, were not as commonly found in the backgrounds of politicians for numerous decades after 1920. Eighty years later, however, those linkages are no longer a detriment to a politician's successful national career.

Democracy also has the potential for creating social differences among politicians as compared to those in the predemocratic or transitional eras. Intuitively, one might expect electoral democracy to embrace social breadth among political leaders. Mexico's experience, however, from a social perspective, is that electoral democracy has produced a more socially homogeneous set of leaders, a leadership that is even less representative of the social class distribution of the general population than previously. It has increased the percentage of middle-class politicians while decreasing further individuals who come from working-class families. For decades, the PRI, given its corporatist structure and specifically the importance of labor unions and the teachers' union, as well as its extensive organizational presence in smaller, rural communities, extended leadership possibilities to a slowly decreasing minority of politicians who came from humble backgrounds, especially rural settings. The majority of these individuals have pursued successful political careers in the legislative branch. PAN, given its urban origins and its antiunion campaign pledges, would not be a particularly inviting organizational setting for politicians boasting working-class credentials.

As has been demonstrated, electoral democracy does not ensure the complete decentralization of institutions and political careers. Among the significant exceptions to that statement is a definitive shift in the impact of leading regional versus leading national positions. Cabinets have played the crucial role in determining Mexican presidential leadership. For decades, beginning with the first presidential race after the formation of the PRI through 2000, every successful PRI candidate came directly from the cabinet, even though a number of the early presidents had been governors earlier in their careers, as was the PRI candidate in 2000. Among PAN presidential candidates, no clear pattern emerges, but among those with recent political experience, most served in congress and a number held important party posts, including that of president. Since the democratic period, however, governors have provided most of the leading presidential candidates from the major parties.

Governors, as the career most likely to lead to a national party nomination for president since 2000, offer many differences from their executive branch counterparts. Among the most important differences, several of which distinguish general patterns among all politicians in the post-democratic era, are (1) the fact that they have had far more extensive experience in local politics; (2) they are much more likely to have held multiple elective offices, both at the local and national levels; and (3) they have been active party militants with numerous party leadership posts locally and regionally.

Democracy is enhancing an increase in politicians' experiences and credentials typically associated with a democratic process, including negotiating and bargaining skills. On the other hand, democracy also has increased significantly party militancy and consequently the level of partisanship, not only among governors but among politicians holding important national positions, including members of congress. Increased partisanship has not been conducive to legislative accomplishments in either the Fox or Calderón administrations. By increasing significantly the level of partisanship, democracy introduced a variable that creates a serious obstacle to its success, leads to a depreciation of the legislative branch in the public's eyes, and increases the tenuousness of popular support for democratic politics.

Democratic politics also has increased the diversity in the backgrounds of political leadership by further opening the door to successful female leaders who are well represented in the judicial branch, the legislative branch, and party leadership. Diversity should not be measured based on gender alone but on equally important differences in background characteristics represented by women and men. Women, who have long been more successful in legislative careers in Mexico and elsewhere, have enhanced overall the greater presence of elective offices in the backgrounds of all

national figures. Moreover, they boast greater experience with other affiliated political organizations, such as unions, and have more involvement
with nongovernmental and civic organizations. Finally, women have
increased the diversity of educational backgrounds, introducing numerous specialties that have not been as well represented among men. Each of
these qualities also increases the importance of those institutions that are
responsible for these new and different credentials, institutions that are
likely to have consequences for years to come.

Last, individual generations, given their origins, political experiences,
and recruitment practices, can set in motion decisive changes that impact
the importance of specific political institutions and the contributions
such institutions make to the formation of national leadership and policy-
making outcomes. The Alemán generation produced such an impact. Their
consequences were long-lasting, resulting in a significant shift favoring the
increased domination of Mexico City in the backgrounds of prominent
politicians. Furthermore, that trend reinforced the growing importance of
national public institutions in the training, socialization, and recruitment of
students with political ambitions. Given the proximity of those educational
institutions to executive branch agencies, and the fact that most members
of the Alemán generation were instructors in those institutions, teachers
and students became the political networking linkage of choice, converting
the capital's public institutions as the informal recruiting agency of a huge
percentage of the national leadership.

These patterns and the biases they represent toward favored institutions
remained in place for decades. Many of the characteristics associated with
the Alemán generation established it as the first "technocratic" generation
in twentieth-century Mexico. Those same characteristics form the basis of
the better-known technocratic wave of national politicians characterizing
the democratic transition. Although Mexico City continues to produce an
increasingly disproportionate percentage of the most influential figures
in the executive branch, other distinctive patterns of this second wave
emerged, including an increased level of education abroad (specifically in
the United States), a growing emphasis on economically trained leaders, a
significant trend away from public to private universities in the capital, an
increase in more specialized educational training, and a decrease in elective experience, local officeholding, and party militancy.

Changes in a political model from a semi-authoritarian to an electoral
democracy demonstrate how political structures and institutions can
produce decisive changes on leadership. It is also important to understand
that within the broader characteristics of those different models, a cohesive group of leaders, linked together by their generational experiences,
can establish equally powerful patterns that define specific characteristics

of the broader political model, suggesting how leaders impact a political system. The Alemán generation established such characteristics for the semi-authoritarian model. It is too soon to tell whether a democratic generation, such as the 1960s generation, will have a similar impact on Mexican democracy. Because electoral democracy incorporates many political parties and their leaders, and because party incumbency is likely to change in the executive and legislative branches, it will be far more difficult for any single group of individuals after 2000 to accomplish comparable changes in institutions and leadership patterns initiated or reinforced by the 1900s generation in the 1940s and 1950s.

Electoral democracy has produced wide-ranging and significant changes in Mexican leadership, some of which are linked to patterns already well developed during the democratic transition and others that were produced in dramatic fashion by a single presidential election (that of 2000).[4] Still other patterns can be traced to the predemocratic era, suggesting that certain characteristics and conditions are fairly impervious to political change, even when that change includes a different political model. These characteristics often tend to be more informal than formal, but informal behaviors can determine the actual consequences of more formalized institutional structures. Such patterns can be found in other societies that have undergone significant changes in their political model. The complexity and breadth of the findings revealed in an examination of Mexican leadership and the alterations effected by electoral democracy unquestionably suggest the importance and value of testing those conclusions in other political and cultural settings to fully understand the interaction between leadership and democracy.

4. Kenneth Greene, in his analysis of the democratization of Mexico's electoral system *Why Dominant Parties Lose: Mexico's Democratization in Comparative Perspective* (New York: Cambridge University Press, 2007), 169, concurs with this view, even arguing that the transition began seriously after 1982, during the extreme austerity program.

# Index